The Procurement and Supply Manager's Desk Reference

The Procurement and Supply Manager's Desk Reference

Second Edition

FRED SOLLISH, MS
JOHN SEMANIK, MBA

WILEY

John Wiley & Sons, Inc.

For general information on our other products and services or for technical support, please contact our Customer Care Department within the United States at (800) 762-2974, outside the United States at (317) 572-3993 or fax (317) 572-4002.

Wiley also publishes its books in a variety of electronic formats. Some content that appears in print may not be available in electronic books. For more information about Wiley products, visit our web site at www.wiley.com.

Library of Congress Cataloging-in-Publication Data:

Sollish, Fred.
  The procurement and supply manager's desk reference / Fred B. Sollish, John Semanik. – 2nd ed.
    p. cm.
  Includes index.
  ISBN 978-1-118-13009-4 (hardback); ISBN 978-1-118-22568-4 (ebk);
  ISBN 978-1-118-23849-3 (ebk); ISBN 978-1-118-26309-9 (ebk)
  1. Industrial procurement—Handbooks, manuals, etc.   2. Purchasing—Handbooks, manuals, etc. 3. Materials management—Handbooks, manuals, etc.   I. Semanik, John.   II. Title.
  HD39.5.S66 2012
  658.7′2—dc23

                                                                        2012004857

Printed in the United States of America

SKY10038865_112422

Contents

Preface to the Second Edition

This book, now in its second edition, is written for the procurement and supply chain management professional needing a reference to the working methods available today for use on the job. It also has in mind the newly appointed executive or the staff member with only a cursory knowledge of the workings of procurement and supply management. It provides, we trust, a complete compendium of the information that is required to effectively carry out the responsibilities incumbent in the procurement and supply management area.

Leading-edge business enterprises constantly look for ways to remain competitive. The procurement and supply chain management processes outlined in this book are just some of the ways business supply managers can make key contributions to their company's bottom line. The modern world of outsourcing requires proficient expertise in procurement and supply chain management that has not been seen in any other period during our lifetimes. The future is bound to rely even more on the expertise of effective leverage and the management of supply resources.

Change is inevitable. And our profession is changing now even more rapidly than it has in the past. Therefore, we also hope this book will enable you to assess the value of new concepts and processes in our field, and assist you in keeping up with these changes. To be successful you must stay well ahead of the curve yet be ever mindful of the responsibility that rests with your choices. Make the right choices and you *will* succeed.

Should you wish to contact us with input, comments, or suggestions about any subject in the book, please e-mail us at custsvc@supplyknowledge.com.

Fred Sollish, MS, C.P.M.
San Francisco, California

John Semanik, MBA, C.P.M.
San Jose, California

Acknowledgments

The information in this book is largely based upon the experience we acquired over several decades as practitioners and teachers.

A thank-you goes out to those we have worked with and those who have taught us, and those professional organizations that have provided support...but mostly we want to thank our students, whose challenging questions sent us scurrying to learn more about our profession.

—Fred Sollish and John Semanik

CHAPTER 1

Procurement and Best Business Practices

The role of the *procurement* and *supply management* professional is rapidly changing. While in the past the procurement professional's area of responsibility was clearly relegated to efficient "processing" of purchase orders, the pace of today's business environment has expanded that role to control of the entire sourcing and acquisition process. To be successful in this rapidly changing, dynamic marketplace requires not only the traditionally disciplined approach to managing critical business relationships but also the ability to quickly understand and employ strategic new methods and technology. Procurement professionals today must have the ability to assess and respond effectively to current market conditions and the foresight to envision the future needs of the organization, setting into motion plans that will respond to the changing dynamics of the continually reinvented organization. Indeed, today's procurement management professional must be a master of change. And to facilitate that dynamic of change, the procurement professional must also be a master of best practices—methods shown to provide outstanding results—to continually ensure that change drives improvement in the business process and does not simply replace one poorly functioning system with another poorly functioning system. That is why we begin this Desktop Reference by reviewing the key elements of those processes and best practices that are fundamental to excellence in procurement.

Understanding Procurement

Effective procurement requires the utilization of sound business practices that maximize value to the organization through the acquisition of goods and services. This follows the old adage that the Procurement Department's role is to deliver the right material (or service) in the right amount to the right place at the right time and at the right price. You can do this by employing well-conceived strategies—a plan to enhance competitive bidding, for example—that leverage clearly defined processes to manage the supply base. As a procurement professional, you will be expected to conceive and implement strategies that employ best practices.

Employing best practices in procurement ensures that the procurement professional and ultimately the organization make correct decisions. This means that an organization must develop plans that are in alignment with its goals and best interests. Frequently, these plans evolve from well-defined sourcing strategies developed to help the organization achieve its overall objectives. In turn, sourcing strategies rely on a clear set of tactical procedures to ensure their implementation. At the root of these tactical procedures are the day-to-day methods the organization employs to convey its requirements to the supplier. Many organizations refer to these processes as *standard operating procedures (SOPs)* and maintain them in formalized document libraries.

Understanding and Conveying Requirements

Sound business practice requires that you understand and can clearly describe to a prospective supplier the requirement of your purchase. Unless you can describe to a supplier exactly what you need, the procurement process will not be successful. As we will detail below, this description often takes the form of a *specification* for materials or a *statement of work (SOW)* for services. Most commonly, it is the internal user who generates this information—often called a *requirement*—and it is the procurement professional's responsibility to ensure that it is properly conveyed to the supplier in the procurement document (such as the purchase order or contract). In the case where a purchase is particularly complex, the process of stating organizational needs is so critical that you may find a face-to-face meeting with your supplier is in order. That way, you can ensure that there are no misunderstandings or faulty interpretations of the requirement. A well-developed and well-stated requirement describing exactly what it is you expect to receive is the key to successful procurement. For this reason, you must ensure that there are systems in place that accurately convey the needs of your customers to you so that you can formalize them into a contract or purchase order. At the minimum, you should include the following elements in your procurement documents when stating requirements.

Material or Service

Describe exactly what it is you expect to receive from the supplier. This description can be provided in the form of a specification, an SOW, a drawing, a part number, or the nomenclature of an *off-the-shelf* or brand name part. Generally, we use a specification to describe a material requirement and an SOW to describe a service. Along with the stated quantity and the quality of the purchase, this can be the basis for approving payment and must be easy for third parties such as receiving personnel, finance, and auditors to understand after the transaction is completed.

Specification

A specification contains a technical description of the material being purchased. In its simplest terms, it can be a reference to a supplier's stock number or a brand name. It can also refer to an engineering drawing (or a set of drawings) provided by the internal user that shows the part or assembly with call-outs for the type of materials required and all necessary dimensions to produce the part. Or, in the case of chemicals and other formulated and processed materials, the specification can be tendered as a recipe or in a compositional format.

Statement of Work (SOW)

Unlike a specification, the SOW describes the requirements for a service. It may be stated in detailed and prescriptive format, describing not only what needs to be done but the method to be used (called a design specification) and how often the service must be done as well. Or it may simply be stated in terms of expected outcomes. Frequently, the SOW also contains a set of metrics describing the level of performance required (called a performance specification). The measurements used to determine the level of performance needed for a specific element are called *key performance indicators (KPIs)* and are often used to assess any performance requiring corrective action or, conversely, when an incentive bonus may be due.

We'll discuss the SOW in greater detail in Chapter 2, "Sourcing Management."

Time of Performance

This indicates the date when you expect to receive the product or service you're procuring in the procurement document. The document must clearly state delivery or work completion dates so that the supplier understands precisely when performance is required.

Expressions such as "Rush" or "ASAP" are inappropriate because they can be open to a variety of interpretations. It requires only a little more effort to specify an exact date. Consider calling the supplier to determine the earliest possible date and pass that along to your internal customer. If the proposed date is acceptable, it should then be included in your procurement document.

Price and Payment Terms

You'll need to include exactly how much your organization has agreed to pay for the specified product or service in the requirement so that you avoid misunderstandings and can clearly determine your organization's financial obligation.

The procurement document should also specify when payment is due. This is usually expressed as a net number of days, such as Net 30 or Net 45. A discount period may be included where the supplier specifies the amount of the discount as well as the number of days the buyer can make payments and still earn the discount. The discount period is often expressed as a formula:

$$2/10 \text{ Net } 45$$

This means that if payment is made within 10 days, a 2 percent discount can be taken, but the total balance is nevertheless due in 45 days. The annualized discount savings for a 2 percent discount for 10 days (in this example) actually equals 73 percent ($2 \times 365 \div 10$)!

Shipping Destination, Method, and Terms

If you're procuring materials and intend to use a specific carrier to transport the purchased material, you should include this in your document as well. You'll need to specify the level of service—overnight air, second-day air, ground, and so on—and indicate if the supplier is to bill your account, pay for it, and then bill your organization or absorb the freight cost outright. In your instructions, include the exact destination of the shipment and the point at which the ownership of the goods, or title, transfers from the seller to the buyer.

Creating Strategic Plans and Tactics

Virtually all organizations develop a set of key goals and objectives to guide their operations and, typically, formulate a broad plan to achieve them. This plan is usually referred to as a *strategic plan*. It focuses activities to achieve the organization's overall mission. So, as each segment of the organization pursues individual commitments to achieve its goals, it generates the need for materials and services from the supply community. The Procurement Department, as the interface between internal departments and their suppliers, then formulates its plans based on meeting these needs in alignment with the various conditions that drive its supply base.

As you look closely at the various missions within the organization based on their functional roles, specific sets of strategies that determine how and when goods or services must be purchased become apparent:

Finance

Strategies involving finance are critical to the organization's success. Cash position relative to the overall economy often determines when new technology can be acquired or when additional product lines can be launched. In a period of declining prices, organizations may want to postpone major purchases for a period of time in the anticipation of lower pricing in the near future. Business organizations with strong cash positions during weak economic times frequently find acquisitions of other companies an attractive way to expand market position. Obviously, these strategies generate procurement requirements that must be dovetailed with overall procurement strategies so that they are properly met with appropriate action when it is needed.

Manufacturing and Operations

Manufacturing and operational strategies develop from the need to meet customer demand. The influx of orders and the development of new product lines generate procurement requirements that are critically time phased to meet current market demands. At various phases of the product life cycle, significantly different requirements must be met, so it is imperative that the Procurement Department develop its strategy accordingly. For example, early involvement in the development phase of a new product can be critical since that is when much of the sourcing, supplier qualification, and contracting activity will take place.

Other strategies developed in conjunction with procurement can similarly support operational strategies. These include *just-in-time (JIT)* delivery, *supplier-managed inventory (SMI)*, and a variety of other programs developed to enhance well-run operations and eliminate waste and non-value-added costs.

Sales and Marketing

Sales and marketing drive product or service adoption and develop strategies that are critical to the organization's revenue stream. Accurately forecasting anticipated volumes provides critical data to operations and can be the basis for developing supply management strategies. The timing of a new product launch typically generates requirements for additional capital equipment and marketing material, so it is important that strategic plans be coordinated with the Procurement Department to the extent that its involvement will be required.

Supply Management

While procurement strategies are generally created to respond to the needs of other internal organizations, it is important for Procurement to develop plans that anticipate changing conditions in the marketplace as well. As a result, you often find strategies for procurement formulated along commodity lines to allow for response to specific trends that may be affecting one industry more than another. Changes in supply or demand can trigger decisions to hold acquisition plans for later or to accelerate them in the face of a temporary opportunity. Prices are rarely in equilibrium, so commodity-specific strategies must be developed to react quickly to changing supply-and-demand conditions.

Typically, supply management strategies focus on key areas of spending and technology, seeking formularies to balance various needs at any given time. Thus, it is important to have well-conceived decision-making strategies for favoring one aspect over another. For example, it must be clear to the individual buyer whether the acquisition of advanced technology overrides the need to reduce costs when the organization's strategy seeks to gain greater market penetration of its products or services based on price competition. You can easily see how the interpretation of this strategy can affect supplier selection, favoring a supplier with superior technology over a supplier with best pricing (or vice versa). Supplier selection or sourcing, therefore, becomes one of the key elements in the Procurement Department's strategic plan.

In the final analysis, the key to effective strategy for procurement is the proper alignment of procurement activity with the strategic plans of its internal customers and conditions in the supply base. This will be manifest in both long-term and short-term commodity plans that relate procurement decisions to individual market conditions and specific internal needs.

Finding Innovative Methods and Exploring Alternatives

Closely linked to the development and implementation of procurement strategy is the traditional role of the Procurement Department as a strategic tool itself. In most organizations, policy requires the implementation of business processes through procurement activities that reduce cost and increase life-cycle value. Later in this chapter, we explore some of these methods in more detail, but for now it would be valuable to point out that the strategies just outlined require specific tactics to ensure favorable results. A program to reduce the purchase prices of a specific set of materials may best be implemented through a competitive bidding process—as a tactical tool—whereas the co-development of new technology that requires prodigious engineering costs from a potential supplier might be more easily gained through negotiation.

To be effective, the procurement professional must continually explore new methods and seek out alternatives that will improve existing processes. In turn, these improvements will spawn new strategies. Tactics and strategies thus feed one another in a cycle of *continuous improvement*.

Providing Procurement Services

The decision to initiate a particular purchase develops in a variety of ways and from a variety of circumstances. Usually, purchases are initiated by an internal user based on some planned and budgeted need that can be justified by a specific operational purpose. For example, new technology may require the purchase of new manufacturing equipment, or the development of a new product line may require building models or ordering special tools. In a manufacturing environment, raw material needs are generated through a formal planning process based on incoming customer orders and forecasts of anticipated production needs.

For the purchaser, it is important to understand the overall needs and responsibilities of the internal customer so that when requirements are generated, they can be fulfilled in the most expeditious manner possible. Often, this requires the development of close relationships with those staff members responsible for generating the procurement requirements you will be handling. It also involves understanding the supplier community and its marketplace, including an in-depth knowledge of industry standards and methodologies, so that you can best advise your internal users on which supplier may be best able to handle a specific requirement or how to develop a requirements statement using language common to the industry. While you are rarely expected to provide technical expertise, your customers should be able to rely on you and your team to find new suppliers, assist in the selection of an existing supplier for a specific job, and advise them on which supplier provides the best business solution in any given situation.

Your customers will frequently have specific goals that relate to how and where purchases are made, such as the development and use of a new source for advanced technology or the use of a supplier who is willing to undertake the co-development of new engineering processes, that will enable your organization to develop a better position in the marketplace for its products or services. Often, the need will arise to use *minority business enterprise (MBE)* suppliers, which are classified as minority or disadvantaged businesses or sources within a certain geographical region or national boundary, to enhance your organization's own competitive position in these areas. Your sensitivity to such issues and ability to enhance these positions will help build strong relationships within your customer base that will open further opportunities for your involvement in their business processes.

You and your team will also be responsible for evaluating overall supplier performance and developing ways to work with suppliers to improve that performance. If you can do this effectively, you will add measurable value to your internal customers' mission.

Accepting Orders

Requests to purchase or contract for materials and services can be submitted to the Procurement Department in a number of ways. However, regardless of the method of submission, a number of common elements define the process and requirements in most organizations:

1. The procurement staff must have documented evidence that the order has been duly authorized in accordance with prescribed organizational policy prior to processing it for placement.
2. The information outlined in the "Understanding and Conveying Requirements" section that originates with the requestor must be present, along with any required accounting data, user information, and known supplier sources. Briefly summarized, this information includes:
   The user's name and department.
   The cost code, general ledger (GL) account, or budgeting center being charged.
   A description of the purchase in terms that can be understood by the supplier.
   The quantity needed (and the amount of acceptable overage or underage, if applicable).
   The date required.
   Estimated cost (if not exactly known).
   Suggested suppliers (and justification if a specific *sole source* is required).
   The shipping address or location where the materials are to be delivered or where the work is to be performed.
3. The order must not have been placed previously without proper procedural due diligence by the Procurement Department. In most organizations, the Procurement Department is the only authorized buying entity, and purchases made outside the authority of the Procurement Department are considered unauthorized and are frequently referred to as *maverick purchases*.

Order Approval and Authority

Most organizations designate individuals or job positions within each department that are authorized to approve requests for purchases. Often, this authority is hierarchical, requiring increasingly higher approval according to an existing chain of command and depending on the spending amount represented by the request.

In most organizations, all but a few specialized spending requirements must be placed by the Procurement Department. Buying through other channels is usually considered unauthorized spending and is strongly discouraged. There are a number of important considerations for this. First of all, spending outside of the recognized procurement channels cannot benefit from negotiated discounts accorded the larger volumes that are placed within the system, and the volume of these purchases does not count toward further discounts since they are often purchased from noncontractual sources. Second, these purchases do not benefit from the trained due diligence performed by the professional buyer and can result in liability for the organization. Third, they are not likely to be properly captured in the budget and so cannot provide visibility for future requirements and expense allocations. And, finally, they are not likely to be placed with the most qualified supplier because the maverick buyer will have few resources or incentives to perform more than the most perfunctory competitive analysis.

Types of Purchase Requests

Purchase requests can be generated in a number of different ways depending on the organization's level of automation and the nature of the purchase. We'll discuss some of the more commonly used processes, such as requisitions, catalog ordering, material requirements planning (MRP), and system-generated orders.

REQUISITIONS *Requisitions* are documents generated by the user or user department containing the specific information outlined in the preceding paragraphs. They may be submitted as a paper form through standard internal distribution channels or as an electronic document through an existing computerized system, often linked to the organization's primary data system. Sometimes organizations use e-mail to transmit them.

Note

Paper requisitions usually contain the written signatures of the approving professionals, whereas electronic requisitions are signed digitally. In general, today's electronic systems automatically route user requests to the approval authority based on an existing workflow hierarchy. Approval dates and times are maintained in a workflow database within the system and kept for future audit reference. Appendix A on the companion website contains a sample material requisition.

CATALOG ORDERING The *electronic catalog* is another automated method for ordering standard products. Here, the user accesses a listing of products available for ordering within the organization's electronic requisitioning system (usually available as a distinct section on the organization's internal network or *intranet*). By using a search engine that returns data stored by key words or product categories, users can find products they are authorized to purchase and in some systems perform side-by-side comparisons of pricing, features, and functions from competing suppliers in order to make the appropriate selection.

There are numerous ways to generate and store electronic catalog data, depending on the system being used. However, the Procurement Department (or a cross-functional team led by Procurement) generally selects the suppliers in advance; negotiates the prices, terms, and conditions; and processes whatever contractual documents are needed. In many systems, the supplier actually maintains the data, either outside or inside the organization's firewall, depending on security requirements. Changes to the data can be made in real time (that is, immediately) or at periodic intervals and typically require the designated buyer's approval.

Systems are available today that enable users to "punch out" of the existing electronic catalog and access a supplier's website catalog (or a group of catalogs) directly, often through common tools such as a Web browser. Once accessed, items can be captured and moved directly into the user's system and then processed as a normal catalog order. This can be as simple as dragging a desired item into the user's requisitioning system. As convenient as this sounds, there is a catch: The supplier must be prequalified since significant work is required in advance to ensure compatibility between the systems of each party.

Note

Appendix C on the companion website contains a sample electronic catalog page.

ELECTRONIC DATA INTERCHANGE (EDI) *Electronic Data Interchange (EDI)* and its European counterpart maintained by the United Nations (*EDIFACT*) is a process widely used by large organizations and government entities and their trading partners. Its primary function is to exchange data related to procurement between computers. EDI, along with other procurement standards and processes is covered in Chapter 7.

MRP AND SYSTEM-GENERATED ORDERS *Material requirements planning (MRP)* systems or the somewhat newer version, *manufacturing resource planning (MRPII)*, typically used in manufacturing operations, generate automated requisitions or special electronic listings of current and planned requirements that can be transmitted directly to a supplier. Overall requirements are based on a combination of incoming customer orders and forecasts of customer orders and can be time phased so that material reaches the organization at a specific time. (We will review this in more detail in Chapter 18.) Each product (or line of products) has a distinct *bill of materials (BOM)*, a formulary of the parts that constitute the final product, from which detailed requirements can be quantified and summarized by the supplier. These summaries are usually transmitted electronically.

Table 1.1 contains an exploded BOM, with a brief summary of the combined requirements by the supplier in typical printed format. As you can see in Table 1.1, in a simple listing, parts are grouped by level. In most production environments, the final product is composed of a number of *subassemblies*, sections that must be assembled or manufactured separately before being built into the product being sold, so the order in which they are assembled is designated by a level number. Thus, Level 5 parts in a subassembly are put together before Level 4 parts, and so on. This table lists the parts by their order of assembly but does not show their relationship to one another. A listing such as this shows the number of common parts being used and their specific order of assembly. Note that Part Number 34009-40023, a hex nut, is listed on both Level 2 and Level 5. Another type of listing would list the BOM by specific part number so that total requirements for the product could be determined.

TABLE 1.1   Bill of Material: Swing Arm Task Lamp Assembly (Listing)

Level	Part Number	Revision	Quantity	Unit of Measure	Description	Supplier
1	15400–10000	A	Parent	Each	Lamp assembly	Make
2	24001–30010	A	1	Each	Lamp switch	Delta
2	25950–40010	B	1	Each	Lamp switch housing	Delta
2	34009–40023	A	2	Each	10–32 hex nut	Omni
2	35010–45098	B	2	Each	10–32 bolt	Omni
3	40900–10000	C	1	Each	Light socket assembly	Delta
4	60902–29845	B	1	Each	40-watt light bulb	Consolidated
4	48098–60090	B	1	Each	Lamp cone assembly	Delta
5	89009–34896	D	1	Each	Swing arm assembly	Marsten
5	34009–40023	A	10	Each	10–32 hex nut	Omni
5	35010–45098	B	10	Each	10–32 bolt	Omni

Table 1.1 also shows the format used for a simple listing of a BOM. It shows the assigned part number, the engineering revision number, the quantity (and the unit of measurement), along with their nomenclature and the supplier.

Figure 1.1 shows where the parts from the Table 1.1 BOM are actually used in relation to one another. This view of the lamp assembly BOM shows the relationships between individual parts in their subassemblies and how they roll up into the final product.

Placing Orders

There are two key considerations that must be addressed in any system for placing orders with suppliers: first, the format used to convey the order to the supplier, and second, the priority of placement. We'll discuss these issues in this section.

Ordering Formats

A number of different formats can be used to convey purchase orders (POs) to the supplier, depending on the circumstances and the nature of the requirement. Each method has its own specific requirements, as you can see from the following: POs, blanket POs, contracts, credit cards, and system-generated orders.

STANDARD PURCHASE ORDERS   The *purchase order* is likely the most commonly used form of procurement document. As a contractual document, the PO contains all of the information outlined in the requirements section, along with the organization's standard *terms and conditions* boilerplate. POs are numbered for unique identification and audit control and, in paper format, usually contain a number of copies

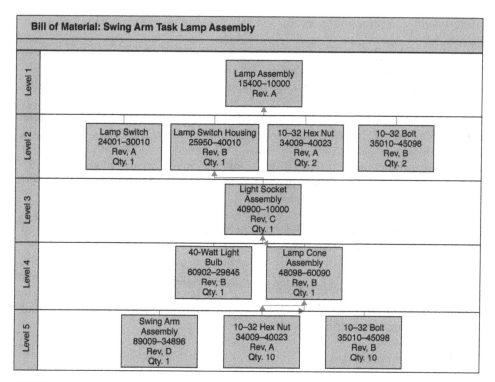

FIGURE 1.1   Diagrammatic Bill of Materials (BOM)

for distribution to the supplier, the Accounting Department, the original requestor, and the files. POs can be transmitted by any common form of mail, by fax, or by a variety of other electronic processes, including e-mail.

BLANKET PURCHASE ORDERS   The *blanket purchase order* covers a procurement commitment to a supplier for specific products or services at an agreed-upon price for a set period of time or for a limited quantity or spending amount. Commonly used to eliminate many smaller orders so as to minimize the amount of paperwork processed, the blanket PO, once placed by the Procurement Department, can be used by other groups within the organization to set releases as frequently as needed and when needed.

CONTRACTS   A *contract* generally covers services or other complex purchases that require special legal language or terms and conditions beyond the scope of a typical PO. A contract is also used when requirements extend over periods of time longer than a year or when automatic renewal may be required to ensure continuing operations.

Under the broader heading of contracts, we can include a number of similar documents used in the normal course of business, such as the *memorandum of understanding (MOU)* and the *letter of intent (LOI)*. Many organizations also have specialized agreements used for particular purposes, such as an agreement for *consignment* or a *master supply agreement*. We discuss these in more detail in Chapter 5.

PROCUREMENT CARDS OR CREDIT CARDS   Issued to specific users within the organization whose duties require making frequent small purchases, the *procurement card (P-card)* or credit card can effectively reduce the clutter of low-value requisitions and purchases processed by the Procurement Department that can interfere with efficient supply management. Used mainly for incidental purchases associated with nonproduction or *maintenance, repair, and operations (MRO)* products, P-card purchases can be controlled through limits placed by the organization for specific products or services (or classes of products and services), or even through limits on the industry type or individual supplier.

The card also reduces the time it takes to place an order as well as the cycle time for payment to the supplier, reducing (or eliminating) the typical cost associated with the buying and payment of POs.

Estimates of the transactional cost of the PO and payment process vary widely, often ranging from $50 to $250. According to the National Association of Purchasing Card Professionals (NAPCP, www.napcp.org), purchasing card efficiencies result in savings ranging from 55 to 90 percent of this transactional cost. NAPCP adds that additional savings can accrue through:

- Supply base consolidation.
- Reinforcement of general purchasing best practices.
- A significant source of spend information.
- Streamlining payees in the accounts payable system.
- An opportunity for suppliers to streamline their processes.

Of course, one of the major drawbacks to use of the P-card is the limited amount of control over where purchases are made. When an organization is attempting to consolidate suppliers for better pricing, Procurement has no way to ensure that existing suppliers under contract are used.

SYSTEM-GENERATED ORDERS   There are a variety of orders that are generated internally through various planning and scheduling systems such as MRP or other automated inventory replenishment systems. For the most part, organizations using these systems issue documentation electronically as agreed upon with the supplier in advance (and usually according to a contract). MRP and system-generated orders have already been described in this chapter.

Externally managed inventory through a formal SMI program is a relative of system-generated orders, insofar as replenishment signals are controlled by the supplier based on a negotiated level of inventory or the receipt of incoming orders.

Placement Priority

Electronic catalog and system-generated orders are most commonly transmitted in real time directly to the supplier through electronic media. A manually generated order, however, requires buyer intervention to accomplish several tasks. With a manually generated order, the buyer must determine proper authorization, establish the source of supply, and review requirements for legality and conformance to applicable regulations such as those related to the *Environmental Protection Agency (EPA)* or the *Occupational Safety and Health Administration (OSHA)*. A manually generated order also requires that the buyer convert the requisition to a PO or contract. Because buyers typically have backlogs of multiple orders to place, some process for determining the order and timing of their placement must be implemented.

FIRST IN, FIRST OUT (FIFO)   Using the *first in, first out (FIFO)* method, orders received in the buyers' queues are prioritized by order of receipt so that the oldest one becomes the next to be placed. While this sounds fair, it could adversely affect operations if applied too blindly because it ignores the need for urgency in the case of emergencies or critical outages.

PRIORITY SYSTEM   Using a *priority system* method, priorities are established within the department to address specific needs. For example, conditions that could create a line down condition in a manufacturing operation or situations that may immediately jeopardize employee health require immediate attention, and buyers are required to put other work aside to address them. Separate priority is often assigned to orders with specific lead times so that user needs can be uniformly accommodated. Items with the longest lead time may be placed soonest.

CYCLE TIME   In some organizations, buyers' performance metrics include the *cycle time* for orders based on the date and time received and the date and time placed with the supplier. Buyers are measured on how long it takes, on average, for a particular individual to place orders during a specific time period. Obviously, if this becomes the key consideration, it will provide incentives to the buyers to place the easy orders first—the ones requiring the least amount of sourcing or negotiation—to reduce the average turnaround time in the queue. However, as a measure of internal service, cycle time and customer satisfaction with the procurement process go hand-in-glove.

Mastering Procurement and Business Tactics

Procurement tactics naturally follow the course established by organizational and departmental strategies. Indeed, you might well consider that tactics are the methods and processes through which we implement effective strategies. A buyer may develop the most appropriate and innovative strategies, but unless they can be effectively executed through practical measures, the organization may never realize their benefits.

In this section, we explore how business and procurement strategies are generally applied.

Budgets and Expense Allocation

Most organizations implement critical strategies through some form of spending. Typically, this spending comes in the form of the purchase of capital equipment or the hiring of additional staff and their accompanying support materials and services. It may also be reflected in larger spending on new product development or through additional marketing and advertising. All of these are strategic efforts that are usually implemented through Procurement.

A budget can be viewed as an organization's spending plan. Usually, budgets are allocated (or funded) to specific departments or functional areas, cost centers, or projects, and incoming goods and services are charged against those accounts. To a large extent, an approved budget may be the final authorization to proceed with expenditures.

Because adherence to an established budget can mean the difference between profit and loss in a business organization, or the continuation of operations in a nonprofit, management takes the budget seriously and pays close attention to individual areas of conformance. This may explain the sensitivity that internal users often manifest when ensuring that expenses are charged to the correct cost code.

The Finance Department usually manages the control and allocation of expenses and is responsible for categorizing and reporting actual expenditures. Finance is also responsible for paying suppliers and requires that specific criteria be met prior to disbursing the organization's funds. For materials, accounting practice typically requires that a duly authorized PO and a Receiving Document, along with the supplier's invoice, are in place prior to payment. (In the case of services, usually a sign-off on the supplier's invoice by the budgeting manager or department head indicating satisfactory completion of the service is required in lieu of a receiving document.) This is commonly referred to as a *three-way match*.

Finance, along with internal and external auditors, verifies that purchases are made in accordance with approved policies and procedures. To the extent that Procurement implements (or at least touches in some significant manner) most of these procedures in its dealing with suppliers, it becomes an instrument of the organization's financial apparatus and undergoes periodic audits to ensure proper conformance. Public companies must meet regulatory audit requirements under the *Sarbanes-Oxley Act of 2002 (SOX)*. SOX determines that corporate management is responsible for establishing and maintaining adequate controls and procedures for financial reporting. Maintenance of procurement policies, procedures, and records is included among these responsibilities.

SOX was passed to ensure that senior corporate executives would be held responsible for any financial misconduct within the organization. It also requires that organizations develop and implement reporting processes that safeguard financial integrity. A summary of the act can be found at www.sec.gov/about/laws/soa2002.pdf.

Internal Control Systems

An effective internal control system enables you to manage significant risks and monitor the reliability and integrity of financial and operating information. It also ensures that the audit committee acts as a powerful and proactive agent for corporate self-regulation. The Committee of Sponsoring Organizations of the Treadway Commission (COSO, www.coso.org) developed a list of internal control questions to help senior executives and directors gain a better understanding of their organizations' control systems.

The COSO framework is summarized as follows:

In an "effective" internal control system, the following five components work to support the achievement of an entity's mission, strategies and related business objectives.

Control Environment

- *Integrity and Ethical Values*
- *Commitment to Competence*
- *Board of Directors and Audit Committee*
- *Management's Philosophy and Operating Style*
- *Organizational Structure*
- *Assignment of Authority and Responsibility*
- *Human Resource Policies and Procedures*

Risk Assessment

- *Company-Wide Objectives*
- *Process-Level Objectives*
- *Risk Identification and Analysis*
- *Managing Change*

Control Activities

- *Policies and Procedures*
- *Security (Application and Network)*
- *Application Change Management*
- *Business Continuity/Backups*
- *Outsourcing*

Information and Communication

- *Quality of Information*
- *Effectiveness of Communication*

Monitoring

- *Ongoing Monitoring*
- *Separate Evaluations*
- *Reporting Deficiencies*

Source: www.firstload.com/?ir=1&fn=coso+framework+download

Establishing Procurement Methods

Many systematized processes exist for placing POs, as outlined earlier in this chapter. But far more important than simply determining the appropriate document or format for a particular purchase, the Procurement Department also has responsibility for actually driving the deal. By this we mean that the procurement professional has a fiduciary obligation to ensure that goods and services are acquired in accordance with the best interests of the organization. This can be accomplished either through negotiations (bargaining) or through some form of competitive bidding process, or a combination of both.

Procurement Negotiations

Negotiation, in its simplest form, can be a way of striking a deal through a process of give and take. Buyer and seller each have specific objectives in developing the bargain, and generally accepted best practice indicates that, in a successful negotiation, each party achieves an equal measure of satisfaction. Techniques and methods for accomplishing this, so critical to maintaining a competitive, motivated supply base, will be discussed in Chapter 9.

Competitive Bidding

Another common way to strike a procurement agreement with a supplier is through the competitive bidding process. The typical objective of competitive bidding is to ensure that the buying organization receives the lowest market pricing for a given purchase, with all other terms and conditions remaining equal. To do this, the buyer needs to ensure that a number of conditions are present:

- **Competition.** The marketplace contains a reasonable number of qualified or qualifiable suppliers who are willing to compete. The more suppliers available (within manageable degrees), the greater the competition will be. Competition is the buyer's best friend.
- **Value.** The goods or services have significant enough value to make the bidding process worthwhile.
- **Savings.** The bidding has the potential to result in lower prices.
- **Requirements.** A clear specification or SOW (or industry standard) is available to all bidders.
- **Contract.** The suppliers have the capability and are willing to commit to furnishing the goods or services at the price bid and under.
- **Time.** There is sufficient time to conduct a fair and impartial process.
- **Corrections and clarifications.** A process exists to provide suppliers with answers to questions or corrections to specifications. Answers to questions asked by one supplier must be shared with all others.

Tips and Techniques

Buyer Beware of Competitive Bidding Traps

Unscrupulous suppliers have developed an onerous repertoire of dirty tricks to circumvent the competitive bidding process. We refer to these as traps.

One competitive bidding trap occurs when a supplier intentionally bids for a new product without including associated tooling or startup costs, thus providing a price that the more forthright competition cannot possibly meet. However, the price offered is usually somewhat above the normal cost associated with production. In this way, the supplier can gradually recover the tooling costs over a period of several years, while at the same time always excluding competitors who will be unable to match the price without absorbing the tooling or startup costs that are continually rising due to inflation. As the years go on, the supplier not only recovers the full cost of the tooling, but can also charge a significantly higher price for the materials as long as it stays just below the next lowest bid (which includes tooling).

Another competitive bidding trap occurs when the supplier realizes that the specifications will require further change after the bid is awarded. This is often the result of improperly designed products or an ill-conceived SOW, although it sometimes results from a simple mistake made by the buyer. The supplier makes the original quote at below cost and reasonable market prices. However, the inevitable changes are then quoted on a substantially higher basis than would ordinarily be justified (since there will be no other bidders at that point), and thus the supplier can recover the difference and earn a handsome premium as well.

Note

We'll discuss competitive bidding in more detail in Chapter 2.

Reverse Auction

Although not as popular as it once was, an automated process known as the *reverse auction (RA)* has enabled the acceleration of bidding from what formerly took months to a mere few days. It is called a "reverse" auction because the roles of buyer and seller are reversed, requiring the *suppliers* to bid down the price, and the *lowest* price, rather than the highest price, wins the bid. (In a more typical auction, the seller puts an item up for sale, multiple buyers bid for the item, and depending on the nature of the auction—English or Dutch—one or more of the highest bidders buy the goods at a price determined by the bidding.)

Note

Auction types are described in Appendix D on the companion website.

The RA provides an electronic marketplace where prequalified suppliers can bid on a buyer's requirements in real time instead of through a delayed process and, most importantly, can determine their position in the overall bidding process so that they can improve their bids as they deem appropriate. An auction serves the additional benefit of ensuring to the buyer that a fair and reasonable price has been established.

Internal Cost-Related Analysis Tools

A number of tools and methods are used internally to track the performance of the Procurement Department relative to the nature of the organization's *costs*. For the procurement professional to effectively manage this critical area requires a detailed knowledge of the various aspects of costs and how they are calculated.

Costs are categorized and defined both in terms of their method of calculation and their relationship to the organization's balance sheet. Following are some of the more common ways accountants characterize them.

Direct Costs

Direct costs are those expenditures directly incorporated into the product or service being delivered to the end customer. Typically, these costs are generated only when there is a product or service being sold, or when *finished goods* inventory is being built in the anticipation of future demand. This implies that without sales there will be no direct costs.

In most manufacturing operations, it is common to account for and distribute the total company *overhead* (see the next section) as a percentage *burden* added to each separate product or product line. That way, the total cost of producing a specific product can be calculated on a stand-alone basis.

Indirect Costs

The elements of cost that are associated with the organization's operation but not directly with a specific product or service are classified as *indirect costs*. These costs can be further subdivided into three other categories: fixed, variable, and semivariable.

FIXED COSTS   Costs that remain relatively constant within a specific range of operations, regardless of changes in production or service volumes, are considered fixed costs. When calculated on a per-unit-produced basis, they increase and decrease with corresponding variations in volumes. Examples of such expenses include rent, facilities maintenance, nonproduction-related service contracts, and administrative support from information technology providers. They are usually expenses committed by management as part of the general planning process and are often reallocated to various departments based on a standard financial formula.

VARIABLE COSTS   Variable costs are costs that increase or decrease in relation to production or service volumes. When calculated on a per-unit-produced basis, they remain relatively constant regardless of the organization's output. Examples of these expenses include consumable materials and spare parts used in manufacturing. Variable costs are typically incurred in relation to some specific reaction to a change in demand and so are accountable at the consuming departmental level.

SEMIVARIABLE COSTS   *Semivariable costs* are costs that change in response to changes in operational levels but not necessarily on a uniform basis. They exhibit qualities of both fixed and variable costs, having elements of both. Managerial bonuses might be considered an example.

Overhead

Overhead costs, usually called *general and administrative expenses (G&A)* on the *profit-and-loss statement (P&L)*, are those costs generally connected with the operation of the organization as a whole and cannot be directly connected with any specific operational activity. Examples include equipment depreciation, utilities, interest expense, outside auditing, and legal fees. Commonly, overhead and indirect costs are kept separate.

Overhead expenses are usually allocated back to the various operational units or product lines on a percentage basis. Some organizations use direct labor for the method of calculation, while others may use direct materials or even machine hours.

Total Cost of Ownership

The total cost of acquiring and using a material or service is sometimes called the *total cost of ownership (TCO)*. Total cost methods typically track all the additional costs beyond the purchase price that are associated with the life cycle of the materials or services purchased by an organization. This can include the cost of transportation and customs duties—called the *landed price*—to acquire the product; installation and maintenance (in the case of equipment); training; rework; inventory carrying and storage costs; handling; and, finally, disposal at the end of life, as illustrated in Figure 1.2. As you might surmise, the typical life-cycle costs far outweigh the simple purchase price. Figure 1.2 illustrates what a typical breakdown might look like for capital equipment. Notice that the actual purchase price accounts for just over one-fourth the total life-cycle costs.

The TCO calculation can be used to assess direct and indirect costs as well as benefits related to a particular purchase covering not only the cost of the initial purchase, but all aspects in the further use and maintenance of the equipment.

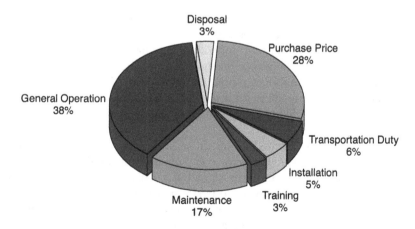

FIGURE 1.2   Total Cost of Ownership Buildup

Typically, this includes installation, ongoing maintenance, and training of support personnel and the users of the system, as well as end-of-life disposal.

TCO can be a useful tool when evaluating various alternative solutions to a particular acquisition requirement and when demonstrating or comparing return-on-investment alternatives. Figure 1.2 illustrates how the TCO buildup takes place.

Standard costs are the planned costs to manufacture specific products or to provide a unit of service, as defined for a specific time, either at the present time or for some specific date in the future. In the case of a newly introduced product or service, they are often based on engineering estimates. Standard costs typically determine the selling price of an item or operating budgets and projected cash flow. They are also used as benchmarks and to set goals for cost reduction efforts.

The *purchase price variance (PPV)* is the reported difference between the actual price paid by the organization and the standard cost shown in the Bill of Materials. Despite the fact that it is widely used to measure procurement performance, there are numerous, often indeterminate reasons for a typical PPV, many of which are the result of market conditions or engineering changes that are beyond the control of the procurement professional.

Hard and Soft Costs

Internal savings are frequently calculated on the basis of reduced labor requirements or the elimination of certain building space. Unless these savings actually result in the elimination of cost—that is, reduced head count or lower rent—they are considered *soft costs*. Soft costs may or may not result in a benefit to the organization. Savings that are actually reflected in a lower price paid for an item or the elimination of specific head count are considered *hard costs*. In the calculation of a savings contribution to the organization, the procurement professional must consider the relevancy of the cost.

Accounting Systems

Virtually all organizations use an accounting system to maintain their financial records. The system usually incorporates a *chart of accounts* to classify expenditures and determine how to allocate individual purchases. The chart of accounts simply lists the names and numerical designations of the various expense codes such as office supplies, telephone, travel, or equipment. When combined with a specific *cost center* (the designation for a section or department within the organization), the expenses can be clearly categorized and allocated to a specific department or individual.

Budgets are ordinarily created along these lines and so actual expenses can be rolled up into the same categories for comparison. Individual accounts are then rolled up into the P&L statement on the same basis. This method enables organizations to control spending and to evaluate performance to original budgets.

One method for allocation in common use today is *activity-based costing (ABC)*. This method allocates expenses from a company-wide cost center—Utilities, for example—to the actual project or operation using it. Often, these allocations are based on a business unit so that management can determine the profitability of one unit compared to another.

Utilizing Financial Tools

When we refer to financial tools, we typically mean the methods used to analyze the financial performance of the organization or a particular activity within the organization. These methods are often expressed in terms of a specific ratio. Here are some common examples you should understand.

RETURN ON INVESTMENT (ROI) *Return on investment (ROI)* describes the effectiveness of a particular investment in terms of how long it takes to recover (or earn back) the initial funding. ROI can be calculated as the *net present value (NPV)* of the revenue created divided by the initial investment:

$$\text{ROI} = (\text{Savings} \times \text{Time}) - (\text{Discount Rate} \times \text{Time})$$

RETURN ON TOTAL ASSETS (ROTA)/RETURN ON NET ASSETS (RONA) *Return on total assets (ROTA)* and *return on net assets (RONA)* are measures used to determine how effectively capital is deployed within the organization. Here, net income (that is, revenue less expenses) is divided by the value of assets in operation to determine effectiveness:

$$\text{ROTA} = \text{Net Income/Total Assets}$$

NET OPERATING MARGIN (NOM) *Net operating margin* (NOM) reflects the profitability of the organization by calculating the percentage of its *total operating income* (sales less direct costs) to its overall sales:

$$\text{NOM} = \text{Net Operating Income/Revenue}$$

CURRENT RATIO The current ratio is calculated by dividing current assets by current liabilities and is used to measure a company's liquidity. A higher current ratio indicates a greater cushion between current obligations and a company's ability to pay them.

QUICK RATIO The quick ratio is a measure of a company's financial strength (or weakness); it is also known as the "acid test." It is calculated by taking liquid assets (which are current assets less inventories), divided by current liabilities. By excluding inventory, this key liquidity ratio focuses on the company's more liquid assets and indicates the firm's ability to pay off short-term obligations without relying on sale of inventories. This ratio is also used to determine creditworthiness.

The procurement professional uses these measures both internally for gauging the organization's performance and externally for assessing the performance of suppliers. Often, these measures help select or qualify suppliers on the basis of their financial strength and leverage.

Note

A description of commonly used ratios can be found in Appendix E on the companion website.

Keeping Supplier Information

One of the key responsibilities of the Procurement Department is the maintenance of ethical and sound business relationships with the organization's suppliers. In this pursuit, it is especially important to note the adage that "perception is everything." In ordinary dealings with suppliers, the procurement professional must always ensure that there is not the least compromise of integrity or even the perception of impropriety. (We cover this more in the section covering ethical principles in Chapter 4).

Confidentiality

Confidentiality is a mutual responsibility and a critical obligation, both legal and ethical, that buyer and supplier owe each other. Maintaining confidentiality becomes especially important when the information one has received or is divulging can affect the organization's competitive position and result in financial loss. Typically, organizations sign a contractual document—called a *nondisclosure agreement (NDA)*—legally binding them to maintaining each other's intellectual property.

The procurement professional must ensure that no one in the organization discloses information about one supplier to another, such as bids, pricing, manufacturing methods, designs, plans, formulas, nonpublic measures of performance, or any other form of intellectual property. Both Procurement and Legal have an obligation to instruct and inform all personnel in the organization who come into contact with suppliers or the general public about these obligations and to conscientiously protect supplier information from compromise through special care and diligence.

Business Reports

The Procurement Department maintains a variety of reports covering supplier performance, such as cost profiles, quality records, and on-time delivery performance. It is important that the department uses this information properly and confidentially. Internal users with access to this information should be similarly informed.

Samples and Returns

Samples should be accepted from suppliers only when there is a specific need for evaluation, and following evaluation, they should be returned. If there is no immediate need or internal request for the particular sample, it should not be accepted in the first place. The organization should pay for any samples that it keeps.

It is also good business practice and the Procurement Department's responsibility to ensure that rejected or excess goods for which credits have been issued by the supplier are properly returned. Many times credits are taken by Procurement and sent to Accounts Payable before the supplier has authorized returns. This practice simply messes up the books of the respective organizations and creates a great deal of ill will. For continued good business relations, it is important that organizations keep their financial accounts in proper order.

Summary

In procurement, best practices generally cover the creation of strategic and tactical plans for the acquisition of goods and services that align with the organization's mission, as well as implementing those plans in a manner that provides added value. Best practices in procurement also cover the processing of user requests to purchase goods and services.

In order to meet their responsibilities effectively, the procurement professional must be an enabler capable of matching the needs of internal customers with what is available to purchase in the marketplace. The Procurement Department requires effective and efficient operation through its interface with suppliers to ensure that critical requirements are conveyed properly and in a timely manner.

The procurement professional should also demonstrate the ability to use the tools available to obtain the best value for organizations in dealings with suppliers. These tools include methods for financial analysis and determining total cost of ownership, as well as processes to develop competition that results in greater purchased value to the organization. The procurement professional also needs to have a strong understanding of accounting methods and techniques so as to add further value to internal customers and to make sound judgments in the application of fiduciary responsibilities.

In addition, the procurement professional must ensure that all personnel in the organization honor the dictates of good ethical practices and that information furnished by suppliers is maintained in confidence.

CHAPTER 2

Sourcing Management

In this chapter, we introduce you to some of the most valuable tasks performed by the Procurement Department: developing bids and proposals, evaluating suppliers' responses, and selecting the supplier that provides the greatest value to your organization. The procurement professional is expected to ensure that this process results in fair and consistent supplier selection that is fully aligned with organizational objectives.

To manage this effectively, you will also need to know how specifications, statements of work, and performance criteria are commonly developed, along with your role in properly conveying them to the supplier. Since you will also have responsibility for ensuring compliance to laws and regulations throughout this process, you will be required to have a working knowledge of how they affect the selection and contracting process.

Included in this chapter is a review of the various supplier classifications and their general requirements and how this information is maintained for internal use.

Finally, for future reference, we have included a section on the elements of strategic planning and how they are implemented through operational planning.

Establishing Requirements

As noted in Chapter 1, a description of the organization's detailed needs for any purchase consists of a number of elements, including terms and conditions, lead time, and technical requirements. In order for the organization's procurement team to select the most appropriate source for any specific purchase or for any potential supplier to submit an accurate bid or proposal, these elements must be available for documentation. So let's examine how to generate and document requirements, convey them to suppliers, and use them in your supplier selection process.

Creating and Organizing Requirements

In most organizations, especially those in the manufacturing sector, new requirements are developed by the *using department* (the department that will actually receive the goods or services) in conjunction with other interested parties. Similarly, existing specifications are periodically reviewed by the using group, and any changes generated are conveyed to the Procurement Department prior to any subsequent purchases. Specifications and subsequent changes for standard products and services are usually documented and filed by the *document control* section responsible for physically maintaining the organization's specifications. However, when there are no formal processes within the organization for developing specifications, it is the responsibility of the *requisitioner*—the individual initiating the request—to supply sufficient information to the Procurement Department so that the correct product or service is purchased.

Roles and Responsibilities

The responsibility for creating and maintaining specifications generally resides with the user or the using department. For direct materials used in a manufacturing organization, that usually means an engineering group or research and development group closely associated with making the product being shipped to the organization's final customer. In other cases, the department responsible for the budget is also responsible for the specifications. When a statement of work (SOW) for a service used by the entire organization is being purchased (for example, travel, consulting services, or telecommunications), most commonly an administrative department, such as Finance, Human Resources, or Information Technology, will take responsibility.

Project Team

The development of complex requirements often takes on a project-oriented nature, and a cross-functional team is chartered with the responsibility to define and document the organization's specific need in that particular situation. This team is composed of technical experts, users, and, of course, the Procurement Department. On occasion, outside information sources may be required, and consultants may be engaged to assist the project team. Frequently, it is this team that actually makes the final supplier selection.

Customer Inputs

In situations where the components or service being performed is critical to the operations of the organization, customers may play an important role in the development of specifications. It is not uncommon in high-tech industries, for example, where speed of product development and time to market introduction can be critical for success, to have representatives of the organization's final customer participating in the development of specifications. Occasionally, customers will actually determine the specifications themselves if they are critical.

Other Inputs

Besides the internal user or engineer, the most common additional information detailing the specification or SOW comes from existing or potential supplier(s) of the item to be purchased. Based on the degree of collaboration, it is common to find suppliers participating actively in the development of specifications. While this may sound like a conflict of interest, the supplier is usually in the best position to help formulate requirements, especially where there is no internal core competency in a particular commodity area. This collaboration often leads to a more complete understanding of the user's requirement on the part of the supplier and substantially lowers the risk of receiving inadequate product or service quality.

It is also not uncommon, as noted previously, for organizations to engage third-party consultants who are experts in a particular industry or commodity to assist with the development of requirements and the writing of the specification due to their unique domain knowledge, especially when there is insufficient expertise within the organization and where cost or overall risk is substantially high.

In addition, there are many third-party organizations that provide industry standards for products or services in common use. Such standards exist for a large number of commodities—fasteners, lubricants, and grades of ore, to name a few—and can be used to speed the development process or align specifications with commonly employed definitions. Standards are often in place for an entire industry, making the specification process fairly straightforward.

Developing Specifications and Formats

Detailed requirements are typically documented in a written specification (in the case of materials) or a statement of work (for services). These describe the precise parameters or standards that a supplier must meet in order for the purchase to be accepted by the buyer. Having a "tight" specification, that is, one that clearly and completely defines the organization's intended purchase, helps prevent problems later on. First of all, it creates the need to fully develop and define the purchase requirements internally so that they can be clearly documented by the Procurement Department on orders or contracts. Second, it enables the supplier to have a full understanding of what your organization expects to receive so that the supplier can properly meet your requirements. In both cases, documentation is important in avoiding future conflict because a clear, unambiguous description is difficult to dispute after the receipt of the goods or services.

Specific formats vary from organization to organization and can range from a variety of written descriptions to detailed drawings or even actual samples. The key is to convey your requirements so that they cannot be misunderstood by the supplier. The old carpenter's adage, "Measure twice, cut once," also applies to the value of well-developed specifications. It is far less costly to develop a clear description of your requirements in the first place than to have to go through the return and repair process because they were not specific enough or presented clearly enough to ensure complete conformance.

There are two elements to consider when developing a specification. First, there is the actual description of the product or material in terms of its physical characteristics, what it looks like, or how it functions. Second, there is an element of quantification that evaluates the level of performance. Certain measures of quality, such as the frequency or *mean time between failure (MTBF)* for equipment and the allowable number of rejected *parts per million (PPM)* for purchased parts, are typically systematized into an inspection process for determining acceptance at delivery and subsequent payment.

TABLE 2.1   Sample Technical Specifications

Item	Specification
Display area (mm)	170.9 (H) × 128.2 (V) (4.5-inch diagonal)
Number of dots	640 × 3 (H) × 480 (V)
Pixel pitch (mm)	0.267 (H) × 0.267 (V)
Color pixel arrangement	RGB vertical stripe
Display mode	Normally white
Number of colors	262,144
Contrast ratio	450
Optimum viewing angle (contrast ratio)	6 o'clock
Brightness (cd/m^2)	450
Module size (mm)	199.5 (W) × 149.0 (H) × 11.5 (D)
Module mass (g)	360 (Typ)
Backlight unit	CCFL, 2 tubes, edge-light, replaceable
Surface treatment	Antiglare and hard-coating 3H

Specifications are typically created using one of the following three approaches, depending on the organization's objectives:

Technical Specifications

Technical specifications describe the physical characteristics of the material or product being purchased, such as dimensions, grade of materials, physical properties, color, finish, and any other data that define an acceptable product. Written technical specifications may be supplemented by drawings or samples. Table 2.1 demonstrates an example of a technical specification.

Functional Specifications

The function of a product can be defined in terms of its actual role and what it is intended to do. *Functional specifications* define the job to be done rather than the method by which it is to be accomplished. Typically, functional specifications do not limit the supplier to providing a specific solution, as in the case of a technical specification, thus enabling the supplier to create the best possible solution. For example, a functional specification may require "the safe and efficient movement of passengers from Zone A to Zone B" at an airport.

Functional specifications are typically used to solicit suppliers' proposals for further evaluation by the procurement organization when a specific solution is not known. They are often combined with performance specifications, outlined next, to create a more detailed requirement.

Performance Specifications

While technical specifications define the product's physical characteristics, and functional specifications describe what role the product plays, neither describes just how well the product must perform. This is the purpose of a *performance specification*, which describes the parameters of actual performance the item or service must meet. With a performance specification, you are primarily interested in results rather than in method.

In the example just given of passenger movement at an airport, a performance specification might call out just how many passengers must be moved in any particular time period, or it may state the number of hours the device must be operational in any specific period.

Performance specifications can be described by a virtually unlimited choice of criteria. However, they must be capable of some clearly stated measurement. Some of the more common parameters include:

- **Speed.** Product must travel at 20 miles per hour.
- **Output.** Product must produce 400 acceptable parts per hour.
- **Quality.** Product must be capable of 2,000 operational hours before failure.
- **Efficacy.** Product must reduce rejected parts by 20 percent.

Tips and Techniques

Be sure to keep the specification types clear in your mind. There are subtle differences that may be confusing. For example, performance characteristics *can* be included in a technical specification, and technical data *can* be included in a performance spec. The purpose of the specification must be made clear.

Standards

Using preestablished standards is another way of describing specifications or supplementing the description when that is appropriate. Literally dozens of organizations provide published standards available for general use, including the American National Standards Institute (ANSI), the National Institute of Standards and Technology, and the Society of Automotive Engineers (SAE), to name just a few. A detailed listing of military and industry standards and specifications has been assembled by the Los Angeles Public Library and can be found on the Internet at www.lapl.org/resources/guides/standards.html.

Benchmarking

In its simplest form, a *benchmark* provides a measurement as a guide for establishing a specific requirement. However, benchmarking can also be a detailed process for determining how one organization is performing in relation to other organizations. For example, your organization's cost for packaging a particular product is 12 percent of its total cost. Are you overspecifying your packaging requirements? Obtaining data or finding a benchmark from other organizations in your business sector might indicate an opportunity to save costs by reducing specifications to less expensive alternatives. The organized use of methodologies that focus on the function of a material, process, or service in providing value to the customer is also called *value analysis*.

Quality Control

Most people readily agree that quality is less costly when controlled within the initial process itself rather than through some form of inspection at a stage following manufacture or shipping. Prevention is less expensive than finding a full-blown cure.

Methods of *quality control* typically include automated controls to measure compliance to specification and site inspection at the point of manufacture where corrections can be made. It also includes control of the process through a continual sampling and measurement discipline known as *statistical process control (SPC)*. This process relies on a variety of data collection and measurement systems, reports using run data and flowcharts, and diagrams showing the actual distribution of measures in relation to process control limits. Figure 2.1 shows the actual time taken to process a work package in relation to the *upper control limit (UCL)* (the highest point of measurement at which performance is acceptable) of 17.5 days and the *lower control limit (LCL)* (the lowest point of measurement at which performance is acceptable) of 1.5 days. The average for the period shown is described by a line at 9.4 days. Whenever a statistically significant number of occurrences fall outside this range—1.5 to 17.5 days—the process being used is out of control and will need to be reengineered.

One of the more commonly used tools in SPC is the measurement of *process capability (C_{pK})*. This compares the actual process range of the supplier's manufacturing capability with the buyer's acceptable range of variation. A C_{pK} of 1.00 means that the supplier's actual variation range and the buyer's allowable variation range are the same. A C_{pK} of more than 1.00 indicates that the supplier's process is in

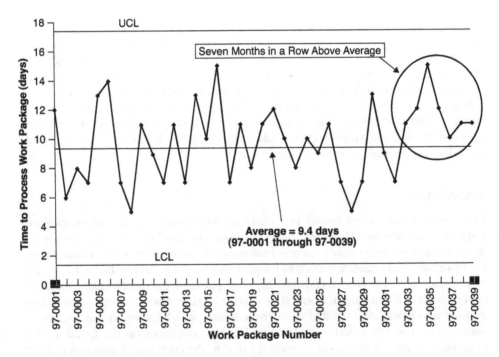

FIGURE 2.1   Statistical Process Control Chart

better control than the buyer requires, while a C_{pK} of less than 1.00 indicates that the supplier will produce greater variation than the buyer will allow. Ideally, the process yields a C_{pK} of 1.33.

Statement of Work

A *statement of work (SOW)* outlines the requirements for a purchase of services rather than a product. Nevertheless, like a specification, it defines exactly what is needed in enough detail so that disputes will be avoided when it comes time for payment for the services performed.

All SOWs, whether simple or highly complex, usually contain a number of common elements. They often include the following:

Description of the Work to Be Performed

This is often task oriented and provided in sequential terms following some logical, defined process of workflow. For example:

- Generate a detailed design for the lab work area.
- List all work to be performed by the nature of the subcontract required.
- Submit work specification to at least three applicable subcontractors for each major trade.

Timeline

Each section of the work must be completed within a specific time. The timeline details the expected completion times of each element in the workflow and ensures that the project finishes on time. Often, the timeline specifies the points at which approval is required before proceeding further to ensure that requirements for one section are met before proceeding on to another. Timeline approval points may also trigger payment to the suppler for acceptable work performed.

Performance

The SOW must clearly define the parameters for acceptable quality and performance and the metrics by which they will be determined. Subjective terms such as "good" or "best" should be avoided whenever possible and replaced with more objective measurements such as "100 percent" or "within two hours of notification" so that it is clear to both parties if (or when) the requirements have been met.

Tips and Techniques

Statement of work and *scope of work* are interchangeable terms. You might notice the use of both in other books and materials about procurement.

Terms and Conditions

As an adjunct to both specifications and statements of work, terms and conditions, which were discussed in Chapter 1, define the contractual obligations of the supplier and the procurement organization. To the extent that your organization's standard terms and conditions will be included in all solicitations for quotations, they should be considered an integral part of the specifications.

While terms and conditions naturally vary from organization to organization, each generally uses a set of standard terms and conditions for purchase requirements, modified from time to time by terms and conditions tailored specifically for a given purchase. Typically, these are included in the boilerplate on the reverse side of a purchase order or in the standard library of contracts prepared by the Legal Department.

Standard terms and conditions usually include sections covering warranties, liability, indemnity, payment terms, legal jurisdiction, contingencies, cancellation, shipping requirements, and inspection. For a more complete picture, you may want to look at the back of one of your organization's purchase orders or one sent in by a customer. Terms that are customized for a particular purchase and tend to apply uniquely to that specific purpose may include such provisions as installation, acceptance criteria, training, and timelines. These are often added as amendments to the standard contract or in the wording on the face of the PO.

On the face of a PO, special terms and conditions are usually included as a subset of the item's description. For example, you might have a description in the PO such as "Valve, pneumatic as described in the attached specification." And then following that description, you might see a list like this in the PO:

The following additional terms and conditions apply:

- Approval by Robert Johnson required prior to payment.
- Delivery no later than July 23.
- Call 24 hours before delivery: (234) 555-1212.

Specification Traps

There are a number of traps that purchasers unknowingly build into their specifications. Some increase cost unnecessarily while others unwittingly ensure that the best solutions are not accepted. We discuss these traps in this section.

Uneeded Customization

This trap arises from the mistaken assumption that the product being purchased must be customized to conform to user requirements. *Customization* typically adds cost so the purchaser is well advised to investigate if this is truly required. An internal change in process with little or no resulting cost can often eliminate the need for customization. The term *standardization* also refers to the methods used to reduce or eliminate custom, one-time, and seldom-used components and processes that introduce variability and can potentially create added cost and quality problems.

Disregarding Performance Requirements

Specifications unnecessarily stricter than actual performance would require simply adding cost without adding benefits. They may also eliminate potential suppliers who are unable to perform to the higher requirements and thus eliminate price-reducing competition.

Conversely, specifications that are too open or loose, or with important details missing, tend to invite unacceptable quality and can create costly mistakes. The supplier can provide a product or material that meets the specification precisely but will not perform in its intended function. Often, a supplier will "low-ball" an initial bid, purposely bidding well below market price to buy the business knowing that a *change order* request will follow. Having already received the contract, the supplier is then relatively free to charge any amount it wishes and thus recover its loss on the initial bid.

Brand Name

Specifying a *brand name* limits competition and thus increases the likelihood of higher prices. Brand names may or may not improve the chances of receiving better quality; nevertheless, they typically cost more as a result of higher advertising costs to create the brand name in the first place and because of users' perception that substitutes will not perform as well. One way to avoid this trap is to specify the brand name and include the verbiage "or equivalent" to allow for greater competition. This means that any product meeting the same specifications as the brand name will be acceptable to the purchaser.

Tips and Techniques

The Hidden Cost of Using Brand Name Products

Companies spend a great deal of effort and money creating a brand name that is indistinguishable from the actual process being performed. A case in point is Xerox. So common has this name become that we use it as though it were a verb: "Please Xerox five copies for me."

We once received an order for several testers that were called out by brand name. Checking with the user, we discovered that he was simply using shorthand for the function and that there were many brands that would perform as well and be equally acceptable. Subsequent bids from competitors produced a savings of $70,000 on an original request for $300,000.

Locating and Developing Sources of Supply

In its traditional sense, *sourcing*, the identification, evaluation, and development of potential suppliers, has been the fundamental strategic role of the procurement activity. Today, this role has expanded to a broader level and includes the understanding and analysis of the specific market from which the purchase is being made, as well as developing and employing various processes to enhance competition. In this section, we examine the basic elements of finding potential sources.

The nature of the source from which the purchase is made can vary widely and be dependent on the nature of the purchase, the nature of the industry in which the purchase is being made, and the size of the purchase. The procurement professional must develop an understanding of how various supplier types can affect sourcing decisions.

For instance, a buyer needs to know whether to use a local source as supplier or whether location is irrelevant. The buyer should also be concerned with the size of the supplier; perhaps the organization would receive better service from a smaller supplier, where the volume of business might be more significant for the supplier and the buying organization would have more leverage. The buyer should also determine whether the organization should use a distributor or a manufacturer.

Local, Domestic, or International

Sourcing decisions based on the suppliers' location can often provide distinct advantages in specific situations. A local supplier, for example, may feel a greater obligation to maintain higher levels of service because it shares the same community as the buyer. And buying organizations may have the same preference for supporting other members of the immediate community. Local suppliers, too, can frequently provide faster response time as well as lower freight costs.

The buying organization can develop greater competition simply by expanding the geographical range of its sourcing to national sources that may provide better pricing and wider choices.

Similarly, there are numerous trade-offs to consider when making a decision to source domestically or internationally. Typically, communications and delivery are more reliable with domestic sources, whereas international sources can usually provide lower prices due to reduced labor costs.

There are also payment methods to consider when evaluating offshore or domestic sources. Commonly, sellers will want overseas buyers to guarantee payment through some form of bank document, such as a *letter of credit (LC)*. An LC usually contains provisions triggering an automatic payment from the buyer's bank upon documented proof of shipment or at some specific predetermined time intervals. This can be a relatively costly process and can tie up cash or credit lines for an inordinate period of time.

In addition, considerations regarding additional risks due to fluctuations in currency exchange rates must also be taken into account when purchasing internationally, and long-term contracts often contain a clause that adjusts the selling price based on any significant change in the exchange rate at the time of delivery.

Finally, you should also take into account logistical issues such as customs duties, taxes, *tariffs,* and added shipping costs.

DUTIES   Most governments, including the United States, charge taxes for the import and export of certain types of goods. There are three major types of duties in common use:

- *Ad valorem* duties are duties charged as a percentage of the shipment's value (e.g., 10 percent). Ad valorem is the most commonly assessed form of tariff.
- *Specific duties* are duties imposed as a flat rate for some specified measure of goods, for example, $6 per ton.
- *Compound duties* combine both ad valorem and specific duties, such as $6 per ton *and* 10 percent of the total value of the shipment.

SHIPPING The procurement professional has to consider the additional costs of shipping as well as the potential delays and risks of conducting business along an extended supply chain when making a decision to source overseas. Goods that are sensitive to environmental conditions or are needed in a reliable and timely manner are often shipped by air since the alternative, ocean freight, can be very slow. This can add significantly to shipping costs.

INVENTORY Longer supply chains typically require higher levels of inventory to buffer the long lead times and potential fluctuations in demand. The longer pipeline may also contain several weeks of inventory in various stages of manufacture or shipment if it is a regularly used product. Because most products are paid for at the time of shipment, this can tie up significant amounts of the organization's cash and can result in increased costs for carrying the inventory.

DOCUMENTATION Goods traveling across international borders often require special documentation and licenses or must comply with certain restrictions. The most common of these include export and import licenses, commercial invoices, certificate of origin, insurance certificates, and international bills of lading. The *Convention on Contracts for the International Sale of Goods (CISG)* establishes uniform regulations in an attempt to standardize the rules governing international commerce but has not yet found universal acceptance. The *United Nations Commission on International Trade Law (UNCITRAL)* publishes an updated list of countries that have adopted the CISG at www.uncitral.org.

Size

As a procurement professional, you should consider the size of the organizations you are sourcing from before making a final decision to choose a specific source. Smaller-sized organizations often have a greater incentive to provide more customized and personalized service than larger ones since they rely more heavily on individual accounts. Larger organizations, however, may have greater technical resources and may be better able to respond to wide swings in demand.

Original Manufacturer or Distributor

Distributors frequently service the spot buying market and typically maintain substantial inventories in order to better service their clientele. As a result, they must often charge somewhat higher prices than the original manufacturing sources. Consequently, the procurement professional's decision should take into consideration the volume of the purchase. The greater the volume, the more likely you are to obtain lower prices directly from the manufacturer. However, if you need small quantities of many different products (hardware, for example), your advantage may lie with a local stocking distributor.

Types of Competition

Supplier selection is also determined to a large extent by the nature of competition, whether that competition is established directly by the buyer as an offshoot of an organizational policy or as a result of conditions prevailing in the industry. In the following section, we will define the various competitive conditions that you may encounter.

Open Competition

Open competition is said to exist when there are multiple suppliers available to fill your specific requirements, and they are willing to vie for your business. When strong competitive factors exist in the marketplace, the buyer's negotiating position is stronger, and there are greater opportunities for gaining concessions in price as well as in payment terms, service, and support. To continue to foster robust competition, the buyer will want to avoid customization so that as many companies as possible can easily supply the product or service and maintain the widest possible area of source selection to keep the number of competitors high.

Sole Source

What if only one source is capable of meeting the buyer's needs? Then you have a *sole-source* situation—the exact opposite of open competition. Sole-source situations are often the result of a government-created monopoly, such as a local utility, and there is little the buyer can do to gain concessions. Typically, in this kind of situation there is formal oversight by some governing body to ensure customers get fair treatment, but beyond such public regulation, there is sometimes little incentive on the part of the sole source to negotiate.

Single Source

A *single-source* situation is similar to the sole source but is a condition created by the buying organization, either through product customization where only one supplier is capable of producing the product, or through some predefined collaborative relationship that by its nature excludes competition. In this case, the benefits of the relationship itself provide a competitive advantage—such as a supplier-managed inventory program or joint development of new technology—that outweighs the benefits of open competition.

Technical or Limited Competition

Technical competition (also known as *limited competition*) is created when only a limited number of suppliers are available for a particular product due to patents or limited production capability. Competition in a particular industry can also be limited to only a few suppliers within a geographical area, commonly due to the existence of franchises or large initial investments required to enter the business, and the buyer can find it financially impractical to extend procurement beyond the limited area.

Partnership/Joint Venture

On occasion, organizations will form a *joint venture* to create a source of supply when none exists or to jointly share the expenses of developing new technology. While not specifically limiting competition, the investing organizations have little or no incentive to purchase outside the bounds of this partnership because the costs of development have already been invested and there are no other ways to recover the investment.

Co-Sources

Multiple sources are sometimes used by the same organization, either to foster competition or because no single supplier is capable of fulfilling 100 percent of the requirements. Frequently, multiple sources will be maintained to reduce the risk of interrupted supply, and there are also situations when some percentage of the business may be set aside for small or minority enterprises.

Consortium

In some industries, small groups of buyers band together to purchase jointly and contract with suppliers as a single entity. This enables each of the organizations in the *consortium* to buy at a rate that they would ordinarily not receive. There are a number of legal considerations that vary by state so you will want to engage your legal advisor prior to participating in or forming a buying consortium.

Requirements Integration

Sometimes organizations will choose to combine the requirements of a class of products or services—maintenance, repair, and operations (MRO), for example—and source them through one supplier. Doing so can consolidate and leverage spending in many commodity areas that would ordinarily produce little discount and marginal service. By integrating supply, buyers can often provide service benefits, such as desktop delivery for office supplies or online procurement.

Locating Suitable Suppliers

There are so many ways to locate potential suppliers; it is hardly possible to list them all. Our methods have ranged from using online search engines and business directories to calling colleagues and attending networking activities at our local *Institute for Supply Management (ISM)* affiliate. There may also be sources of information available to you through the technical staff within your own organization, and that is often the best place to begin your supplier sourcing activity.

In this section, we'll discuss some of the more common methods of locating sources.

Directories and Industrial Guides

The most traditional means of locating potential suppliers is through industry-focused directories and buyers' guides. These are typically published in conjunction with a trade magazine or an industry association and contain listings of suppliers grouped by specialty or geographical location. These directories also often contain information about the supplier's products or services, capabilities, and size and market segment, along with contact names and telephone numbers.

One of the most commonly used directories is the *Thomas Register*, a general directory covering several hundred industries and hundreds of thousands of suppliers. Other directories are focused more specifically on one particular industry, such as those published by *Ceramic Industry* magazine directed at the ceramic manufacturing industry and the Buyers' Guide published by *Electronics Weekly* magazine.

There are also the ever-popular telephone directories such as the local Yellow Pages. These provide listings of businesses for a local calling area by category but typically provide no specific information beyond the advertising paid for by the organization. Regional business directories published by local newspapers to promote business in the readership area are also popular.

Internet Search Tools

Today, it is common to use the Internet to search for suppliers. Using easily accessed search engines such as Google, you can locate multiple suppliers for any product or service simply by entering product key words in the search box. The problem, as you may have already experienced, is that there is so much information available on the Internet that it can be impractical to search through it all. For example, a Google search for the phrase "paper cup manufacturer" returned 130,000 entries in less than one second.

Trade Associations/Trade Shows

Trade organizations typically sponsor magazines and online directories that help the buyer find sources. More importantly perhaps, these organizations sponsor local or national trade shows that bring together all of the significant suppliers within a specific industry for several days of workshops and exhibits where buyers can effortlessly contact a significant number of suppliers in one location. An example is WESCON, an annual exhibit held on the West Coast for electronic component suppliers. This is a trade show that brings together hundreds of established and newly organized companies that supply the electronics OEM (original equipment manufacturer) marketplace and is cosponsored by several professional organizations, including the *Institute of Electrical and Electronic Engineers (IEEE)*.

Governmental Agencies

Many governmental agencies provide information and directories that can be used for sourcing. The most commonly available are those published by the U.S.

Department of Commerce and the U.S. General Services Administration's Federal Supply Service.

Minority Supplier Directories

For those seeking minority suppliers, there are literally dozens of minority business directories available, many through local minority business councils. One of the most useful directories is released by the U.S. *Small Business Administration (SBA)* online at www.sba8a.com.

Consultants

When a significant or critical need arises and there are no internal resources to provide adequate sourcing activities, procurement professionals often reach outside the organization for proven expertise. Engaging consultants that are industry experts can save the time it takes to find and prepare detailed studies and comparisons of sources since they already have substantial knowledge of suppliers and can leverage their expertise to shorten the time it takes to develop the best supplier fit. While this might appear to be an expensive approach, in the long run it can save valuable time and expense.

Market Analysis: Determining Changing Marketplace Factors

One of the most significant determinants of sourcing decisions generates from the nature of changes in the market. Supply and demand continually interact to produce varying pricing profiles. When product is in short supply or production resources come under threat (e.g., oil and the Middle East), prices can rise dramatically and capacity limits may, in addition, create supply *allocations*. Organizations wishing to continually work with the most price competitive suppliers who stay up-to-date on the latest technological advances and business methods must maintain an aggressive review process that periodically surveys the market as conditions change.

Economic Conditions

Supply and demand continually drive prices up and down. As economic conditions change, demand increases or declines, generating shortages or excesses in supply at any given time. As previously noted, increased supply or decreased demand (or combinations of both) generally lead to reduced prices. What drives these fluctuations can be a mystery. However, the astute procurement professional can take advantage of these conditions by seeking increased competition during periods of abundant supply and declining prices when suppliers are more anxious to seek new business or, conversely, by locking in prices through contracts when facing periods of shortage or inflationary pricing.

MARKET COMPLEXITY The extent to which an organization's economic strategy can be employed—for example, when to lock in prices through extended contracts or when to pay more for higher quality levels—depends somewhat significantly on the complexity of the market. Markets with few suppliers and little potential for product substitution tend to offer only limited opportunities for the buyer to use competition to advantage. However, markets in which competitive forces exist and shortages in one product can be easily offset by substituting another—that is, markets with greater complexity—provide the buyer with a great deal of leverage to gain improvements. Cost reduction efforts can produce the greatest results in industries with broadly diverse alternatives, so the buyer's sourcing effort should always begin by determining the nature of the market.

NATURE OF COMPETITION   The nature of competition in any particular market varies. Are there many technical solutions available or only one or two? Is the market characterized by geographical limitations with very high transportation costs? If, for example, the product being purchased is covered by a patent or controlled by patented manufacturing technology, competition will be unlikely. Similarly, when startup costs are high, such as those that occur in the development of proprietary tooling, competition tends to become constricted once the initial sourcing decision is made. It is always wise to understand the nature of competition in this regard before committing to generating short-term cost reductions since the sourcing effort will likely require major engineering efforts.

When dealing with sources of critical supplies or services, the buyer needs to maintain continual vigilance for potential traps, such as absorbing tooling costs to "buy the business" with the intention of recovering the cost in future years, that will unknowingly limit the nature of the competition for that particular product or service.

Technology

When technological change drives conditions in the market, new sources of supply must always be under consideration. New technology frequently generates new opportunities for capital investment, and emerging businesses tend to spring up everywhere. The buyer should be sensitive to these opportunities but be able to balance them with the need for maintaining long-term relationships that produce value beyond price or the latest fad in technology.

With critical supplies and services, one should always monitor the supply base to ensure that existing sources are keeping abreast of technology and adding improvements as necessary. Suppliers that do not constantly upgrade their processes to take advantage of new technology could easily fall by the wayside. The buyer should consider ways to continually monitor existing suppliers and their technological position relative to their competitors so that failures to keep up with important changes in technology do not adversely affect their own organization's competitive position.

Performance

Just as economic conditions can change for the worse, so can supplier performance. Suppliers under continual pricing pressures due to emerging global markets, for example, may tend to sacrifice some of the quality that helped select them for your business in the first place. Delivery delays, cuts in services, and quality failures are often the early signs of declining performance due to economic hardship. Companies providing critical supplies and services need to be continually measured against industry performance standards. Initial signs of deteriorating performance should be met with clear improvement projects and, depending upon the rapidity of decline, additional sourcing activities.

Obtaining Bids and Proposals

Bids and proposals are integral elements in the procurement process. When a clear specification or SOW exists, the buyer will typically solicit a competitive bid or a *request for quotation (RFQ)*. When specific information does not exist or when there are a number of potential ways to meet the user's requirements, proposals are often requested through a formal *request for proposal (RFP)* process. How the buyer structures the bidding or proposal strategy depends on a number of factors outlined in the next section.

Bidding Guidelines

Bidding is a competitive process that enables the buyer to leverage several potential sources of supply through a single activity to obtain the most favorable business terms. In order for this process to be successful, a number of conditions, such as those outlined here, must be met.

Provide Clear Content

A solicitation for bids should provide sufficient information about the requirement so that a supplier will be able to offer exact pricing and provide whatever other detailed information is required to successfully obtain the business. Typically, this will include facts such as the exact specification of the required goods or an SOW for a service, the quantity required, payment terms, the expected time of performance, necessary quality levels, and shipping or performance location. The solicitation must also include a deadline for submission.

Determine Compressible Spending

Before engaging in the solicitation process, the buyer is responsible for determining if market conditions will support a reduction in price or an improvement in terms. Unless favorable market conditions are present, competitive bidding will not be worthwhile. While there is no precise way to ensure this under all conditions, benchmarking industry trends, whenever possible, might provide some guidance.

Ensure Responsive, Responsible Competition

When selecting potential suppliers or candidates to which bids will be sent, it is important that the buyer prequalify them to ensure that the bids returned will be responsive to the organization's needs. This means that the supplier has the means to fully understand the buyer's needs and can, under normal business conditions, fulfill the requirements.

The buyer should ensure that the suppliers are in a position to meet any procurement requirements; that, for example, they have the necessary financial means to produce the product being specified or that they have the equipment needed to meet the requirement in a timely manner. If tooling is required, the buyer must be careful to ensure that the supplier is not using a bidding trap by absorbing the cost of the tooling as a way of keeping out the competition.

Enable Fair and Ethical Bidding Processes

As a buyer, your job is to properly ensure ethical conduct in the solicitation and acceptance of bids, making sure that all suppliers are provided with exactly the same information and have an equal amount of time to respond. Answers to questions submitted by one supplier need to be distributed to all bidding suppliers to further enhance the competitive process.

Suppliers should also be made aware of the process for awarding the business by the buying organization, whether it is the lowest price or some combination of terms, as well as the criteria for making the final selection. Many organizations use a weighted-average scoring process developed by a cross-functional internal team to select suppliers for complex services, since it can be extremely difficult to unilaterally evaluate and select the best supplier.

Hold an Open Prebid Conference

A prebid conference, where all potential suppliers have the opportunity to receive a briefing on the bid package from the buying organization's staff, should be used when the requirement is relatively complex. Usually, this is held for all potential suppliers at one time and provides an opportunity to review the specifications, time frames, drawings or blueprints, and to meet the staff. The prebid conference also provides an opportunity for suppliers to become familiar with the organization's policies and procedures, payment practices, and code of conduct, as well as any special requirements that relate to the particular procurement.

Although this practice in the bidding process can enhance competition through personal contact and expedite the process through real-time resolution of questions, it can also be time consuming for both parties. For this reason, it is important to schedule the conference far enough in advance so that all parties may attend and so that you can have the right personnel available to provide answers. This is especially relevant when the prebid conference is mandatory or when the requirements are particularly complex.

Formulating the Bid or Proposal Type

There are a number of procedures that can be used in the solicitation of bids and proposals, depending on the nature of the requirements and the objectives of the bidding process. Some widely used solicitation types include sealed bids, offers to buy, RFPs, and RFQs. Each of these has a variety of potential applications, so choosing the optimal method for obtaining a specific bid requires a clear understanding of its advantages and limitations. The section that follows provides the background for making the best selections.

Sealed Bid

Typically used in government-related contracting, the *sealed bid* is an offer submitted in a sealed envelope that is opened with other bids at a previously designated time and place. This method is used when the buyer does not wish to publicly reveal any of the bids prior to a specific deadline to prevent others from leveraging it to unfair advantage. There are two types of sealed bids that are used frequently in procurement: *open bidding* and *restricted bidding*.

The bidding process may be open to any qualified supplier (open bidding) that wishes to enter a bid. In most cases, qualification takes place at an earlier date and the supplier must be approved by the time the bids are sent out. Or the bidding process may be open only to a specific group of suppliers (restricted bidding) due to the requirements of a regulatory process (e.g., minority or small business set asides) or to ensure that sensitive information does not get into the wrong hands.

Posted Offer to Buy

Government contracting requirements are often posted in a public bidding document or online. This ensures that the general public has open access to the process. In common usage, this notice is referred to as a *posted offer to buy*. This process is not used by commercial organizations much, although notices on Procurement Department websites open to the supplier community are now becoming more common. Figure 2.2 illustrates a typical online posting as an invitation to bid. Notice that some of the business requirements, such as the due date and required format, are posted outside of the actual specifications as a way of calling particular attention to them.

Automated Bidding

It is common today to generate automated bids using a number of computer-based processes. In addition to submitting and receiving bids and proposals directly through the Internet, some organizations are turning to the *reverse auction* process to enhance competition.

A reverse auction is typically an event that enables prequalified suppliers to submit many bids in sequence with the objective of outbidding their competitors and thereby winning the business. Outbidding in this case means submitting real-time offers that go below the prices submitted by their competition. The bidding process ends at a specific time, and usually the lowest bidder obtains the order. On occasion, the business may be divided among several bidders on a percentage basis, with the lowest bidder receiving the largest allotment.

Request for Information (RFI)

The *request for information (RFI)* is used by organizations seeking to develop a bid list or prequalify potential suppliers. Generally, the RFI asks suppliers to submit

INVITATION FOR BID
XYZ IFB 11-02

| NOTICE TO PROSPECTIVE BIDDERS

February 18, 2011

You are invited to review and respond to this Invitation for Bid (IFB), entitled **"IFB 11-02 Armored Car Service"** In submitting your bid, you must comply with these instructions.

This contract is for a daily armored car service pickup at one location. Monday through Friday between 12 PM – 5 PM, excluding State Holidays and days mandated off due to any Executive Orders. The duration of the contract is for thirty-six (36) months.
Note that all agreements entered into with the State ... will include by reference, General Terms and Conditions ... and Contractor Certification Clauses ... that may be viewed and downloaded at Internet site.... If you do not have Internet access, a hard copy can be provided by contacting the person listed below.
If you have questions or should you need any clarifying information, the contact person for this IFB is:

> Contract Analyst
> Department of Programs
> (906) 555-1212
> tsmith@xyz.or.gov

Please note that any *verbal* information given will not be binding upon the State unless such information is issued in writing as an official addendum.

Sincerely,

Contracts Manager

FIGURE 2.2   A Sample Invitation to Bid

general information about their companies, such as size, financial performance, years in business, market position, product lines, and a variety of other information that can determine the supplier's suitability for participating in some future competitive event. Of the three requests we discuss in this section, the RFI is used the least because of the advent of the Internet and how easy it is to gather information now.

Request for Proposal (RFP)

The RFP is used when a specification or SOW has not yet been developed, or when the buyer has a general requirement and wants to solicit various ideas on how that requirement can best be met. Included in the RFP are typical objectives of the future contract and as much of the background behind the requirement as is already known. The language of the RFP usually allows the supplier some freedom in determining the most effective solution and often enables the supplier to actually establish the specifications. Sometimes prices are requested along with the proposal, and sometimes suppliers are specifically requested not to submit price quotations.

Tips and Techniques

Two-Step Bidding

When RFPs are not used to solicit price quotations, the buyer may use a two-step process. In this procedure, the buying organization generally assembles a specification or SOW based on the collective responses of the suppliers (or a modification of the most agreeable solution) and then submits the requirement back to the suppliers for a price quotation.

The time required to fully implement this process is often a factor limiting its use. In a complex RFP, it is not uncommon to allow suppliers three to four weeks to respond, so it is easy to see that the overall time to progress through a two-step process can take several months, considering the time it takes to formulate the initial proposal, then work it into a specification and resubmit it for quotes. However, for extremely large acquisitions, for example, construction of an office complex, this process is undeniably worthwhile.

Request for Quotation

The RFQ is virtually no different from the second part of the two-step bidding process just described. It is used when a specification or SOW has already been formulated and the buyer needs only to obtain price, delivery, and other specific terms from the suppliers in order to select the most appropriate source. The specifications are sent to prequalified suppliers soliciting price and other terms and conditions.

Managing Sourcing Data

Most organizations maintain listings of suppliers with whom they have established some form of business relationship. These listings, often referred to as a sourcing list, provide other internal users and buyers with both the current status of a particular supplier and whatever historical data may be available. Historical data are particularly useful as a method of avoiding duplication of effort, since the organization's prior records can tell a buyer if the supplier is qualified for a particular purpose. This prevents having to gather the usual information needed to qualify that supplier.

There are numerous ways to designate and list suppliers. Outlined next are a few of the more common ways.

Categories of Existing Sources

To enhance their usefulness, supplier listings are usually developed according to some form of commodity categorization—in addition to the product or service they supply—indicating their current supplier status. Some of the more common listings in use include the *approved supplier list (ASL)*, along with listings of certified, qualified, preferred, and disqualified suppliers. These lists are usually developed and maintained by the Procurement Department but are considered an integral part of the quality control process. Let's describe these in more detail.

Approved Supplier List

One type of list the buyer keeps is an approved supplier list (ASL), which contains a listing of suppliers who have met the organization's compliance criteria and are qualified to provide specific direct materials, controlled *materials*, or manufacturing-related services to the organization. ASLs are usually used in manufacturing environments where technical and quality control requirements are necessary. Suppliers are often expected to pass on-site inspections and to maintain preestablished levels of quality, service, and on-time delivery. Suppliers listed on the buyer's ASL are considered first-tier suppliers.

Certified Suppliers

When the need to integrate the quality standards and systems of multiple organizations exists so that inspection and training costs can be held to a minimum, procurement departments often establish a listing of suppliers that have met these particular requirements. *Certified suppliers* are suppliers that do not furnish direct materials and are, therefore, not appropriate for inclusion on the ASL. This designation might apply to suppliers removing hazardous waste or specially licensed consultants, as well as companies supplying certain types of telecommunications or network hardware.

Qualified Suppliers

Qualified suppliers are those that have successfully completed a formal screening process but may not yet have been qualified for the ASL or that may be supplying a product or service that does not require the stringent supplier site inspection criteria used to establish eligibility for the ASL. These are usually suppliers who meet all of the business requirements of the organization and are approved by the Procurement Department for future business that may arise.

Preferred Suppliers

A *preferred supplier* listing generally includes suppliers who have proven capabilities that make them especially valuable to the buying organization. Often, they are suppliers who provide exceptional service or favorable pricing. They may be suppliers already under contract to provide particular products or services, so the Procurement Department will encourage their use.

Preferred supplier listings may also include minority- or female-owned and disadvantaged businesses, and companies that are engaged in contractual (or similarly formalized) partnerships, as well as good customers or clients of the buying organization.

Tips and Techniques

Watch out. Subtle differences in terminology usage regarding the supplier's actual status may confuse you. Remember that the approved supplier list is used in audit-controlled environments.

Disqualified Suppliers

On occasion, a supplier will be unable to meet the organization's requirements, have a contract terminated for violations, or consistently fail to maintain acceptable performance or quality levels. Under these circumstances, suppliers will often be barred from conducting further business for a period of time and will be added to a listing of *disqualified suppliers*. This listing may be further reinforced by a reference stating "Do Not Use" following the supplier's name in the buying organization's computer system.

Maintaining Sourcing Lists

To take full advantage of the value inherent in maintaining sourcing lists, buyers must take special efforts to keep them up to date. Fortunately, computerization and *enterprise resource planning (ERP)* software has greatly aided this process. Keep in mind that some listings, such as the ASL, are auditable for compliance with *ISO (International Organization for Standardization)* certification. Some of the other considerations you may want to keep in mind include the following:

Electronic Tools

Most computer-based procurement systems in use today enable the buyer to include special status in the *supplier master record*, the database that maintains information about the supplier such as their address, key contact personnel, and payment terms. Reports can then be run listing suppliers by specific sourcing list status such as commodity or small business type. This can be extremely useful when sourcing requirements dictate using suppliers from one of these categories.

Contracts Database

Organizations that do a substantial portion of their business through contracts often maintain a database where they are centrally stored. This is useful not only in providing historical guidance to the buyer but in assisting with future sourcing decisions and avoiding duplication of effort in the formation of contract language.

The Strategic Sourcing Plan

When in place and understood by all stakeholders, a strategic sourcing plan provides guidance to those responsible for implementing acquisition policy. As with any plan, it should be well documented and systematically refer to the organizational mission and vision. The plan must also clearly take into account customer requirements that are identified in the organization's broader strategic business plan.

Plan Elements

Many organizations use a standard format in which to create departmental strategic plans. This uniformity helps when various plans are consolidated, since each of the plan elements is treated in a similar order. It also helps to ensure that critical path segments are not overlooked.

The common elements of a strategic plan can be outlined as follows.

MISSION AND VISION Traditionally, any strategic plan begins with a statement of vision and mission. The mission statement must set the tone for the objectives within the plan. The strategic sourcing plan should also contain a mission statement, and it should clearly align with the organization's business mission statement. It also needs to identify what value will be added by the sourcing group.

Equally important is to communicate the statement to all cross-functional departmental personnel. Most internal organizations that we work with dutifully create the plan and place the document on a shelf. Very few cross-functional personnel outside of those who have contributed to the plan even know it exists. On one occasion, one of the authors recalls asking the CEO of a company he worked for to describe the organization's objectives. "Sorry," the CEO said. "That information is confidential."

Do *you* know your organization's mission statement? It's not surprising to find that very few employees know, much less understand, the mission of their organization. In class after class, the authors asked how many attending knew their organization's mission statement well enough to recite it. We considered it fortunate to find more than two in any class of 30+.

ENVIRONMENTAL ANALYSIS An environmental analysis is another traditional element of the strategic sourcing plan. The environmental analysis describes current conditions within the organization, as well as with its primary customers, its supply chain, and the overall market. This provides the background against which the plan is developed. Its importance lies in tying objectives to current business conditions; if conditions change significantly, the plan may require revision.

In our analysis, we must also take into account conditions across the entire supply chain that can impact our supply strategy. If we are a semiconductor manufacturer, we must consider our customers' demand for advanced technology and time our development process to coincide with their plans and technology roadmaps.

SWOT ANALYSIS The plan should include a comprehensive SWOT (strengths, weaknesses, opportunities, and threats) analysis traditionally used to guide plan implementers toward defining objectives. A SWOT analysis helps identify potential roadblocks (weaknesses and threats) and prepares the way for dealing with them through organizational strengths. It can also identify potential opportunities that help to implement the plan strategy. In the strategic sourcing plan, it is important to identify these roadblock conditions since they invariably affect meeting key objectives. In fact, it is probably a good idea to describe all objectives as they relate to the SWOT analysis.

ASSUMPTIONS While it is ideal to have all of the detail needed to formulate the plan, this is rarely the case. Market dynamics will continue to change throughout the plan's period, and new conditions will arise that are unlikely to be foreseen. So what isn't clearly known or capable of forecast needs to be assumed so that the plan can go forward. These assumptions must be documented since, just as with environmental conditions, they are used as "just-in-case" placeholders. When we can replace assumptions with known facts, we can then make whatever adjustments to the plan are required.

OBJECTIVES Within the strategic sourcing plan, we can outline specific business objectives that we expect to achieve. *Objectives*, as we use the term here, are the expression of specific targets that will advance our mission by adding value to the organization. They are tied to the overall mission statement and take into account environmental conditions, our SWOT analysis, and any assumptions we make.

The plan describes objectives in clear and directive language. For example, our customers may be demanding environment friendly products. Do we need to move more aggressively into a green sourcing program?

When developing objectives, it's important to include measurements that go along with them. If you can't measure it, how will you know when you have achieved it?

Obviously, not all goals are of equal importance, and we know that in many cases, our resources will be limited, so it's important to prioritize all goals. Those that are most important are given the highest priority for achievement. We can also consider any objectives that can be achieved without using significant resources, perhaps in the course of fulfilling our general responsibilities.

Objectives for a strategic sourcing plan might include (as examples):

- A specific amount of cost saving.
- An improvement in customer support through reduced lead times from suppliers and better on-time delivery performance.
- Development of new supplier alliances and partnerships.
- Reduction of inventory levels through, for example, consignment.
- Development of new demand management planning tools and models.

STRATEGY Sourcing strategy must be developed within the scope of the overall mission statement and to ensure, to the extent possible, achieving our objectives. For example: "We will actively support the organization's 'first to market' objectives." This simple statement can then be used to create a strategy. First to market may require *early supplier involvement (ESI)*. This in turn may generate the need for close alliances with key suppliers so that we can develop early involvement. (Early involvement is rather difficult if we are competing all of our purchases and can only make an award once the bids are analyzed.) For the sourcing team, strong business alliances as opposed to full bidding competition on all purchases, for example, represent a distinct strategy.

We must also ensure that our strategy addresses developments throughout the supply chain; it may be economic conditions or it may be category or commodity shortages that escalate market pricing. We may have solid data or we may need to make some critical assumptions. If we forecast an economic downturn, for example, we will likely want to reduce inventory in our suppliers' inventory pipelines.

Within the plan, we must initially identify cross-functional team members and describe their key roles and responsibilities. Particularly important are responsibilities for supplier negotiations and analysis for implementation; that is, developing and interpreting relevant data, and implementing actions such analysis generates. These efforts will likely be parsed out to existing commodity teams, so we will want to determine if we have the right people in the right places at the right time.

IMPLEMENTATION   Keep in mind, the strategic sourcing plan establishes a high-level approach that does not delve into the details of tactical methods. So to implement our strategy, we require an operational strategy and a tactical approach to achieving our goals. This begins with an operational analysis that serves to bridge the strategic plan and the operational tactical plan.

Opportunity Analysis

The strategic sourcing plan needs to address procurement commodities or categories where potential opportunities for improvement have been identified. Improvements can take the form of lower prices, better quality, reduced inventory, and so on. We develop these through an opportunity analysis, typically an extension of the overall sourcing plan into areas managed by commodity or category groups. This analysis should be conducted by a cross-functional strategic sourcing team, preferably before finalizing the plan.

The opportunity analysis often uses industry benchmarks to determine where gaps exist between best practices and current practices in our organization. (We'll outline the gap analysis methodology in the section that follows.) These benchmarks, developed by commodity, category, or industry, take into account our total annual volume (past and projected) so that we can be sure they are relevant in scope. We also need to know our historical experience with price increases within the commodity or with a specific supplier and what earlier cost and price improvements have been made.

The opportunity analysis and the benchmarking process are often by-products of the market analysis (which we addressed earlier in this chapter) that takes place prior to the development of the strategic plan. Keep in mind that there may be a significant number of opportunities that have been identified subsequent to the previous strategic sourcing plan, but we are, for now, only interested in those opportunities that align with the organization's objectives. Based on the data gathered through our opportunity analysis, we should be able to project the degree to which our plan will support the overall organizational plan.

Typically, the opportunity analysis will cover several elements:

- **Determine how and with whom we are spending our funds.** Known as *spend analysis*, this process reviews the organization's detailed spending history as a means of finding common items that can be consolidated by using fewer suppliers. The added volume for the suppliers we do use should provide additional price reduction negotiation opportunities.
- **Review spending history to find multiple items that are very similar and can be respecified to a single item.** We refer to this as part standardization or value engineering and, as with spending analysis, we can leverage the larger consolidated spending as a way to generate price reductions. This is an especially productive area when the organization operates from multiple locations or when a merger or acquisition occurs.
- **Identify poor supplier performance.** Especially in areas that directly support the organization's mission, we should review suppliers' history to pinpoint those that are well below our expectations. We can later determine if improvement is possible or if any supplier(s) need to be replaced.

  In relation to performance, we want to review (and perhaps benchmark) the measurements we use to assess supplier performance via a "scorecard." Are the supplier(s) still relevant? Do our metrics provide an accurate picture of how well the supplier is meeting our needs? And, perhaps more importantly, are we monitoring the supplier for contract compliance and performance to agreed upon service levels?
- **Improve competition.** Are there important elements of our procurement strategies that lack robust competition? Do suppliers of these items routinely raise prices regardless of market conditions? Do we have suppliers who believe they are certain to continue to receive our business regardless of business conditions? Do we have products or services that have not been supply competed for several years? A "yes" to any of these questions may mean that we need to reformulate our supply strategy for achieving the best value from these suppliers as a reward for earning our business.
- **Investigate outsourcing opportunities.** Outsourcing, in general, and business process outsourcing (BPO) specifically, is a well-established, significant component of strategic sourcing. As its title implies, the focus of BPO is on services. Some of the more commonly outsourced services include information technology (although often assigned to its own category), accounts payable, customer support, legal services, design and engineering, research and data analysis, logistics, security, facilities management, financial services, and procurement itself. The primary objectives of outsourcing are relatively clear: reduced cost through lower wages for labor, an extension of the organization's capabilities, a more specialized workforce, greater spend visibility, up-to-date technology, temporary personnel (and recruiting) and, importantly, the ability to meet variable demand without having to add employees.

  In addition to business processes, organizations are also engaged in outsourcing elements of manufacturing. In fact, assembly operations under subcontracts are likely the earliest example of outsourcing, tracing its roots to the traditional "make or buy" practice that would determine if a manufactured part or a manufacturing process could be converted to a purchase. Oddly enough, in the early days of assembly line manufacturing, vertical integration—that is, incorporating all elements of the end product's production within the company—was the rule rather than the exception.

The outsourcing opportunity analysis should take into account geographical considerations, including the pros and cons of offshoring (outsourcing to companies based in other countries) or nearshoring (outsourcing to companies within the organization's national borders). Some aspects to consider in globalizing sourcing activities are the complexity and costs of currency exchange rates, taxes, transportation, and logistics (including customs), overcoming cultural and language differences, and the risk factors inherent in the local economy and political climate. (Outsourcing will be covered in more detail in Chapter 16 where we discuss make-or-buy decisions.)

- **Capture additional spending.** It is not uncommon for organizations to tolerate spending by any number of departments without procurement involvement, sometimes called "maverick buying." Capturing this spending by the sourcing and procurement teams can lead to a number of benefits for the organization, such as improved pricing through negotiation, better value through competitive bidding, and tighter control of supplier performance. And capturing this spending can assist the sourcing and procurement group in achieving strategic supply savings goals.

- **Improve internal processes.** In many cases, opportunity means "work." Organizations sometimes find themselves in the peculiar position of having more cost-saving opportunities than there are staff members to implement them. However, if we can find ways to improve our internal procurement process, it's possible that we can free up resources to engage in cost savings or standardization projects. As an example, Figure 2.3 shows that our model allocates 5 percent of its spending (in dollars) to the MRO (maintenance, repair, and operations) or indirect category. But in actual procurement volume, this category would likely account for nearly 50 percent of the ordering volume. Do we really want to allocate 50 percent of our staff to 5 percent of the spending?

During one recent assignment, our consulting team discovered a situation similar to the one outlined earlier. In developing a spending analysis, it was found that the MRO category accounted for about 8 percent of the procurement spending, with just over 45 percent of the transactions. Half the procurement staff (eight buyers) was allocated to this category of spending. Automating this very-low-risk category produced significant savings. The "liberated" team members went on to assist commodity groups harvest the identified savings possibilities.

By now, many organizations recognize the value gained by using purchasing cards. P-cards virtually eliminate the need to generate a purchase order since the card issuer can provide detailed spending reports that can be approved by management. Similarly, most automated purchase requisitioning systems provide the internal user with a catalog of suppliers with items that they may purchase in various spending categories. Their supply request is routed for approval and, once the proper approvals are obtained, then goes directly to the

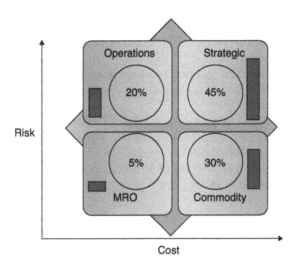

FIGURE 2.3   Supply Positioning

selected catalog supplier. Each supplier has obligated responsibilities under a master supply agreement or a similar contractual arrangement, which lowers business risk substantially.

- **Review of current market conditions.** For the sourcing team to identify opportunities that exist in the market, outside of the relatively limited picture taken from the organization's experience, a thorough analysis of external market conditions must be taken. This is perhaps the most important step in the planning process since, ideally, it will provide critical benchmarks used to identify areas of supply opportunity when compared with our own organization's overall performance. There are many significant fundamentals that we can examine. Here are some that are perhaps the most common:
  - **Competitive positioning.** To what extent does supplier competition exist? Are there many suppliers or very few? Many suppliers would result in robust competition and the opportunity to leverage and improve our overall cost position. Fewer suppliers might lead us to a strategy of placing more of our other types of purchases with these suppliers to gain overall financial leverage, depending on the scope of their business. Similarly, we should know who the major buyers are that create market demand and what likely impact they will have on our sourcing strategy.
  - **Cost profiles.** We need to understand the drivers of market pricing and the likely trends in those areas. This will define our supplier negotiation timing strategy: Rising prices might signal longer-term contracts to lock in current pricing; falling prices may lead to a strategy of spot or one-time buying.
  - **Risk.** Identify significant market and/or political risks affecting our key purchases and develop a strategy to deal with them. We also want to determine how this type of risk will impact our inventory goal positions. Do we need more or less safety stock or altered lead times?
  - **The supply chain.** For critical items and categories, we want to understand the extent that factors in our extended supply chain will impact our key critical

path suppliers. Depending on the length of the supply chain, transportation and logistics costs can be an area for further negotiation, as well as continued monitoring and analysis.

- **Technological trends.** We need to understand how rapidly the technology changes in major sourcing categories so we can determine areas that are due for a turnover or retooling.
- **Financial profiles.** As part of our market review, we should not overlook an analysis of the financial position of our suppliers. This means looking at market trends in profitability, accounts receivable aging, accounts payable aging, cash flow and short-term obligations, and comparing our suppliers to the trends in their market segment.

Operational Sourcing Strategy

Strategic sourcing, as a plan, must be implemented, that is, set in motion, through operational executed activities. A practical way to guide this process is to develop an implementation initiative. This initiative outlines those specific operational activities that will support the strategic sourcing plan. By operational executed activities we mean those day-to-day functions common to most procurement organizations: issuing purchase orders, ordering or releasing direct materials to plan, forecasting volumes, monitoring supplier performance, tracking spending patterns, assessing supply risk, resolving contractual issues, arranging the return of unused product, and reconciling invoices.

Having an operational plan in place will help to significantly reduce (or even eliminate) the common fire drill approach to acquisition.

Steps to Implementing the Plan

The strategic sourcing plan is useful in guiding operational tactics without actually defining them. But there are some important details that should be identified when developing an operational sourcing strategy:

- **Current conditions.** For each of the stated strategic objectives, the authoring team needs to examine existing conditions and describe them in enough detail so that they are easily understood. If the "as-is" situation is not described in the SWOT analysis, this may generate a need to conduct research. For example: The organization needs a 20 percent reduction in procurement governed spending. This is one of the strategic plan's objectives. However, it is quickly discovered that three primary suppliers are operating at a loss (and unable to provide further discounts), and other potential low-cost suppliers lack the capacity to handle additional volume. Think about how you might handle this situation.
- **Gap analysis.** Current conditions and our stated objectives are obviously *not* in alignment in the example provided. There is a gap between our needs and the situation in the market. We need to identify this gap in specific terms. For example: What percentage of our total spending do these suppliers account

for? If it's 10 percent of our total spending of $70 million, we have lost an opportunity to meet the organization's objectives by $1.4 million:

10% of $70 million = $7 million in spending × 20% required savings = $1.4 million.

- **Plan to bridge the gap.** Are any price concessions available? Can we find another way, outside of additional discounts, to narrow the gap? Since our primary suppliers are suffering, could we offer an expedited payment arrangement in exchange for some measure of discount? That is one approach popularized during recessions.

We can also look at areas where cost avoidance is possible. A typical method might be to make up the gap in other areas of spending, perhaps reducing travel expenses by conducting online meetings. And there may be other potential solutions. The point is that we must include the intended areas of savings or cost avoidance in our plan.

If our spending profile looks like that in Figure 2.3, where else would you suggest looking for savings? (Hint: Where is the most likely spending that is not presently managed by our procurement group? By capturing this spending, could we effect further cost reductions?)

Figure 2.3 shows a hypothetical breakdown of organizational spending, divided into four categories.

Operational Objectives

Generally, we implement operational objectives through the use of tactics. What we mean by "tactics" is employing the appropriate means available to meet the goals defined in our sourcing strategy. For example, if an organization's long-term strategy is to gain market share through aggressive price competition, its sourcing strategy would likely include robust competition throughout the supply base. In terms of tactics, we would require that each purchase be competed primarily on price (although other factors must be present as well) and that some relinquishment of longer-term supplier relations would be acceptable as a natural outcome.

So from a tactical perspective, we can achieve our supply objectives through a number of key operational activities. These activities should align with our strategic objectives as we have defined them in the strategic sourcing plan. The section that follows will briefly examine some of the most common operational objectives to be considered.

ENSURE SUPPLY   One of the first considerations in operational supply management activities is to ensure that the necessary goods and services are available when needed. There are any number of events that can jeopardize the smooth flow of goods and services. To this extent, procurement personnel must continually monitor the working status of requirements within the supply base. Naturally, it would be impossible to monitor the status of each and every order placed, at least with current technology, so close monitoring would only apply to critical items.

What makes an acquisition critical? There are a number of factors we can point to:

- **Items that directly support the organization's primary business.** Raw materials, production supplies, energy, and outsourced services. Without these, the organization would not be able to function in its market.
- **Items that are tailored to the organization's specific requirements.** These might include special tooling and parts, customized software, components of customers' special orders, and specialized employee benefit plans.
- **Items that cannot be substituted.** These are generally materials and services that cannot be produced by another party due to specialized labor, equipment, or patents. Essentially, these are sole-sourced items; that is, only one supplier can provide the product or service.
- **Items whose demand is difficult to forecast.** To meet highly variable demand, we need to be able to forecast usage within the supplier's lead time for production. If we cannot provide accurate forecasts, we must supplement our requirements through safety stock or with other hedging methods.

Ensuring supply also works hand-in-hand with supply risk assessment (which we'll go into in the next section). We must enable enough flexibility in our operations to recover from natural disasters (*force majeure*), catastrophic events, and unanticipated failures within our supply base. As you will discover, compensating for these circumstances can often become impossible, so what is really needed is an early assessment and an operational strategy that can accept only a specific level of risk.

IMPROVE VALUE   Organizations today are beginning to turn away from simply finding the lowest price and looking more carefully at how the entire spectrum of value plays out. Best value includes the traditional concept of total cost of ownership (TCOO), in which the entire product life cycle cost is considered, but expands the concept to supply intangibles as well. Using best value means we also measure on time delivery, quality levels, risk factors, supplier innovation, technology, service (and flexibility) along with TCOO.

Employing a best value concept does not negate other cost-saving approaches. One of the most common tactics is to consolidate spending and leverage it to effect price reduction. This is a recognized and legitimate way to gain additional value. To do this, we must assemble data on our total volumes (and how they compare with other buying organizations), historical price changes, and operational improvements initiated by the supplier. We must then decide if our contract terms are adequate, if we are properly positioned to leverage our volume, and where we stand in relation to our competitors. Not an easy task to measure supply value.

REDUCE SUPPLY RISK   Managing supply risk is a complex operational business activity that until recently has been largely ignored in sourcing and procurement. In reality, it is a major factor in supplier selection and thus an integral part of sourcing activities.

Risk reduction has a number of specific features, beginning with identification of potential risks, methods to mitigate it or to develop contingency plans, in proportion to the potential severity of the consequences of the risk event. For the most part, sourcing strategy must set limits on the level of risk within the organization's acceptable operational range. Operational strategy calls for constant monitoring and reassessment of risk levels, as well as continuous scanning in critical areas for new threats.

From a strategic sourcing perspective, assessing and managing risk is an activity that derives from market analysis and supplier selection methods. We'll examine this in later chapters that deal with each of these topics and expand the concepts into actionable elements.

COORDINATE SUPPLIER ACTIVITIES While this is not a complex process, it is often overlooked in sourcing and procurement activities. Coordinating the activities of suppliers requires an effective planning group and relatively accurate forecasts that are updated in a timely manner. It also requires specific metrics to define the supplier's commitment. We use metrics in a number of different ways, but in this context we are referring to most common service levels such as on-time delivery, quality levels, and price reductions. We should also monitor supplier communications with our cross-functional internal users so we understand any issues that arise and can take relatively quick action to resolve them.

ADMINISTER CONTRACT COMPLIANCE Once a supplier contract is signed, it often gets filed and never looked at again. What a mistake! Contracts must be properly administered to ensure that the supply organization achieves its part of the bargain. Typically, this task goes to the internal user who, more often than not, is far too busy to monitor contract compliance in all but the most strategic areas. The sourcing group, teaming with the end-user and other stakeholders, must establish a contractual *service-level agreement (SLA)* that sets forth the key metrics that the supplier is required to meet over time. Procurement or Contract Administration groups must then administer the contract by monitoring the supplier's performance to the metrics established. If we are paying for two-week delivery from the time the order is placed, for example, why would we accept delivery in three weeks on a regular basis? If three weeks is fine with the internal users, that's what we should have contracted for and possibly paid less.

Summary

Sourcing is one of the most important functions performed by the Procurement Department. The procurement professional with a thorough knowledge of how to effectively find, develop, and manage sources of supply will truly add value to the organization.

A key activity in sourcing is to ensure that your internal users establish and effectively communicate their requirements to the suppliers. When obtaining quotations or proposals, it will be your task to objectively analyze supplier responses so that when a decision is made to use a particular source, the organization can be assured it will obtain optimal value in the procurement. This often involves gaining a thorough understanding of the marketplace and the economic factors that prevail. It also requires that you fully understand the various methods for obtaining information and competitive bids from suppliers and when to use them.

The procurement professional is also responsible for ensuring the development and maintenance of sourcing lists so that others within the organization will have access to up-to-date information about which suppliers are qualified for any particular purchase.

Closely related to sourcing activities are regulations and laws governing the conduct of business, such as the Uniform Commercial Code and the various antitrust acts. It is important that you understand how these laws affect the sourcing decisions you make and how they may impact ongoing relationships with suppliers so that you are able to minimize the risk of the negative impact a violation would have on your organization.

For reference, we included a number of planning topics: the mission and vision statement, environmental analysis, SWOT analysis, assumptions, objectives, strategy, and implementation.

We examined the process of operational analysis and the formation of operational plans and objectives. This section included spending analysis, supplier performance issues, competition, and outsourcing opportunities. We also touched upon capturing additional spending and improving internal processes, following which we outlined the analysis of market conditions.

In the section on operational sourcing strategy, we covered the steps needed to implement the strategic plan and performing a gap analysis. Operational objectives were also noted, including processes such as ensuring supply, improving value, reducing supply risk, coordinating supplier activities, and administering contract compliance.

CHAPTER 3

Solicitation of Bids and Proposals

The next step in the sourcing process is the solicitation phase. Solicitation, in simple terms, is the process of requesting bids or proposals from potential suppliers. Once the supplier research and market analysis is complete, and we have identified several suppliers that are well positioned in their markets and appear to have the qualifications we need, the sourcing team can develop a solicitation plan. The plan should establish the method to be used for the solicitation and, when applicable, the type of contract to be used.

In this chapter, we will examine the solicitation plan and the methods of solicitation.

Solicitation Planning

To a large degree, the solicitation plan is driven by the nature of what is being acquired and the makeup of the supply base in the particular market in which we are sourcing. In the process of developing the plan, we must evaluate the nature of the acquisition as a way of narrowing the sourcing possibilities. Keep in mind that there are sourcing and procurement actions that fall outside the requirement for solicitation, such as purchasing card transactions and spot or micro-purchases that may simply be "shopped" by the procurement group.

Product or Service Characteristics

In an earlier chapter, we noted that the goods and services we typically source will have one of three possible general characteristics, determined by the statement of work or specification, and the nature of the market we discover during the market analysis phase. We based this division on the Federal Acquisition Regulations (FAR), which outlines the three main categories of product. The product categories outlined in the FAR can be applied to commercial sourcing as well. For simplicity, we have included services as well and provided a bit of paraphrasing to help keep it that way:

1. The product or service is commercially available, meaning that it can be purchased by the general public in its present form. Another way of saying this is that the product or service is available "off the shelf."

2. The product or service is commercially available but will need some modification to meet our requirements or specifications. An example of this would be a field generator requiring balloon tires so that it can be towed through a sandy or swampy area; the generator is standard but the tires will have to be sourced separately.

3. There is no commercially available product or service that can be used to meet our requirements; we will require one that is fully customized to meet the specific need.

Here's why we simplified our definitions. This is the official U.S. government definition of a commercial item, as specified in FAR PART 2—DEFINITIONS OF WORDS AND TERMS, Subpart 2.1—Definitions:

"Commercial item means—

(1) Any item, other than real property, that is of a type customarily used by the general public or by non-governmental entities for purposes other than governmental purposes, and—

  (i) Has been sold, leased, or licensed to the general public; or

  (ii) Has been offered for sale, lease, or license to the general public;

(2) Any item that evolved from an item described in paragraph (1) of this definition through advances in technology or performance and that is not yet available in the commercial marketplace, but will be available in the commercial marketplace in time to satisfy the delivery requirements under a Government solicitation;

(3) Any item that would satisfy a criterion expressed in paragraphs (1) or (2) of this definition, but for—

  (i) Modifications of a type customarily available in the commercial marketplace; or

  (ii) Minor modifications of a type not customarily available in the commercial marketplace made to meet Federal Government requirements. Minor modifications means modifications that do not significantly alter the non-governmental function or essential physical characteristics of an item or component, or change the purpose of a process. Factors to be considered in determining whether a modification is minor include the value and size of the modification and the comparative value and size of the final product. Dollar values and percentages may be used as guideposts, but are not conclusive evidence that a modification is minor;

(4) Any combination of items meeting the requirements of paragraphs (1), (2), (3), or (5) of this definition that are of a type customarily combined and sold in combination to the general public;

(5) Installation services, maintenance services, repair services, training services, and other services if—

  (i) Such services are procured for support of an item referred to in paragraph (1), (2), (3), or (4) of this definition, regardless of whether such services are provided by the same source or at the same time as the item; and

(ii) The source of such services provides similar services contemporaneously to the general public under terms and conditions similar to those offered to the Federal Government;

(6) Services of a type offered and sold competitively in substantial quantities in the commercial marketplace based on established catalog or market prices for specific tasks performed or specific outcomes to be achieved and under standard commercial terms and conditions. For purposes of these services—

   (i) "Catalog price" means a price included in a catalog, price list, schedule, or other form that is regularly maintained by the manufacturer or vendor, is either published or otherwise available for inspection by customers, and states prices at which sales are currently, or were last, made to a significant number of buyers constituting the general public; and

   (ii) "Market prices" means current prices that are established in the course of ordinary trade between buyers and sellers free to bargain and that can be substantiated through competition or from sources independent of the offerors.

(7) Any item, combination of items, or service referred to in paragraphs (1) through (6) of this definition, notwithstanding the fact that the item, combination of items, or service is transferred between or among separate divisions, subsidiaries, or affiliates of a contractor; or

(8) A nondevelopmental item, if the procuring agency determines the item was developed exclusively at private expense and sold in substantial quantities, on a competitive basis, to multiple State and local governments.

"Commercially available off-the-shelf (COTS)" item—

(1) Means any item of supply (including construction material) that is—
   (i) A commercial item (as defined in paragraph (1) of the definition in this section);
   (ii) Sold in substantial quantities in the commercial marketplace; and
   (iii) Offered to the Government, under a contract or subcontract at any tier, without modification, in the same form in which it is sold in the commercial marketplace; and

(2) Does not include bulk cargo, as defined in section 3 of the Shipping Act of 1984 (46 U.S.C. App. 1702), such as agricultural products and petroleum products."

A fourth option that we generally exclude from these categories is the acquisition of professional services, such as engineering or consulting. We will address this separately at the end of this section.

Solicitation Types

The characteristics or categories outlined will each lead to a somewhat different set of solicitation possibilities, although in some cases the same method can be used in more than one category.

COMMERCIALLY AVAILABLE PRODUCT/SERVICE Products and services that are off the shelf share the same characteristics and are, for the most part, interchangeable if there is more than one supplying producer. As a result, the acquisition decisions will focus on elements such as pricing, terms and conditions, availability, return policy, and so on.

In a competitive market, we have several viable options for solicitation:

- *The invitation for bid (IFB)* is used by government procurement, usually for requirements over $25,000. The bidder responds with a sealed bid to be opened publicly at a stated date and time. It is primarily a price competition and the lowest bid will win.
- *The request for quotation (RFQ)* is used by both government (usually under $25,000) and commercial organizations. The RFQ simply requests a quotation for price and delivery where other terms are already specified, as in the case where master supply agreements or master service agreements are in place. (The acronym RFQ is sometimes used to mean request for qualification, a request similar to the RFI, request for information.)
- *A reverse auction* enables suppliers to bid against one another in a real-time bidding "event." Bidders are blind to one another but everyone can see the current lowest bid price. The auction is typically hosted by a third party, although there are a number of software systems that enable buyers to work directly with suppliers. Here again, terms and conditions are already specified, so the lowest price wins the business.
- *Competitive negotiations* are held with suppliers whose bids are the most favorable. It is a process that is rarely used for simple acquisitions, since negotiations typically follow the suppliers' submission of bids and can have the undesirable effect of suppliers "padding" future bids to enable the buyer to negotiate back to its intended pricing.

If goods or nonprofessional services are being procured, negotiations are conducted with each of the favored providers. Price is important, but need not be the only factor in our negotiation. After negotiations have been conducted with each supplier, the sourcing team recommends the one that offers the best value.

In a noncompetitive market for commercial goods or services, one characterized by a sole source (only one supplier in existence), there is no option for competitive bidding. As a result, there must be some form of negotiation if we intend to achieve lower costs or improved business terms. Many sole source suppliers, however, are not inclined to negotiate, and since they have a legal monopoly, there is little we can do in this regard during sourcing operations. We do, however, submit a request for quotation in most cases, unless there is a published price covering our volume.

In the case of a single source, where the market is competitive but we choose to use only one supplier, there are often more options available than with a sole source. But if the decision has already been made to use a particular supplier, competitive bidding would be unethical since there is no chance of an award going to a different supplier. We do issue an RFQ and conduct negotiations, though, unless we have an existing master agreement that already covers the common element for which we would typically negotiate. We will address negotiation strategies for single-source acquisitions in Chapter 9.

COMMERCIALLY AVAILABLE PRODUCT/SERVICE REQUIRING MODIFICATION   In a situation where we require a nonstandard modification made to an existing commercial item, we will likely have the same options as we have with a commercial item. But unless we have a precise specification for our requirement, we will also have the option of using a request for proposal (RFP) where there is competition in the market.

REQUEST FOR PROPOSAL   The RFP is used primarily to solicit proposals for services. Since services are generally tailored to the organization's special needs, the statement of work becomes the focal point document. However, where modification is required to a product to meet some specific requirement and we have no particular solution in mind, an RFP should be used to solicit proposed solutions to the modification.

The RFP generally follows a standard format that contains the statement of work or some similar expression of need.

An RFP is often composed from existing data for the requirements or statement of work/specification. It typically consists of three sections. The first can be called an introduction since it describes your organization and the purpose of the RFP. This is followed by the requirements section, which can range from a simple compilation of existing known information and a description of likely needs, across the spectrum to a fully detailed statement of work. The requirements section will then be followed by the attachments (or addendums) section listing existing information or describing previous history.

The RFP often provides a framework that you can use to compare proposed solutions and evaluate proposals and to help you and your team select the most qualified source.

You can also use RFP responses to develop a statement of work (where none exists) by combining proposals from several suppliers, selecting the most appropriate elements from each. In this case, you would then perform a two-step bidding process and follow the suppliers' RFP submissions with your own specification in an RFQ.

The RFP can also be used as a means of preparing the way for the actual contract formation. You will want to include a copy of your organization's standard terms and conditions and ask the supplier to determine if they are acceptable. Or you may want to get even more specific, for example, and include a requirement for payment terms of net "X" days. Then, based on the responses you receive, you will be able to determine if there are suppliers willing to meet those terms.

And through the process, you will find the opportunity to get to know some of the supplier's staff that you will likely be working with once you award the contract. It is important to use these opportunities to build collaborative, rather than adversarial relationships that will serve both organizations, reducing the ramp-up time once the contract has been signed. The following is a summary of the three sections of the RFP:

1. **Introduction.** The introductory section will contain general information about your company that will help the prospective supplier better gauge your needs. It will also clearly state the problem or situation that gives rise to the requirements and what the present status is. In providing useful information about your organization, you might consider elements such as years in business, gross revenue, profitability, employee count, product lines, market share (for main products or

services), number of customers (and notable customers and locations of operation).

It is important to be factual while, at the same time, using this as an opportunity to present your organization in its most favorable light. The responding supplier will most often have to expend some significant effort in answering your request, so this information might be helpful in making its decision to respond or not.

The introductory section also outlines some of the requirements for response submission including deadlines, timelines if multiple stages of fact-finding and proposal are being considered, along with any legal disclaimers that may be appropriate. One commonly used disclaimer reserves the rights of your organization to make an award or not to award at all, as it so chooses. Often this section will include any supplemental material required from the supplier, such as the requirement to provide references from other customers.

It is often productive to advise the potential bidders of the evaluation criteria, without becoming overly specific. For instance, you might include a statement to the effect that a suitable technical solution is critical to the project and will be the primary consideration for an award, followed, let's say, by pricing and proven track record.

2. **Requirements.** The requirements section is typically a statement of need, which describes in detail the specific objectives of the purchase. This is almost always prepared by the using department since it is the group with the proper expertise. However, since the procurement group is responsible for making the supplier selection and the award, you should become familiar with these requirements.

In the requirements section, you will want to ensure that all the known details regarding the work to be performed have been included. This most likely will include elements such as time requirements and operational frequency, known constraints, quality requirements, and the elements that will be measured. One way to do this is by creating a work breakdown structure that lists each of the deliverables required.

To the extent possible, group the criteria in a logical context that follows some easily understood format and insist that the supplier respond in that format. This way you won't have to chase through several unformatted responses to dig out the information you need.

In stating the requirements, avoid establishing restrictive criteria that are out of alignment with current industry practices—another good reason for you to research the market prior to issuing the RFP. Be aware that the requirements do not generate a sole source selection situation, where only one supplier is capable of fulfilling the requirements.

3. **Attachments.** The attachments section commonly includes boilerplate terms and conditions and other contractual requirements. If available, perhaps even a copy of a standard contract can be included so that the supplier has a chance to determine if there are any issues that will develop during the contract formation phase. Often, the RFP will contain a request to indicate if these are acceptable terms and conditions and if not, where there are potential areas for negotiation.

If you have one, include a template for the supplier to use to submit its response. It's also useful sometimes to provide a sample service-level metric so that the supplier understands the level of detail you will be evaluating.

NO COMMERCIAL ITEM AVAILABLE: REQUIRES CUSTOMIZATION It is always a challenging endeavor when sourcing (and soliciting proposals) for a product or service that does not yet exist. How do you know where to start? Well, it may take a bit more work, but for a customized *product*, it really is not that difficult. In fact, virtually all industries have numerous suppliers that specialize in providing customization. For companies that have the resources and facilities to accommodate custom-built products—we often refer to these specialists as "job shops"—it can be a profitable business. As a general rule, where there is profit, there is competition.

Some industries are actually built around custom products. Injection molding (and its accompanying tool making), application-specific integrated circuits (ASIC), and metal stamping, just to mention a few, serve the custom need for producing specialized components in practically all industries.

Where technical specifications and drawings exist, the solicitation is straight-forward. We would use a typical sourcing process, and once potential suppliers are identified and prequalified, we can use an *RFQ*, conduct a *reverse auction*, or engage in *competitive negotiations*, as outlined in an earlier section.

Where no specifications exist, just a concept, we would use an RFP, following the guidelines provided earlier. Once the proposals are in, we may consider a two-step process where we develop the specifications from the supplier proposals or even competitive negotiations. And certainly do not rule out the reverse auction, although in most cases it can take more effort and produce marginal results.

Customized *services* must be handled somewhat differently. With services, supplier prequalification during the sourcing process can require a great deal of extra effort. Outsourcing a customer service function or an IT operation that is organization-specific, for example, requires far more due diligence simply because there are significantly more elements involved in the qualification process. Customized services usually begin with extensive supplier contact to determine how the supplier "fits" with our organization. Often, there are formal preproposal briefings to flesh out the requirements so that suppliers can get a fuller picture of what is needed. Typically, in such cases, the entire acquisition process is conducted by a cross-functional team and formally managed as a project.

The solicitation mechanism for customized services always requires an RFP. Because each supplier's proposal is going to be different, and sometimes radically so, it may require additional steps. Here we can use a two-step sourcing process. We can also use a process developed by the federal government called "competitive discussions." Discussions are not negotiations (and this should be made very clear for the supplier) and so require a greater degree of collaboration. Included in these discussions will be a good deal of fact-finding and questioning regarding proposed solutions, along with staffing, timing, and service levels. The purpose is to gain a better understanding of the supplier's position and capabilities. The end product should be a clearer assessment of each proposer's strengths and weaknesses.

We can follow the proposal (or secondary bid process) and competitive discussions with negotiations by soliciting improvements in areas where a particular supplier's proposal is weak. Our RFP should clearly state that we are under no obligation to accept a proposal on face value and that we may not even make an award as a result of the process.

TABLE 3.1   Types of Solicitations and Where Used

Product/Service Type	Competitive Market	Noncompetitive Market
Commercial	IFB, RFQ, RFI, sealed bid	RFQ
Commercial with modification	IFB, RFP, RFI, sealed bid	RFP
Customized	IFB, RFP, RFI, sealed bid	RFP

REQUEST FOR INFORMATION (RFI)   The RFI is a tool used in sourcing to help determine a supplier's capabilities and financial health, although our experience shows that most responses to an RFI by suppliers tend to become sales pitches. However, using an RFI is more relevant to the sourcing process itself than to the actual solicitation, so perhaps this is not inappropriate. But keep in mind, the RFI is a formal process that can actually become part of the contracting process to the same extent a supplier's quote or proposal may contain legally binding elements. It must be handled equitably, with the same request provided to all potential suppliers, and any clarifications made to one participant must be passed on to all.

SEALED BID   Any RFQ, RFP, or IFB can call for a sealed bid, depending upon the nature of the acquisition and the market. A sealed bid is one that is not opened until a specific date and time and, for the most part, the opening is conducted publicly. It is not a solicitation process in itself; rather, it is a method of response to a solicitation. Sealed bids are used primarily in high-value government contracts to maintain the confidentiality of the bids (and the bidder) and to ensure an equitable award to the lowest bidder.

Table 3.1 provides a summary of solicitation types.

Solicitation Methods

Now that we have an understanding of the types of solicitations we can use, let's turn our attention to the methods we can use to deploy them. Essentially, we will examine the communication tools available for distributing and responding to the RFQ, IFB, and RFP.

Mail or Courier

Possibly the simplest means for distribution is the traditional method of mailing or distribution by couriers such as FedEx or UPS. The only issues that typically arise from this method are ensuring that the request gets to the right individual and the answers get back to the originator. It is also a comparatively slow method when compared with the tools available in the electronic age.

Published Posting

In this method, an "expression of interest" is solicited through newspaper ads or through industry and government publications. An interested supplier follows the instructions for getting detailed requirements and bid documents from the buyer. It is not in widespread use today and is found mostly in cases where the method is required by law.

Web-Based Portals

These are buyer or collaborative group websites that serve the area of solicitation primarily as static tools for distributing solicitations in any format to the supply base. They are generally maintained by the buying organization, but there has been increasing movement toward consolidated sites that have developed relationships with communities of suppliers and communities of buyers. They are used to prepare and publish electronic solicitations to participating suppliers and, sometimes, to accept their responses. Very often, this service also includes a range of software tools that are subscribed to as software as a service (SAAS).

An early example of a Web-based industry portal is Covisint, which began operation in the 1990s as a means for the auto industry to collaborate with its suppliers and has subsequently expanded into a number of other industries. Surprisingly, it is still in operation. Other early consolidators providing sourcing, solicitation, and collaboration tools include SciQuest (for the biotech and pharmaceutical industries), Ariba (one of the first to provide software as a service for its customers), Oracle, and SAP, just to mention a few. Most Fortune 500 companies maintain their own supplier portals—Intel, Cisco, HP, Procter & Gamble, and so on.

E-Mail Solicitations

Instead of using postal mail or couriers, solicitations are often sent directly to the supplier's sales contact by e-mail. Other than the method of distribution and response, the e-mail solicitation is handled in exactly the same manner as any other type of solicitation; the method leverages commonly used technology to reduce the cost and time required by older methods.

The only potential issue with using e-mail for the solicitation process is the maintenance of security to ensure that confidentiality is not violated and that the information in any documents is not compromised.

Telephone

For simple or low-cost acquisitions and for acquisitions competitively bid among suppliers with master agreements in place, a telephone solicitation may be appropriate. Here we will typically adopt the format of a typical RFQ for a known item. There are some caveats, however:

- It is recommended that the individual conducting the solicitation operate from a "script" to ensure that all competitors receive exactly the same information.
- If any questions arise that might affect the bid, all of those solicited must be notified of the question and its response, as in any formal process.
- Keep good documentation of whom you spoke with, when the conversation took place, and the exact bid that was received.

- In the interest of ethical behavior, never reveal the bids of other suppliers (or even who they are) in any form, and never coach a bidder to provide a quote lower than the others.
- Confirm the accepted bid in writing.

Mailing Lists

Many organizations maintain an extensive bidders' list of companies that have a previous history with the sourcing organization or have responded well to earlier solicitations. Often, this list can be used in place of extensive market research and prequalification processes so that the sourcing individual has only to conduct a brief survey of the market to determine current conditions and to see if any significant changes have occurred in the supply base. All other elements of a standard solicitation would apply.

Crowdsourcing

This is a relatively new and increasingly popular avenue for sourcing and solicitation of relatively simple services. It is a method that also leverages current technology.

In its basic form, crowdsourcing works through posting a set of requirements on a specialized job board. Members with access to the site (which is usually open to the public) can offer bids using a simplified online form by responding with their prices, lead times, and credentials. These bids are often sealed to the extent that they can only be seen by the buyer.

On many sites, members are given a page to include their qualifications and references, along with feedback from previous customers. It is proving to be a viable tool for freelancers in service areas such as website development, simple programming, writing, graphic design, marketing collateral, and various administrative support jobs. One of the more interesting aspects of this process is that responses can come from anywhere in the world, since virtually all of the work can be conducted remotely.

Some of the sites that are available include Amazon's Mechanical Turk with its proprietary system called HITs—*human intelligence tasks*—which are individual tasks that can be worked on remotely. Another system that has been in existence since late in the last century is Elance, specializing in a narrower form of crowdsourcing focused on categories of expertise. Others include Sologig.com, Guru.com, and Freelancer.com—and this is just a partial list.

Summary

This chapter focused on the types and methods of solicitation. We began with an overview of solicitation planning, describing the product or service categories and characteristics as we see them. We examined the three categories—commercially available product/service, commercially available product/service requiring modification, and no commercially available product/service which requires complete customization. We then went over the various solicitation methods in use today such as postal mail or courier, publication posting, Web-based portals, e-mail, telephone, mailing lists, and the latest method, crowdsourcing.

CHAPTER 4

Supplier Selection Criteria

The Procurement Department is expected to lead the process of evaluating competitive offers and selecting the supplier for any particular contract. The methods used for selection are some of the most important elements of the procurement professional's skill set. Indeed, effective supplier management, one of Procurement's most vital functions, truly begins with establishing the proper initial selection criteria and ensuring that the right supplier gets chosen. Too often, inadequate preparation and effort goes into this process with predictably disastrous results: the wrong supplier chosen or disappointing supplier performance. Even worse, in too many organizations a weak and poorly trained buyer staff has virtually no input into supplier selection and contract awards in the first place, yet is expected to manage ongoing supplier performance. That is why it is critical that you clearly understand the methods available in supplier selection and employ them professionally.

This chapter introduces you to evaluating and selecting suppliers for specific contracts and some of the methods available to measure and manage a supplier's ongoing performance.

Selecting the Supplier and Awarding the Contract

You cannot make a silk purse out of a sow's ear. To produce a specific result, you must choose the correct mechanism. The supplier is the fundamental resource employed by your organization to meet its requirements, and if you do not select correctly, you will never achieve satisfactory results.

Proper supplier selection, despite requiring a strong measure of distinctly human intuition, must be performed systematically and to the most objective criteria you are capable of developing. As you read the steps to selecting the right supplier outlined in this section, think about how your organization might benefit from a more rigorous approach to this discipline.

Evaluating Offers

Before selecting an offer, every buyer should employ some process of evaluation to ensure adequate consideration that all aspects of the organization's needs are being optimized. Evaluating a supplier's offer means not only evaluating its bid or proposal from a cost perspective, it also means evaluating the supplier's ability to perform to the required level of speed and quality. You need to evaluate offers in terms of potential risk as well as potential benefits. In providing incentives to obtain the contract by reducing the price, for example, will the supplier continue to maintain the level of quality the organization requires? Issues such as this will be merely one among the many you will have to consider during the supplier selection process.

Tips and Techniques

In contract law, the term "offer" has a specific legal meaning. We discuss some of the legal aspects of contracts in Chapter 5. For our purposes here, we are using the term more loosely to mean any valid bid or proposal submitted by a supplier.

In performing proper *due diligence*, the buyer reviewing a supplier offer evaluates three key criteria before reaching a decision to award the contract to a specific supplier: responsiveness, capability, and competitive value. Because of the inherent subjectivity of much of evaluating suppliers, there is strong evidence to show that a thorough review process produces the most reliable results when it involves several individuals from a cross section of functional departments. In fact, we generally find that the evaluation process can be best performed in a cross-functional team environment where individuals perform separate evaluations but come together to develop a consensus opinion.

Here, then, are the guidelines for determining responsiveness, capability, and competitive value that you will want to consider when awarding a supplier contract.

Responsiveness

Most obviously, the basic criteria for receiving the award will be the supplier's ability to perform to the specification or scope of work contained in your request for proposal (RFP). In high-value or high-profile contracts, it is wise to actually visit the supplier's facility and physically inspect the facility (we'll discuss qualifying when we discuss site visits later in this chapter) to qualify the supplier and determine its ability to meet your requirements.

In many situations, however, site visits may be physically or financially impractical, so other methods to confirm the supplier's ability to respond should be used. For instance, you might consider contacting a supplier's references to ask about similar work performed in the past. This is frequently an effective way of determining overall supplier competency. You may also want to review the response document to ensure that the supplier has answered all the questions in your bid proposal and successfully addressed any mandatory requirements you may have set forth. While oversights sometimes occur, it is not a good sign to discover that some of the key elements of your requirement remain unaddressed. Offers that do not answer your specific questions should be considered *nonconforming* and rejected.

The thoroughness of the supplier's response and the level of detail the supplier provides generally signifies the supplier's level of understanding of your requirements and its expertise in providing workable solutions, services, or conforming parts.

You should also determine the extent to which the supplier's proposal conforms to your organizational business and to environmental and ethical policies and procedures. Does the offer appropriately address warranty and replacement issues? Does it conform to your organization's policy regarding commercial liability and *damages*? Is it signed by the proper authority? Are the correct documents, such as evidence of insurance certificates and copies of applicable licenses, attached?

Perhaps even more significantly, how closely do the supplier's terms and conditions match those of your organization? You may want to keep in mind that reconciling conflicts in terms and conditions can require a great deal of negotiation effort and typically requires participation by your risk management and legal organizations.

Capability

While many capable suppliers may respond to your proposal, your task will be to determine which supplier is the most qualified for this particular contract award. In your evaluation, you should consider several critical factors, which we'll discuss in this section.

OPERATIONAL CAPACITY   One of the key considerations in award determination will be the supplier's physical capacity to meet your needs as promised. You do not want to select a supplier that could have difficulty meeting the required volume due to capacity constraints or conflicts with the scheduling of other jobs. A simple ratio of current output to capacity can provide a valuable indication of this ability. Your risk of on-time delivery failure increases when a supplier's loading for your products or service exceeds 90 percent of capacity, especially in industries where skilled labor or production capacity can be difficult to obtain.

You will also need to ensure that the supplier has the ability and systems to properly schedule orders and keep track of current production operations to meet its customer's commitments. With little or no technology to assist in the scheduling process, the supplier may have difficulty keeping track of its customer order obligations and may prove unreliable in meeting delivery promises. You should be able to benchmark this through the customer references the supplier provides.

Past performance, while not necessarily a clear predictor of future performance, can provide some further insight into the supplier's operational capability. You may be able to develop data on this from your own organization's internal records such as supplier delivery efficiencies or your own production lead times, if applicable. If not, you may need to perform some benchmarking activities and, certainly, check with as many referenced accounts as possible.

Tips and Techniques

Avoiding the Obvious

We recall a situation when our contract award team prepared a recommendation to select a particular supplier for a molded plastic part. High quality was critical since this particular part held a key function in the assembly, and its failure in the field could create enormous problems. This supplier produced far and away the best quality we could find for this particular material. Pricing was competitive, and the company agreed to all our terms and conditions.

It was just prior to issuing the purchase order that one of our team members discovered a startling fact. Our annual volume for this part was approximately $3 million. The company chosen had sales in the prior year of just over $7 million, putting in question the supplier's capacity to handle this award in an orderly manner. Upon further questioning, we learned it was the supplier's intent to subcontract a good deal of the work to another shop, one we had previously declined to qualify for this particular project since it did not have the ability to meet the exceptional quality requirements needed for this part.

We decided to award the entire contract to the runner-up, although there was much discussion about using the first supplier we selected for part of the contract so that we could include them on our list of approved suppliers. However, we chose not to do so since we did not want to dilute the volume by awarding business to two suppliers and thus potentially increase the price.

From this exercise, we learned to include a clause in future RFPs indicating that subcontracting would not be allowed without our express written permission.

TECHNICAL CAPABILITY   Another key capability to be evaluated is the supplier's technology and technical ability. Does it have the necessary equipment, tools, and talent to meet your requirements? This can be determined not only through site visits but through historical performance records and active participation in industry events. How many patents does the company hold in comparison to its competition? How often does it lead the market with the introduction of new products? To what extent is it funding its research and development efforts?

You might also consider supplier certification as an adjunct to technical enablement. Does the supplier have the necessary licenses, insurance, and certifications required to ensure regulatory compliance? This not only reduces the supplier's liability, in many cases it may reduce the liability of your own organization, too, because lawsuits directed at your supplier while they are performing your contract will potentially bring your organization into potential litigation as well.

FINANCIAL ANALYSIS   In the modern global sourcing environment, it has become increasingly important to perform financial analysis in order to assess overall supply base risk factors. Financial analysis demonstrates a sound fiduciary responsibility to shareholders and may be required in order to meet audit compliance requirements.

When we refer to financial analysis tools, we typically mean the methods used to analyze the financial performance of an organization or a particular activity within the organization. These methods are often expressed in terms of a specific financial ratio. Presented in this section are some of the more common measures you should have the ability to analyze and understand.

In sourcing, we use financial ratios both internally for gauging our own organization's performance and externally for assessing the performance of suppliers. Often, these measures help select or qualify suppliers on the basis of their financial strength, competitive advantage, and financial leverage.

To properly evaluate individual financial ratios, it is important that they be viewed with respect to the historical performance of the supplier or the ratios of similar firms in the industry. Ratios must be viewed as "indicators" rather than absolutes, so a proper evaluation will require comparison of a set of values, rather than just one or two. Keep in mind that ratios are dependent on generally accepted accounting principles (GAAP) used, which may vary somewhat based on how the company chooses to present its data. Such financial data should be considered a snapshot of a period in time—so it's important to view financial trends, rather than individual measurements.

Measures of Liquidity

Liquidity ratios indicate an organization's ability to meet short-term financial obligations. Since they are of special interest to credit organizations, they may reflect the organization's ability to borrow funds to meet the shortfall in its current time horizon.

- **Current ratio.** The current ratio tells you whether an organization is able to meet its current financial obligations. It measures an organization's ability to meet short-term debt obligations; the higher the ratio, the more liquid the organization from a cash flow perspective.

    The *current ratio* is calculated by dividing current assets by current liabilities. Current assets are those that can be converted to cash within a year; typically, cash, marketable securities, inventory and accounts receivable. Current liabilities are those that are due within a year; typically, accounts payable, accrued salaries and wages, outstanding lines of credit, and the principal of long-term loans.

    The standard current ratio for a healthy business is two, meaning it has twice as many assets as liabilities.

- **Quick ratio.** Very closely related to the current ratio, the quick ratio measures an organization's ability to fund its short-term financial obligations through its most liquid assets. It is also called the acid test.

    The quick ratio is calculated by taking current assets *less inventories*, divided by current liabilities.

    A low quick ratio (below 0.5) indicates an organization may be slow in paying its obligations. A quick ratio of 2.0 or more is desirable.

- **Receivables turnover ratio.** This ratio calculates how many days it takes the organization to receive payment from its customers.

    Receivables turnover is calculated by dividing net sales (in dollars) by receivables.

    The faster accounts receivable are converted to cash, the greater the ability of the organization to meet its current liabilities.

- **Payables turnover ratio.** This ratio indicates how long it takes, on average, for an organization to pay its bills. It is a calculation of how often payables turn over during the year.

    It is calculated by dividing the cost of goods sold by payables.

    A high ratio means there is a relatively short time between purchase of goods and services and payment for them. A low ratio may be a sign that the company has chronic cash shortages.

- **Debt to equity ratio.** This ratio indicates how much the company is leveraged (in debt) by comparing what is owed to what is owned. Equity and debt are two key figures on a financial statement, so lenders or investors often use the relationship of these two figures to evaluate risk. The ratio of an organization's equity to its long-term debt provides a window into how strong its finances are.

  Equity will include goods and property, plus any claims it has against other entities. Debts will include both current and long-term liabilities.

  Debt to equity is calculated by dividing total liabilities by total equity.

  A high debt to equity ratio could indicate that the company may be over-leveraged.

Measures of Profitability

Profitability ratios are used to determine if adequate profits are being generated based on the investments made in the corporation. Profitability reflects the organization's ability to generate enough income to maintain its financial health and growth in both the near term and long term.

- **Gross profit margin ratio.** The gross profit margin ratio indicates how efficiently a business is using its materials and labor in the production process. It shows the percentage of net sales remaining after subtracting cost of goods sold. A high gross profit margin indicates that a business can make a reasonable profit on sales, as long as it keeps overhead costs in control.

  It is calculated by dividing gross profit by total sales.
- **Net operating margin (NOM).** *Net operating margin* (NOM) reflects the profitability of the organization by calculating the percentage of its *total operating income* (sales less direct costs) to its overall sales:

$$NOM = Net \ Operating \ Income/Revenue$$

- **Return on assets (ROA) ratio.** This calculation shows how effective an organization is at using its assets. The ROA is a test of capital utilization—how much profit (before interest and income tax) a business earned on the total capital used to make that profit.

  Return on assets is an indicator of an organization's profitability.

  It is calculated by dividing earnings before interest and taxes (EBIT) by net operating assets.
- **Return on total assets (ROTA)/return on net assets (RONA).** *Return on total assets (ROTA)* and *return on net assets (RONA)* are measures used to determine how effectively capital is deployed within the organization. Here, net income (that is, revenue less expenses) is divided by the value of assets in operation to determine effectiveness:

$$ROTA = Net \ Income/Total \ Assets$$

- **Return on investment (ROI).** *Return on investment (ROI)* describes the effectiveness of a particular investment in terms of how long it takes to recover (or earn back) the initial funding. ROI can be calculated as the *net present value (NPV)* of the revenue created divided by the initial investment:

$$ROI = (Savings \times Time) - (Discount \ Rate \times Time)$$

Financial Data Sources

Some useful information sources include the following:

- Dun and Bradstreet: www.dnb.com
- EDGAR: www.sec.gov/edgar/searchedgar/companysearch.html
- Hoovers: www.hoovers.com
- MarketWatch: www.marketwatch.com
- Standard and Poor's: www.standardandpoors.com
- Moody's: www.moodys.com

Operational Measures and Measures of Efficiency

Organizations operating at high to maximum efficiency levels can increase the capacity of their business and thereby leverage their capabilities to operate at minimum cost. Often, this translates into lower prices for the buyer. Thus efficiency is really a measure of how effectively the production or service offerings of the business can support its customers.

Efficiency is one of the more difficult aspects of a business organization to assess from the outside. However, there are a number of measures that can be used in most cases.

Productivity

Often, productivity can be assessed through a number of the financial measures cited above. To these, we can add a quick evaluation by calculating the net revenue per employee. It is easily calculated by dividing the supplier's pretax profit (earnings before taxes) by the number of employees in its company. Although not a sophisticated measurement, when evaluated in comparison to other potential suppliers, it can point out suppliers that operate more efficiently than their competitors, and vice-versa. This measure can be skewed, however, if the organization relies on outsourcing to any great extent since those employees would not be included in the count.

Two other measures commonly used to calculate productivity are:

1. **Receivables turnover ratio.** This is a measure of how fast the organization is able to collect its outstanding accounts receivable, often a reflection of the liquidity of its customer base.

   Receivables turnover is calculated by dividing the current accounts receivable amount by the annual credit sales divided by 365. It can also be stated as 365 divided by the receivables turnover.

2. **Inventory turnover ratio.** This ratio calculates how many times a business's inventory turns over—that is, was sold and replaced—during the year. Generally, a higher number indicates that inventory is moving quickly and being minimally stocked.

   Inventory turnover is calculated by dividing the cost of goods sold by the average value of inventory.

   An inventory period ratio can be calculated as 365 divided by inventory turnover.

Market Share

In simple terms, market share is the percentage of the total available market for a given product or service that the supplier has captured. It can be measured in terms of revenue (supplier's revenue divided by total market revenue) or, if a product, by units (supplier's unit sales divided by total market unit sales). Market share is a useful measure since it eliminates most of the effect of up and down economic conditions when considering the supplier's position in its market. A supplier with a small market share may be devoting its resources to other areas, thus providing very little support for that product or service; high market share may indicate sizeable purchases by large companies and the potential for ignoring the needs of those with less purchasing power. Neither of these positions are universal, so checking is required.

Service

When you evaluate service, you will look at a number of factors:

- Full support for just-in-time delivery.
- The flexibility to accommodate rush orders.
- Strong engineering and design support.
- An accommodating credit policy or a guarantee of satisfaction.

Buyers also evaluate how well the supplier responds to unexpected situations, such as accepting return of slow-moving or obsolete parts. From the customers' perspective, service is the element that bonds the organization to the supplier. In developing relationships with customers, the supplying sales team generally strives to develop a perception of responsiveness to problems and issues. But in your evaluation, you should evaluate the selling organization's proactive efforts in avoiding problems in the first place.

Quality Management Process

There is a dual aspect to the characteristics of quality that most of us immediately recognize: First, quality means conformance to specifications. Conformance to specifications is another way of saying that we get exactly what we ordered. Second, quality also means perceived value and desirability, such as an expensive, high-end automobile compared with a relatively low-priced, basic model.

Here we are primarily concerned with conformance to specifications; we discuss value in a later section. We employ *quality control* as a way of ensuring that we receive the product or service we specify and that we expect—to a degree that is measureable. Thus, we measure incoming product quality or the quality of services that have been performed. We must also consider how quality is controlled at the source by the provider so that the likelihood of receiving faulty products or services can be minimized, without the cost of performing incoming inspections.

Although typically quality is an operational concern, generally managed by the internal using group, supplier quality engineers are becoming increasingly common. Their role is to ensure the selection of quality capable suppliers and to maintain metrics on failure rates so that corrective action, when needed, can take place as soon as possible.

In Chapter 12, we will cover quality in more detail.

Customers and Reputation

It's important to know who the supplier's customers are so that you can avoid any potential conflict of interest with one of your competitors, especially where proprietary information can be compromised. It is also important, as noted above, to know what share of the supplier's market your business will bring so that you can determine how well your voice will be heard.

Determining a supplier's reputation is important in understanding how well it services the market and how reliable its products or services are in the eyes of its customers and industry analysts. Here, for the most part, a measure of research will be needed to gain a clear picture of how the company is regarded.

Reference checks are another, very important way of determining a supplier's reputation. You should be prepared to interview several of the supplier's existing customers, asking for input regarding service reliability, quality, price escalation, and response to special needs. You can ask for reference contacts from the company or get a list of current customers and find the buyer yourself. It is important, though, to ask the exact same questions of each person you contact so that your "picture" of the supplier is as objective as you can make it.

If the supplier is controlled by any government regulatory agencies (such as the Environmental Protection Agency), it will be possible for you to check public records for a history of violations. A consistent record of violations, or violations that have not been resolved, should raise a red flag.

You might also consider whether or not the supplier has an effective procedure to monitor the satisfaction of its customers. Customer feedback helps in establishing a system and method by which the supplier will satisfy the needs of its customers. Without such processes in place, there is little assurance that the supplier has, in fact, fully responded to the requirements of its customers. Determine the frequency of the surveys to establish the supplier's seriousness in conducting the process, what percentage of the customer base was included, and when the last survey was taken.

Applying Selection Criteria

Qualifying a supplier requires the disciplined application of an objective process. While in the previous section we broadly outlined the various assessment elements that can be used to qualify a supplier, here we will provide more detail that can be used as a checklist. A checklist typically includes a set of criteria appropriate for that particular supply segment to which some form of measurement can be added. Evaluation is most commonly performed by a cross-functional team with members chosen from the various departments or *stakeholder* groups affected by the choice of supplier. It is the team's job to develop the final supplier selection through some method of achieving consensus. Commonly, consensus is generated through the application of a scoring evaluation matrix that averages the inputs from each of the team members. We'll discuss consensus matrices and other methods for supplier selection in this section.

Qualifying the Supplier

Clearly, the site visit is conducted to qualify or continue the qualification status of a particular supplier. It is a formal process and should be well prepared for in advance. And since it can be somewhat costly considering travel expenses, the team should develop a process that will enable it to come away with as much information as possible.

By way of a checklist, here are several key areas you should cover during the site visit, which we will discuss here in this section.

ORDER PROCESSING AND FULFILLMENT   Order processing and fulfillment covers the methods by which the supplier receives, processes, and schedules incoming customer orders. It includes shipping and tracking records. Some of the specifics you should cover include the efficiency and effectiveness of the following:

- Systems employed for entering and verifying customer orders, level of automation, and reliability.
- Methods used to prioritize orders.
- Processes used to schedule orders and monitor delays.
- Comparative length of backlog.
- Cycle times.
- Flexibility in meeting spikes and valleys of incoming orders.
- Training and expertise of the staff.

OPERATIONS   The areas of operations you should consider reviewing for a supplier audit include manufacturing, technical document control, engineering, facilities management, and procurement. Specifically, you should be concerned with the following:

- Capacity (the current level of operation as a percentage of the maximum level of operation).
- Degree of automation and technological enablement.
- Complexity of the product line.
- Flexibility to fulfill additional requirements.
- *Work-in-process (WIP)* tracking and lot tracking ability.
- Inventory management.
- Preventive maintenance.
- Record keeping including technical specification control.
- Production flexibility.
- Reliability of suppliers and methods used to improve performance.
- Training and expertise of the staff.

QUALITY SYSTEMS   Quality systems generally consist of the methods used to ensure current quality and the processes employed for longer-term improvement. A buyer performing a supplier audit should review the following in regard to quality systems:

- Systems used to evaluate and control quality (including testing).
- Management commitment to quality improvement.

- Processes employed for continuous improvement.
- Record keeping.
- Compliance control.
- Internal and external audit procedures.
- Measures and methods used to determine customer satisfaction.
- Supplier quality engineering.
- Communications programs.
- Training and expertise of the staff.
- Training programs for employees.

COST CONTROL The method used for controlling costs is one of the key elements that should be covered in a site visit, largely because the suppliers' ability to manage cost will indicate its future viability as a partner. To a large extent, your organization's ability to compete with others in your market depends on the effectiveness of your suppliers and their ability to keep pace with market pricing. Some of the most important areas you should review include:

- Ability to properly account for cost by job.
- Systems used to allocate costs by task.
- Effectiveness of cost control initiatives.
- Process documentation.
- Engineering support.
- Performance of value analysis.
- Adherence to accepted standards of cost accounting.
- Establishment of aggressive company-wide goals.
- Ability to manage cost variances to limit margin loss.

FINANCE How an organization manages its finances generally determines how long it will stay in business. Today, the U.S. government sets strict rules for financial accountability, and site inspections can effectively determine the efficacy of government regulations. Look for evidence of the following:

- Effective profitability management.
- A strong balance sheet.
- Excellent credit ratings.
- Sarbanes-Oxley compliance (for public companies).

For publicly held companies, you can use a number of reports (some of which are available online) to determine an organization's financial condition, including the following:

- **Annual statements and reports,** some of which are available for free online at www.prars.com.
- **10-K reports** filed with the *Securities and Exchange Commission (SEC)* are available online at www.sec.gov/edgar.shtml.
- **Ratio of current liabilities to current assets** (also called *current ratio*) are available online through any financial report search engine, such as finance.yahoo.com—just enter the ticker or company name.

- **Earnings per share of stock.** Found on any financial report search engine, such as finance.yahoo.com—just enter the ticker or company name.
- **Return on net assets (RONA).** Found on any financial report search engine, such as finance.yahoo.com—just enter the ticker or company name.
- **Ratio of debt to assets.** Found on any financial report search engine, such as finance.yahoo.com—just enter the ticker or company name.

Other generalized ratio categories include the following:

- **Leverage ratios.** Show the extent that debt is used in a company's capital structure.
- **Liquidity ratio.** Presents a company's short-term financial situation or solvency.
- **Operational ratios.** Use turnover measures to show how efficient a company is in its operations and use of assets.
- **Profitability ratios.** Employ margin analysis to show the return on sales and capital employed.
- **Solvency ratios.** Provide analysis of a company's ability to generate cash flow and pay its financial obligations.

FINANCIAL REPORTING MECHANISMS   All U.S. publicly held corporations are required to file certain financial reports with the SEC. Although specific line items may differ from company to company, these reports follow a roughly standardized format that allows for relatively easy comparison.

You will likely need to examine three specific items in order to get a full picture of an organization's financial health: the balance sheet, the income statement, and the cash flow statement. Following are examples.

- **Balance sheet.** Provides a snapshot of an organization's financial position in terms of its liabilities, assets, and equity on a specific date (see Figure 4.1).
- **Income statement.** Also known as a profit-and-loss statement or statement of operations; shows an organization's income and expenses for a given period, along with the associated net profit or loss. Most of the ratios noted above are drawn from this information (see Figure 4.2).
- **Cash flow statement.** A report showing the organization's movement of money. It presents cash receipts and cash expenditures for a particular period, detailing any changes in the cash position from the previous statement. It appears in the general format shown in Figure 4.3.

MANAGEMENT   You should evaluate the management team and its style of management to determine an organization's compatibility with that of your organization. Some things to consider in relation to management include the following:

- Management policies, for instance, whether they reflect honest dealing and strong adherence to an ethical code of conduct.
- Management's commitments to other customers and to suppliers.
- Management's maintenance of long-term and short-term needs.
- Management's commitment to sound environmental practices and adherence to a code of ethics and social responsibility.

CONSOLIDATED CONDENSED BALANCE SHEETS
(In millions)

	July 31, 2010 (unaudited)	October 31, 2009
ASSETS		
Current assets:		
Cash and cash equivalents	$ 14,718	$ 13,279
Short-term investments	5	55
Accounts receivable	15,621	16,537
Financing receivables	2,799	2,675
Inventory	7,206	6,128
Other current assets	14,016	13,865
Total current assets	54,365	52,539
Property, plant, and equipment	11,477	11,262
Long-term financing receivables and other assets	11,681	11,289
Goodwill and purchased intangible assets	42,494	39,709
Total assets	$ 120,017	$ 114,799
LIABILITIES AND STOCKHOLDERS' EQUITY		
Current liabilities:		
Notes payable and short-term borrowings	$ 7,842	$ 1,850
Accounts payable	14,885	14,809
Employee compensation and benefits	3,703	4,071
Taxes on earnings	947	910
Deferred revenue	6,583	6,182
Other accrued liabilities	15,328	15,181
Total current liabilities	49,288	43,003
Long-term debt	12,204	13,980
Other liabilities	15,690	17,052(a)
Stockholders' equity		
HF stockholders' equity	42,535	40,517
Noncontrolling interests	300	247(a)
Total stockholders' equity	42,835	40,764
Total liabilities and stockholders' equity	$ 120,017	$ 114,799

FIGURE 4.1   Balance Sheet

Quantitative Analysis   There's an old adage: "If it's worth doing, it's worth measuring." (Or sometimes alternatively expressed: "Nothing that can't be measured is worth doing.") This measurement process is called *quantitative analysis* to indicate that the analysis is provided in mathematical terms. With quantitative analysis you will apply statistics and analytical matrices to suppliers.

Well in advance of any site visit, the team should establish the criteria it will use to evaluate and select a supplier. To the extent possible, you should conduct this evaluation using objective, quantitative methods so that you can easily present data that require a minimum amount of interpretation.

Balanced Scorecard   Robert Kaplan (of Harvard Business School) and David Norton introduced the "balanced scorecard" in the early 1990s, and it has gained widespread

CONSOLIDATED CONDENSED STATEMENTS OF EARNINGS
(Unaudited)
(In millions except per share amounts)

	Three months ended		
	July 31, 2010	April 30, 2010	July 31, 2009
Net revenue	$30,729	$30,849	$27,585
Costs and expenses:[a]			
Cost of sales	23,402	23,601	21,031
Research and development	742	722	667
Selling, general and administrative	3,154	3,064	2,874
Amortization of purchased intangible assets	383	347	379
Restructuring charges	598	180	362
Acquisition-related charges	127	77	59
Total costs and expenses	28,406	27,991	25,372
Earnings from operations	2,323	2,858	2,213
Interest and other, net	(134)	(91)	(177)
Earnings before taxes	2,189	2,767	2,036
Provision for taxes[b]	416	567	365
Net earnings	$ 1,773	$ 2,200	$ 1,671
Net earnings per share:			
Basic	$ 0.76	$ 0.94	$ 0.70
Diluted	$ 0.75	$ 0.91	$ 0.69
Cash dividends declared per share	$ 0.16	$ –	$ 0.16
Weighted-average shares used to compute net earnings per share:			
Basic	2,322	2,345	2,382
Diluted	2,376	2,406	2,436
(a) Stock-based compensation expense was as follows:			
Cost of sales	$ 43	$ 48	$ 41
Research and development	11	16	12
Selling, general and administrative	111	136	94
Acquisition-related charges	1	–	3
Total costs and expenses	$ 166	$ 200	$ 150

FIGURE 4.2   Income Statement

recognition as a key management tool. Essentially an analysis technique, it was designed to translate an organization's mission statement and overall business strategy
into specific, quantifiable goals and to monitor the organization's performance in
terms of achieving these goals. The balanced scorecard outlines what organizations
need to measure from a financial perspective so that they can work toward achieving a "balanced" operation. It is a means of translating strategic planning from an
academic exercise into a fully functional operational process.

    The balanced scorecard method suggests that we consider and manage the
organization from four perspectives, and that we develop metrics and collect and
analyze data relative to each of them:

1. The learning and growth perspective.
2. The business process perspective.

CONSOLIDATED CONDENSED STATEMENTS OF CASH FLOWS
(Unaudited)
(In millions)

	Three months ended July 31, 2010	Nine months ended July 31, 2010
Cash flows from operating activities:		
Net earnings	$ 1,773	$ 6,223
Adjustments to reconcile net earnings to net cash provided by operating activities:		
Depreciation and amortization	1,210	3,556
Stock-based compensation expense	166	547
Provision for bad debt and inventory	56	249
Restructuring charges	598	909
Deferred taxes on earnings	95	(191)
Excess tax benefit from-stock-based compensation	(20)	(283)
Other, net	44	193
Changes in assets and liabilities:		
Accounts and financing receivables	(864)	845
Inventory	(791)	(981)
Accounts payable	1,420	(128)
Taxes on earnings	(85)	641
Restructuring	(270)	(1,053)
Other assets and liabilities	(59)	(1,756)
Net cash provided by operating activities	3,273	8,771
Cash flows from investing activities:		
Investment in property, plant, and equipment	(1,130)	(2,901)
Proceeds from sale of property, plant, and equipment	85	353
Purchases of available-for-sale securities and other investments	(22)	(50)
Maturities and sales of available-for-sale securities and other investments	94	197
Payments made in connection with business acquisition, net	(1,505)	(4,017)
Proceeds from business divestiture, net	125	125
Net cash used in investing activities	(2,353)	(6,293)
Cash flows from financing activities:		
Issuance of commercial paper and notes payable, net	3,138	4,993
Issuance of debt	71	121
Payment of debt	(1,030)	(1,274)
Issuance of common stock under employee stock plans	241	2,507
Repurchase of common stock	(2,568)	(7,079)
Excess tax benefit from stock-based compensation	20	283
Dividends	(205)	(590)
Net cash used in financing activities	(333)	(1,039)
Increase in cash and cash equivalents	587	1,439
Cash and cash equivalents at beginning of period	14,131	13,279
Cash and cash equivalents at end of period	$ 14,718	$ 14,718

FIGURE 4.3   Cash Flow Statement

3. The customer perspective.
4. The financial perspective.

The authors outline its intended approach as follows:

The balanced scorecard retains traditional financial measures. But financial measures tell the story of past events, an adequate story for industrial age companies for which investments in long-term capabilities and customer relationships were not critical for success. These financial measures are inadequate, however, for guiding and evaluating the journey that information age companies must make to create future value through investment in customers, suppliers, employees, processes, technology, and innovation.[1]

WEIGHTED AVERAGE SCORECARD When evaluating a supplier, you may often use a rating matrix called a *weighted average*. A weighted average defines critical areas and attempts to develop an objective, average score based on the opinions of the various team members. Table 4.1 shows you an example of part of a typical weighted-average evaluation chart. Although the category titles and values will vary widely depending on what is being evaluated, the format will likely always look similar.

During the initial development of the weighted-average matrix, the team assigns percentages to each of the major sections. In the example shown in Table 4.1, these major categories are cost, quality, technology, and service. The categories are then broken down into subsets composed of each of the individual elements being scored. Each is assigned a portion of the total percentage allocated to the broader category. In a simple analysis, there may be only two or three subsets, while in a complex analysis there may be dozens.

Each member of the team, represented by letters A–E in the table, prepares a separate rating, evaluating any of the categories they are qualified to assess. Assessment is made on a sliding scale and scored accordingly. Some scales use a 1–3 rating system; others use 1–5. Occasionally, you see scales of 1–10, but that gets far more complex than necessary. Some users prefer scales with even numbers (such as 1–6) so that individuals are forced onto one side or another and cannot select a midrange score to remain neutral. All relate the numbers to some measure of judgment, for example, 5 = excellent and 1 = inadequate.

Individual scores are then tallied into a master score sheet, averaged by subset, and then weighted by the percentage allocated to it. As an example, let's say that the

TABLE 4.1 Supplier Evaluation Matrix Example

	Overall Weight	Supplier "A"	Supplier "B"	Supplier "C"
Price	35	2.80	1.90	3.25
Quality	30	2.70	2.00	2.80
Service	20	1.60	1.60	2.20
Technology	15	1.65	1.55	1.80
TOTAL		8.75	7.05	10.05

team decides quality should be given an overall value of 25 percent and one of its subsets, SPC measurement systems, should be given 6 percent. The five individuals (A–E) rate the subset on a scale of 1–5, as follows: A. 5, B. 3, C. 3, D. 4, and E. 2. The average of the five ratings comes to 3.4 (17 / 5). This average is then multiplied by 6 percent (.06), the amount allocated to the subset, to determine its total value: $3.4 \times .06 = .204$.

The sum of the subsets equals the total percentage score for each category. The total scores for each category then add up to the supplier's total rating. However, a word of caution is in order: Regardless of the number of team members used to develop the rating, it will still be a subjective rating. As a result, you should consider a wide margin of error when evaluating scores, and only when the order of magnitude clearly separates one supplier from the rest should you consider using this as an absolute selection criterion. If, for example, your team evaluates six suppliers, five of which score in the 50–60-point range and one that scores 87 points, you have a clear mandate. On the other hand, if three score in the 50–60-point range and three score in the 75–85-point range, you may simply have developed a short list of suppliers in the top range for further evaluation.

WEIGHTED BID ANALYSIS Another method for comparatively evaluating suppliers' offers can be implemented through the use of a *weighted bid analysis*, or *cost-ratio analysis*. This method is also known as *transformational bidding* because it weighs one supplier's bid in comparison to others by transforming the value of their offer to some equivalent percentage based on their demonstrated performance or added value.

In simple terms, let's say you know from past experience that Supplier A's billing process results in more errors than Supplier B's. You have been able to measure the additional cost and found it adds about 1 percent to the cost of all the products you purchase from Supplier A. You also know that it costs 2 percent more for shipping from Supplier A than from Supplier B. Therefore, you transform their bids to equivalency by adding 3 percent to Supplier A's bid.

Here's the math for this example:

Supplier A's total bid = $142,000
Supplier B's total bid = $144,000
Supplier A's transformed bid (adding 3 percent) = $146,260
Supplier A's bid is actually higher than Supplier B's using this method.

Site Visit

The site visit is one of the more common tools used to develop an evaluation of a supplier. While not every member of the team will attend the site visit, it is important that at the least representatives of the user group, the quality group, and supply management attend.

In addition to performing an inspection to audit the supplier's facilities (and perhaps records), the site visit provides an opportunity to establish or further develop working relationships with staff that you may not get to know under arm's-length circumstances. If you use this effectively, it may save time in the future when you need a problem solved quickly.

Reviewing, Approving, and Issuing the Contract

Once the scoring or other method for determining supplier selection has been completed and approved by the team, the contract may need to be reviewed and approved by other internal groups or individuals according to company policy. If the contract is for tangible goods covered by the UCC, chances are good that the organization's standard *purchase order (PO)* terms and conditions will apply and the issuance of a PO will be all that is required. In this case, any further approvals needed depend on the PO value. Some organizations require a procurement professional's approval prior to the issuance of a PO if it exceeds a certain value. Since the budgeting manager has already approved the expenditure, the procurement professional reviews the PO for its conformance to organizational policy and good business practices.

In the case of contracts for services not covered by the organization's standard terms and conditions, the buyer may have to write up a special contract. Typically, organizations rely on a previously developed set of contracts for each particular category of service—construction or consulting, for example. These contracts will have already had legal review. However, should the supplier wish to change any of the clauses in the contract that may impact its legal value, a further legal review will be required.

Depending on company policy and procedure, most POs can be signed by an authorized buyer. Contracts, however, are usually signed by an officer of the company or a senior manager as a means of ensuring one last sanity review. A PO often must be issued even with a contract in place, so that it can be recorded on the organization's financial system for payment.

Administering the Contract

Once the contract has been approved and implemented, the procurement professional is in charge of providing continuous supplier evaluation and performance improvement in relation to the contract. Your objective is not only to measure current performance, but also to identify areas for improvement and collaboratively develop programs to implement improvement. We will discuss this in Chapter 14.

Ethical Principles

Would you recommend doing business with an organization that utilizes child labor? Would you recommend doing business with a supplier that evades taxes by hiding revenues in another country? Would you approve a supplier that pays substandard wages? Some of these actions may not actually violate a law, but they may violate the law of your conscience.

So how do you regulate conformance to a set of moral expectations that may or may not violate any laws? You can do so by establishing a set of ethical principles governing your expectation of how suppliers will behave. These, if you like, are the rules *buyers* expect suppliers to meet.

Ethical principles are usually issued in the form of a document, such as an *ethical code of conduct*, outlining the organization's expectations for employees and suppliers. Sometimes this document is the same for both groups; sometimes organizations will write them separately.

The ethical code of conduct is usually organized by specific subject matter such as legal compliance, working conditions, financial accounting practices, and so on. There is no clear formula, and different organizations emphasize different elements.

Note

Here are URLs for two examples of organizations with ethical codes of conduct that you might find useful:

1. HSBC is a globally positioned bank headquartered in the United Kingdom: http://www.hsbc.com/1/2/purchasing/ethical-code-of-conduct
2. Hewlett-Packard is a well-known global supplier of computers: www.hp .com/hpinfo/globalcitizenship/environment/

Managing Records and Data

Most organizations have policies regarding the management and retention of records. Some of these policies are based on legal requirements (e.g., the Internal Revenue Service requires documents relating to taxes be stored for seven years), and others are based on good business practices, such as keeping journals of engineering activity to limit future liability and to prove the development history of a particular patent.

Those policies notwithstanding, it is important that you maintain historical data indicating supplier performance so that there can be no misinterpretations and disputes in the conduct of the evaluation process.

Summary

Supplier evaluation and selection is one of the key organizational functions led by the Procurement Department. It is critical, therefore, that the procurement professional develop and implement effective processes for qualifying suppliers and determining the award of business. We have explored how supplier responsiveness and capability can be evaluated and how these attributes need to be combined with the elements of value to ensure that your organization receives the best return for its expenditure.

There are many ways to evaluate supplier performance, but we strongly recommend using a quantitative approach. This approach generally requires team input to gain appropriate objectivity and, in the case of key suppliers, data should be gathered from physical visits as well as from the evaluation of written offers. Most commonly, supplier selection data is put into a weighted-average matrix as a means of comparing various suppliers and their offers.

Ongoing contract administration requires the use of continuous improvement methods to generate greater value for your organization. Here, too, the use of a weighted-average method for evaluating performance is strongly recommended. You will also find that customer surveys can provide important feedback when measurement is not altogether practical.

Organizations must strive to develop sound business practices that conform to applicable law as well as fundamental ethical principles. It is a key function of the procurement professional to ensure that there is alignment between the requirements of their organization and that of the supplier.

Note

1. Kaplan, Robert S., and David P. Norton, *The Balanced Scorecard: Translating Strategy into Action* (Boston: Harvard Business School Press, 1996).

CHAPTER 5

Contracts and the Legal Aspects of Procurement

In this chapter, we focus on reviewing key aspects of creating and managing various types of procurement contracts and documents. As a procurement professional, you are required to understand the nature and purpose of contracts and what constitutes a legally binding obligation. You will also need to become familiar with a variety of standard elements that are required for contracts and what types of contracts should be used in any particular procurement transaction.

As you probably know by this time, forming and administering contracts covers a broad range of the department's responsibilities and constitutes a major investment of required talent. Problems with document verbiage, issues regarding unclear specifications, lack of supplier performance, and unseen financial obligations plague many organizations. The vast majority of these contractual problems, however, can be reduced or even eliminated by establishing clear process requirements for developing them and ensuring they receive appropriate approval and legal review.

Properly administering purchase orders (POs) and contracts also requires close attention to detail so that the supplier's compliance with the terms and conditions adds the full measure of value that was originally intended by the organization. This often involves resolving discrepancies and expediting deliveries, as well as handling disputes and contractual violations. Establishing procurement policies and practices that conform to ethical behavior and enhance the organization's integrity are keys to the Procurement Department's effectiveness in performing these obligations.

Contract Essentials

The Procurement Department is responsible for the issuance and management of a variety of procurement contracts and documents. Since they generate both legal and financial obligations for the organization, the buyer needs to apply due diligence to their formation and management.

Tips and Techniques

In its basic form, a contract represents a legally binding agreement made by two or more parties to complete a specified action at a specific point in time. It represents a bargain that is valid in a court. Contracts may be generated to cover the purchase of either goods or services.

In this section, we will review the basis for forming contractual obligations and the key elements that provide their validity.

Contracts cover the purchase of both goods and services. Services are generally covered by state laws (known as common law or case law), which establish precedents that can help resolve disputes. Goods are considered personal property and are covered by Article 2 of the Uniform Commercial Code (UCC). You will recall from Chapter 2 that the UCC was developed to provide a measure of standardization in the laws of commerce between the states and has been adopted by 49 U.S. states (all states except Louisiana) and the District of Columbia. One other body of law, known as *statutory law*, covers acts and regulations enacted by the U.S. Congress and state legislatures.

Written Contracts

In broad terms, contracts can use either written or oral formats. While from a procurement point of view written contracts pose the least amount of risk, it is important to understand that oral contracts can be equally enforceable if they meet a common set of conditions. However, the *Statute of Frauds*—laws designed to prevent fraud—requires certain types of contracts to be validated in written form:

- Contracts for goods sold under the UCC exceeding $500 that are not specifically manufactured for the user. (This amount will likely increase to $5,000 under pending proposals.)
- Contracts for the sale or transfer of real estate.
- Contracts to assume the debt or duty of another.
- Contracts that cannot be completed within one year, either by their own terms or because they are objectively impossible to complete.

Agreements required to be evidenced in writing (such as those just listed) do not have to take a specific contractual form. However, at the least, the writing must contain:

- Identification of the other party as the individual responsible for the contract.
- Some form of signature of the above.
- A clearly identified subject of the contract.
- Specific terms and conditions.
- Identification of the consideration (as an exchange of value).

There are a number of exceptions to the written requirements of the Statute of Frauds under which an oral contract will be enforced, including the partial completion of an oral contract up to the point of performance. If, for example, a contract to buy $10,000 worth of parts has not yet been committed to writing and is canceled by the buyer after $2,000 worth of parts has been received and accepted, will the seller be able to force the buyer to honor the entire contract? The answer is no. Since the value of the remaining portion of the contract exceeds $500 and there is no evidence in writing of any contract, the buyer is under no obligation to honor the original agreement. Similarly, the seller would not be responsible for delivering any more than that already shipped.

Oral Contracts

The principle of *detrimental reliance* applies when it can be shown that reliance on the oral promise will produce substantial or unconscionable injury to the promisee or will unjustly enrich the promisor. The fact that the promisee relies on the oral promise to its detriment is generally not considered sufficient reason to entitle it to enforce an oral contract. However, when customized products are made for a buying organization under an oral agreement and cannot be sold to any others, the contract is enforceable by the seller.

If an oral contract not required to be in writing (e.g., for goods under $500) is modified to the extent that it falls within the Statute of Frauds, then the contract must be in writing to be enforceable. For example, if $200 worth of goods is added to an oral contract already totaling $450, it's required that the entire contract be put in writing since the total amount ($650) exceeds the limit of $500 for an oral contract.

Also considered in the formation of a contract is the law of promissory estoppel. An oral contract unenforceable under the Statute of Frauds may be enforced under the doctrine of promissory estoppel if one party made an oral promise and the other party relied on that promise and performed part of or its entire obligation. Under these conditions, the oral promise cannot be rescinded simply because it is not evidenced in writing.

Tips and Techniques

The Trouble with Electronic Procurement

Electronic procurement is a relatively new process that has yet to be fully recognized under the UCC or the Statute of Frauds. The primary issue concerns the ability of one party to fraudulently alter a document after agreement has been reached. While faxed signatures and documents, along with electronic data interchange (EDI) transactions, are generally considered reliable evidence of contractual obligations, other forms such as e-mail have yet to be fully accepted as legal. Parties using electronic transmission for business are usually counseled to initiate some contractual documentation, such as a formal trading partner agreement, outlining the processes and obligations that will govern them.

Contract Requirements

In order for a contract to be legally enforceable, it is commonly agreed that four key elements need to be demonstrated: mutual agreement, legality, consideration, and capacity. Let's discuss each of these in more detail:

1. **Mutual agreement.** As evidence of a "meeting of the minds," *mutual agreement* includes an *offer* and its *acceptance*. When a buyer places a PO, for example, it is considered an offer to buy, and the seller's acknowledgment is generally considered an acceptance. An acceptance can also be demonstrated by actual performance, such as a shipment of materials or some constructive action of service that indicates such acceptance. This is called a *unilateral contract*, whereas a contract containing both an offer to sell and an agreement to buy is considered a *bilateral contract*.

   If a seller extends an offer in the form of a quotation but the buyer requests modification to some of the terms, it is considered a *counteroffer* rather than an acceptance. By requesting modification, the buyer, in effect, rejects the original offer and proposes a new one.

   If a buyer issues a solicitation for a certain quantity of materials and a seller provides a quotation, does it signify a contract exists? No, because a solicitation is not necessarily an offer to buy.

2. **Legality.** A contract requires a legal purpose. Contracts that violate a legal statute or are against public policy are invalid.

3. **Consideration.** Consideration means an exchange of anything of value. To be valid, a contract has to show evidence that an exchange of some value for a promise is part of the agreement. Consideration does not necessarily have to be exchanged in the form of money. It can also be in the form of various types of services rendered.

Tips and Techniques

One way to think of consideration is by referring to the Latin term quid pro quo. Translated literally, quid pro quo means "this for that" or "something for something." While we generally consider this to mean something of equal value, it is also generally considered that value is subjective and must be determined by the parties to the exchange.

4. **Capacity.** Parties to a contract need to be legally *competent* to enter into it and perform its *obligations*. Minors, for example, are not considered legally competent. A person who is legally insane cannot be a valid party to a contract.

Contract Types

Typically, a Procurement Department will use a wide variety of contractual documents during the normal course of business. The exact document you choose will largely depend on the business needs of your organization and the type of purchase being made. Outlined in this section are the contracts that are most commonly used.

Purchase Orders (POs)

In almost all environments, the PO is the most common procurement document available and is, in effect, a contract. As a standard form, it is the easiest way to order purchased materials and services and provides the most commonly required audit trail. A standard PO can be used for recurring or repetitive purchases as well as one-time purchases. In addition to stating the specific requirements for the purchase, the PO usually conveys your organization's standard terms and conditions, sometimes termed a "boilerplate."

The PO can be both an offer and a means of acceptance, depending on the existing circumstances. When issued in response to a solicitation for bids, it can be considered evidence of contract formation. However, when sent to a supplier without having previously received a quote or proposal, it may be considered simply an offer to buy.

In addition to standard terms and conditions covering remedies, warranties, liabilities, rights of inspection and rejection, ability to cancel, and other typical clauses (usually transmitted by the fine print on the reverse side of the PO), the PO will generally describe on its face what is being purchased, the price being paid, the terms of delivery, and any other instructions needed to describe the specific requirements of that particular order.

Blanket POs, also known as indefinite delivery contracts, are used when the buyer wishes to establish set pricing and terms but does not yet wish to place orders for specific quantities or delivery times.

Requirements or Indefinite Delivery Contracts

Requirements contracts or *indefinite delivery contracts* are used when the buyer wishes to lock in pricing or lead time in exchange for a commitment to purchase all of the organization's requirements (or at least some described minimum and/or maximum amount) but specific quantities and delivery dates are not yet known. Sometimes, the requirements contract will be used to make commitments to a supplier for a certain line of products (e.g., office supplies) in exchange for a specified discount level or for some other consideration such as setting up an automated, online ordering program.

Definite Quantity Contracts

A *definite quantity contract* specifies the amount being purchased during a given time frame but not the specific delivery dates. This type of contract is also known as a *take or pay* contract because the buying organization cannot cancel it and must pay for it at the end of the contractual period even if it is not used.

Fixed-Price Contracts

Fixed-price contracts are the most commonly used contracts in typical business environments. Most fixed-price contract types are defined in the Federal Acquisitions Regulations (FAR) as they apply to government purchases; however, they are commonly adapted for commercial use by procurement departments. Essentially, they are contracts in which prices are agreed to in advance of performance. There are five types of fixed-price contracts that we will discuss in more detail here.

FIRM FIXED PRICE   A *firm-fixed-price contract* is exactly what its title states: The price is not subject to adjustment. The buyer and seller agree to performance at the stated price, and the risk of profit and loss passes solely to the supplier.

FIXED PRICE WITH INCENTIVE   For the *fixed-price-with-incentive contract*, a profit formula is established based on target cost and target profit within an agreed-upon maximum price. The final price is established by adjusting the actual profit the supplier receives based on the difference between the final cost agreed to by the parties and the original target cost. Typically, the amount saved by reducing the cost is shared by both parties. In other words, this contract type provides an incentive to the supplier to hold down the costs and thereby increase its profit.

FIXED PRICE WITH ECONOMIC PRICE ADJUSTMENT   The *fixed-price-with-economic-price-adjustment contract* allows pricing to be adjusted upward or downward based on established contingencies such as escalating labor and material rates. Changes in actual costs beyond the supplier's control or reasonable ability to foresee, above or below the contract's baseline, can lead to an adjustment reflected in the supplier's pricing. This method is frequently used for multiyear contracts or when economic conditions are unstable. Often, this is a standard contract with the inclusion of a clause allowing *escalation* or *deescalation* of prices under agreed-upon conditions. When it is difficult to calculate actual prices, adjustments are sometimes based on some readily available business or financial index.

FIXED PRICE WITH PRICE REDETERMINATION   Similar to the economic price adjustment contract, the *fixed-price-with-price-redetermination contract* is used when prices are anticipated to change over time but the extent of those changes cannot be predicted, such as during startup operations. Generally, the specific time for redetermination will be included.

FIXED PRICE, LEVEL OF EFFORT   The *fixed-price, level-of-effort* method of pricing, although relatively uncommon, is usually used in situations when the precise amount of labor or materials is unknown but the parties can agree on a standard level of effort (such as the type and quantity of tools to be used or the rated proficiency of the employees) and a given price. Thus the fixed-price, level-of-effort contract is similar to the concept in the time and materials contract, which will be discussed shortly.

Cost Reimbursable Contracts

Cost reimbursable contracts are primarily used by government organizations and large corporations as an inducement for supplier participation in situations where the initial research and development engineering or capital investment may be very high and the financial risk great. These contracts assure the supplier that the buyer will cover, at a minimum, agreed-upon costs up to an agreed-upon monetary ceiling. The supplier may not exceed that amount without prior approval, unless it wishes to go forward at its own risk. Cost reimbursable contracts are used in a variety of ways, as you will see in this section.

Cost Plus Fixed Fee

The *cost-plus-fixed-fee contract* is a cost-reimbursement contract that allows the supplier to recover actual costs plus a fee negotiated prior to the contract's inception. The fee is considered fixed because it does not vary from the amount of the cost, although further negotiation of the fee based on changed conditions can be considered.

Cost Plus Incentive Fee

The *cost-plus-incentive-fee contract* is another reimbursable contract that, like the fixed-price-plus-incentive contract outlined previously, provides an initially negotiated fee with a formula-based adjustment that reflects the relationship of total allowable cost to total target cost.

Cost Plus Award Fee

The *cost-plus-award-fee contract* provides additional incentive for the supplier to produce excellent results by enabling the buyer to make a financial award in addition to the cost and negotiated fee. It is designed to provide the supplier with a financial incentive for excellent performance.

Tips and Techniques

At one time, the federal government used a cost-plus-percentage-of-cost contract. For obvious reasons, this provided the supplier no incentive whatsoever to hold down costs. The Government Accounting Office (GAO), the federal watchdog agency, caught on and banned this practice with legislation as of November 14, 2002.

Cost Sharing

A *cost-sharing contract* is generally used in a partnering relationship where all parties share the cost and the accruing benefits according to a negotiated formula. The costs are typically limited to a specific amount or an *in-kind exchange* that is defined at the contract's formation. In many ways, this type of contract is similar to a *joint venture,* where all parties own a portion of the operation.

Cost Only

Used primarily between universities and other nonprofit and research organizations, the *cost-only contract* covers reimbursement only for actual costs, without including a fee. This contract typically supplements one organization's capabilities and enables full utilization of the other's resources that might otherwise remain idle.

Tips and Techniques

Incentive Contracts

We have outlined two commonly used incentive contracts in this section, the fixed-fee-plus-incentive and the cost-reimbursable-plus-incentive contracts. These are based primarily on cost reduction. However, there are often other reasons to provide incentives to the supplier, such as when accelerated delivery may be highly valuable (such as in development work) or when specific elements of performance (e.g., quality) are needed. Typically, such contracts fall into the fixed-price or cost-plus categories but contain clauses calling for additional payments for improvements in the negotiated level of performance.

Time and Materials Contracts

Time and materials (T&M) contracts are used when there are no acceptable ways to determine what a fair and reasonable price may be for a particular project, such as a well-digging contract where the exact depth of the water and the composition of the soil may be unknown. With this type of contract, the rates for labor and the markup for materials are initially negotiated with a cap, or *not-to-exceed (NTE)* amount, specified as a limit. In most ways, T&M contracts are similar to cost-reimbursable contracts.

Letters of Intent

A letter of intent (LOI) can be useful when parties are seriously working toward a final contract and wish to proceed with some of their preliminary efforts under a formal agreement. Letters of intent can outline the broad intent of the contract regarding some terms that have not yet been specified or agreed upon. Depending on how complete LOIs are, they can be a legally binding contract between buyer and supplier. They can also induce the supplier to perform some specific action such as reserving production scheduling time or ordering materials in advance of an actual contract. Some of the most common elements of an LOI include:

- **Price and terms.** May include projected costs and how they will be determined. It may also broadly outline the terms and conditions that will apply under a given set of assumptions. In some instances, the LOI may specify the accrual of payment to the supplier for work performed in the development of the contract, such as research needed to validate a statement of work. It may also include payment terms.
- **Obligations.** A section covering obligations is also typically included. This section generally outlines what each party must do prior to proceeding with a contract and which party will pay for what activities.
- **Confidentiality.** Generally, an LOI binds the parties to the same level of confidentiality as a standard contract. This enables the free exchange of proprietary information so that certain elements of the contract can be predefined.

- **Exclusivity.** This section outlines the length of time the parties are bound to an exclusive relationship. Following this period, the parties may enter into agreements with others under preestablished confidentiality conditions and protection of any intellectual property developed.
- **Structure.** Often, the nature of the relationship needs to be stated prior to beginning even basic aspects of the work. This includes defining the nature of the final agreement—for example, the type of contract or the disposition of *intellectual property (IP)*—and what the nature of the relationship will be subsequent to a contract.
- **Time and conditions.** The elements related to time and specific conditions express the parties' intent to form a final agreement by a specific date and under described conditions. These reflect the known conditions that must be present at that time in order to proceed and without which either of the parties are not obligated to form a further contract.
- **Binding or nonbinding clauses.** Included in most LOI documents are statements indicating which portions of the agreement shall be binding and which shall not. For example, the parties may agree to be bound by an IP clause granting the rights to any IP developed to one or the other of the parties.
- **Licensing agreements.** When another party has secured ownership rights to specific IP—such as an invention or a software program—through a *patent* or *copyright*, your organization will need to obtain permission to use it. Usually, this permission is given in the form of a *licensing agreement*, a contract for which the licensee will pay either a fixed fee or a *royalty* based on usage. A royalty is similar to a commission insofar as it is generally calculated as a percentage of gross sales. There are a number of different formats you may encounter, but the more common ones you will likely come in contact with include the following:
  - **Exclusive license.** Grants usage rights to only one party so that no others may be so licensed.
  - **Nonexclusive license.** Grants usage rights to a party but does not limit the number of others that may be similarly licensed by the owner.
  - **Partially exclusive license.** Grants exclusive rights to use the patent within a geographical area or for specific products.
  - **End-user license agreement (EULA).** A three-way contract among the manufacturer, the author, and the *end user* written to cover proprietary software. It is often attached to a program that requires you to check a box indicating acceptance of the terms prior to being able to use it.

Tips and Techniques

Intellectual Property

In general, IP is protected in the United States by specific law and a number of registration processes. The more common of the registration processes are outlined below:

PATENTS A patent is generally considered a set of exclusive rights granted by a government to an inventor for a specified period of time. In the United States, this is usually for 20 years. For the period of time covered by the patent, the patent holder owns a monopoly, and others wishing to use it must obtain a license. Patents are granted for inventions and processes, as opposed to copyrights, which are granted to written documents, designs, and software; or trademarks, which identify products.

COPYRIGHTS Copyrights grant ownership of various forms of expression such as works of art, literature, software programs, or audio/visual material (and similar forms of expression). Ownership enables the exclusive right to publish, sell, or license it.

TRADEMARKS A trademark is a word or symbol that identifies a particular brand, product, or business. Like a patent, it can also be registered with the U.S. Patent and Trademark Office so that exclusive ownership can be reserved.

Consigned Goods Contracts

It is becoming increasingly common for organizations to require suppliers to stock inventory at the buyers' sites in order to support rapid delivery. These arrangements are called supplier-managed inventory (SMI) and are included in a contract covering specific conditions, such as when and under what conditions the transfer of ownership from the supplier to the buyer takes place, which party bears the financial liability of loss during storage or potential obsolescence, and the general payment terms.

Other Contract Types

A wide variety of contracts are employed in special circumstances that broadly outline the terms and conditions of ongoing relationships outside of any specific statement of work. There are so many types that it would be impossible (and beyond our scope) to list them all. For reference, here are just a few:

- **Master supply agreement.** Covers special terms and conditions for the purchase of critical materials. You may also find this listed under *master supply agreement* in directories of legal agreements.
- **Master services agreement.** Addresses terms and conditions related to the purchase of nontangible goods. Since the UCC does not cover services directly—except when the major portion (greater than 50 percent) of the contract is actually for goods—it is always a good idea to have an overriding contract in place for each significant service purchased by your organization.
- **Construction contract.** Used for significant building and facilities improvement contracts where special risks of performance and liability exist.
- **Nondisclosure agreement (NDA).** An NDA or *confidentiality agreement* protects sensitive information from disclosure to third parties or the general public.

An NDA can be unilateral, that is, binding on only one party, or mutual and binding on both parties.

■ **Commercial lease agreement.** Forms a contract for equipment owned by one party and used by another for a fee. Leases are essentially rental agreements that outline the responsibilities and liabilities assumed by each of the parties. Terms generally state which party is responsible for maintenance and upkeep as well as the conditions for use and warranties.

Methods of Exchange

As discussed earlier in this chapter, a contract requires both an offer and acceptance in order to be legally enforceable. Questions often arise regarding how to handle disparities between the form of the contract and the form of its acceptance, one issued by the supplier and the other by the buyer. If the terms of the two differ, which should prevail? This brings up the topic referred to as the "battle of the forms."

Battle of the Forms

Typically, for low-value goods orders, the buyer will issue a simple PO containing the organization's standard terms and conditions in the form of a boilerplate on the reverse side. The supplier acknowledges the order issuing its own form with a corresponding boilerplate on its side. In common practice, neither party reads the other's boilerplate. But what happens when the two sets differ?

The answer to this gets rather complicated and has created some confusion. Section 2–207 of the UCC looks at this from three different perspectives:

1. Do the conflicting forms establish a contract?
2. If a contract does exist, what terms are then enforceable?
3. If a contract does not exist, but the parties have performed anyway, what are the terms of the contract established by their performance?

While many courts have ruled on these questions, there seems to be no uniform conclusion. For material goods, what appears to emerge is the concept that if one party *says* it accepts an offer, a contract exists even though the terms may be different or additional terms are included in the acceptance. But how are the additional terms or conflicting terms handled?

To complicate the answer to this question, Section 2–207 indicates that additional terms included by the seller in its acknowledgment become part of the contract unless the buyer's contract expressly prohibits such additions or if they materially alter the original contract. If not, the added terms become part of the contract unless the buyer specifically objects within a reasonable time frame. Thus, the additional terms are added to the buyer's contract.

Conflicting terms, however, are generally considered self-canceling, that is, they do not apply. Instead, under most circumstances, standard terms contained in the UCC become the default provisions.

Mirror Image Rule

Because the UCC does not expressly apply to services, the battle of the forms does not arise when services are contracted. Instead, the *mirror image* rule applies under the Statute of Frauds. This requires that offer and acceptance match exactly, that is, be mirror images of each other, before a contract can be enforced. If the acceptance differs from the offer, it is considered a counteroffer. However, if either of the parties initiates performance following such counteroffer, it is considered an acceptance.

Tips and Techniques

Careful: Actions speak louder than words. Initiating any act that indicates the existence of a contract can be tantamount to accepting the other party's terms.

Acceptance of an Oral Agreement

Under the terms of the UCC, oral agreements require written confirmation if they are for material goods with values greater than $500. If they are and the confirmation has been offered, the party receiving the written confirmation has 10 days from the receipt of such confirmation to object. Otherwise, the contract is considered accepted.

Other Contract Elements

As you may imagine, numerous important legal elements are included in every contract. Each of these varies with the nature of the particular situation for which the contract is being written. Let's discuss some of the more common ones.

Revocation

In most cases, an offer may be revoked by the party making it any time before it is accepted. The revocation can take any form that expressly or implicitly indicates that the party making the offer is no longer willing or able to enter into a contract. A clear example of this would be the incapacity of the seller to perform as a result of a fire that destroys its facility or the sale of the item being offered to another party.

An action inconsistent with the offer is also considered a revocation if notice of the action is provided to the other party prior to acceptance. If, for example, we offer to perform a service for your organization next week and, before you can accept, leave you a voice mail that we have gone on vacation, we have then revoked the offer.

Change Orders

Common in construction projects and other services, change orders present another issue. Having established a contract with your organization, is the supplier required to accept changes to the SOW? Most service contracts include appropriate criteria for making unilateral changes, including the method of pricing them. Without such protection, the supplier is under little obligation to accept changes or to price them in relation to its initial contract pricing. Change orders are subject to the same requirements of writing as the original contract.

Dispute Resolution

Most contracts, including POs, contain legal remedies should a dispute arise. Many contain mediation or arbitration clauses or some other method for resolving them, such as a formal appeals process. In commercial transactions, disputes may ultimately come to a court for resolution.

Note

Section 2–207 of the UCC can be a handy reference for further detail regarding contract modification, rescission, and waiver.

Legal Authority and the Buyers' Responsibilities

In dealing with contracts, there are some specific principles you will need to keep in mind so that you fully understand your role and responsibilities, as well as the limits of your authority. Agency, authority, and financial responsibility are discussed in the following sections.

Agency

An *agent* is an individual with the authority to act on behalf of a principal, in most cases an employer. This means that your organization may be legally bound by the terms of any contract you have formed. The law of agency covers the legal principles governing this relationship and the buyer's relationship to the supplier. As an agent, however, *you* will not be held *personally* liable for such acts, providing you have not violated the law or your organization's express business and/or ethics policies.

AUTHORITY As an agent, the buyer is required to perform certain duties. Within the scope of these duties the buyer is given certain authority, both by role and by specific designation.

APPARENT AUTHORITY *Apparent authority* comes with the role of buyer. It differs from *actual authority* insofar as no specific charter is given to perform designated duties other than those typically associated with buyers' duties through common business practice. In effect, it is an implied authority but one on which third parties may legally rely. The title of buyer (or any similar association) will generally be taken to mean that authority has been granted to contract and buy goods and services for the organization. The buyer's spending limit is technically controlled only by internal policy, meaning that a supplier may rely on the buyer's authority even if it exceeds the amount allowed by the organization.

Tips and Techniques

If you place or authorize an order in an amount that exceeds your authority, your organization will likely be bound by the amount since, in your role, you have apparent authority. However, your organization may hold you personally responsible for any amount exceeding your designated authority should any liability arise.

LIMITED AUTHORITY   Limited authority means that the agency may be limited within the scope of an individual's responsibility. Most commonly, in commercial environments, the agency of a salesperson is specifically limited. Sales representatives are hired to solicit business and coordinate activities between the respective organizations and thus have limited authority. They are not empowered through the agency to commit their company to any specific obligations. For this, you will need to find an individual who is at least designated as a manager.

Ratification

When an agent acts beyond the designated scope of its responsibility, the contracting organization may nevertheless choose to ratify the action. This ratification thus binds the obligations created by the contract and releases the agent from personal liability.

Financial Responsibility

At all times, the buyer, as an agent, holds a position of *fiduciary* trust, as well as business responsibility, toward the principal. Thus, the buyer is expected to act prudently and in the best interest of the organization, especially in carrying out financial duties. This responsibility covers conformance to legal, as well as ethical, principles. Needless to say, the exercise of good judgment and integrity are paramount to meeting this responsibility.

Sarbanes-Oxley

Corporate financial malfeasance has resulted in several scandals over the years and, as a reaction, Congress enacted the Sarbanes-Oxley Act (or SOX, as it is called). This law, passed in 2002, affects only publicly traded corporations for now but will likely expand to include all corporate entities that have dealings with them, whether public or private. Section 404 of the act requires, among other things, that corporate policies and procedures be documented and that key accounting and finance processes be clearly stated. More importantly, the act requires that CEOs and CFOs attest to the veracity of the financial statement in a written statement. The firm's financial reports must include disclosure of all financial obligations, including procurement contracts that could create a liability for the shareholders. Penalties for violation include very stiff prison sentences.

   The impact that this will have on procurement activities is still being sorted out, but it is clear that all risks associated with any significant supply agreement will need to be disclosed and steps taken to mitigate the risk included in reporting documents. For example, any high-dollar "take or pay" contract requiring payment regardless of whether or not the products or services are needed (often used as an inducement to the supplier to invest in capital equipment or engineering) will need to be disclosed, along with the rationale for entering into such agreement and the steps that can be taken to minimize the loss to shareholders should the need for cancellation arise.

Reviewing Contracts for Legal Requirements

Legal decisions are typically based on historical precedent—how prior cases regarding the same circumstances have been resolved by the courts. Unfortunately, as a procurement professional you are not always aware of the most recent decisions and how they might affect your contract since you are primarily focused on the business issues. Before issuing a contract, therefore, you should ensure that it conforms to appropriate legal requirements in addition to the business needs of your organization. To this end, it is best to obtain legal input prior to its writing. In fact, many organizations have policies requiring that only their Legal Department can draft contracts.

In some organizations, standard contracts drafted by legal counsel are available for your use when needed. Whenever possible, you should use these rather than the contracts submitted by the supplier since they likely offer more specific protection in your circumstances. It is never a good idea to simply sign a contract presented by the supplier.

Legal counsel provides assurance that the contract conforms to applicable law and regulations and that your organization's liability is minimized. In addition to this, you may also want to employ counsel for a number of specific circumstances, such as those listed below:

- **Intellectual property rights.** As just discussed, you need to be certain that your organization does not infringe on any IP rights legally granted to others and that you have properly protected its own IP rights through proper disclosure processes.
- **Legal venue.** Your legal counsel will require language in the contract to determine which state's laws will be considered and in which state's court action will be taken should litigation be required.

    This can be quite difficult when dealing with international suppliers. Some countries recognize the rules established by the United Nations Convention on Contracts for the International Sale of Goods (CISG) as discussed in Chapter 20, but others do not. Your counsel may wish to obtain advice from a local attorney in the country in which you are conducting business.
- **Assignability.** Legal review may also be required to ensure that the contract will be transferable to any future business interests your organization may acquire (such as through acquisition, merger, or the creation of a subsidiary) and, at the same time, limit the supplier's ability to transfer the contract without prior approval.
- **Insurance.** For some contracts, you will want to be certain that the supplier carries the proper insurance, such as worker's compensation, so that additional liability does not accrue to your organization. Legal counsel will often require that you obtain copies of the supplier's certificate of insurance as evidence that

it is in place. In some cases, in addition to insurance, a performance bond may be required. These bonds are usually purchased to insure against the buyer's loss should the supplier default in providing the agreed-upon services.

- **Reviews and claims.** Under certain circumstances, you may wish to include a process for review should there be a dispute regarding the contract. This benefits both parties. Reviews are generally a form of mediation and often simply refer questions and decisions to more senior management or to corresponding company counsel. In government environments, however, the process is generally more formal and will often involve an actual review board convened for the express purpose of reviewing supplier protests and claims.

- **Parol evidence.** The rule of *parol evidence* prevents the use of oral testimony to alter a written contract. This means that any oral promises made by the supplier during the contracting process must be put in writing or they will not apply. Only the written contract can be used as evidence of an agreement. As a result, it is extremely important to review the deliverables with legal counsel to ensure that all commitments are accurately reflected in the document.

  Keep in mind that the parol evidence rule also requires any amendments or changes to an existing written contract to also be in writing and be certain that this is clearly written into your contract to avoid disputes when field personnel become involved and begin to make *ad hoc* changes.

- **Reservation of rights.** Your legal counsel will also want to similarly review any clauses that specifically limit your organization's rights to the full performance of the contract. This will include a requirement that no changes can be made in the contract without the express consent of the buyer.

- **Liability limitations.** Suppliers typically want to limit liability to replacement of a product or service under the terms of the warranty. Depending on the circumstances, however, this may limit your organization's rights to claim *incidental damages* such as transportation or special handling costs. In some cases, *consequential damages*—including lost revenue or profit, damage to property, or injury to persons—may be in order. Clauses covering these conditions are often contentious and best left in the hands of your attorney.

- **Liquidated damages.** It will often be impossible to calculate the actual monetary damage or loss suffered under certain circumstances. In such situations, the parties will agree to a predetermined amount—known as liquidated damages—to be paid in the event of default. This is also a contentious process and so requires input from legal counsel. It is important to determine a reasonable amount for damages in any particular case so that it will be upheld if the argument goes to court.

- **Regulated materials.** Laws governing the transportation, use, and disposal of regulated and hazardous materials, such as the Toxic Substances Control Act (1976) and the Resource Conservation and Recovery Act (1976), require special attention since these substances can create exceptional liability for your organization. Special legal and technical expertise is definitely required when dealing contractually with any material that might fall under these regulations. These are high-risk areas and, at the minimum, require that the roles and responsibilities of the parties be clearly defined.

- **Force majeure.** *Force majeure* identifies acts or events that are outside the control of human beings, such as wars, natural disasters, fires, floods, and the like. Typically, either or both parties to a contract are relieved of performance when such uncontrollable actions occur and are not held liable for damages. It is important, however, to be certain proper legal language is included in your contract since there are no automatic provisions covering this.

Aligning Contracts and Practices with Policy

Most organizations maintain a set of documents governing the practices conducted by the Procurement Department. These usually take the form of written policies or operating procedures. They are designed to provide effective guidance in the conduct of activities so that employees understand their obligations to the organization. In scope, these policies and procedures vary, but they typically cover elements such as procurement authority, supplier management, quality standards, records retention, conformance to law, and good business and ethical practices.

The procurement professional is expected to bring to the job sufficient expertise to interpret and enforce these policies and may expect to be called upon for input when they are being created or revised. In some organizations, the procurement professional will have the additional responsibility of actually writing and maintaining the procurement portion of organizational policy.

Conformance to Law

At the minimum, organizations are required to conform to antitrust, environmental, and health and safety laws. As you will recall, antitrust regulations were covered in Chapter 2, and some of the laws covering environmental and health and safety processes were outlined above. In addition, there are numerous laws governing intellectual property (which we discussed earlier in this chapter), and there are rules governing confidentiality such as the *Uniform Trade Secrets Act (UTSA)* that define rights for particular trade secrets. As a procurement professional, you will be required to have a working knowledge of all of these laws and regulations.

In addition, you should become familiar with the activities and regulations of certain governmental agencies that are empowered to protect the rights and welfare of the general population. One of these organizations, the Environmental Protection Agency (EPA), is charged with enforcing federal laws relating to hazardous materials, clean air, and water and waste disposal. Many of the regulations and laws enforced by this agency carry criminal charges if violated, so you should become very familiar with their overall requirements.

The Occupational Safety and Health Act gives rise to a variety of rules and regulations governing safety in the workplace. Under certain circumstances, your organization will want to include a clause in its contracts that essentially shifts the burden of compliance to the supplier. A clause in the contract requiring compliance with applicable laws is generally sufficient protection, but it must be crafted by legal counsel since regulations are quite formal in this area.

Ethical Principles

The Institute for Supply Management (ISM) maintains a set of ethical standards for the supply management profession entitled "Principles and Standards of Ethical Supply

Management Conduct." These are excellent guidelines to use as a basis for your organization's business ethics policy and as individual guidelines for the staff. In light of continuing scandals involving the questionable integrity of corporate officers and the subsequent U.S. requirements for reporting imposed by SOX, we cannot emphasize enough the importance that you understand, adopt, and strictly adhere to the covenants of a viable code of ethics.

Following are some areas that should be of particular concern:

- **Conflict of interest.** Occurs when procurement employees conduct the organization's business in such manner as to further their own personal gain or that of their families and friends. This includes providing insider tips on activities that would affect the price of stock, or buying and selling from relatives. It also includes owning a share of any organization that conducts business with the organization that employs you.
- **Bribery.** It is illegal to accept *bribes* and *gratuities* in the form of money or any other valuable goods or services with the intent to influence decisions. You probably understand this. However, it is important to also understand that even the perception of unethical conduct must always be avoided. This includes accepting frequent meals and entertainment from suppliers or any gifts that could be considered to have even nominal value. In a position of financial trust, one must exercise impeccable judgment.

  Similarly, it is also illegal for the buyer to offer bribes to others. Although in some countries, gratuities are customary for work performed in the normal course of duties, it is clearly a violation of U.S. law to offer a bribe to any government or business official to influence a decision, regardless of the country in which it takes place.
- **Personal purchases.** Be certain that any purchases you make for your personal use from a supplier conforms to the organization's policy and that it is fair to the supplier and others in your organization. Some organizations encourage this as a means of supporting valued suppliers and gaining benefit for their employees; others look upon it as a conflict of interest.
- **Proprietary information.** You will be expected to maintain confidentiality at all times and to protect the *proprietary information* in the possession of your organization, regardless of its ultimate ownership. This includes maintaining the confidentiality of plans and intentions. If you must disclose information to a supplier or other third party in the normal course of your business, be certain that you obtain a signed confidentiality agreement or nondisclosure agreement before so doing.

Note

The Institute for Supply Management (ISM) provides excellent references for codes of ethics in their "Principles of Social Responsibility and Principles and Standards of Ethical Supply Management Conduct." You can find these documents on the ISM Web site at: www.ism.ws/ISMMembership/PrincipleStandards.cfm.

Maintaining Procurement Documents and Records

To comply with standard records retention programs and legal processes, you are required to know how to maintain certain documents and for what specific period of time they must be retained. Some of the requirements are mandated by law (such as those outlined by the Internal Revenue Service [IRS]), while others are based on organizational policy and sound business practices. Keep in mind it is equally important to know when *not* to keep documents as it is to know when they should be kept. There is no inherent value to storing records that will never require access if it is not a legal or regulatory requirement. You must ask if the records are worth the cost and space of storage and if you want to keep them on-site or at a third-party storage facility. You must also determine if they should be kept in printed format or in electronic media.

Not all documents related to contracts and POs will be maintained by the Procurement Department. In some organizations, it is common for the Legal Department to hold all documents related to written contracts. Also, equipment records and related drawings are often kept by the using department. However, it is more typical to find that most of these are stored by the Procurement Department if they are related to procurement activities.

Examples of the kind of records generated and maintained by the Procurement Department include the following:

- **POs and contracts.** Includes quotes and acknowledgment history. POs and contracts are typically filed by *open orders* (those that are still active) and *closed orders* (those that have been fully received or have expired). Today, of course, many of these records are being maintained electronically and require no filing space.

  POs are kept for a six-year period (following their expiration) as required by most taxing authorities, including the IRS. The UCC, it should be noted, requires that POs for goods be kept for only a four-year period.
- **Supplier qualification records and periodic reviews.** Historical records containing the original qualification data and supplier ratings and reviews. They are typically maintained as long as the supplier is active. Also included here might be the records of previous negotiations. All of these records are retained in accordance with organizational policy.
- **Catalogs.** Generally maintained in a central library, although it is becoming less common for organizations to keep printed catalogs because so many are available online or in electronic format. This media certainly reduces the storage and filing requirements and is preferred since it is typically more up-to-date. Electronic catalogs also do not vanish, as do some of their more popular paper counterparts.
- **Inventory records.** These records, such as traveling requisitions and historical ordering data by part, are also likely to be found in many procurement departments. Commonly, today, these records are maintained on computer systems. These are kept for a relatively short period of time and only as required by organizational policy.
- **Project files.** Kept when appropriate and when they are for projects led by the Procurement Department, such as cost reduction or quality improvement programs. These are also kept for a relatively short period of time and only as required by organizational policy.

It may be worth mentioning that records are stored in a variety of formats, including paper and electronic media such as tape, floppy disks, and compact discs (CDs). In some environments, they are also stored on microfilm (or microfiche). From a record retention and legal perspective, the media should make little or no difference to the storage policy.

Summary

One of the primary responsibilities of the Procurement Department involves creating and issuing purchase orders. Since contracts (and, of course, POs) are considered legally binding documents, the procurement professional must become familiar with the basic principles of contract formation. These principles are founded on the basic requirements that are needed in order for a contract to be legally binding: mutual agreement, legal purpose, consideration, and the capacity to enter into a contract.

There are numerous types of standard procurement contract types available based primarily on payment schema. Contracts generally fall into two major categories: fixed price and cost reimbursable. To a large extent, the payment method selected determines the way that risk is shared between the contracting parties. In addition to these major categories, agreements are commonly developed for licensing intellectual property, maintaining confidentiality, leasing buildings and equipment, and consigning goods.

Buyers, as agents, are granted certain legal authority to commit the organization to a contract, but this authority also generates a measure of fiduciary responsibility to the employer. It is important, therefore, that in complex situations you seek legal review and proper approval prior to signature. It is also important that you align your contracts to conform to applicable law and organization policy. Today, ethical behavior is one of the key issues in business, and it is critical that you understand your obligations. A good reference point is the "Principles and Standards of Ethical Supply Management Conduct," a set of ethical standards published by the Institute for Supply Management (ISM).

Finally, the Procurement Department is also responsible for maintaining and retaining files and records commonly associated with procurement activities. You should become familiar with your organization's policy regarding records retention.

CHAPTER 6

Supplier Diversity

The concept of supplier diversity programs to support economically disadvantaged groups in the United States was born from the American sense of fairness and equality, and supported by numerous government-sponsored programs that have been legislated into law. But many of us are not familiar with the nature and benefits of a diversity supplier program and, importantly, many do not fully understand how their organization can support and benefit from these programs.

As it relates to sourcing management, supplier diversity programs expand the organization's supply base by developing new sources of sustainable supply as a means to expand competition. Diversity programs support a supply base that is generally more representative of the community than without such programs. We call this process "inclusion." Fostering inclusion supports the economic welfare of the community and promotes the availability of a viable workforce. Thus by increasing the diversity of the supply base, we also increase its overall health. That is why we chose to include the process in our examination of best practices in sourcing management.

To be effective in developing a supplier diversity program, most organizations fund a comprehensive annual supplier diversity operating budget. The goal of the budget is to execute stated long- and short-term objectives for the inclusion of a diverse supply base for sourcing. Usually, cross-functional teams within the enterprise are assembled in order to develop and implement plans to meet supplier diversity sourcing goals.

The need for professional support in the management of diversity programs is rapidly becoming a significant corporate objective, so much so that the Institute for Supply Management has recently launched a certification program for individuals working in this field:

ISM Launches Certified Professional in Supplier Diversity™ (CPSD™)

"Those who hold responsibility for supplier diversity have for some time asked ISM to define the body of knowledge necessary to do this job professionally and successfully," says ISM CEO Paul Novak, CPSM, C.P.M., A.P.P., MCIPS. "We have captured the body of knowledge that is required for supplier diversity efforts not only in the United States, but also wherever efforts are practiced that are inclusive of minority and women suppliers."

www.ism.ws/about/MediaRoom/newsreleasedetail
.cfm?ItemNumber=21029

Diversity Programs

When we speak of "diversity," we refer primarily to historically underrepresented segments of our society, initially small businesses owned by minorities. Government has expanded the definition to include other segments of small business that require special consideration: service-disabled veteran-owned small business, disabled veteran–owned small business, veteran-owned small business, and women-owned small business. Also included are small businesses located in specific historically underutilized business zones called HUBZones. As a group these are referred to using the acronym MWDBE: minority, women, and disadvantaged business enterprises, or sometimes just SDBs (small, disadvantaged business) and MBEs (minority business enterprise).

Definitions and Certification

There are two major entities that define what type of business is part of a disadvantaged business group: the U.S. Small Business Administration (SBA) and the National Minority Supplier Development Council (NMSDC).

THE U.S. SMALL BUSINESS ADMINISTRATION (SBA)   The SBA administers two particular business assistance programs for small disadvantaged businesses (SDBs). These programs are the 8(a) Business Development Program and the Small Disadvantaged Business Certification Program. Until recently, the SBA certified small businesses that were "disadvantaged." Presently, this process has been suspended and organizations seeking to do business with the federal government as a small, disadvantaged business can self-certify for any of the protected categories. The 8(a) Program, however, is still in effect.

The 8(a) Program—named for Section 8(a) of the Small Business Act—is a business development program created to help small disadvantaged businesses compete in the marketplace. A Certified 8(a) firm is a company owned and operated by socially and economically disadvantaged individuals and eligible to receive federal contracts under the Small Business Administration's 8(a) Business Development Program. Suppliers wanting to conduct business with the federal government apply for a designation through the Central Contractor Registration (CCR). Firms that are certified receive assistance and counseling in a structured developmental process over a nine-year period. Maintaining this classification requires an annual review.

The SBA has established numerical definitions, called "size standards," for every private-sector industry in the U.S. economy; the North American Industry Classification System (NAICS) is used to identify the industries. An industry is coded with a six-digit number, such as 541330 for Engineering Services. A size standard, which is usually stated in number of employees or average annual receipts, represents the largest size that a business (including its subsidiaries and affiliates) may be to remain classified as a small business for SBA and federal contracting programs. All federal agencies must use SBA size standards for contracts identified as small business.

Table 6.1 shows the most commonly used size standards within an NAICS industry sector. If the size of a business exceeds the size standard for its overall industry sector, it may still be a small business for the specific six-digit NAICS industry. Some industries have higher size standards than the general one for the

TABLE 6.1   Small Business Size Standards

NAICS Industry Sector	Size Standard
Manufacturing	500 employees
Wholesale Trade	100 employees
Agriculture	$750,000
Retail Trade	$7 million
General and Heavy Construction (except Dredging)	$33.5 million
Dredging	$20 million
Special Trade Contractors	$14 million
Travel Agencies	$3.5 million (commissions and other income)
Business and Personal Services Except:	$7 million
Architectural, Engineering, Surveying, and Mapping Services	$4.5 million
Dry Cleaning and Carpet Cleaning Services	$4.5 million

industry group. SBA's Table of Small Business Size Standards lists size standards by six-digit NAICS industry codes.

Other definitions provided by the SBA include the following:

- **A woman-owned business** is defined as a business that is owned and controlled 51 percent or more by a woman or women. Currently, a woman-owned certification process is not required for federal contracts.
- **A veteran-owned business** is defined as a business that is owned 51 percent by a veteran(s). There is no veteran-owned certification process to complete; self-certification is sufficient.
- **A service-disabled business** is defined as a business that is owned 51 percent by one or more service-disabled veterans. The Veterans Administration confirms service-related disability.
- **A HUBZone business.** SBA's HUBZone (historically underutilized business zone) Program is designed to promote economic development and employment growth in distressed areas by providing access to more federal contracting opportunities. Certified small business firms have the opportunity to negotiate contracts and participate in restricted competition limited to HUBZone firms.

THE NATIONAL MINORITY SUPPLIER DEVELOPMENT COUNCIL (NMSDC)   NMSDC has standardized procedures to assure consistent and identical review and certification of minority-owned businesses.

A minority-owned business is a for-profit enterprise, regardless of size, physically located in the United States or its trust territories, which is owned, operated and controlled by minority group members.

"Minority group members" are United States citizens who are Asian (Asian Pacific and Asian-Indian), Black, Hispanic and Native American with at least 25% minimum (documentation to support claim of 25% required from applicant).

Ownership by minority individuals means the business is at least 51% owned by such individuals or, in the case of a publicly-owned business, at least 51% of the stock is owned by one or more such individuals. Further, the management and daily operations are controlled by those minority group members.

Note: *Asian-Indian American* refers to a U.S. citizen whose origins are from India, Pakistan, and Bangladesh. *Asian-Pacific American* refers to a U.S. citizen whose origins are from Japan, China, Taiwan, Korea, Vietnam, Laos, Cambodia, the Philippines, Samoa, Guam, the U.S. Trust Territories of the Pacific, or the Northern Marianas. *American Indian* refers to a person who is a Native American Indian, Eskimo, Aleut, or Native Hawaiian and regarded as such by the community of which the person claims to be a part. Native Americans must be documented members of a North American tribe, band, or otherwise organized group of native people who are indigenous to the continental United States and proof can be provided through a Native American Blood Degree Certificate (i.e., tribal registry letter, tribal roll register number).

U.S. Small Business Support

What is a small business? The SBA defines a business concern as one that is organized for profit; has a place of business in the United States; operates primarily within the United States or makes a significant contribution to the U.S. economy through payment of taxes or use of American products, materials, or labor; is independently owned and operated; and is not dominant in its field on a national basis. The business may be a sole proprietorship, partnership, corporation, or any other legal form.

The federal government's size definitions are much more complex: Generally, the standards used are either 500 or more employees or revenue over $750,000. Variations are based on the specific industry as summarized in Table 6.1.

Statistics
- Represent 99.7 percent of all employer firms.
- Employ half of all private sector employees.
- Pay 44 percent of total U.S. private payroll.
- Generated 65 percent of net new jobs over the past 17 years.
- Create more than half of the nonfarm private GDP.
- Hire 43 percent of high-tech workers (scientists, engineers, computer programmers, and others).
- Are 52 percent home based and 2 percent franchises.
- Made up 97.5 percent of all identified exporters and produced 31 percent of export value in FY 2008.
- Produce 13 times more patents per employee than large patenting firms.

The U.S. Small Business Administration (SBA)

The SBA was created in 1953 as an independent agency of the federal government to aid, counsel, assist, and protect the interests of small business concerns; to preserve free competitive enterprise; and to maintain and strengthen the overall economy of our nation. We recognize that small business is critical to our economic recovery and strength, to building America's future, and to helping the United States compete in today's global marketplace. Although the SBA has grown and evolved in the years since it was established, the bottom-line mission remains the same. The SBA helps Americans start, build, and grow businesses. Through an extensive network of field offices and partnerships with public and private organizations, the SBA delivers its services to people throughout the United States, Puerto Rico, the U.S. Virgin Islands, and Guam.

Some of the services offered by the SBA include help with the following:

- Starting your business.
- Managing your business.
- Marketing your business.
- Technology for your business.

Technical Assistance (Training and Counseling)

The SBA offers specific technical assistance in areas that are commonly problematic for small business owners. For example, training and counseling topics include the following:

- Entrepreneurial development.
- Entrepreneurship education.
- Native American affairs.
- Women's business ownership.
- International trade.

Financial Assistance

Financing is a critical factor in developing a small business. The SBA provides a number of programs and areas of assistance in an effort to help entrepreneurs get their businesses on a solid financial footing, including the following:

- Loan programs.
- Specialty loan programs.
- Financial assistance.
- Investment.
- Surety guarantees.

Contracting

The determination to make a small business set-aside is usually made unilaterally by the contracting officer. However, this determination may also be joint. In this case, it is recommended by the Small Business Administration procurement center representative (PCR) and agreed to by the contracting officer.

Set-Asides and Quotas

The regulations specify that, to the extent practicable, unilateral determinations initiated by a contracting officer, rather than joint determinations, should be used as the basis for small business set-asides:

Contracts of $0–$2,500: No set-asides available.

Contracts of $2,500–$100,000: Under the set-aside program, every acquisition of supplies or services that has an anticipated dollar value between $2,500 and $100,000 (except for those acquisitions set aside for very small business concerns, as described below) is automatically reserved exclusively for small businesses. However, every set-aside must meet the "Rule of Two," which requires that there must be a reasonable expectation that offers will be obtained from two or more small business concerns that are competitive in terms of market prices, quality, and delivery. If only one acceptable offer is received from a responsible small business concern in response to a set-aside, the contracting officer is required to make an award to that firm. If no acceptable offers are received from responsible small business concerns, the set-aside will be withdrawn and the product or service, if still valid, will be solicited on an unrestricted basis.

Contracts over $100,000: In addition, the contracting officer is required to set aside any contract over $100,000 for small businesses when there is a reasonable expectation that offers will be obtained from at least two responsible small business concerns offering the products of different small business concerns and that the award will be made at fair market prices.

Partial Set-Asides: A small business set-aside of a single acquisition or a class of acquisitions may be total or partial. The contracting officer is required to set aside a portion of an acquisition, except for construction, for exclusive small business participation when:

A total set-aside is not appropriate.

The government's purchase requirement is severable into two or more economic production runs or reasonable lots.

One or more small business concerns are expected to have the technical competence and productive capacity to satisfy the set-aside portion of the requirement at a fair market price.

The acquisition is not subject to simplified acquisition procedures.

Qualified Products List (QPL): Any products on a QPL are not set aside for small business.

Award Requirements

To get this type of contract, a business must perform at least a given percentage of the contract. This provision limits the amount of subcontracting a concern may enter into with other firms when performing these types of contracts. The provisions are as follows:

- *Construction.* For general and heavy construction contractors, at least 15 percent of the cost of the contract, not including the cost of materials, must be performed by the prime contractor with its own employees. For special trade construction, such as plumbing, electrical, or tile work, this requirement is 25 percent.

- *Manufacturing.* At least 50 percent of the cost of manufacturing, not including the cost of materials, must be done by the prime contractor.
- *Services.* At least 50 percent of the contract cost for personnel must be performed by the prime contractor's own employees.

The Business Case for Diversity

The Chubb Group of Insurance Companies states the business case (on its website) with elegant simplicity:

> *Those who perceive diversity as exclusively a moral imperative or societal goal are missing the larger point. Workforce diversity needs to be viewed as a competitive advantage and a business opportunity. That's why Chubb makes diversity a business priority and strives to achieve a fully inclusive diverse workforce.*

Many other organizations echo this concept. For example, Sears Holdings' diversity statement posted on its website includes this:

> *Sears Holdings endeavors to provide minority, women, small, HUBZone, veteran or service-disabled veteran businesses with the maximum opportunities to participate as suppliers and contractors for merchandise, supplies and services used in all Sears Holdings business units.*

> *We recognize that supplier diversity adds value to our business. A diverse supplier base stimulates growth in our communities while helping us bring a wide variety of diverse merchandise and services to our customers.*

Thus it is clear that while organizations sincerely acknowledge the "moral imperative" to engage diversity in their supply base, they also seek to create a competitive advantage and business opportunity.

Objectives

The key objective in conducting a supplier diversity program is to qualify and purchase from small, disadvantaged businesses. As noted, organizations do so in their own self-interest in order to create opportunity for groups that are historically underrepresented, increasing their economic viability and thereby helping to create new markets for their sponsoring organizations. Businesses also hope to benefit through an increased market share within multicultural and disadvantaged communities. There is also the important consideration that companies doing business with most U.S. and local government entities are evaluated on their ability to contract with diversity enterprises for a measurable portion of their supplies and services. Typically, this requirement is mandated by law.

Measuring Success

To be fully effective, a supplier diversity program must have measurable goals. Measurable goals communicate the program's expectations and provide a framework to measure progress. Typically, goals are established in the strategic planning process for the sourcing organization. These goals should include implementation timetables as well as quantitative goals such as annual purchase dollars, percent of total purchases, and the number of diversity suppliers contracted with.

The NMSDC suggests establishing the following measurable goals:

- Performance milestones or in-process review/benchmarks to ensure that adequate bidding opportunities are offered to MBEs
- Quantitative goals that reflect the corporation's use of minority suppliers/contractors (i.e., annual purchase dollars, percent increase over previous year purchases, percent of total purchase value, etc.).
- Qualitative goals that reflect progress in implementing specific minority business development strategies (i.e., mentoring, joint venturing, strategic alliances, education, financial assistance, etc.).

Supplier Diversity Best Practices

Recognized best practices maintain that organizations should have and adhere to a diversity *business development policy statement* that is signed by the CEO. This policy statement should guide sourcing operations and should be a requirement in the contracting process. Best practices also include a contract flow-down clause requiring the implementation of similar policies by the supplier in its contracting activities.

Best practices suggest organizations should demonstrate a number of specific characteristics in their diversity programs. As stated by NMSDC, this includes:

- Commitment on the part of the chief executive officer and his or her senior officers.
- A minority business development director specifically assigned the responsibility for implementing the program.
- Minority business development goals that are established and monitored the same as other corporate goals and objectives.
- A corporate culture that promotes innovative techniques to develop minority businesses.

To undertake a minority business development program without making it a part of the day-to-day business of the organization is to condemn it to almost certain failure. But by careful planning, policy formation, goal setting, implementation, monitoring, and accountability, the program can reach its goals and produce significant benefits for the corporation and the community.

Like all corporate policies, a minority business development policy must have the backing of the senior line officers if it is to be implemented effectively throughout the organization. Through written and verbal communication, the CEO should emphasize to senior officers that purchasing from minority businesses is beneficial to the company in many ways.

Support for Diversity Suppliers

Establishing programs that support diversity supplier development should not end (as it too often does) with a policy statement. There are many ways to support the diversity supplier community through mentoring and inclusion in the organization's processes:

- **Financial assistance.** Funding is possibly the single most critical issue that small, disadvantaged businesses must deal with. The buying organization can offer substantial assistance in getting working capital by issuing advance purchase orders that the supplier can use to obtain funding. The organization may also consider providing loan guarantees or even financing loans itself. In fact, some organizations have actually hosted their developing suppliers as a form of incubator, providing facilities and administrative support at low or no cost.
- **Training and mentoring.** Support through inclusion in organizational training programs, especially those encompassing management training, business planning, human resources, finance and managing cash flow, sourcing and procurement methods, and so on.

  Organizations can also assist their diversity suppliers by helping them to identify areas where they are deficient and where training may be required, perhaps providing appropriate staff members to conduct the training.
- **Technical assistance.** Buying organizations can provide a number of technical services from engineering development to establishing a quality control function. This can operate either in the form of low-cost technical services or assistance with product development.
- **Registration.** Organizations with viable supplier diversity programs provide Internet access to their program and a means of Internet-accessible registration to incorporate those firms registered in a sourcing database. Often this is a simple process that requires little more than identification of the supplier, its diversity category, and the products or services that it provides. The database is searchable by the sourcing and the procurement groups.

Other Best Practice Elements

There are a number of other elements you may want to consider applying to diversity sourcing operations. These will include:

- Integrating supplier diversity goals and strategic plans.
- Establishing annual goals for purchases from diversity suppliers and developing mechanisms to track spending.
- Achievement of annual goals included in individual performance measures and tied to compensation.
- Incorporating the consideration of diversity suppliers as a standard element in the sourcing process.

- Educating internal customers on the benefits of diversity sourcing; providing training for using groups and sourcing and procurement personnel.
- Developing outreach and communications programs to attract potential diversity suppliers to register for solicitation opportunities, including visibility on the organization's website outlining the sourcing program for diversity suppliers.
- Active participation by the senior sourcing manager in diversity councils.
- Creating an internal supplier diversity council to help guide diversity program policy.
- Incorporating flow-down provisions in contracts encouraging the use of second-tier diversity suppliers with specific goals.
- Requiring prime (first-tier) suppliers to report on second-tier outreach metrics and progress to goals using a supplier portal.
- Rewarding diversity suppliers that demonstrate innovation with an outlet for their ideas; especially seeking to adopt breakthrough innovation in supply management.
- Holding business and technology roadmap workshops for the small businesses that have been engaged by your organization; providing the opportunity to exchange plans for the next period of time so that your organization and its suppliers can synchronize collaborative efforts.
- Encouraging and supporting continuous improvement processes in the diversity supply base.
- Paying less attention to total spend with diversity suppliers and more attention to how that spend is distributed.

Global Supplier Diversity

As we have pointed out, supplier diversity programs are developed to create equal social and economic opportunity for classes of small, disadvantaged businesses. The current approach has proven very effective in the United States with many government organizations and their suppliers meeting their objectives on a continuing basis. Can this process be extended globally?

Many U.S. organizations doing business in multinational environments have initiated programs for "global diversity." However, we could find no definition of the term and note that many companies carry over the same U.S. language used for supplier diversity. This is likely a good start, but it's difficult, we feel, to apply U.S. criteria directly to international conditions. Simply combining the term "diversity" with "global sourcing" can be misleading and confusing.

Our Definition of Global Supplier Diversity

Consequently, in promoting a global philosophy of economic inclusion, which enables all business organizations to freely and equally engage in commercial activities within their scope, it seems appropriate to have a formal definition. We propose the following:

> *Global supplier diversity (GSD) is a formal program actively engaged in by a buying organization to support and encourage the development of small businesses*

owned by members of economically disadvantaged groups within a country or defined geographical area.

GSD is sustained through the award of business, mentoring, and technical and financial assistance consistent with the culture and legal requirements in which it operates.

An economically disadvantaged, diversity small business is one without equal access to business opportunities as a result of the ethnic, social, religious, handicapped, or gender class of its owner.

A small business is defined as one with less than 250 employees and gross income below $1 million per year.

This definition enables the business organization to operate its program within the scope of supplier diversity principles already in existence in the United States but with activities specific to the country or geographical area in which they are conducting business.

Some Efforts Are Encouraging

Despite the lack of clarity, there is one very significant effort being made by a number of companies who have been working together toward developing a workable program. Cisco is a founder and sponsor of the Minority Supplier Diversity (MSD) China organization, a nonprofit set up to help the development of China's minority-owned businesses by connecting minority suppliers to various companies as a means of providing procurement opportunities.

Significantly, participants in the MSD program include Dell, IBM, Motorola, Intel, Boeing, Johnson Controls, Coca-Cola, ITT, Tianjin Tasly Group, MSD, PepsiCo, Wyndham, and Delphi. The effort also appears to have Chinese government support, so it should be possible to use the project as a model to assist those wanting to initiate a similar program for disadvantaged small business in other countries.

Through its program, MSD has identified 55 ethnic minority groups in China that would be able to benefit from an organized effort to foster diversity; it has established a permanent operating organization and developed a number of outreach programs.

Unfortunately, this is an exception rather than a common situation. There are no other U.S. businesses that we could find that have international diversity programs as far advanced as this.

Diversity Advocacy Organizations

In the United States, there are a number of organizations, both private and public, that advocate and support programs focused on small disadvantaged business. A number of these organizations provide certification/verification of the status of the applicant company, which for many diversity suppliers is the first step toward establishing themselves as eligible for future business as a member of this category.

Verification Organizations

Here is a sampling of certification and support organizations that can be accessed through the Web:

- **National Minority Supplier Development Council (NMSDC),** www.nmsdc .org. "The National Minority Supplier Development Council® (NMSDC®) provides a direct link between corporate America and minority-owned businesses. NMSDC is one of the country's leading business membership organizations. It was chartered in 1972 to provide increased procurement and business opportunities for minority businesses of all sizes."

- **Women's Business Enterprise National Council (WBENC),** www.wbenc .org. "The Women's Business Enterprise National Council (WBENC), founded in 1997, is the largest third-party certifier of businesses owned controlled, and operated by women in the United States. WBENC, a national 501(c)(3) nonprofit, partners with 14 Regional Partner Organizations to provide its national standard of certification to women-owned businesses throughout the country. WBENC is also the nation's leading advocate of women-owned businesses as suppliers to America's corporations."

- **National Gay and Lesbian Chamber of Commerce (NGLCC),** www.nglcc .org. "The NGLCC is the business advocate and direct link between lesbian, gay, bisexual and transgender (LGBT) business owners, corporations, and government, representing the interests of more than 1.4 million LGBT businesses and entrepreneurs. The NGLCC is committed to forming a broad-based coalition of LGBT owned and friendly businesses, professionals, and major corporations for the purpose of promoting economic growth and the prosperity of our members."

- **Central Contractor Registration (CCR),** www.bpn.gov/ccr. "The primary registrant database for the U.S. Federal Government. CCR collects, validates, stores and disseminates data in support of agency acquisition missions."

- **U.S. Small Business Administration (SBA),** www.sba.gov/index.html. "The U.S. Small Business Administration (SBA) was created in 1953 as an independent agency of the federal government to aid, counsel, assist and protect the interests of small business concerns, to preserve free competitive enterprise and to maintain and strengthen the overall economy of our nation."

- **HUBZone Certification,** www.sba.gov/hubzone/. "It is our mission to promote job growth, capital investment, and economic development to historically underutilized business zones, referred to as HUBZones, by providing contracting assistance to small businesses located in these economically distressed communities."

- **VetBIZ,** www.vetbiz.gov/. "Verification of Veteran-Owned and Service-Disabled Veteran-Owned Small Businesses per Public Law (P.L.) 109-461."

Other Support Organizations

In addition to the certification/verification organizations, there are a number of other support groups. Here is just a small sampling of them:

- **DiversityInc,** www.diversityinc.com/. "The leading publication on diversity and business. DiversityInc's CEO and owner is Luke Visconti. DiversityInc was founded in 1998 as a web-based publication; our print magazine was launched in 2002. We reach more than 1 million unique monthly visitors on Diversity-Inc.com, and the magazine has circulation of over 340,000. DiversityInc.com has the largest dedicated career center for diverse professionals."

- **The Multicultural Advantage,** www.multiculturaladvantage.com. "An information site with articles, job opportunities, event listings, research tool, downloads, links and other resources for professionals from diverse background. The site also addresses the needs of diversity recruiting and workplace diversity professionals who are seeking to reach & understand them."
- **Association of MultiEthnic Americans (AMEA),** www.ameasite.org/. An international nonprofit association of organizations dedicated to advocacy, education, and collaboration on behalf of the multiethnic, multiracial, and transracial adoption community.
- **Center for Advancement of Racial & Ethnic Equity, American Council on Education (ACE),** www.acenet.edu/Content/NavigationMenu /ProgramsServices/CAREE/index.htm. Monitors and reports on the progress of African Americans, Latinos, Asian Americans, and American Indians in post-secondary education and works to improve their educational and employment opportunities in higher education.
- **DisabilityInfo.Gov,** www.disability.gov/. This website is an online guide to the federal government's disability-related information and resources.
- **Foundation for Ethnic Understanding,** www.ffeu.org/index.htm. A national nonprofit "dedicated to strengthening relations between ethnic communities." The foundation's work focuses primarily on black-Jewish relations, but has recently expanded to include Latino-Jewish relations.
- **American Indian Business Leaders (AIBL),** www.aibl.org/home/. "The only American Indian nonprofit organization solely dedicated to empowering business students in the United States. Their programs are designed to engage students in activities that stimulate, enhance, and expand educational experiences beyond traditional academic methods. All students are encouraged to participate in AIBL regardless of race, academic major, or career objectives.
- **National Black MBA Association® (NBMBAA®),** www.nbmbaa.org. "Dedicated to develop partnerships that result in the creation of intellectual and economic wealth in the Black community. In partnership with over 400 of the top U.S. business organizations, the association has inroads into a wide range of industries as well as the public and private sector."
- **ALPFA,** www.alpfa.org/. "ALPFA is the premier Latino organization for professionals and students in business, finance, accounting, and related professions. ALPFA has active members, committed business partners, and quality programs."
- **Minority Professional Network,** www.minorityprofessionalnetwork.com /nonprofit.asp. "The Global Career, Economic, Lifestyle & Networking™ Resource Connection for Progressive Multicultural Professionals. Robust Online, E-marketing & Offline Branding, Recruiting, Event Support, Training and Related Advertising & Outreach Solutions."
- **Workforce Diversity Network (WDN),** www.workforcediversitynetwork.com. "The nation's leading network of professionals and organizations dedicated to professional development, understanding, promotion and management of diversity as an essential part of business success."

- **National MultiCultural Institute,** www.nmci.org/. Founded in 1983, the National MultiCultural Institute (NMCI) is proud to be one of the first organizations to have recognized the nation's need for new services, knowledge, and skills in the growing field of multiculturalism and diversity.
- **DiversityBusiness.com,** www.diversitybusiness.com. Launched in 1999, DiversityBusiness, with over 50,000 members, is the largest organization of diversity-owned businesses throughout the United States that provide goods and services to Fortune 1000 companies, government agencies, and colleges and universities. DiversityBusiness provides research and data collection services for diversity including the "Top 50 Organizations for Multicultural Business Opportunities," "Top 500 Diversity Owned Companies in America," and others. Its research has been recognized and published by *Forbes* magazine, *BusinessWeek*, and thousands of other print and Internet publications. The site has gained national recognition and has won numerous awards for its content and design.

Corporate Supplier Diversity Programs

A number of major corporations currently have ongoing supplier diversity programs. Listed below are just a few examples:

- AT&T, www.attsuppliers.com/sd/
- Apple Computer, www.apple.com/procurement/
- Bank of America, www.bankofamerica.com/supplierdiversity
- Bosch, www.bosch.us/content/language1/html/3182.htm
- Bristol-Meyers Squibb, www.bms.com/ourcompany/diversity/supplier_diversity /Pages/default.aspx
- Chevron, www.chevron.com/productsservices/supplierdiversity/default.aspx
- Cisco, www.cisco.com/web/about/ac50/ac142/sdbd/index.html
- Coca-Cola, supplierdiversity.coke.com/Pages/Default.aspx
- Diebold, www.diebold.com/aboutus/sba/commitment.htm
- General Electric, www.ge.com/citizenship/metrics/suppliers.html
- Georgia Pacific, www.gp.com/supplierdiversity/ourprogram.asp
- Hertz, www.hertz.com/rentacar/b2b/diversityOverview-b2b
- Hewlett-Packard,   www.hp.com/hpinfo/globalcitizenship/09gcreport/society /supplychain/supplierdiversity.html
- Marriott, www.marriott.com/diversity/supplier-evaluation.mi
- Merck,   www.merck.com/about/how-we-operate/diversity/supplier-diversity. html
- New York Life, www.newyorklife.com/supplierdiversity/
- Nordstrom, shop.nordstrom.com/c/diversity-supplier-program?origin = customerService
- Pacific Gas & Electric, www.pge.com/b2b/purchasing/supplierdiversity/
- PepsiCo, www.pepsico.com/Purpose/Responsible-Sourcing.html
- Pitney Bowes,   www.pb.com/cgi-bin/pb.dll/jsp/GenericEditorial.do?catOID= -18268&editorial_id=ed_SupplierDiversity&lang=en&country=US
- Shell Oil,   www.shell.us/home/content/usa/aboutshell/who_we_are/supplier _diversity/

- Silicon Graphics, www.sgi.com/company_info/supplier_guidelines/diverse_smbwo.html
- Sprint, www.sprint.com/companyinfo/scm/supplierdiversity/index.html?ECID= vanity:supplierdiversity/
- Telcordia Technologies, www.telcordia.com/aboutus/supp_div/index.html /aboutus/supp_div/index.html
- Time Warner, www.twsupplierdiversity.com/
- Verizon Communications, www22.verizon.com/about/community/supplier _diversity/
- Wells Fargo Bank, www.wellsfargo.com/about/diversity/supplierdiversity /overview.jhtml

Summary

In this chapter, we examined the nature of supplier diversity programs beginning with definitions and the process of certification. We then looked at making a business case for diversity and how some organizations have approached the process. From there, we covered supplier diversity best practices, including the types of support available to diversity suppliers and a number of other best practice elements.

We concluded with a discussion of the status of global supplier diversity, along with our own definition, and gave an extensive listing of organizations providing certification and support to diversity suppliers.

CHAPTER 7

Risk Management

Risk is probably one of the most pervasive topics today in sourcing and supply management. The reason for this is quite logical: The more dependent on its suppliers an organization becomes, the more likely that a disruption in supply anywhere along its supply chain can result in the organization's failure to meet its commitments. This is compounded in operations that conduct a "lean" approach to resources, where shortages can shut down production, as well as in operations that are environmentally or politically sensitive, where failure can impact an entire nation or geographic area.

In this chapter, we examine the nature of *risk* in sourcing operations and how organizations are (or should be) dealing with it.

The Nature of Risk

While definitions of risk are abundant, let's begin our exploration with two definitions that will be useful as we go forward:

- *Simple definition*: Risk is the chance of something happening that will have an adverse impact upon our objectives.
- *More complex definition*: Risk is a measure of the inability to achieve program objectives within defined cost, schedule, and performance constraints.

In this chapter, we use these two definitions interchangeably. They serve as an anchor point in our illustrations.

Why Is Understanding Risk Important?

Risk affects many aspects of the sourcing process; it is a guiding consideration when selecting suppliers. We select those suppliers that are most likely to meet our stated requirements: suppliers with low risk. Risk is also an overriding consideration in ensuring ongoing supplier performance and our continued operation without interruption due to a supplier's failure to meet its commitments.

We also recognize that uncertainty in the statement of work we issue with our contracts can add to the price of a service by a supplier through hold backs or contingency accounts due to vague or complex requirements. This is especially true in construction and R&D projects. And risk can add to supply interruption or increased cost through contract breach or default, or a supplier's inability to fund its commitments.

We also base many of our key business decisions on the level of risk involved in an action or activity, or in the choice of a design solution or a technology. We consider risk as an evaluation factor in choosing between alternative courses of action, often seeking the alternative with the least amount of risk. Thus we typically see risk as a critical aspect of business operations that must be properly managed in order to remain in a tolerable range.

Clearly, effectively monitoring and managing risk is costly when the risk is high and consumes large amounts of critical resources, yet the customer is often blind to the value this produces. As a result, risk management processes must be well understood so that they can be implemented with minimum cost.

Risk Management Principles

With an effective process in place, risk can be managed so that the impact of a potentially catastrophic event can be minimized or avoided altogether. In order to help you establish this process, there are several fundamental principles that you should recognize and understand first.

When a formal risk management process is first put in place, there is a cultural shift from putting out fires and crisis management within the organization to a much more proactive decision-making method that seeks to avoid problems. Systematically anticipating what events might occur to thwart our objectives becomes a part of everyday business, and the management of risks becomes as integral to sourcing as any other process.

What Is Risk Management?

Risk management is the process of identifying, assessing, and controlling risks arising from operational factors and making decisions that balance risk with offsetting benefits (or rewards). It is a systematic approach used to identify, evaluate, and reduce or eliminate the possibility of an unfavorable deviation from an expected outcome.

Risk management is also a process wherein the program or project team is responsible for identifying, analyzing, planning, tracking, controlling, and communicating effectively the risks (and the steps being taken to handle them) within the team's environment. This outcome of this process is communicated to management and stakeholders.

Risk management is also a continuous, iterative process used to manage risk in order to ensure that activities achieve their intended objectives. It should be a key element and an integral part of normal program or project management and engineering planning.

Risk Identification

Identifying specific risks is the first step in any risk management process. Let's look at some of the more common categories of risk to consider:

- **Financial risks.** These risks can range from an unexpected and unfavorable change in exchange rates all the way to a supplier's bankruptcy. Some examples of financial risks include budget overruns, funding limitation, unauthorized (constructive) changes, and missed milestones requiring additional funding. Financial risks also encompass unexpected cost overruns that may be linked to other risk factors such as changes in the scope of work required to successfully complete the activity.

- **Scope or schedule risks.** Largely a result of poor project definition or a poorly worded statement of work, these are primarily risks that threaten the timeline, but as noted previously, they can also have cost implications. Schedule changes are often the result of a natural disaster such as hurricanes, fire, or flood, or as a result of noncompliance issues generated by the supplier. Scope risk can occur as a result of changes that are required when the initial SOW becomes unworkable or due to technological changes generated by the market.

- **Legal risks.** Legal and contractual risks are often related to disputes or different interpretations of contractual obligations, or from not meeting a requirement included in the terms and conditions. Use or misuse of intellectual property can also be considered a legal risk, especially when patent infringement is a possibility. We can also include in this category violation of laws or regulations and obligations created as a result of changes in the law, as well as civil lawsuits.

- **Environmental risk.** In the sourcing process, it is critical to evaluate the risk to the environment created by your supplier or contractor. Environmental risk includes the organization's negative impact on water, air, and soil as a result of discharges, emissions, and other forms of waste. As we note in Chapter 8, greenhouse gases and ozone-depleting chemicals have become a serious threat to the planet. Industrial waste, too, has to be considered of major concern. Threats to the natural habitat are also coming under very close scrutiny and regulation. Where these factors are present or potentially present, you must monitor them closely; governments worldwide are regulating these conditions to a much greater extent, which may result in significant interruptions should a supplier be affected.

- **Sociopolitical risk.** When the regulatory environment changes in response to a new government or to increasing awareness of inequitable social conditions, many existing institutions experience difficulty in adapting. Sourcing efforts, especially those in low-cost countries, must consider the impact of these changes on the culture and business operations within that environment. Stability comes with a price.

- **Project organization risk.** These are generally a result of not having the right people or equipment in the right place at the right time. You might also consider this as a planning risk.

■ **Human behavior risks.** Not surprisingly, human behavior risks are the most difficult to assess. Sometimes the project or activity may be placed in jeopardy due to an illness or injury or due to the departure of key personnel; sometimes it may be the result of poor judgment or bad decisions.

Risk Varies

Risk increases with the complexity of any given situation, the number of unknown factors, and the potential consequences of failure.

In addition to the categories just outlined, our assessment should identify if the risks to be considered are internal risks (risks related to our own operations) or external risks related to conditions outside of our organization, such as market factors, political climate, regulatory environment, economic circumstances, and so on. More specifically:

■ **Internal risks** are risks that you can control or influence. Internal risks include cost estimates, staff assignments, schedule delays, and product design.
■ **External risks** are risks that you as a contract manager cannot control or influence. External risks include governmental actions relating to taxes that could affect a financial contract, weather delays that could affect a construction contract, and a change in currency rates that could affect the value of an international contract.

A number of techniques and tools may be useful in helping you identify risks. You can adapt these are techniques and tools to your current situation:

■ **Expert knowledge.** Expert knowledge relies on the experience of people who have worked on similar sourcing operations in the past. Interviews with individuals, stakeholders, and experts are good methods to use to gather expert knowledge. Interviews with subject matter experts may uncover risks not previously considered.
■ **Historical information.** You or your colleagues may have compiled a historical database of risks encountered in previous sourcing efforts and contracts. It will be useful if you organize this database by contract type and include a list of the problems encountered that can be identified as risks, their sources, and the events that precipitated them. Include also the mitigation plan put in place to deal with the risk, and the success of that mitigation plan if it was actually applied to an event. Records of previous contracts can also provide historical information. These records may be kept in a database, or they may be paper files. If you don't currently have a process that captures historical risk information, you should consider developing one.
■ **Brainstorming.** Another technique frequently noted is to identify risks and sources of risk by conducting a brainstorming session. Gather a group of subject matter experts who have an understanding of the nature of risk; include

stakeholders as well as those who will not be directly affected by your activities as a way of maintaining relative objectivity. This activity will make it possible to create a broad list of potential risk events and their sources. You can then apply them to your specific conditions in order to refine the list.

A variation of brainstorming often used is called the *Delphi method*, a means of leveraging the collective judgment of specialists and/or management (often referred to as "expert judgment"). We use this process primarily when objective and quantitative data for measurement and decision making doesn't exist (or possibly even make sense). You can use this technique to determine outcomes like how long it might take to draft a contract, what penalty limits you should set, or how long negotiations may last. This technique consists of three simple steps:

1. Ask participants to estimate a value for some occurrence, usually anonymously on paper.
2. Consolidate the results and ask participants with responses outside the norm to justify their positions for each participant's benefit and/or reconsideration. You ask all participants to estimate the value of the occurrence.
3. Consolidate the results from Step 2 and repeat the process until you reach a reasonably close value.

- **Simulations.** There are several analysis tools commonly available for providing simulations. One that is frequently used is the Monte Carlo simulation. Monte Carlo simulation provides the user with a range of possible outcomes and the probabilities that they will occur for any choice of action. There are a number of software products available that help develop models; several of them work with MS Excel. The *decision tree* diagram is also a useful simulation tool that can depict key interactions among decisions and associated chance events. An example is shown in Figure 7.1.
- **Checklists.** Through research, you may be able to develop a useful checklist to run through whenever needed during sourcing activities. You can use historical data that applies to similar activities in your organization or find related information through a well-directed Web search.

As you conduct your sourcing activities, you can go over this list to determine if any apply to current activities and if the sources being considered pose potential risks for this contract. Although checklists can be useful tools, they should not replace close analysis of the conditions you might encounter. It is also unlikely that even the most detailed checklist will include every potential risk in a particular situation.

Risk Assessment

Risks such as these are closely related to the circumstances of the project or an activity, and the implications of their impact vary widely from situation to situation. Consequently, it is incumbent on sourcing personnel to review the specific situation in terms of the categories noted previously in order to define the risks that may apply in any given case. This is the first step in the assessment process, but it can also be the most complex since many of the situations we must work with are quite fluid and ever changing. When we add in the many variable factors in most sourcing

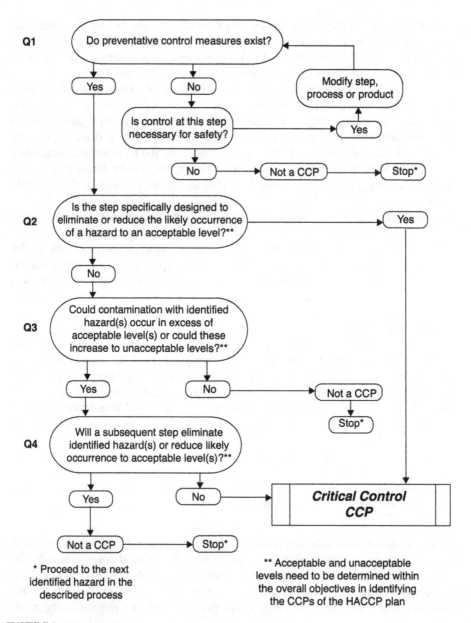

FIGURE 7.1   Decision Tree

Source: United Nations Food and Agriculture Organization

plans, we understandably find that an assessment of risk is often simply a matter of guesswork since what we can observe is lacking any discernible pattern.

Probably the best we can do is to keep it simple. Once the elements of potential risk have been identified, we will need a very simple method of evaluating or measuring them to determine which require our attention, now and in the future. In simplifying our assessment, we will generally have to abandon the interaction of individual elements with one another and opt for examining them, for the most part, in isolation. It would be virtually impossible, given the common tools we have available, to try to examine the impact, let's say, that a decision by a supplier to take on additional work beyond its capacity would have on its ability to commit funds to our project. So we are forced to look at each one—exceeding capacity and committing funds—separately.

There is a very simple method used in common practice to do this. We examine each element of risk in terms of its likelihood of occurrence: the probability that a program or project will experience an undesired event and its impact; the consequences or severity of the undesired event, should it actually occur. Some examples of an undesired event include a cost overrun, schedule slippage, safety mishap, health problem, malicious activities, environmental impact, or failure to achieve a needed scientific or technological breakthrough.

A brainstorming-based *risk assessment* facilitated session with stakeholders, team members, and infrastructure support staff is the most common technique used to identify risks and evaluate their potentials. The primary source of information is historical data developed from activities similar to the one we are evaluating, with an added element of human judgment and intuition. This form of facilitated session is also known as *force-field analysis*. By using qualitative terms such as *very high, high, moderate, low,* and *very low* to identify the probability of risk occurring, you can prioritize the risks associated with sourcing and with the contract that follows, then map the analysis to specific phases of the contract, specific business units, parties to a contract, and so on.

Once we have identified individual risk characteristics, we can then assign some relative criteria to each of the categories. Along with the descriptions, we will include a relative measure. Table 7.1 is an example of what that might look like, beginning with descriptions of each probability and consequence.

The criteria and scale shown in Table 7.2 is an example of a calculated risk assessment. Very simply, we multiply the probability factor by the consequence factor. As you can see, at the time of this particular assessment, the risk of design failure is the most significant. In fact, we would likely consider any score above

TABLE 7.1 Simple Method of Rating Risk

Probability		Consequence	
Rating	Description	Rating	Description
Almost certain (.90)	Will occur in most instances	Catastrophic (.90)	Will cause cancellation of the project
Likely (.70)	Could occur in most instances	Major (.70)	Significant time or cost overruns
Moderate (.50)	Should occur at some time	Moderate (.50)	Some time or cost overruns
Unlikely (.30)	Might occur occasionally	Minor (.30)	Some inconvenience
Rare (.10)	Will only occur in exceptional circumstances	Insignificant (.10)	Little noticeable effect

TABLE 7.2   Scoring Risk Using a Simplified Method

Risk	Description	Probability	Consequence	Score
Design	Fails to work effectively	0.60	0.90	0.54
Key personnel	Lead engineer leaves	0.40	0.50	0.20
Ramp up	Late delivery of equipment	0.50	0.50	0.25
Production	Lower yield than expected	0.40	0.40	0.16
Sales	Not marketable at price	0.20	0.40	0.08

.35 as sufficient to require ongoing tracking. For this particular situation, sourcing activities based upon design criteria would be a bit premature, although some market analysis would still be in order as a means of gaining a head start should the current design be released. Keep in mind, though, that as time progresses, additional criteria may surface and the ratings shown may change.

Risk Control

Every contract has a product or service around which the contract is written. The nature of that product or service has a major effect on the risks identified. If the product has been successfully provided many times in the past, there will be fewer unidentified risks and you will have a history of dealing with them.

After identifying and categorizing the risks, you must take steps to control the risks. The notion of control acknowledges that you may not be able to *eliminate* risk entirely in many situations.

Instead, you may be able to minimize the risk or mitigate it by taking action to handle the unwanted outcome in an acceptable way. Options may also be available that will enable you to avoid the risk altogether or transfer the risk to your supplier when beneficial to both parties.

The approach or tool you use for control will largely depend on the stage in the contract where a risk appears and on the amount of information available regarding the source or impact of that risk. Regardless of the conditions, however, effective control requires a plan or at the very least an outline of actions we should be taking and the circumstances under which we should take them.

As you develop a plan, you must take into account the goal, scope, and objectives of the sourcing activity. You must clearly understand the product or service being provided, its purpose, and the expectations of the customer or stakeholders regarding the product. You also need to understand how the contract and its product support your organization's strategic goals and business plans. This knowledge will help prioritize your activities.

For guidance, some of the key elements of a risk control plan will likely consist of one or more of the following concepts.

RISK TRIGGERS   A risk trigger can be defined as a "precursor to an actual risk event." It lets you know a risk event may be about to occur. You should identify triggers for each significant risk, and you should monitor those triggers, being alert to their appearance as you manage a sourcing operation or contract.

For example, cost overruns on early activities may be a signal that cost estimates were poorly developed, and the contract is trending toward being over budget. The person responsible for monitoring the risk would be tracking the costs on those early activities. Cost overruns by a specified date would indicate that cost estimates should be reevaluated.

Another example: A vendor missing a scheduled ship date may be a signal that hardware will not be delivered on time to meet the contracted date. The risk monitor would be responsible for checking with the vendor to make sure items were shipped on the specified date.

MONITORING Monitoring includes tracking current conditions through reports or through physical access to the source. It also includes updated assessments of probability and consequences, as well as uncovering conditions that were not previously apparent.

You monitor risks to ensure that:

- Risk responses have been implemented as planned.
- Risk responses are as effective as you expected them to be. If they're not, you may have to develop new responses.
- Any documented assumptions remain valid.
- Risk exposure has not changed from its prior state. If it has changed, additional analysis is needed.
- No risk trigger has occurred. If a trigger has occurred, contingency plans must be put in place.
- Proper policies and procedures are followed.
- No risks have occurred that were not previously identified. Again, if new risks have arisen, they must go through the same review and analysis process as previously identified risks.

MITIGATION Risk mitigation involves lessening the impact or magnitude of a risk event. You can do that by reducing the probability that the risk will occur, reducing the risk event's impact, or both, to an acceptable level. One way to reduce the probability of a risk occurring is by using proven technology to lessen the chances that the product of the contract will not work. If the contracted service is a software application, you could elect to develop on a platform that you've used successfully in the past rather than on a platform with which you have little or no experience. Purchasing insurance to protect against weather damage on a construction project is a way to mitigate the financial impact of a risk event related to bad weather.

As you mitigate risks, you may end up trading one risk for another. For example, a buyer may choose to mitigate a cost risk by asking for a fixed-price contract, but that may cause a schedule risk if the contractor is not able to provide the service in the desired time frame for the fixed price.

Costs for risk mitigation should be in line with the probability and consequences of the risk. In other words, you'll spend less time and money planning for risks with low probability and low impact than for risks with high probability and/or high impact. To aid decision making about risk reduction, you must take into account the cost of reducing the risk. We call "risk leverage" the difference in risk exposure divided by the cost of reducing the risk. In other words, risk reduction leverage is:

$$\frac{(\text{Risk exposure before reduction}) - (\text{Risk exposure after reduction})}{(\text{Cost of risk reduction})}.$$

CONTINGENCY PLANS A common method of mitigating the impact of a risk event is to develop a contingency plan in advance of the possible occurrence, usually shortly after the risk is identified. The purpose of this plan is to enable the sustained execution of mission-critical processes and information technology systems in the event of an extraordinary event that causes these systems to fail minimum requirements. The contingency plan will assess the needs and requirements so that your organization may be prepared to respond to the event in order to efficiently regain operation of the systems that are made inoperable from the event.

The plan includes specific actions to be taken should a risk event occur, such as identifying an alternate source should the selected source become unable to meet its contractual obligations or a substitute part should the primary part become unavailable.

AVOIDANCE Eliminating the cause of the risk can sometimes remove a risk that you can specifically identify. For example, if the lack of skilled resources causes an identified risk, you can eliminate the risk by having the supplier hire the skills needed to perform the contracted services. Risk avoidance techniques also include reducing the scope of the contract to avoid high-risk elements, adding resources or time to the contract, avoiding suppliers or contractors with unproven track records, and using a proven approach instead of a new one.

ACCEPTANCE You may choose to accept the consequences of the risk event. Risk assumption can be active, as in developing a contingency plan for execution should the risk event occur, or passive, as in deciding to deal with the risks and their consequences when or if they occur, but not planning for them in advance.

TRANSFER Transferring the risk occurs by allocating risks to other entities or by buying insurance to cover any financial loss should the risk become a reality. In some situations, your supplier may be better suited to dealing with a particular risk, so transferring it through negotiations might be in order. There is a caveat, however: Risk transfer may come with additional cost, such as the cost of insurance or an additional amount tacked on to the pricing by the supplier in order to be able to deal with the event should it occur.

Resources for Additional Information

Before concluding this chapter, we thought it useful to provide some additional resources in the form of websites where you can find relevant articles and information from organizations that manage risk.

Articles Related to Supply Management Risk

- **"Risk in supply networks—seeing it all, or not?"** This article is an outline of risk management topics that provides another perspective on risk types. www.husdal.com/2009/05/24/risk-in-supply-networks-seeing-it-all-or-not/

- **"Supply Chain Risk Management."** Outlines the exposure to risk in supply chain network design along with the top pressures driving supply risk management. www.slideshare.net/anandsubramaniam/supply-chain-risk-management

- **"Procurement Capability in CSR Part 3: Risk Management."** Examines risk from the perspective of the broad categories of management such as industry risk management and enterprise risk management. purchasingpractice.com /procurement-capability-in-csr-part-3-risk-management/

- **"Keeping Ahead of Supply Chain Risk and Uncertainty."** This is a comprehensive article that describes how Accenture and Oracle provide a point of view that will help companies understand the nature of supply chain risk—and what they can do to mitigate it. www.accenture.com/us-en/Pages/insight-keeping -ahead-supply-chain-risk-uncertainty.aspx

- **"Avoiding Supply Chain Breakdown."** This article, published in *MIT Sloan Management Review*, presents a comprehensive practice-oriented framework for managing supply chain disruptions. The framework covers everything from risk analysis to the selection of the risk mitigation strategy. scrmblog.com/categories/14-Business-Research-Tools

- **"Supply Chain Risk Management Tools."** This is a white paper by consulting firm MBtech outlining its approach to managing risk with specialized software tools. www.slideshare.net/Bobtb/microsoft-powerpoint-supply-chain -risk-management-tools

- **"Global Manufacturing Outlook: Relationships, Risk and Reach."** Global research commissioned by KPMG International from the Economist Intelligence Unit. www.kpmg.com/Global/en/IssuesAndInsights/ArticlesPublications /diversified-industrials-publication/Documents/global-manufacturing-outlook -sept-2010.pdf

- **"Checklist: Four Steps to Mitigating Supplier Risk and Protecting Your Supply Chain."** An article in *Supply & Demand Chain Executive* magazine defines risk "as the process of predicting and preparing for the probability of variables which may adversely or favorably affect the supply chain. Supplier risk management is not a new concept; however, the type of risk that can affect the supply chain and the way in which these risks are managed and mitigated has evolved significantly. The need for proactive and predictive management strategies is ever present in business today." www.sdcexec.com/print/Supply -and-Demand-Chain-Executive/Checklist–Four-Steps-to-Mitigating-Supplier-Risk -and-Protect-Your-Supply-Chain/1$12265

- **"Mitigating Supply Risk: Managing Supply Variability in the High Technology Industry."** This article by Guy Schlacter, director of high-technology industry marketing and strategy at Oracle, examines how the impact of disruption in supply or demand can have a range of negative effects, but those with proper plans and tools in place can often minimize disruption. www .oracle.com/us/corporate/profit/opinion/o32911-gschlacter-351070.html?msgid= 3-3828664956

- **"How Do You Manage Transportation Risk in a Sustainable Supply Chain?"** "More strategically focused organizations are evaluating business sustainability risks that extend beyond the walls of the company." blog .taigacompany.com/blog/sustainability-business-life-environment/0/0/how-do -you-manage-transportation-risk-in-a-sustainable-supply-chain

Links to Providers of Risk Management Solutions

- **Supplier Risk Manager by Dun & Bradstreet, Inc.,** www.dnb.com/supplier -risk-manager-locator/14899977-1.html
- **Supply Chain Risk Management Solutions from Kinaxis,** www.kinaxis .com/operations-performance-solutions/supply-chain-risk-management.cfm
- **LAVANTE SIM™ Supplier Information Management,** www.lavante.com /supplier-information-management
- **Cortera, Inc.,** cortera.com/company-profiles/
- **Dow Jones Supplier & Risk Monitor,** www.dowjones.com/research /DJSRM.asp
- **"Accenture Launches Risk Management Consulting Service Line,"** newsroom.accenture.com/article_display.cfm?article_id=4938
- **Aravo Solutions Inc.,** www.aravo.com
- **HICX Solutions Ltd.,** www.hicxsolutions.com
- **Hiperos LLC,** www.hiperos.com
- **Zycus Inc.,** www.zycus.com

Summary

While this is by no means an exhaustive study of risk in sourcing operations, we trust we have touched upon the key points so that you can gain an understanding of the nature of risk and its associated elements.

We began this chapter with some definitions and an explanation of the nature of risk, covering why an understanding of risk is important. Examining risk management principles, we categorized risks as related to financial, scope or schedule, legal, environmental, sociopolitical, project organization, and human behavior factors; we also pointed out the difference between internal and external risk factors. From there we turned our attention to tools that can be useful in identifying risks, such as leveraging expert knowledge and historical information, brainstorming and using the Delphi technique, and the use of simulations and checklists. Following this, we examined risk assessment and simple methods used to evaluate risk such as using the probability/consequence matrix to identify the level of risk we may be facing.

Looking at risk control, we pointed out the importance of planning. We then covered the elements of risk control, such as identifying risk triggers, monitoring risk, mitigating risk, and developing contingency plans. Finally, we noted the characteristics of risk avoidance, risk acceptance, and risk transfer. We ended the chapter with links to useful articles and providers of software and consulting services.

CHAPTER 8

Sustainability

B y now it is clear to almost everyone that the earth's environment is facing some very significant challenges, considered by most to be the result of human activity and waste. We somehow need to reverse these trends so that available resources, including the very air we breathe and the water we drink, are available to future generations. We call this concept *Sustainability*.

The Institute for Supply Management (ISM) defines the term *sustainability* as follows:

> *Sustainability is the ability to meet current needs without hindering the ability to meet the needs of future generations in terms of economic, environmental and social challenges.*

The philosophy of sustainability revolves around the general concepts of social responsibility in terms of how we use our earthly resources. In supply management, we have simplified the term for this philosophy as "green sourcing."

Sustainability requires commitment by management and employees alike. New global and national standards for socially responsible and environmentally sound practices are continually being developed, and to maintain effectiveness, organizations must constantly adapt and stay a step or two ahead of the changing dynamics.

It is very difficult to identify best practices that are themselves sustainable. But clearly it is still in every organization's best interests to review its operations and determine what can be done to meet the current demands of its industry, its business partners, and its shareholders.

In this chapter, we will examine the important areas to consider when sourcing that must embrace principles of sustainability and, to the extent we have clear data, what is being done to address this area of concern.

Issues in Sustainability

There are numerous areas where social responsibility and environmental concerns impact the process of sourcing, and each of them has a somewhat varied set of challenges. In general, however, we can identify three specific areas where issues in the commercial sphere are abundant:

1. **Materials.** Issues concern eliminating waste, recycling materials, reducing the rates of natural resource depletion, including food, and eliminating the dangers of hazardous materials (HazMat) and the effects of natural disasters created by humankind.
2. **Toxic discharge.** Poor air quality issues are associated with greenhouse gases, ozone depletion, and air pollutants as they relate to global climate warming. We must also consider waste discharge into waterways and ground water table contamination. Universal waste reduction programs are currently characterized by an astounding lack of action and petty bickering between nations.
3. **Energy consumption.** Here the issues revolve around finding alternative sources of energy to replace nonsustainable fuel sources such as oil, coal, and gas. These are issues faced primarily by the developed (and to some extent, developing) countries.

As we go forward with our examination of sustainability, we will review each of these areas in more depth as they apply to global sourcing and effective supplier management. Although they are critically important to the environment, we will not examine government, municipal, or household waste streams and reduction initiatives.

Materials

As previously noted, there are a substantial number of environmental issues relating to how we use materials. Achieving sustainability in our current business and governmental environment appears to be largely a matter of customer demand, so the sourcing team can have a significant impact by establishing or adhering to relevant environmental standards.

WASTE AND WASTE REDUCTION   The reduction of waste in all forms is central to sustainability. Unfortunately there is no universal standard for either defining waste or reducing waste, although countless initiatives exist at regional, national, local, corporate, and even personal levels.

Waste, in most circumstances, can be difficult to identify but as defined by the European Union, it can be viewed as follows:

> *"Any substance or object the holder discards, intends to discard or is required to discard" is WASTE under the Waste Framework Directive (European Directive (WFD) 2006/12/EC), as amended by the new WFD (Directive 2008/98/EC, coming into force in December 2010).*

> *Once a substance or object has become waste, it will remain waste until it has been fully recovered and no longer poses a potential threat to the environment or to human health.*

This definition includes solid waste, liquid waste, and airborne waste. We can also apply the term *waste* to scrap and rework common to manufacturing industries.

Today, most waste is disposed of in landfills, through incineration, or in oceans and waterways.

Recycling is the most widely used tool to reduce waste, followed by reduced consumption and detoxification of airborne and liquid waste streams. Here, too, governments (at all levels) and various industries have developed their own sets of standards and reduction goals, so it's quite difficult to determine a standard for reduction goals. For the purposes of sourcing, it will be necessary to determine the amount of a supplier's current waste and decide if its goals for reduction are in line with its industry standards or your own organization's goals. In another section of this chapter, we will review ISO environmental standards and the UN's Global Compact.

In terms of waste reduction *processes*, the EU, while it fails to state measurable objectives, offers this set of instructive guidelines:

The European Union's approach to waste management is based on three principles:

1. **Waste prevention.** *This is a key factor in any waste management strategy. If we can reduce the amount of waste generated in the first place and reduce its hazardousness by reducing the presence of dangerous substances in products, then disposing of it will automatically become simpler. Waste prevention is closely linked with improving manufacturing methods and influencing consumers to demand greener products and less packaging.*

2. **Recycling and reuse.** *If waste cannot be prevented, as many of the materials as possible should be recovered, preferably by recycling. The European Commission has defined several specific "waste streams" for priority attention, the aim being to reduce their overall environmental impact. This includes packaging waste, end-of-life vehicles, batteries, electrical and electronic waste. EU directives now require Member States to introduce legislation on waste collection, reuse, recycling and disposal of these waste streams. Several EU countries are already managing to recycle over 50% of packaging waste.*

3. **Improving final disposal and monitoring.** *Where possible, waste that cannot be recycled or reused should be safely incinerated, with landfill only used as a last resort. Both these methods need close monitoring because of their potential for causing severe environmental damage. The EU has recently approved a directive setting strict guidelines for landfill management. It bans certain types of waste, such as used tyres, and sets targets for reducing quantities of biodegradable rubbish. Another recent directive lays down tough limits on emission levels from incinerators. The Union also wants to reduce emissions of dioxins and acid gases such as nitrogen oxides (NO_x), sulfur dioxides (SO_2), and hydrogen chlorides (HCL), which can be harmful to human health."*

ec.europa.eu/environment/waste/index.htm

RENEWABLE RESOURCES AND HABITATS *Renewable resources* are those that are replaced by natural processes faster than they are consumed or destroyed through human activity. This is a major area of concern since many of our natural resources and areas of wildlife habitats are rapidly disappearing. To maintain sustainability, the guiding principles are those of long-term conservation that ensure the environment is able to maintain its supply of the materials necessary to sustain life.

Resources   Typical renewable resources that we depend upon, and that are currently threatened, include a number of commodities such as forest products, agricultural products, potable water, soil, marine species, and biomass. Also included on our list are some renewable resources that are not inherently threatened, such as wind power and solar energy.

We must also closely consider the use of nonrenewable resources, those that are not being replaced as they are consumed, such as oil, coal, and gas. Sourcing professionals must assess their suppliers' use of these elements along with their efforts to replace them with renewable sources. Again, unfortunately there are no global standards for slowing the depletion of natural resources.

Habitat   In addition to sustaining wildlife, natural habitats are an important form of resources for humans, as well. Many environmentalists believe that we can only maintain a natural balance on the earth if existing species are able to survive so that we can maintain our system of biodiversity. They believe that, globally, we are inextricably linked to the well-being and continuation of diverse species.

We know, too, that the disappearance of jungle and forest lands will have an adverse effect on our quality of life since the forests' greenery replaces harmful carbon dioxide with the oxygen we need to breathe.

Forest Depletion

One lumber buyer we know tells us that in the 1960s and 1970s he would travel to Brazil to select hardwoods, such as the then-popular rosewood. He would fly into Rio, stay the night, and the next morning he would take a two- to three-hour boat trip to the sawmill.

By 1997, the same trip to the sawmill would take three days: a flight to Rio, an overnight stay, another four-hour flight to a commercial hub, another overnight stay, and then a six- or seven-hour boat ride to the sawmill.

The reason? Forest land has increasingly vanished as a result of clear-cutting for lumber and agriculture, and industrial mining.

HAZARDOUS MATERIALS   Definitions of hazardous materials (*HazMat*) are bountiful, but collectively they describe the same concept: any substance or compound that has the capability of producing adverse effects on the health and safety of human beings. In most parts of the world, the use and disposal of materials that have been classified as hazardous has become closely regulated and, as a result, sourcing professionals must determine the extent to which their organization and their suppliers are required to comply with existing regulations. Noncompliance increases the risk of supply interruption and extensive liability.

In the United States, there are a number of regulatory agencies at the federal level, and virtually all states and many local governments have passed regulations restricting their use, transport, and disposal. Some of the key U.S. agencies requiring regulatory compliance include:

- **Department of Transportation.** DOT regulates the transport and temporary storage of hazardous materials. "The Hazardous Materials Regulations (HMR) are issued by the Pipeline and Hazardous Materials Safety Administration and govern the transportation of hazardous materials by highway, rail, vessel, and air. The HMR address hazardous materials classification, packaging, hazard communication, emergency response information and training." For a list of applicable regulations, see www.phmsa.dot.gov/hazmat/regs.
- **Occupational Safety and Health Administration (OSHA).** In addition to the DOT, the U.S. Department of Labor (OSHA) maintains a listing of the standards set forth by federal regulation.

  In order to ensure chemical safety in the workplace, information must be available about the identities and hazards of the chemicals. OSHA's Hazard Communication Standard (HCS) requires the development and dissemination of such information:
  - "Chemical manufacturers and importers are required to evaluate the hazards of the chemicals they produce or import, and
  - Prepare labels and Material Safety Data Sheets (MSDS) to convey the hazard information to their downstream customers.
  - Any employer with hazardous chemicals in its workplace must have labels and MSDSs for their exposed workers, and train them to handle the chemicals appropriately."[1]
- **Environmental Protection Agency (EPA).** The EPA is primarily concerned with the handling and disposal of hazardous waste. It defines hazardous waste in these terms:

  Hazardous waste is waste that is dangerous or potentially harmful to our health or the environment. Hazardous wastes can be liquids, solids, gases, or sludges. They can be discarded commercial products, like cleaning fluids or pesticides, or the by-products of manufacturing processes.

  You can find a list of important references, including materials that are classified as hazardous, on the EPA website at: www.epa.gov/osw/hazard/index.htm.
- **United Nations.** Internationally, many sets of regulations exist regarding the transportation of hazardous goods by rail, sea, and road. However, the United Nations has developed a set of guidelines for international use (primarily in Europe) that can be accessed here: www.unece.org/trans/danger/publi/manual/Rev4/ManRev4-files_e.html.

  The UN has also developed a set of model regulations to be used as a further guideline: It can be accessed here: www.unece.org/trans/danger/publi/unrec/rev15/15files_e.html

MAN-MADE DISASTERS   The U.S. Department of Health and Human Services defines man-made disasters in the following terms:

> *Man-made disasters are events which, either intentionally or by accident cause severe threats to public health and well-being. Because their occurrence is unpredictable, man-made disasters pose an especially challenging threat that must be dealt with through vigilance, and proper preparedness and response.*

Its listing of man-made disaster categories covers chemical agents, radiation, pandemics, and forms of terrorism. To this list we should add oil and chemical spills and accidental nuclear discharge and accidents. Perhaps even more significantly, we should include wars and other armed conflicts.

Suppliers located in areas prone to these events have a much higher risk of operational interruptions and therefore must have contingency plans in place. Similarly, if you are sourcing in these areas, you should put in place a contingency plan as well should a supplier experience a work stoppage due to one of these events. More information is available on the Web at: www.hhs.gov/disasters/index.html.

TERRORISM   A newly recognized category must now, unfortunately, be added to the section on man-made disasters. The FBI defines terrorism as "the unlawful use of force or violence against persons or property to intimidate or coerce a government, the civilian population, or any segment thereof in furtherance of political or social objectives." The FBI further classifies terrorism as either domestic or international, depending on the origin, base, and objectives of the terrorist organization.

The 9/11 catastrophe that brought down the World Trade Center towers and several notable incidents before and after clearly illustrates the destructive potential of terrorist acts of violence, and the extent to which terrorist organizations can affect our daily lives.

Threats can take many forms from the use of ordinary weapons and explosives to biological, chemical, nuclear, and radiological dispersion methods. FEMA (Federal Emergency Management Agency) provides this list of potential terrorist activities: "Acts of terrorism include threats of terrorism; assassinations; kidnappings; hijackings; bomb scares and bombings; cyber attacks (computer-based); and the use of chemical, biological, nuclear and radiological weapons."[2]

FEMA goes on to state: "High-risk targets for acts of terrorism include military and civilian government facilities, international airports, large cities, and high-profile landmarks. Terrorists might also target large public gatherings, water and food supplies, utilities, and corporate centers. Further, terrorists are capable of spreading fear by sending explosives or chemical and biological agents through the mail."

The U.S. Department of State maintains a fairly extensive list of known foreign terrorist organizations along with lists of countries that support them and individuals considered terrorists under Executive Order 13224. For specific detail, visit www.state.gov/s/ct/list/index.htm. It is advisable to check these lists before engaging in overseas sourcing.

NATURAL DISASTERS   The United States Depart of Health and Human Services (HHS) also defines and tracks major natural disasters such as earthquake, fire or wildfire, flood and dam failure, hurricane and high wind, landslide, thunderstorm, tornadoes, tsunami, volcano, extreme cold, and extreme heat. To this list we can add nuclear energy accidents, avalanches, mudslides, and blizzards.

Toxic Discharge

To some extent, we have discussed toxic discharges in the preceding section; however, a number of other factors that affect the environment that were not discussed also relate to the very important concerns regarding global warming and ongoing sources of environmental pollution.

GREENHOUSE GASES So much has been written about global warming and the effect of greenhouse gases that adding to the topic seems unnecessary. "Global warming" is the term most commonly used to describe the gradual warming up of Earth's atmosphere as a result of increased greenhouse gas emissions.

From a sourcing perspective, you must be alert to any potential toxic discharge generated by a supplier, including gases that help create the greenhouse warming effect. Where potential for discharge exists, risk increases exponentially and should be included in your supplier selection decision criteria. Despite the current international bickering over quotas for carbon emissions, limitations will eventually find universal adoption.

CARBON FOOTPRINTS AND CO_2 REDUCTION Scientists for the most part agree that the key to reversing the global warming trend that threatens our extinction is to reduce so-called greenhouse gases. A primary greenhouse gas has been identified as carbon dioxide (CO_2), and its emission is known as a "carbon footprint." This is a measure of the amount of greenhouse gases produced through burning fossil fuels and other human activities, converted to tons of carbon dioxide equivalent that we individually produce. You can calculate any carbon footprint by visiting this (or similar) site: www.carbonfootprint.com/calculator.aspx.

Carbon management has recently taken the form of "cap and trade" legislation. This is a market-based system whereby companies are provided with a quota based upon a calculated baseline from which they can sell or buy emission credits depending upon their usage. In the case of the European Union Emission Trading System, which is reported to cover more than 10,000 installations, large organizations are required to monitor their carbon emissions and provide reductions according to a rather complex, country-by-country reduction plan. Similar legislation is in process for the United States and other countries in accordance with the United Nations' Framework Convention on Climate Change (UNFCCC, 1992) or the *Kyoto Protocol*.

What is potentially significant for sourcing activities in this process is that emissions footprints may be tied to an organization's entire supply chain. Largely, this will be calculated on the basis of shipment size and mileage. Since truck transportation accounts for a very significant portion of carbon emissions, there are currently a plethora of new software applications designed to calculate the truck transportation footprint and suggest possible methods for reducing it. One possible reduction method would be to switch from truck to rail transport, which, per unit, has a significantly lower footprint. Another method might be to switch to local production to reduce the need for lengthy transportation and/or to switch to other materials that have lower emissions.

Another proposed method is a straightforward carbon tax. The Carbon Tax Center regards this method as more predictable and having less impact on pricing. You can find a more detailed discussion at the CTC site, www.carbontax.org.

Interestingly, the U.S. Environmental Protection Agency has been working in the background for a number of years to develop methods for the reduction of greenhouse gases in general. If you recall, it was the EPA that led the initiatives for the reduction of acid rain emissions.

The following is an outline of the EPA's WARM system, which provides a method for calculating the overall emission of greenhouse gases including methane and nitrous oxide, other greenhouse gases, rather than just carbon alone:

EPA created the Waste Reduction Model (WARM) to help solid waste planners and organizations track and voluntarily report greenhouse gas (GHG) emissions reductions from several different waste management practices. WARM is available both as a Web-based calculator and as a Microsoft Excel spreadsheet (355K WinZip archive). The Excel-based version of WARM offers more functionality than the Web-based calculator.

WARM calculates and totals GHG emissions of baseline and alternative waste management practices—source reduction, recycling, combustion, composting, and landfilling. The model calculates emissions in metric tons of carbon equivalent (MTCE), metric tons of carbon dioxide equivalent (MTCO2E), and energy units (million BTU) across a wide range of material types commonly found in municipal solid waste (MSW).

WARM is periodically updated as new information becomes available and new material types are added. Users may refer to the model history to better understand the differences among various versions of WARM. WARM was last updated August, 2010.[3]

OZONE DEPLETION Another significant issue is related to the earth's ozone layer (in the stratosphere), which protects us from harmful ultraviolet rays generated by the sun. It has been thinning at an accelerated rate, and the "holes" in the ozone layer around the polar regions have been growing larger. In simple terms, ozone depletion is the result of emissions of chlorofluorocarbon (CFC) compounds called freons and bromofluorocarbon compounds called halons at the earth's surface.

Ozone depletion has been identified as the major contributor to climate change. Climate change is the term used to describe how the weather and climate patterns are changing as a result of global warming. To simplify: Global warming and ozone depletion both contribute to climate change.

POLLUTION In addition to global warming and climate change, sustainability in the supply chain also includes eliminating other sources of environmental pollution, including air pollution, water pollution, and ground contamination. In these areas, numerous global initiatives are underway to eliminate waste at its source through the use of nontoxic substances, modification of production processes, conservation methods, and recycling. The elimination of waste of all types has long been a recognized factor in cost reduction and improved manufacturing productivity since the introduction of *just-in-time* concepts in the late 1950s.

Worldwide, there are several treaties and regulations aimed at reducing the amount of waste that contributes to pollution. In the United States, the Pollution Prevention Act of 1990 seeks to establish a collaborative effort with industry and the EPA. The goal of this legislation is to reduce pollution at its source. While compliance is currently voluntary, the act creates the potential for a future enforcement-oriented attack by the government in its efforts at pollution prevention.

The EPA's approach establishes reduction of pollution at its source as the most effective approach, with recycling and treatment following. The EPA defines source reduction as any practice that:

- Reduces the amount of any hazardous substance, pollutant, or contaminant entering any waste stream or otherwise released into the environment (including fugitive emissions) prior to recycling, treatment, or disposal.
- Reduces the hazards to public health and the environment associated with the release of such substances, pollutants, or contaminants.

Reduction practices that are emphasized include modifications to equipment, processes and procedures, product design and modifications, substitution of materials, and better housekeeping.

Energy Consumption

Sustainability also encompasses the use of renewable energy sources, those that cannot be depleted, such as wind power, solar energy, hydropower, geothermal energy, nuclear energy, hydrogen fuel cells, biological-based sources, and other natural resources. This is a high priority for many governments and industries, considering that the world's current reliance on fossil fuels (petroleum) is no longer sustainable much past mid-century at its current rate of consumption. However, many of these sources require significant investments in order to convert from current oil-based processes to efficient renewable energy. While the development of these sources is clearly underway, it has not reached the point where it is practical in most situations and where it can be legislatively mandated.

The dilemma for the sourcing team, then, is how to evaluate compliance with the use of renewable energy sources when virtually no standards or requirements exist. Most of the initiatives we see in the United States are directed toward existing power suppliers, requiring that a percentage of their energy come from renewable sources. These are called renewable portfolio standards (RPS) and have been established in the United States by a majority of states. The problem is that they are focused on the most cost-efficient methods such as wind and methane from landfills but fail to provide adequate support for smaller scale methods such as solar energy, largely due to cost considerations.

A recent survey conducted by the *Environmental Leader* and *Retailer Daily* found that:

Of all the varying factors that go into an enterprise's decision to enact renewable energy program—brand image, corporate responsibility, and future viability of fossil fuel—finance is the most important of all, as would be expected of a business decision.

In virtually every question asking respondents why they did (or did not) make a certain decision regarding a renewable energy implementation, a financial consideration was the top answer. This applies whether respondents purchase renewable energy from a third party, RECs, or generate their own renewable energy on site. It also applies to respondents who have not yet implemented renewable energy, whether they plan to in the future or not.

From the "Enterprise Renewable Energy Adoption Survey," available at
reports.environmentalleader.com

Guidelines

Many global initiatives are currently underway that seek to remedy the issues in sustainability, so it is incumbent on the sourcing team leader to determine which ones may apply to its suppliers and the extent to which each is in compliance. This is not going to be an easy task since there are so many government and industry standards. And to further complicate matters, many of these are still in their early stages and will continue evolving. Reviewed here are two key sets of guidelines that comprehensively address sustainability.

ISO 14001 Guidelines

ISO 14001 (and its update, ISO 14001:2004) sets out requirements for an environmental management system (EMS) that can be used by an organization to measure and document its environmental compliance. The key advantage to looking for ISO environmental requirements is that compliance can be externally audited and certified by an accredited certification body. In fact, there are a number of tools available for organizations (and sourcing teams) to conduct a self-assessment to determine if they are compliant and can be certified.

List of ISO 14000 Series Standards

- ISO 14001 Environmental management systems—Requirements
- ISO 14004 Environmental management systems—General guidelines
- ISO 14015 Environmental assessment
- ISO 14020–14025 Environmental labels and declarations
- ISO 14031 Environmental performance evaluation
- ISO 14040–14049 Life cycle assessment
- ISO 14050 Terms and definitions
- ISO 14062 Improvements to environmental impact goals
- ISO 14063 Communication
- ISO 14064 Measuring, quantifying, and reducing greenhouse gas emissions.
- ISO 19011 Audit protocol for 14000 and 9000 series standards.

United Nations Global Compact

Rather than attempt to summarize the United Nations' initiative on supply chain sustainability, due to its importance in defining governing principles of supply chain sustainability, we have decided to print it here for reference.

The Ten Principles

The UN Global Compact's ten principles in the areas of human rights, labour, the environment and anti-corruption enjoy universal consensus and are derived from:

> *The Universal Declaration of Human Rights*
> *The International Labour Organization's Declaration on Fundamental Principles and Rights at Work*
> *The Rio Declaration on Environment and Development*
> *The United Nations Convention Against Corruption*

The UN Global Compact asks companies to embrace, support and enact, within their sphere of influence, a set of core values in the areas of human rights, labour standards, the environment and anti-corruption:

Human Rights

> *Principle 1: Businesses should support and respect the protection of internationally proclaimed human rights; and*
> *Principle 2: make sure that they are not complicit in human rights abuses.*

Labour

> *Principle 3: Businesses should uphold the freedom of association and the effective recognition of the right to collective bargaining;*
> *Principle 4: the elimination of all forms of forced and compulsory labour;*
> *Principle 5: the effective abolition of child labour; and*
> *Principle 6: the elimination of discrimination in respect of employment and occupation.*

Environment

> *Principle 7: Businesses should support a precautionary approach to environmental challenges;*
> *Principle 8: undertake initiatives to promote greater environmental responsibility; and*
> *Principle 9: encourage the development and diffusion of environmentally friendly technologies.*

Anti-Corruption

> *Principle 10: Businesses should work against corruption in all its forms, including extortion and bribery.*

The Global Compact

The Global Compact encourages signatories to engage with their suppliers around the Ten Principles, and thereby to develop more sustainable supply chain practices. However, many companies lack the knowledge or capacity to effectively integrate the principles into their existing supply chain programmes and operations. In particular, a challenge remains to ensure that sustainability considerations are embedded within all sourcing processes.

To assist companies in improving their processes, the Global Compact and partners are currently developing guidance on how to take a more proactive approach to integrate the Ten Principles into supply chain management practices. Because supply chain sustainability is a cross-cutting issue, this work is closely coordinated with the strategy and work done in the four Global Compact issues areas (human rights, labour, environment and anti-corruption).

The Global Compact Office has entered into a strategic partnership with BSR (Business for Social Responsibility), a global business membership network and consultancy focused on sustainability, to develop an implementation guide and a learning and assessment tool for Global Compact signatories. . . .

Background

Corporate supply chains have grown in scale and complexity globally over the past decades. Open markets have enabled companies to source from suppliers in developing and emerging economies, or to move or outsource production, because of the cost advantage these regions offer. As a business strategy, this can deliver significant benefits such as reduced costs, and enhanced profitability and shareholder value. At the same time, it can contribute to much needed economic and social development, and higher standards of living for millions of people.

However, widespread concerns about poor social and environmental conditions in companies' supply chains have emerged. Weak implementation of local social and environmental regulation has forced companies to address issues that traditionally have been seen to lie outside of their core competencies and responsibilities.

Moreover, public scrutiny of business behaviour has led to rising expectations that companies are responsible for the environmental, social and governance (ESG) practices of their suppliers. Failure to address suppliers' ESG performance can give rise to significant operational and reputational risks that can threaten to undermine any potential gains from moving into these markets. As a result, a company's overall commitment to corporate citizenship can be seriously discredited if low standards of business conduct are found to persist in their supply chain.

Supply Chain Sustainability

Corporate buying practices can impact suppliers' ability to improve their business conduct. Downward pressure on cost and efficiency can force suppliers to contravene some of their own ESG standards in order to meet their buyers' commercial requirements. At the opposite end of the scale, companies can use their purchasing power to help instill good ESG practices in small and medium-sized companies across the developing world.

Today, successful supply chain managers must increasingly think beyond short-term financial considerations to building relationships that can deliver long-term value along the entire supply chain. This includes incorporating sustainability issues into the company's sourcing and purchasing practices. In fact, companies that do engage with their suppliers around these issues constitute one of the most important drivers for spreading corporate citizenship principles around the world.

The business case

Incorporating environmental, social and governance considerations into supply chain management can deliver a range of business benefits:

> *Risks are better anticipated and managed (risk is spread out across different players)*
> *Reduced operational risks such as disruption to supply, increased cost and lack of access to key raw materials*
> *"Informal" or "social" license to operate within communities, legal systems and governments that otherwise might be antagonistic*
> *Reduced costs and enhanced efficiency and productivity*
> *Improved working conditions can reduce turnover and improve quality and reliability*
> *Environmental responsibility improves efficiency and profitability*
> *Corporate brand and values, and customer and consumer confidence and loyalty are protected and enhanced*
> *Process and product innovation. Empowered suppliers uncover opportunities for developing sustainable products and services*
> *Examples from leading companies show that good supply chain management can increase shareholder value.*[4]

Lean Six Sigma

Six Sigma uses statistical methods to systemically analyze manufacturing processes in order to reduce process variation and is often used to support continual improvement activities. It is being used by some companies to assess areas of waste to which lean methods can be applied as solutions.

According to the EPA, the potential benefits of applying Six Sigma processes to waste reduction are described as follows:

By removing variation from production processes, fewer defects inherently result. A reduction in defects can, in turn, help eliminate waste from processes in three fundamental ways:

> *1. Fewer defects decreases the number of products that must be scrapped;*
> *2. Fewer defects also means that the raw materials, energy, and resulting waste associated with the scrap are eliminated;*
> *3. Fewer defects decrease the amount of energy, raw material, and wastes that are used or generated to fix defective products that can be re-worked.*

Six Sigma tools can help focus attention on reducing conditions that can result in accidents, spills, and equipment malfunctions. This can reduce the solid and hazardous wastes (e.g., contaminated rags and adsorbent pads) resulting from spills and leaks and their clean-up.

Six Sigma techniques that focus on product durability and reliability can increase the lifespan of products. This can reduce the frequency with which the product will need to be replaced, reducing the overall environmental impacts associated with meeting the customer need.[5]

Protection from Natural Disasters

Natural disasters occur daily in every conceivable form and in virtually every geographical location: a hurricane in New Orleans, a tornado in Missouri, a flood in China, a tsunami resulting from an earthquake in Japan, a volcanic eruption in the Philippines, a devastating heat-wave in Europe ... just to mention a few that occurred recently.

Very often, recovery from such disasters is painfully slow, and sometimes an area never recovers. So the procurement and sourcing professional must find a way to protect the buying organization from any significant disruption in operations, to the extent possible. This begins with a risk assessment that identifies potential natural disasters in the region, determines their potential impact, and formulates plans to mitigate the impact. Most commonly, in areas where the risk is relatively high, we develop a second source as a backup in a location that would not be affected by the particular disaster we are mitigating.

Criteria for Supplier Evaluation

As we noted in earlier chapters, supplier evaluation is generally best tailored to a specific organization and a specific requirement. However, if you are considering evaluating sustainability as part of your supplier selection criteria for the first time and would like a starting point, consider including these elements in your solicitation:

- Do you have a full-time sustainability manager?
- Detail the key elements of your environmental management system (EMS).
- Please provide a copy of your company's corporate social responsibility policy.
- What is your organization's current carbon footprint, and how you are planning to comply with global warming initiatives?
- Identify any toxic materials used in your processes and how you are controlling them.
- Do you currently generate nonrecyclable waste? Please list.
- Describe your program for reducing waste.
- List your accomplishments and goals for converting to sustainable energy sources.
- What significant amounts of recycled materials do you use in your operations?

TABLE 8.1   Criteria and Measurements for Supplier Evaluation

Element	Unit of Measure	Current Emission	Initial Baseline	Objective
Direct Greenhouse Gas Emissions (Kyoto)	Metric Tons CO_2 or equivalent			
Indirect Greenhouse Gas Emissions (Kyoto)	Metric Tons CO_2 or equivalent			
Hazardous Waste Disposal	Metric Tons			
Nonhazardous Waste Disposal	Metric Tons			
Electric Energy Usage	Giga-Joules			
Fuel Energy Usage	Giga-Joules			
Renewable Energy Use	Giga-Joules			
Waste Material Recycled or Reused	Metric Tons			

- Is your organization currently certified to an environmental standard (such as ISO 14001–2004)? Please list.

If possible, you should also consider the use of hard measurements in your evaluation. Table 8.1 lists some of the criteria and measurements that you can use.

Institute for Supply Management's Principles of Sustainability and Social Responsibility

In response to the need for organizations to develop specific guidelines that address sustainability and social responsibility, ISM offers a standardized version that may be used in its entirety or as a starting point, or to complement existing principles.

ISM outlines its intent in the preamble to the principles:

ISM believes the supply management profession is a strategic contributor in the development and implementation of sustainability and social responsibility programs and behavior. Supply professionals are in a unique, critical position to impact the global supply chain. Supply management professionals are encouraged to promote sustainability and social responsibility through participation on appropriate committees, boards and panels of governmental and nongovernmental organizations.

Creating principles across social, industry, public and private, profit and nonprofit, political and country boundaries is daunting. Additionally, laws, regulations, trade agreements, customs and practices pertinent to sustainability and social responsibility must be considered in the development and implementation of business strategies, policies and procedures.

The published principles are the following:

1. Community. Community initiatives provide resources to support the community in which the company or organization operates.
2. Diversity and Inclusiveness—Supply Base. Supply base diversity and inclusiveness refers to efforts to engage different categories of suppliers in sourcing processes and decisions.
3. Diversity and Inclusiveness—Workforce. Workforce diversity and inclusiveness refers to efforts to attract and retain a workforce that represents the varied backgrounds of the customer and community in which the organization operates.
4. Environment. Supply management actions and decisions that promote protection and preservation of the health and vitality of the environment within which the organization operates.
5. Ethics and Business Conduct. Ethical behavior and business conduct is a critical element impacting personal, business (public and private), supplier and governmental relationships and governance.
6. Financial Responsibility. Financial responsibility refers to understanding and applying financial concepts to supply management decisions to address allocation of funds, accurate reporting and management of risk.
7. Human Rights. Human rights refer to the concept of human beings having universal natural rights, or status, regardless of legal jurisdiction or other localizing factors.
8. Health and Safety. Health and safety refer to the condition of being protected or free from the occurrence of risk of injury, danger, failure, error, accident, harm or loss.
9. Sustainability. Sustainability refers to the ability to meet current needs without hindering the ability to meet the needs of future generations in terms of economic, environmental and social challenges.[6]

For further reference, here are the applicable URLs:

- **ISM Principles of Sustainability and Social Responsibility,** www.ism.ws /files/SR/PrinciplesSSR.pdf
- **ISM Principles of Sustainability and Social Responsibility with a Guide to Adoption and Implementation,** www.ism.ws/files/SR/SSRwGuide Book08.pdf

Examples of Corporate Sustainability Efforts

Many organizations have adopted well-thought-out standards to address sustainability. A random sample includes the following:

- **Sustainability at Skyworks Solutions, Inc.**

  Skyworks Solutions is committed to operating under business practices that 'meet the needs of the present without compromising the ability of the future generations to meet their own needs.' Our sustainability efforts include policies and programs that encompass a wide variety of elements ranging from environmental to labor, health and safety, and ethics.[7]

■ **The Procter & Gamble Company**

> *"By urging collaboration and unlocking innovation to create meaningful environmental progress, the initiative has already been a success and is just another example of how we strive to touch and improve the lives of more consumers, more completely, in more parts of the world," said Dr. Len Sauers, Procter & Gamble's vice president for global sustainability. "Working with our external partners is clearly critical to realizing our long-term environmental vision as a company, and this scorecard is a helpful tool to facilitate that collaboration. After all, using 100% renewable or recycled materials for all products and packaging will only be achieved through strong collaboration with our business partners.*
>
> . . .
>
> *"By assessing the total environmental footprint of suppliers, this initiative encourages continued improvement by measuring energy use, water use, waste disposal, and greenhouse gas emissions on a year-by-year basis. More than 20 leading supplier representatives globally, who form the P&G Supplier Sustainability Board, participated in the creation of the scorecard. 'This isn't simply about collecting data,' said Rick Hughes, P&G's chief purchasing officer.' The scorecard is the right tool to give us that snapshot across our supply chain so we can identify where to focus our collective supply network sustainability efforts, develop ideas to work on together, and reward those who excel.'"*[8]

■ **CSRware**

> *CSRware is committed to delivering innovative and user-friendly software to promote environmental sustainability and energy efficient solutions to ensure customers conduct business in a way that preserves our resources for future generations. Our core business strategy is to deliver solutions that integrate sustainability principles in all aspects of a business operation. As an early market leader, CSRware is proud to continue its influence on the carbon and energy management markets and supply chain sustainability management.*[9]

You can find additional information regarding sustainability with more detail at these URLs:

- **Global Institute of Sustainability—Arizona State University:** sustainability.asu.edu
- **Global e-Sustainability Initiative:** www.gesi.org
- **Network for Business Sustainability:** www.nbs.net
- **Sustainable Plant:** www.sustainableplant.com
- **Sustainable Supply Network Consulting Group:** www.sustainablesupplynetwork.com
- **Sustainability Program of EPA's Office of Research and Development:** www.epa.gov/sustainability/
- **The Sustainability Consortium:** www.sustainabilityconsortium.org

- **United Nations Global Compact:** www.unglobalcompact.org
- **World Business Council for Sustainable Development:** www.wbcsd.org

Summary

We began this chapter with some definitions of sustainability and then went on to outline some of the important issues. These relate to the use of materials, toxic discharge, and energy consumption. In the materials section we described the various methods available for waste reduction, the use of renewable resources and protecting habitats, hazardous materials regulations, and man-made and natural disasters. The section on toxic discharge examined greenhouse gases, carbon footprints, ozone depletion, and pollution. We then described the issues around energy consumption and evolving standards such as RPS.

The next section reviewed currently available standards for sustainability such as ISO 14001, the United Nations Global Compact, and Lean Six Sigma. We also included the ISM's Principles of Sustainability and Social Responsibility. This was followed by an outline of criteria for supplier evaluation and several examples of organizations that have adopted sustainability programs. Our chapter concluded with a short list of resources for finding additional information.

Notes

1. OSHA's Hazard Communication Standard (HCS), www.osha.gov/dsg/hazcom/index.html.
2. Federal Emergency Management Agency, www.fema.gov/hazard/terrorism/index.shtm.
3. EPA, Waste Reduction Model (WARM), updated August 2010, www.epa.gov/climate change/wycd/waste/calculators/Warm_home.html.
4. United Nations' initiative on supply chain sustainability, www.unglobalcompact.org/Issues /supply_chain/index.html, last updated March 16, 2010. For more information contact Cecilie Hultmann, UN Global Compact, hultmann@un.org.
5. EPA, "Lean Thinking and Methods," updated November 10, 2011, www.epa.gov/lean /environment/methods/sixsigma.htm.
6. ISM, "Principles of Sustainability and Social Responsibility," www.ism.ws/files/SR /SSRwGuideBook08.pdf.
7. Skyworks Solutions, Green Initiative, www.skyworksinc.com/GreenInitiative.aspx.
8. "P&G First Year Supplier Sustainability Scorecard Results in Collaboration and Innovation," April 7, 2011, www.prnewswire.com/news-releases/pg-first-year-supplier-sustainability -scorecard-results-in-collaboration-and-innovation-119405714.html.
9. CSRware, www.csrware.com.

CHAPTER 9

Negotiation

Your organization naturally seeks to obtain the maximum value for its investment in goods and services. Not surprisingly, so does your supplier; both organizations seek to gain the highest possible benefit from all of their business transactions. So when there is much value at stake, both parties generally come together to reconcile their differing positions. This process is referred to as *negotiations*.

As you have learned in previous chapters, any business transaction involving commercial buying and selling requires both a valid offer and acceptance. Between these two elements, however, there typically lies a gap of expectations and requirements: Your budget, for example, allows a certain amount of spending for a particular purchase, but the supplier's offer contains a significantly higher amount. Obviously, this creates a gap. How do you reconcile these two seemingly oppositional positions so that each organization can achieve its respective goals? In these circumstances it is critical to engage the supplier in some form of negotiations.

A major portion of the buyer's time will be spent conducting negotiations with suppliers to obtain more favorable terms for their organization. That is not to say that you continually engage in petty haggling with your suppliers. However, when the outcome of a procurement activity is critical to the organization's goals, a successful conclusion can never be in doubt: You will need to meet the goals and expectations of your organization as well as ensuring that the supplier continues to value your business. Negotiation is most likely to occur when the conditions for competitive bidding (see Chapter 3) are not present, such as when there is a sole- or single-source situation. It may also be required even when competitive bidding has taken place. Despite the fact that you have issued a request for proposals (RFP) and selected the most appropriate supplier, there may still be gaps in filling all of your organization's needs. Negotiation, therefore, requires much additional planning, research and, most importantly, precise execution in order to achieve a successful outcome and meet your organization's objectives. How this is accomplished and the sequence in which it logically progresses is the subject of this chapter.

Assessing the Negotiating Environment

It is important that you first assess the current situation prior to conducting actual negotiations. Assessing the negotiating climate typically involves gaining an understanding of market conditions for the particular commodity or service being

TABLE 9.1 · Understanding the Competitive Environment

Competitive Condition	Degree Fostering Competitive Bidding
Multiple *qualified* or *qualifiable* suppliers	High
Contracting is feasible	High
Competitive environment is regulated	Medium
Contract recently negotiated	Medium to low
Product or service is covered by patents	None
Clear specifications or SOW exists	High
Government-controlled resource	None
Attractive volume	High
Only one source of supply	None

purchased and the position of the supplier in that market. Market conditions generally refer to circumstances such as the availability of supply in relation to actual demand or the number of suppliers in the marketplace available to create a competitive situation. What is the market share for each of the major players, and how aggressive is the battle for market share? How profitable are companies in the industry, and what constitutes a typical profit margin? What is the economic outlook for this particular segment of the economy?

In addition, it is important for you to assess the relationship you have with the supplier. Often, this can determine the atmosphere during the negotiation and have an important impact on how you and your team develop your negotiation strategy. With this information come insights into the supplier's objectives and, as a result, many clues that tell you what supplier strategies to expect during the negotiations.

In this section, you will explore the nature of the competitive environment and how your understanding of it can assist you in your negotiations.

The Competitive Environment

When the competitive environment is limited by the lack of qualified suppliers or by intellectual property rights, competitive bidding is unlikely. In this circumstance, negotiations may be the only way to achieve organizational objectives. You can assess the likelihood of conducting competitive bidding by using the checklist in Table 9.1. This table describes the specific circumstances in the marketplace and the degree to which their presence fosters competitive bidding. Keep in mind that, as mentioned in the table, there can be no bidding if only one supplier can meet your requirements.

Nature of Competition

Competition is available in virtually all markets for goods and services. What you have to assess is the nature of that competition so that you can effectively formulate your procurement strategies. Higher competition generally results in lower prices and a greater willingness by suppliers to provide additional services.

Competition can be evaluated from a number of perspectives:

- **Number of qualified or qualifiable suppliers in the market.** Higher numbers generally foster greater competition.
- **Impact of the buyer.** Greater procurement volume encourages vigorous competition for your business in markets where competition exists.
- **Barriers to entry for the particular product or service.** The lower the cost to establish new businesses in the particular market, the greater is the competitive pressure.
- **Capacity.** Often related to the number of suppliers, higher levels of unused capacity within an industry can foster greater competition.
- **Dominant brand.** Effective branding strategies that make one supplier or one product more desirable than others result in less vigorous competition.
- **Ability to substitute.** Products or services that are easily substituted by those from other industries are more highly competitive.
- **Role of market forces.** When analysts speak of market forces, they generally refer to factors—economic, physical, and political—influencing and affecting buying and selling at a particular time. These factors may exist within a specific industry or a geographical location or over the course of an entire economy. To some extent, the very nature of competition itself is dynamic and in continual flux so that when you evaluate a given set of conditions—capacity or barriers to entry, for example—at any specific time, you do little more than freeze a frame in a never-ending film.

From the point of view of procurement function, supply and demand are two of the most important market force factors, and you need to pay attention to them very closely. Often in flux, supply and demand influences prices in many different ways. While supply and demand will theoretically reach equilibrium over time so that the supply of a given item exactly matches the demand for it, in reality this is rarely the case. More often than not, the ratio of supply and demand continually moves higher and lower, with fluctuating prices reflecting any imbalance. Figure 9.1 shows how prices can increase as a result of reduced supply because buyers tend to bid up prices to meet their requirements. Buyers compete with one another to obtain scarce goods and services. Keep in mind, however, that as prices increase, with all other factors remaining constant, new capacity will usually enter the market to take advantage of the perceived profit, eventually creating additional supply that once again brings prices lower. The ratio of supply to demand always affects prices. When supply is more plentiful than demand, suppliers must lower prices to make buying more attractive; when demand outstrips supply, buyers compete for the few available resources and prices rise.

Tips and Techniques

Supply shortages can also result from an unexpected increase in demand or some physical situation such as a plant shutdown that severely limits production.

In Figure 9.1, the point P_e represents the equilibrium point at which supply and demand are equal—shown by their intersecting lines. When the available supply

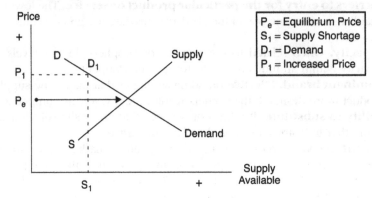

FIGURE 9.1   The Effect of Supply Shortage on Price

decreases along the line S to the point S_1, well below the demand line, prices rise to P_1.

Early Involvement

Early involvement by the procurement group is one of the fundamental keys to employing successful negotiation strategies. The later the involvement of the Procurement Department in sourcing decisions, the less leverage will be available for negotiating favorable terms. In other words, the greater the supplier's certainty that it will receive the order, the less likely it will be to engage in serious negotiations.

Early involvement is essential to avoiding being locked into a single source prematurely without sufficient negotiating leverage to influence critical terms of the contract. This is especially true during the new product development cycle and when engaging a new supplier. Figure 9.2 depicts graphically how the influence of the Procurement Department diminishes as the course of the supplier engagement progresses. As you can see, involvement during the initial phases of the engagement allows the Procurement Department to exercise greater influence and incorporate more robust processes than it can when it is engaged later in the development process. Furthermore, the actual impact of that engagement also diminishes with later involvement.

Gathering Information and Analysis

Information, as they say, is power. Having the right information available when needed is always critical to a successful approach to strategy formulation. It is

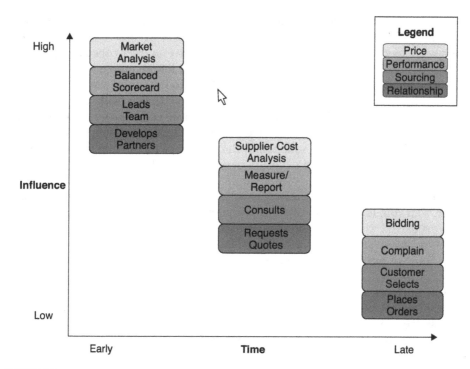

FIGURE 9.2   Factors Influenced by the Procurement Department's Early Involvement

important to know at least as much (and perhaps more) about the conditions that may influence the negotiation of the supplier. By being informed, your team will be able to develop realistic and workable strategies and avoid the embarrassment of establishing unreachable goals. Having the right facts can also preclude the supplier from springing negotiation surprises as tactics.

Each team member should be responsible for gathering a portion of the information that is needed to adequately prepare for both developing strategies and actually participating in the tactical negotiations. Price analysis and market conditions, noted previously, are just a few aspects of your analysis, but there are many more outlined next.

Analyzing the Supplier's Situation

In gathering information, you might first want to consider looking at the situation from the supplier's point of view: What motivates their position and what are they likely to value the most? Conversely, what concessions might they be willing to make to achieve their goals?

FINANCIAL NEEDS   It is relatively easy to assess a U.S. corporation's financial condition if it is *publicly held* (with stock trading on an open stock exchange) since the Securities and Exchange Commission (SEC) regulations require public disclosure of important financial data. From publicly accessible reports such as those filed with the SEC and from the reports of market analysts tracking its stock performance, it will be possible to gain some relative understanding of the supplier's financial picture and insight into its level of motivation to obtain your business. Obviously, the greater the financial need, the greater is the supplier's incentive to offer concessions.

With a privately held organization, gathering this information may be difficult. You will often need to obtain information available through an industry organization or professional association or through other sources familiar with the supplier's operations. The supplier's competitors will often have comparative data to share with you based on marketing surveys they have conducted, but you will naturally want to take into account the source and the simple fact that suppliers are not in the habit of passing along good news about their competition.

EXISTING RELATIONS   There are many reasons a supplier wants to maintain its favored position with you. Replacing a valuable customer can be costly, and the supplier has already "sunk" the costs of acquiring your business. Prior to negotiations, your team should completely analyze the motivational factors that will likely drive concessions to you. Some of the questions you might want to ask in this regard include:

- How much does a supplier value the status of its existing relationship with your organization? Are you a reference account?
- How does your business impact the supplier's bottom line?
- How does your volume affect its position in the marketplace?
- Does your organization require more or less customer service than others?
- Are your business needs relatively easy to forecast?
- Are your volumes consistent over time?
- Do you pay your invoices in an acceptable time frame?
- Are your organizations engaged in joint product development?

Analyzing Your Organization's Position

You will likely know a great deal more about your organization and its specific needs than you will about your supplier's, so the exercise of gathering and analyzing your own position will encourage your team to more clearly identify areas where concessions may be required. This exercise should flag those concerns for further research into the supplier's situation so that you enter the negotiation with at least some understanding of its likely position. This is really the first step in planning the negotiation process and developing a strategy. You will want to cover some of the same areas we discussed in the preceding section on the supplier's needs and will certainly want to review some of the following requirements.

URGENCY   When does your organization need the product or service you will be negotiating? If it is needed urgently, you may want to prepare to negotiate accelerated delivery by trading concessions in other areas such as price or transportation methods. On the other hand, if the requirement can be met over a period of time, allowing the supplier to fulfill it when time and resources are not being otherwise used, this might prove a useful concession to achieve better prices.

PRIORITY OF NEEDS   When you initially evaluated a key supplier, you may have measured its performance on a weighted average matrix to help in the selection process.

TABLE 9.2   Supplier Evaluation Weighting

Category	Percentage
Cost	40%
Quality	25%
Technology	20%
Service	15%

If you recall from Chapter 4, we actually developed a hierarchy of importance by assigning values to each of the categories: cost, quality, technology, and service.

In establishing the priority of needs for a particular negotiation, you will want to review your selection matrix to help determine the approximate priority of the organization's needs. Table 9.2 shows an evaluation matrix similar to the one we developed in Chapter 4. If we assigned the following values to our selection process, then we would likely want to assign a similar set of values to our negotiation priorities.

In terms of concessions, then, we would likely trade elements of service (the lowest value on the list) for pricing concessions (the highest value on the list).

INTERNAL CONSTRAINTS   Unknown conditions within your organization may preclude your team from fully leveraging its negotiating position, and they need to be identified prior to establishing a strategy. For example, it may be impossible to precisely define a scope of work for a construction project renovating an existing building. Contractors rarely know what they will find when opening a wall or ceiling. As a result, you will likely be unable to develop a firm fixed price for the project. Other contracts may be similar: Quality, delivery, and liability are dependent on a set of conditions that are not known at the time of negotiation.

In addition to unknowns, there may internal management pressures to achieve certain goals beyond the value that they may conceivably add. Using a proprietary architectural design to beautify the lobby of the headquarters building may hamper your ability to negotiate with the contractors; nevertheless, it would be unrealistic for a buyer to consider altering an architect's design.

You may also want to consider situations where trade-offs will require an additional investment by your organization. For example, if shortened lead times are critically necessary and the supplier has no flexibility in its manufacturing processes, you may need to develop longer range forecasts. This may require the addition of a staff planner or a more sophisticated software system. With this knowledge, you will be able to properly evaluate the costs of items that will not be effectively negotiated.

Preparing for the Negotiation

Once you have reviewed the general negotiating climate and have a relatively clear understanding of the forces operating behind the scenes, so to speak, you need to prepare for conducting the negotiation itself. This involves a great deal of planning that builds your confidence through a keen understanding of the circumstances you will likely encounter during the actual negotiation. It is also a continual process of fact finding and analysis that leads and guides your strategy.

In preparation, you will likely want to select and orient your cross-functional team to ensure that you are all working together as a team toward the common objectives. With your team in place, the primary focus of your planning will be to carefully review the supplier's proposal from the perspective of your organization's needs. To what extent are your needs being addressed, and where are there critical gaps that fall short of your objectives? The more you know about the contents of the proposal, the less likely you will be caught off guard by any omissions or issues that have not been clearly thought out. Planning for negotiations, in a way, also involves understanding the needs and objectives of your supplier, anticipating its most likely position on any key issue in relation to yours. If you and your supplier can avoid creating surprises with unexpected issues both during and after the contract negotiations, the chances are that the actual performance will run smoothly.

This section will guide you through the processes normally conducted in preparation for negotiations. We will cover some of the ways you might select and assess the team and how you will formulate objectives and develop strategies.

Selecting and Leading the Negotiating Team

In any significant negotiation, you will first want to form a support team composed of technical domain experts, the financial group, and members of the user groups—likely the same people that participated in the preparation of the RFP and the supplier selection. This team should always be led by the senior representative for Procurement that is participating in its activities to ensure that business objectives are met and that the negotiations are conducted in an atmosphere conducive to continued collaboration. The procurement representative will also be responsible to ensure the negotiations are carried out with integrity and in an ethical manner.

SELECTION CRITERIA It is naturally important that key members of the user group—the *stakeholders*, as they are sometimes called—actively participate in the negotiation process for a number of reasons. First, there are technical issues that will arise during the course of discussions that only they will be qualified to answer. Second, as the users, they are in the best position to understand the importance of the various elements of the offer and so can determine when specifications can be relaxed as well as the value of certain trade-offs. Third, as *subject matter experts (SMEs)*, the users are in the best position to evaluate what service levels should be established and the metrics used to evaluate performance. And lastly, the users are the successors of the negotiated bargain—the group that must live with the resulting conditions—and they will inherit not only the wins, but the losses as well.

In addition to members of the user group, you should ensure that you have representation from the various business units such as Finance, Operations, or Facilities. These are the support staff that can provide additional skills—based on their functional roles—to the team when needed. You should select team members according to their behavioral skills as well. Behavioral skills include such qualities as decisiveness, intelligence, business savvy, problem-solving abilities, drive to achieve, patience, and the ability to communicate. It will be up to you to determine what behavioral skills will be needed and who within the broad stakeholder community best demonstrates them.

ASSESSING THE TEAM'S STRENGTH AND WEAKNESSES   It is a good idea for the members of the team to jointly assess its collective strengths and weaknesses in advance. By doing so, team members will develop a more realistic understanding of the constraints they are operating under and what technical skills are available to effectively maneuver to a favorable concession as a result. Externally imposed deadlines can often generate situations that create bad decisions, or the lack of authority to make a decision can lead to a stalemate.

COMMUNICATING WITH TEAM MEMBERS   One of the most important roles the team leader has is that of the communicator and project manager. The team leader is responsible for seeing that participants know what factual information is needed and who should be gathering it. Information should have a clear distribution channel so that everyone can be updated on relevant information as it becomes available. Exercise caution, however, to ensure that there is not so much information generated that it inundates the team and creates data overload.

The team leader also needs to define the individual roles that may be necessary during the course of the negotiation and to help assess which members are best suited to each specific task. This is likely to include deciding who will become the team's spokesperson and how decisions to accept or reject offers will be made. Signals need to be developed that can indicate to other members when offers are acceptable and when they are not, similar to the way they might be used in a sporting event when the coach wants to send a specific play to team members. The team also needs to know who will make the final decisions and the authority level of each of the negotiators.

Formulating Objectives and Developing Strategies

Once the team has been selected and is operationally in place, your next step is to lead the development of a plan for the actual negotiation. It is always best to put this plan in writing so that you and your team members can use it as a guide in future negotiations.

As a first step in developing the plan, team members should list their objectives and the anticipated objectives of the supplier. Objectives can be based on the identified gap between initial expectations in the sourcing process and those actually achieved. Under each objective, indicate the likely impact of not achieving the objective. Then rank the objectives on this list by priority, focusing on developing a strategy for those that are most critical. The strategy will outline what initial offer you can expect from the supplier and what you are willing to counteroffer. (You might call these "take-aways" and "give-aways.") You will also need to determine a position at which you would be willing to accept the offer and one where you would be willing to walk away altogether for each of the key objectives. Your assessment of the situation, such as current market conditions, will play a critical role in this process, for without it you will likely not be able to understand the supplier's needs and motivation.

Tips and Techniques

Gap analysis can be viewed as the process of assessing (measuring) the difference between the current condition and the desired outcome.

It is sometimes helpful to go one step further and have your team run through a mock negotiation exercise where you set the stage by reviewing general market trends and ask some of the team members to assume the supplier's role. What objectives are they likely to have? What concessions are they likely to make? At what point in each of the elements do you feel the supplier will concede, and at what point are you willing to simply walk away?

As you answer these questions for your own position and then compare them to the answers you come up with for the supplier's anticipated position, you will gain a preview of how the actual negotiations may develop and how you can best respond to specific offers or demands. This is much like scripting a football play book where time, field position, score, and other key elements in the game are assessed using a *decision tree* to determine what play should be logically called next. Indeed, you should consider having this script put into written form so that each member of your team has the opportunity to review it periodically during the course of the negotiations.

OBJECTIVES When your supplier selection team established its initial requirements and began the process of determining the most qualified supplier, it also developed a set of expectations. These expectations were based on your organization's needs. Whatever needs are not fully satisfied in the supplier's response, even when that response is the best one received, will need to be further negotiated. You will likely have performed a gap analysis prior to constructing your negotiating plan, so you can compare what you have to what you actually wanted. This can form the basis for determining what you will want to negotiate and your negotiating objectives.

In this section, we'll discuss the few elements you might want to consider including in your checklist such as price, quality, service levels, capacity or volume, the length of the contract, and managing specifications. Shown in Figure 9.3 is an example of a planning template that outlines your organization's objectives and compares it with the likely objectives of the supplier's organization.

Price Despite the fact that you understand the nature of value and the concept of total cost of ownership, the focal point of any negotiation is usually price. The

Negotiations Template Planning Sheet					
Your Major Issues (Ranked in Order of Importance)	Your Goal	Likely Initial Supplier Position	Your Fallback Position #1	Your Fallback Position #2	Your "Walk Away" Position
Delivery	June 30th	August 1st	July 1st	July 10th	July 15th
Payment Terms	2% 10 Net 45	Net 30	2% 10 Net 30	1% 10 Net 30	Net 30
Warranty Period (Months)	12	6	10	9	6
Supplier Spare Parts Response Time (Hours)	8	36	12	15	24

FIGURE 9.3 Negotiations Planning Template

seller wishes to reasonably maximize profit and the buyer wishes to obtain the best possible price. In most cases, the ideal position for both is a fair and reasonable price. For the most part, the best way to determine a fair and reasonable price is through the current pricing in an open market, such as a commodities exchange. On an exchange, commodity prices fluctuate openly in response to supply and demand, so the trading price at any given time reflects the current price a buyer is willing to pay and the current price at which a seller is willing to sell.

In the absence of a public exchange, however, the buyer can turn to the competitive bidding process. When properly executed, the competitive bidding process can approximate an open market exchange. But even when the competitive bidding process is used, there may be some further need to negotiate price. For example, while a specific contract may have an agreed-upon fixed price, the buyer will also want to fix the rates for changes and perhaps prenegotiate the conditions under which the contract may be extended for an additional period of time. This may or may not have been addressed in the initial proposal or competitive bid.

Tips and Techniques

Price Analysis

It is important for the lead negotiator to understand when quoted pricing represents an acceptable offer. The reasonableness of a particular price can be established through an analysis of a number of factors such as market conditions, volume of the purchase, overall volume given the supplier, nature of the specifications, and risk. It can also be determined through benchmarking and whatever other comparative analysis is available to the buyer. Always keep in mind, however, that price is not necessarily directly related to the supplier's cost. In fact, the process of price analysis typically evaluates price without regard to its components of cost and, in most commercial environments, without consideration of the supplier's net profit or operating margin.

When evaluating and negotiating price, you also need to consider some of the auxiliary elements that immediately and directly affect price, such as shipping costs and disposal costs, and the terms of payment. Insofar as these can be directly associated with a clearly measurable price factor, they can be evaluated as part of the price package. Conceding a point or two on the price list in exchange for more favorable payment terms (e.g., Net 30 extended to Net 45) can be calculated as a cash value.

Quality As negotiations progress, you will likely find that increased quality specifications result in higher prices and that relaxing some of the noncritical specifications may result in lower prices. To the extent possible, the technical group on your team should review the specifications as part of the planning process. Knowing where specifications and tolerances can be relaxed and where they cannot needs to be determined largely in advance and should be included in the negotiation plan.

Service Levels In many cases, service levels are included in the statement of work in the form of a service-level agreement (SLA). As with quality specifications, service levels, too, can be relaxed and traded off as a concession to receiving some other benefits in exchange. Required lead time that can be extended through some improved planning on your end and early placement of orders may prove beneficial to the supplier and could result in a greater commitment to on-time delivery. Or you may be willing to make some pricing concessions in order to obtain just-in-time (JIT) delivery or the benefit of establishing a supplier-managed inventory (SMI) program.

Service levels can also be evaluated in terms of engineering support provided by the supplier and the impact of this support on your operations. If one of your organization's key objectives calls for being the first to market, engineering support from the supplier can be a crucial factor in getting you there.

Capacity/Volume   Whenever the potential for limitations in a supplier's production or service levels exist as a result of forecasted changes in market conditions, you will need to address it contractually. During periods of constrained capacity and shortages when suppliers cannot keep up with demand, you will want to ensure that your organization has the protection it needs by locking in specific commitments from the supplier for certain amounts of its capacity or specific volumes based on your anticipated needs. This, of course, is always a trade-off, since in exchange for guaranteed capacity the supplier usually wants a guaranteed volume of business.

Length of Contract   Another point of negotiation occurs when there may be considerable risk involved in the fluctuation of prices and you (or the supplier) wish to lock in pricing for a given period of time. If your team sees prices rising, you will want a longer term for the contract at the current pricing; the supplier, seeing the same trend, will want to shorten the contract period, hoping that increased prices will result in additional revenue. The opposite is true, of course, when prices appear to be falling.

There are many other reasons for negotiations to occur around the length of the contract. The supplier naturally wants to be assured of your organization's business—all other things being equal—for as long as possible. You may want a longer contract period to avoid the additional cost of switching from one supplier to another.

Managing Specifications   The technical users on the team are generally responsible for determining the specifications. Often, you will find that the tighter the specifications are (in terms of typical industrial capabilities), the more you will have to pay. Tighter specifications may also mean additional inspection time (and cost) that interferes with the smooth operation of the supplier's production. It is always advisable, in situations where specifications are critical, to maintain a *want* position, a *need* position, and a *can accept* position so that you are flexible enough to earn concessions for more critical factors.

ESTABLISHING PRIORITIES   As previously described, organizing the priority of your team's objectives can be one of the most important aspects in any negotiation planning process. Based on team discussions and consensus, it is possible to organize each of the stated objectives into a priority list or, at the least, indicate if they are high, medium, or low. During the actual course of negotiations, you will want to be certain to maintain these priorities to avoid wasting time by negotiating for relatively unimportant objectives.

Establishing priorities also relates to determining the amount of time devoted to the actual negotiations. Setting deadlines and the number of sessions reminds everyone that there is an objective to be reached. With this in mind, little time should be devoted to minor issues until the major ones are resolved. However, the order in which you negotiate specific items, critical or minor, can be varied to meet the team's overall strategy.

PREPARING PSYCHOLOGICALLY   Psychological preparation generally means preparing well enough to develop a high level of confidence in the validity of your position. As mentioned earlier in this chapter, confidence develops from having a firm grasp of the conditions in the marketplace and understanding the position of both parties relative to their competitors. Gathering facts and analyzing the supplier's position, as well as your own, leads to a clear understanding of what concessions are required and what concessions are going to be impossible to obtain. Attempting to achieve that which is impossible can only lead to disappointment and confrontation. Conversely, lowering expectations below what is truly possible can lead to demoralization and a sense of loss following the negotiations. The best practices today have buyer and supplier teams working collaboratively so that both achieve the fullest benefit of the bargain.

PLANNING YOUR AGENDA   As part of your psychological preparation, you will want to have your agenda set up in advance. This provides your team with a sense of direction and sets your own pace for the negotiation. The timing of the negotiation is always a critical factor in establishing a strong base for leverage. Timing means not only when the negotiations start and end, but when individual items will be open for discussion. This gives you the opportunity to achieve key objectives first before relinquishing key concessions. Negotiations often move much like card games, where one player can use cards discarded by the other.

CONDUCTING PRACTICE SESSIONS   Finally, it can be quite useful to have your team practice for the actual negotiations by holding some realistic practice sessions. During these sessions, team members can take turns in the anticipated role of the supplier and gain some insight into the situations that are likely to occur during actual negotiations. You can make the process even more realistic by bringing in participants from other groups and creating a somewhat competitive environment by offering relatively substantial prizes.

Conducting the Negotiation

When it is time to actually conduct the negotiation, you will employ a myriad of techniques and tactics. For example, one of the best practices in preparing for and actually conducting negotiations is to continually ask questions whose answers provide a better understanding of the situation and the needs of both parties. Asking questions also helps to control the pace and direction of the negotiations, which can be especially useful when you need to bring the discussion back to its key points.

To a large degree, your tactics will depend on the overall strategy you and your team developed during the planning phase. Implementing your strategy essentially amounts to how you approach the negotiations—cooperatively in a *win-win* mode or win-lose in an adversarial mode. Win-win modes tend to encourage collaboration in the negotiation process. Win-lose strategies tend to rely on power to control the negotiation process.

The following section reviews many of the more traditional tactical aspects of conducting negotiations that you will probably use. Although it is unlikely that they will all fit your personal style of negotiating, keep them in mind and include them as part of your playbook. You never know when you might need a special effect.

Creating the Climate

Establishing the climate is one of your first concerns just prior to and during the negotiation process. Climate refers to the physical aspects of where the negotiations are taking place, as well as the general mood of those conducting the negotiations. It encompasses both the physical atmosphere and the nature of the personal interaction.

Tips and Techniques

Supplier representatives often understand this all too well and have been taught to do as much as possible to keep the lead negotiator or decision maker in a good mood. However, it is generally no longer considered acceptable to conduct serious business negotiations over an expensive lunch or dinner with wine.

LOCATION   There is a maxim in sporting events that the home team has the field advantage. Most of the spectators are fans of the home team and the team likely plays the majority of its games on that particular field. It's hard to say how true this is, but there are some related aspects to consider when choosing the actual location where you will conduct negotiations. Typically, negotiations are held at the buyer's office, although there is no hard and fast rule about that. If negotiations are conducted at your site, you may be subject to more interruptions by routine business matters than you would be at some other place, but you will have the comfort of familiar ground, as well as the convenience of having support staff and records nearby.

In times past, it was thought that there was a critical psychological advantage to holding negotiations in a familiar environment, and you may have heard that the seating arrangements around the conference table can provide an advantage. There may be some truth to this when high-stakes international political outcomes are at stake, but such details rarely influence the kind of business negotiations you will be routinely conducting. This is not to imply that some element of cat-and-mouse intrigue will not be present during your negotiations, since there is often a strong desire on the part of participants to "ink the deal" with favorable terms. It is more important, however, that regardless of where you are, you consider any potential negative impact the environment may have and take whatever steps necessary to counter it.

As part of an awareness of your surroundings, you must also be aware of the body language and the physical actions of those in the negotiations. Learning to read these signs can be useful in determining the mood and status of your supplier's team.

Tips and Techniques

It is universally accepted that the crossed-arm posture (usually sitting with arms folded across the chest, but sometimes seen with the hands held behind the head) represents an unwillingness to listen or to accept what is being said. See what you can do to get your suppliers to open up their posture and demonstrate that they are becoming more receptive to your proposals.

DEVELOPING A COLLABORATIVE ATMOSPHERE A collaborative atmosphere, it is felt by many, is the most conducive to negotiating in environments where long-term relationships are important. While the popularity of win-win negotiations rises and falls with time, there can be little doubt that positional or adversarial contact rarely produces the best results. If your team takes a competitive stance, it is likely the supplier's team will do the same. You should have already developed your priority list of objectives prior to your first session, so you might want to consider that the supplier has done the same. If your discussions are congenial and nonconfrontational and you listen well, you will come away with an understanding very early in the negotiations of what exchanges of value can take place.

That is not to say there is any reason to pretend you and the supplier are best friends. However, you will benefit from good relations if you consider that the supplier's representative is as anxious as you are to do a good job.

You should also keep in mind that sales personnel have generally been given a great deal of training in the tactics of negotiations. Any "tricks" you have learned are likely to be known by one or another member of your supplier's team. Remember, the objective of any negotiation is to reach an agreement, so there is little value in playing games. If your position is firm, let that be known. If you are not clear about the implications of a concession, ask questions and hold a caucus with your team.

An important part of developing a collaborative negotiation is to avoid imposing artificial deadlines. If there are absolute time constraints, you should indicate so at the beginning of your negotiation and stick to them. By the same token, you should not let deadlines be imposed upon you either. To maintain your future credibility, it is critical that you honor your commitments. Do not make decisions before you feel completely ready, regardless of the circumstances.

ALLOWING FOR CULTURAL DIFFERENCES When conducting negotiations with personnel from nations other than your own, the most important rule to remember is that cultural differences will invariably have an impact. Even when the parties are speaking the same language, the native speaker may have a different conception of the terminology than the person speaking a second language. Similarly, body language and expressions take on different meanings in different cultures. The only certain way for you to understand this is to do your homework diligently and become familiar with as many of the nuances of the supplier's culture as you can. Sometimes, it helps defuse this potential problem if you take the initial step (sensitively, of course) of informally discussing these differences together.

Some professional tips include the following:

- Negotiation is always a delicate activity, requiring determination and diplomacy.
- Recognize the cultural principles that negotiators from other countries may be operating under. In the United States, decisions are frequently unilateral, while in Japan, for example, decisions require consensus. Negotiators in the United States value flexibility, whereas their counterparts in Japan find changing a decision to be a sign of weakness.
- Understand the role of relationships in other cultures—some driven by family ties and long-standing friendships—that render negotiations as much a ritual as a pragmatic approach to making a deal.
- Keep a historical perspective. How have the parties, and the countries, dealt with one another in the past? Previous animosities may require special attention.
- Be informed and up-to-date on the legal differences between countries. Often, what is acceptable practice in one country can result in criminal charges in another. Understand the legal obligations in the particular country you are engaged with and how they are adjudicated. Contracts are dissolved under different conditions and with different limitations in various countries, and dispute resolution processes vary widely.

Note

Travelers' guides, such as those published by Fodor and Lonely Planet, are excellent tools for helping you to understand the business and cultural customs in various countries (www.fodors.com, www.lonelyplanet.com).

Adopting a Negotiating Style

While there is an endless array of negotiating styles, and small libraries can be filled with the texts describing them, there are two basic types of negotiators: collaborative negotiators, who seek to develop outcomes that enhance the sense of accomplishment of both parties (win-win), and power (or positional) negotiators, who seek to prevail in achieving their objectives regardless of the impact on the other party. Even after you spend many years in Procurement, it is unlikely you will consistently use one or the other.

TACTICS   The tactics you will likely use for negotiations are closely related to the specific style you adopt, and there appear to be endless compendiums of them strung along like so many proverbs. Here are a few of the more common tactics:

- Generally, more can be gained by listening than by talking. Accordingly, take copious notes and review them frequently.
- Question how your statements will align with your objectives—pronouncements can be pointless or even counterproductive.

- Avoid accepting the first offer.
- Always ask questions, especially when there is useful information to be learned.
- Do not make concessions without receiving equal consideration. This does not necessarily mean that each and every concession need result in some consideration ... but do keep track.
- Attend to deadlines; establish them sparingly and only when necessary.
- Keep your wits about you and avoid reacting emotionally.
- Issues need to be prioritized. When reaching an impasse on one, park it for a while and go on to the next.
- Take breaks whenever you feel the need. Do not attempt to fight fatigue.
- Refrain from bluffing, and use only data you can prove. Imagine the embarrassment and loss of face that could result in being discovered.
- Last and final offers should mean exactly what they say.
- Understand and use body language as a communication tool for your advantage.

SOLE SOURCE TACTICS   Negotiating with a *sole source* can provide a measure of challenge. As long as your organization is able to maintain its objectives from a marketing perspective, you will likely find little to negotiate. Typically, sharing the risk in new product development or distributing the burden of inventory will produce some benefit to both parties. However, if profitability becomes significantly impacted through changing market costs or products reaching their end of life, your organization may want to initiate steps to avoid financial loss prior to discontinuation. In this case, you and the supplier will need to work closely together to monitor the profitability for both sides and make recommendations regarding the timing of any changes in terms and conditions.

Documenting the Negotiation

It is important to properly document negotiation activities so that personnel unfamiliar with the specifics of the project will be able to clearly understand what occurred should the need arise. Documentation should be approached from two points: first, documenting the negotiation plan and its objectives and comparing the objectives to actual outcomes as a way of determining the team's effectiveness; and second, providing an executive summary of the actual negotiation so that auditors will be able to assess its impact, and approving authorities will be able to understand what you are requesting.

The negotiation plan should contain information that describes, at a minimum, the team's objectives, its strategy, and the strengths and weaknesses of its position, along with a similar assessment of the supplier's position. Often, it is useful to include an opening position and bottom-line (least acceptable) position for each of the key objectives. Your team should also prepare likely scenarios for the supplier's position. When the negotiation has concluded, you should review the original planning document and describe where the objectives were met and where they fell short.

The executive summary should describe the objectives of the contract and the negotiation, what was achieved in relation to initial goals, the cost and benefits to the organization, and any alternative courses of action that may be possible. Any future follow-up action should also be included in this summary.

Summary

Conducting successful negotiations requires careful planning and organization. As a first step in your planning process, you should prepare an assessment of current market conditions for the industry and organizations with whom you will be engaged. Assessing the negotiating environment includes developing an evaluation of the competitiveness of the particular industry and what impact you and your supplier have in that market. Be sure to consider aspects such as overall industry capacity, pricing trends, availability of substitute products, and other factors that will help establish an understanding of the competitive forces potentially influencing the outcome of your negotiations.

You will also want to look closely at the supplier's situation to assess elements of its current condition that might affect its motivation. What are its financial needs, and how does your organization fit in with them? Similarly, you will want to have a full understanding of the factors influencing your organization. Establish the urgency of the requirements and a prioritized set of needs and understand any significant internal constraints. Early involvement in the contracting process will assist your efforts to affect a favorable outcome.

If the outcome of the negotiation will significantly impact your organization, you will likely want to form a support team composed of key internal users, a finance representative, and someone from the quality assurance group. With the help of the team, you can then formulate your guiding objectives and strategies using many of the same criteria you used during the supplier selection process.

When it comes time for the actual negotiation, your team should have completed a detailed plan prioritizing needs, outlined roles and responsibilities, selected a location, and discussed the various likely scenarios that might occur and how you will deal with them. You should also consider what negotiating style might produce the best results and what tactics you can use to enhance it.

All of the planning and strategy development should be documented so that others will be able to understand what occurred. Using an executive summary to describe objectives and outcomes will help you gain internal approval and describe any follow-up actions that will be required.

CHAPTER 10

Contract Formation and Administration for Optimum Supplier Performance

C ontract administration officially begins at the time the contract is signed, although the department's involvement may extend into the earlier contract formation phase. Administering contracts to ensure supplier contract compliance and maximum performance is one of the most important responsibilities of the Procurement Department.

The central focal point for contract compliance is meeting the requirements of the internal customer. Procurement departments do not usually have the resources to closely manage the hundreds of suppliers to the organization, nor would it make sense for its staff to even try to do so, since rarely will the Procurement Department be staffed with the same level of expertise as the using or customer department. Instead, you can be best served by relying on your internal customers, those employees and departments directly affected by the supplier's performance, to provide day-to-day operational information such as quality evaluations and on-time delivery reports. Using this information enables you to conduct periodic business reviews with key suppliers to help them understand areas for improvement and how they can best achieve stronger performance. This is the essence of supplier relationship management (SRM), a term coined to describe the activities related to monitoring and improving supplier performance. Integrated with the broader picture will be the Procurement Department's daily tactical activities that revolve around tracking and expediting deliveries as well as responding to supplier-related discrepancies.

This chapter summarizes the broader concepts of contract administration, including how the procurement professional can establish proactive measures to ensure supplier compliance and internal customer satisfaction within the framework of existing contracts. In doing so, the chapter also reviews how to deal with problems relating to supplier payments and how change orders can affect contract terms and conditions.

Managing Contract Compliance

The procurement manager routinely oversees the management of contract administration and supplier relations. Part of this responsibility is to ensure that the terms and conditions of the contract are followed, especially where they may diminish the value of the contract to the organization. Another part involves the continuing effort to improve supplier performance and to maintain strong business relationships. While no procurement professional can be an expert in all areas of the profession, you should constantly strive to provide solid advisement and procurement authority to your organization's suppliers. Handling potential problems early and in a proactive mode will go a long way to defusing problems before they become major issues.

Post–Purchase Order/Contract Administration

Much of the Procurement Department's responsibility lies in the ongoing management of the purchase order (PO) or contract after it has been negotiated and placed with the supplier. This is very much an organic process that takes on a life of its own, which often involves lots of routine work that generally fills much of the tactical buyer's day. To be successful, the procurement professional must set a firm, proactive approach to monitoring day-to-day activities within the context of continuing fiduciary due diligence, ensuring that internal users receive the benefit of the bargain in good faith. Success will also depend in large part on the effective involvement of the using department and those most familiar with the specific requirements of the contract.

The following section reviews many of the routine duties associated with the activities of managing supplier performance to ensure that their contractual obligations are being met.

ENSURING SUPPLIER PERFORMANCE Administering any contract can be a complex, dynamic process requiring skillful attention to detail and thorough familiarity with its objectives and terms and conditions. Therefore, it is important for your internal customers to understand that it is their responsibility to inform you or your staff of any discrepancies or areas of dissatisfaction with the supplier's performance. You may be able to help your customers understand the administration process by reviewing some key contract administration principles with them prior to the contract's actual implementation:

- Clearly define roles and responsibilities in advance so that you can work as a coordinated team.
- Ensure that the Procurement Department is the central body for contract-related communication.
- Read and understand the contract's requirements, if you have not been involved in the formation process. Be certain that the actions you take are in line with its terms and conditions.
- Develop a checklist of areas for periodic review to avert potential problems early.
- Maintain a sound, businesslike relationship with the supplier, instituting clear lines of communication and conflict resolution and avoiding reactive positions.
- Anticipate areas that may require change and develop an understanding of potential cost implications.
- Resolve problems quickly before they escalate or create major issues.

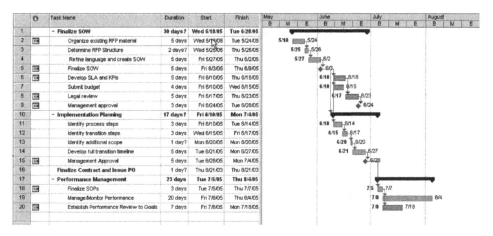

	O	Task Name	Duration	Start	Finish
1		− Finalize SOW	30 days?	Wed 5/18/05	Tue 6/28/05
2	▦	Organize existing RFP material	5 days	Wed 5/18/05	Tue 5/24/05
3		Determine RFP Structure	2 days?	Wed 5/25/05	Thu 5/26/05
4		Refine language and create SOW	5 days	Fri 5/27/05	Thu 6/2/05
5	▦	Finalize SOW	5 days	Fri 6/3/05	Thu 6/9/05
6	▦	Develop SLA and KPIs	5 days	Fri 6/10/05	Thu 6/16/05
7		Submit budget	4 days	Fri 6/10/05	Wed 6/15/05
8	▦	Legal review	5 days	Fri 6/17/05	Thu 6/23/05
9	▦	Management approval	3 days	Fri 6/24/05	Tue 6/28/05
10		− Implementation Planning	17 days?	Fri 6/10/05	Mon 7/4/05
11		Identify process steps	3 days	Fri 6/10/05	Tue 6/14/05
12		Identify transition steps	3 days	Wed 6/15/05	Fri 6/17/05
13		Identify additional scope	1 day?	Mon 6/20/05	Mon 6/20/05
14		Develop full transition timeline	5 days	Tue 6/21/05	Mon 6/27/05
15	▦	Management Approval	5 days	Tue 6/28/05	Mon 7/4/05
16		Finalize Contract and Issue PO	1 day?	Thu 9/21/03	Thu 9/21/03
17		− Performance Management	23 days	Tue 7/5/05	Thu 8/4/05
18	▦	Finalize SOPs	3 days	Tue 7/5/05	Thu 7/7/05
19	▦	Manage/Monitor Performance	20 days	Fri 7/8/05	Thu 8/4/05
20	▦	Establish Performance Review to Goals	7 days	Fri 7/8/05	Mon 7/18/05

FIGURE 10.1   Example of a Timeline for Contract Development

During the course of the contract, and for supplier performance in general, you and core members of the cross-functional supplier management team will likely want to monitor a number of key deliverables for specific performance. Some of the elements critical to successful contract fulfillment include compliance with cost objectives, on-time delivery performance, adherence to quality requirements, and accurate reporting. Specifics on how these elements can be controlled and periodically reviewed by the affected groups are covered in the section on supplier relationship management later in this chapter.

Often, a project management approach to contract compliance can establish a framework and timetable to monitor performance, providing a useful reporting mechanism as well. Project management is the application of knowledge, skills, tools, and techniques to a set of activities in order to meet the detailed requirements of the project.

Figure 10.1 shows a simple timeline approach using a *Gantt chart* that graphically tracks the progress of the project by illustrating on a calendar when events are scheduled to take place, how long they will take, and when they are expected to complete. The Gantt chart also shows the relationship between events, especially which events must complete first before others that are dependent upon them can start. You may also find this method useful for monitoring project management improvement programs.

Maintaining a complete file of reports and correspondence covering actual supplier performance will be useful for conducting subsequent business reviews and for resolving any disputes should they arise. Include in these files progress reports, notes from important meetings, change and amendment history, a log of corrective action issues, and customer feedback. In the case of ongoing supplier monitoring, records will include the history and details of periodic business reviews and documentation of ongoing improvements.

PROCESSING CHANGE ORDERS   Having to process change orders is a typical event during the course of any contract. Formal change orders involving revised specifications or additional requirements are monitored and documented through processes known by a number of names, such as *engineering change order (ECO)* or *specification change order (SCO)*. Usually, these changes are tracked and recorded by the Document Control Department or through the quality engineering group. However, your responsibility will likely include negotiating the additional cost and effect on the delivery timetable with the supplier.

In addition to engineering-generated changes, amendments to the contract are sometimes required to reflect an additional scope of work, such as adding new areas of responsibility to the supplier's duties or redefining a completion timeline or milestone.

A seasoned procurement practitioner is aware of the likelihood of ongoing changes to the contract and negotiates the process in advance, maintaining an awareness of the competitive bidding trap (discussed in Chapter 2) where the supplier underprices the initial contract with an expectation of added profit margin from the inevitable change orders once the contract has been agreed to by the parties. Generally, the mechanics of implementing changes, including allocating their financial impact, can be outlined in the initial contract so that the delivery process works smoothly. To a large extent, this is the responsibility of the Procurement Department representative leading the contract negotiation team and is well facilitated when following the guidelines for internal customer review just provided.

PRICE ADJUSTMENTS   Firm-fixed-price contracts require pricing adjustments only when changes in the specifications or scope of work occur. However, many contracts—especially those developed in government procurement—require price adjustments and fee payments based upon a wide range of conditions and the nature of the contract. (We outlined contract types in Chapter 5.) The most common of these are the economic price adjustments required by escalation contracts or changes in the rates determining baselines in the cost-plus contracts. You will have already defined how and when such changes can be applied in the initial contract and will have linked them to a change in a specific index or a predetermined cost factor.

In most circumstances, escalation changes will be documented by changes in predetermined pricing such as the cost of labor (in union environments) or materials. Often, fluctuations in these cannot be known in advance, and so a contract clause will allow for increases (rarely decreases) to the cost basis beyond a preset trigger threshold. Similarly, when procurement is through international sources, contracts may allow for cost fluctuations based on a predetermined currency exchange rate.

Sometimes the cost basis will be adjusted by increases or decreases in specific published indexes governing labor or materials. Transportation rates, for example, are often based on fuel pricing from a published index and passed through to the buyer as a fuel surcharge.

WARRANTY CLAIMS   A *warranty* is a seller's guarantee to the buyer that if the product or materials being sold does not perform as specified, the seller will take a particular remedial action. Most frequently, the remedy will be to replace the products at the seller's expense. The buyer should be aware of the contractual rights granted by a warranty and practice diligence in exercising those rights.

Warranties and limitations of liability are generally the source of much negotiation during the contract formation process. To reduce their unknown financial exposure, suppliers will generally want to limit their warranties to a specific (and narrow) set of conditions and for a limited time. Often, warranty clauses are taken for granted and not specifically negotiated, becoming additional grist for the battle of the order acknowledgement forms.

The Uniform Commercial Code (UCC) specifically allows a seller to disclaim any or all warranties, but it does not provide any specific rules or guidelines as to how the warranty should be disclaimed. Because of this, the buyer must be aware of the actual language being used to reference or convey the warranty in any particular case. Generally, the seller is required to include a statement specifically disclaiming an actual warranty, such as all goods are sold "as is." Terms such as "no warranties, express or implied" are generally insufficient to disclaim a specific warranty.

Sections 2-312 through 2-318 of the UCC cover commercial warranties for goods and products. Under the UCC, warranties fall into two classifications: express warranties and implied warranties. Let's discuss the more important aspects of each of these in more detail:

1. *Express warranties* provide specific assurances regarding the performance of a product or service. Typically, they are explicitly spelled out within the framework of the contract or purchase order. Created by the words or actions of a seller, an express warranty can be provided either through a specific promise or the description of the product. An affirmative statement or a sample of the product can be considered as the basis for a warranty.

2. An *implied warranty* is provided by rule under the UCC simply by offering goods or products for sale, even when there is no mention of how the product will be expected to perform. As its title suggests, the warranty need not be stated; rather, it is implicit in the offer or acceptance by the seller. The intent of this warranty is to allow buyers to purchase goods and products with reasonable assurance that they will meet certain inherent and basic requirements.

    The UCC creates two distinct types of implied warranties: merchantability and fitness for a particular purpose:

    1. *Merchantability* means that the seller implicitly warrants that the product is fit and suited to be used for the ordinary purposes for which it would be purchased. It also implies that it is of average quality and performs the basic functions that may be stated by the manufacturer.

        The UCC does not intend for a seller to create an implied warranty for goods not normally sold in its regular course of business. For example, a manufacturer of molded plastic parts does not create an implied warranty when it sells one of its obsolete molding machines to another business.

    2. *Fitness for a particular purpose* means that if the seller knows (or has reason to know) the intended use by the buyer for the goods being sold, the seller then warrants that the goods will be suitable for that purpose. A seller, therefore, may not knowingly sell a product that will not do the job and then refute responsibility. In effect, this means that the buyer may rely upon the seller's expertise in selecting a suitable product and seek remedy should the product not perform as intended.

        As in the case of merchantability, the seller need only warrant goods that it would convey during the usual course of its business.

Disclaimer of Warranties/Accuracy and Use of Data/Computer Viruses
Although the data found using the Department of Consumer Affairs' Home Page access
systems have been produced and processed from sources believed to be reliable, no
warranty expressed or implied is made regarding accuracy, adequacy, completeness, legality,
reliability or usefulness of any information. This disclaimer applies of both isolated and
aggregate uses of the information. The Department of Consumer Affairs and the Department
of Consumer Affairs' Home Page provide this information on an "AS IS" basis. All warranties
of any kind, express or implied, including but not limited to the IMPLIED WARRANTIES OF
MERCHANTABILITY, FITNESS FOR A PARTICULAR PURPOSE, freedom from contamination
by computer viruses and non-infringement of proprietary rights ARE DISCLAIMED. Changes
may be periodically added to the information herein; these changes may or may not be
incorporated in any new version of the publication. If the use has obtained information from
The Department of Consumer Affairs' Home Page from a source other than The Department
of Consumer Affairs' Home Page, the user must be aware that electronic data can be altered
subsequent to original distribution. Data can also quickly become out-of-date. It is
recommended that the use pay careful attention to the contents of any metadata associated
with a file, and that the originator of the data or information be contacted with any
questions regarding appropriate use. If the user finds any errors or omissions, we encourage
the user to report them to the Department of Consumer Affairs' Home Page.

FIGURE 10.2   Sample Disclaimer of Warranty and Language

© 2004 State of California

DISCLAIMERS As noted earlier, sellers may disclaim warranties in writing if the writing is specific enough to describe the conditions not being warranted. In addition,
the disclaimer needs to be conspicuous and stand out from other portions of the
contract. That is why you will often see disclaimers written in bold or capital letter-
ing. However, the UCC indicates that a buyer must have some recourse if the goods
received are defective or unusable, and so the seller cannot enforce a clause that
takes all the rights away from the buyer.

Figure 10.2 illustrates a liability disclaimer from the state of California's Department of Consumer Affairs' Web page. Under the title Disclaimer of War-
ranties/Accuracy, you'll notice it disclaims express and implied warranties by specific
reference. This disclaimer also uses capital letters that stand out conspicuously to
state the legal requirements of the warranty.

Supplier Relationship Management (SRM)

Contract management also requires the use of SRM methodology, as well. SRM is
the broad process of aligning the goals of your buying organization and the supplier
community, one supplier at a time. Often, this is a process of tactically aligning the
typical variation in processes between several organizations using analysis, collaboration, and jointly developed action plans.

SRM refers to both business practices and software. Its key objective is to improve the processes between an enterprise and its suppliers and enable them to
operate more effectively. For example, consider the benefits of aligning the planning horizons of buying and supplying organizations so that their forecasts and
operational plans coincide.

SRM practices intend to create a common frame of reference that supports effective communication between the organization and its suppliers who are using different business practices and terminology. As a result, SRM increases the efficiency of processes associated with acquiring goods and services, managing inventory, and processing materials.

In its automated format, SRM can be seen as a way of gathering information from multiple procurement systems in order to develop metrics that measure and evaluate supplier performance. Inherent in the measurement process, however, is the discipline of continuous improvement, the methodology for developing and implementing ongoing improvements in business and operational processes to achieve a specific goal. We will discuss the elements of SRM in more detail in Chapter 14.

Tracking and Expediting Deliveries

In the normal course of daily routine, supplier shipments will not always meet their required delivery dates. Sometimes this is due to errors or damages in shipments; other times it is due to factors such as production delays, miscommunication of requirements, or just Murphy's Law. In any event, as the procurement representative you will be required to assist in resolving them and to handle the communications between the supplier and your internal customers. Two of the most frequent situations that will require your intervention, dealing with shipments and expediting orders, are described in this section.

Tracking and Monitoring Shipments

Fortunately, today, most shipping agencies have automated tracking tools that can immediately report the status and whereabouts of virtually any worldwide shipment. Many of these tools can even be accessed through the Web, and likely many of you have already used the FedEx or UPS tracking systems to locate parcels.

Lost and damaged shipments require the submission of a claim in order to obtain reimbursement. You will likely find this process takes several weeks, so it is best to reorder immediately, keeping in mind that unless you specifically requested shipping terms that require the supplier to maintain ownership title of the goods until actual delivery, your organization will take ownership of the goods at the time of shipment, and it will be your organization's responsibility to file the actual claim with the carrier. In most organizations, however, it will be the Traffic or Receiving Department's responsibility to handle the paperwork, and you will only become involved to the extent that corrective action or expediting is required.

Expediting Orders

Expediting refers to the process of following up with suppliers (through some form of direct contact) to accelerate the shipment of orders or to determine the current status of a particular order and when it will be ready for shipment. It may be counterintuitive, but expediting provides no additional value whatsoever to the product or service and simply increases the associated overhead cost.

Expediting, however, can be required as the result of numerous circumstances and is fairly commonly used. In case you are wondering why it is necessary, some of the typical reasons for expediting include:

- **Late production.** You will expect your supplier to communicate with you in situations where your order has not been shipped (or delivered) as expected. You will need to reestablish a delivery date with the supplier, communicate with your internal customer, and determine if there is any way to mitigate the potential damage to your operations. Some situations may require you to follow up further on subsequent shipments to avoid the situation in the future.
- **Rush orders.** There are times and circumstances that will require you to request shipment in less than the normal lead-time cycle. You may be required to negotiate this with the supplier—offering some future value or additional fees as compensation. We once called a supplier to request a rush status be placed on an existing order. When we made the request to the supplier's customer service representative, she broke out in laughter. We asked what was so funny, and she replied, "Which of these six rush orders I have for you would you like me to do first?"
- **Back orders.** There are occasions when a supplier is only able to ship part of the order by the requested time. This is called a *split order*, and the remaining balance is called a *back order*. While your contract or purchase order may prohibit such practice, you may be willing to bend the rules when you need something urgently rather than see the entire shipment arrive late. You will likely want to flag the order so that you can follow up with the supplier prior to the promised date for shipping the balance to be sure you avoid any further delays.

Tips and Techniques

Who's Responsible for Expediting Orders?

Although it is most typical for the Procurement Department to handle expediting as part of the supplier management process, you may want to keep in mind that it is not always the responsibility of the Procurement Department to handle every circumstance that requires expediting. In some organizations, it is up to the using department to manage this, while in others it may be handled by the inventory planners or the Production Control Department, depending on their level of involvement. However, the stand-alone job function and title of expeditor is rapidly disappearing from contemporary organizations, since we are coming to recognize that prevention is more effective than cure.

You may want to consider the methods your organization uses to perform the expediting to ensure you are using the least costly and most effective method. *Status checks*, for example, may be performed today through some form of electronic media, such as e-mail, that will use fewer personnel resources, reserving personal contact for the more critical conditions. When expediting seems to become a way of life, it is important to develop a continuous improvement program to reduce or perhaps eliminate it altogether.

Handling Supplier-Related Deviations

There are many circumstances—serious and minor—when you will find suppliers are unable to perform adequately or are creating errors that require corrective action. In some cases, issues can be resolved amicably with little lasting effect on the relationship; in others, legal recourse and a permanent parting of the ways may be in order.

In this section, you will find a review of some of the most common situations involving deviations and the typical ways of handling them.

Inadequate performance stems from a wide variety of conditions, some easily remedied while others are more critically serious. The simpler issues can be dealt with by the Procurement Department; the more complex ones may require the intervention of legal counsel. Most performance issues encountered are a result of a lack of clarity in the contract language and expectations that are not incorporated into the contract writing.

Contract Breach

Typically, a supplier's *breach of contract* will occur when it is unable or unwilling to perform to the terms and conditions required by the contract within the agreed-upon time frame. In the case of a shipment of nonconforming goods, however, the supplier has the right to cure or remedy any failure in a reasonable amount of time.

The UCC gives the buyer the right to ask the supplier of goods for adequate assurance that it can perform to the contract, should the buyer have reason to suppose that it will be unable to do so. If the supplier does not respond within 30 days, the buyer may then cancel the contract under the principle of *anticipatory breach.*

Similarly, *anticipatory repudiation* occurs in situations where, prior to the time the performance is required, the supplier informs the buyer that it will be unable to perform. This gives the buyer the right to consider the contract breached and act accordingly.

PURCHASERS' REMEDIES   When a supplier breaches the contract, it is quite likely that the buyer will suffer some form of damage. Under the UCC, the buyer has the right to be "made whole" for its loss. Several common categories of damages may be appropriately claimed by the buying organization as a result of loss:

- **Actual damages.** Cover compensation for the real losses that have been incurred in specific circumstances covered by the contract. However, to be recoverable (and enforceable), they must be capable of precise measurement. *Actual damages* might cover, for instance, the loss of an injection molding tool owned by your organization but stored at the supplier's facility.
- **Consequential damages.** The legal definition of *consequential damages* refers to those losses that arise not from the immediate act of the party but in consequence of such act. For the most part, consequential damages are not going to be included in any form of contract for commercial goods.
- **Liquidated damages.** Provide for a predetermined fixed payment amount in the event of a breach of contract. They typically apply only when the actual

damages would have been very difficult or impractical to determine and when the amount of the *liquidated damages* is reasonable. Courts have generally not enforced a liquidated damages clause when it is intended to be punitive or when it is significantly in excess of a reasonable amount of damages that may have been incurred.

- **Incidental damages.** *Incidental damages* cover the reasonable expenses or costs that result from loss or harm, such as the cost of transportation for replacement products.
- **Cover damages.** May be claimed when a contract is breached (e.g., in the case of late delivery), and the buyer must purchase replacement goods at a price higher than that contracted with the supplier. In this case, the buying organization may claim the difference between what it would have paid under the contract and what it actually paid.

PURCHASER'S BREACH   In addition to the supplier's breach, the UCC also covers the purchaser's breach. The procurement organization can breach the contract in a number of ways. For example, breach may occur if the buyer wrongfully rejects a conforming shipment upon receipt or later rejects the shipment having first accepted it. In the case of *latent defects* that do not show up on original inspection, the buyer is obligated to provide adequate time for the supplier to fix the problem once it has been discovered. The buyer may also establish anticipatory repudiation when it informs the supplier that it will be unable to accept the goods.

In the case of a purchaser's breach, the seller may also apply for remedies. Typical remedies available to the seller include:

- **Contract recovery.** The supplier may claim the entire contract value should the buying organization breach, providing that it makes a reasonable and diligent effort to sell the goods to another buyer. Whatever value the supplier may obtain through scrap is discounted from the total amount claimed.
- **Market value.** The seller may claim the difference between the sale at current market value and the sale to the purchaser.
- **Recovery of lost profits.** The supplier may include lost profit in any legal action to recover damages as a result of the purchaser's breach, although calculating that amount may become controversial.
- **Costs.** The seller may recover the cost of selling or disposing of the goods to another party in the event of a purchaser's breach.

Liability Issues

Liability in a commercial environment generally refers to the legal responsibility for the cost of damages. It is the Procurement Department's responsibility to reduce the risk to the organization whenever potential liability exists.

Potential financial liability can be a significant factor for the purchaser when evaluating risk and should be carefully considered during the contract formation process. It is always advisable, when there appears to be potential for significant liability to arise from a contract, to defer to legal counsel for review and the crafting of proper contract language. Similarly, when issues surrounding liability or potential liability actually do arise, it is always advisable to obtain legal advice.

Actual liability can generate from a number of conditions, including, for example, damage to goods during transit, damage from faulty equipment or workmanship, loss of revenue due to associated production delays, loss or damage due to field failure, loss due to the cessation of the supplier's operation or inability to perform, and legal responsibility for violation of public laws and regulations—to list just a few.

Mitigating Loss

The intent of legal language and the UCC is generally to provide for the recovery of actual losses from transactions involving goods and to compensate the party bearing the loss to the extent that it can be made whole again, or restored to its original position. However, documentation becomes critical in order to prove the value of the damages and to ensure adequate recovery.

This section highlights some specific factors you should be aware of regarding mitigation of loss.

LIMITATIONS The supplier has the right to limit liability for consequential damages and incidental damages in the contract. You need to be certain that the limitations specified are favorable to your organization.

HOLD HARMLESS A common clause in contracts is designed to protect the parties from the responsibilities for damages incurred through the violation of any laws or regulations. The term *hold harmless* refers to the language that places the liability for damages on the other party. Supplier contracts will often require that the buyer hold them harmless from any third-party suits arising from the performance of its obligations. This is especially contentious in cases where product liability due to loss or injury is involved and where each party has an obligation to indemnify the others when they do not contribute to the liability. It is not uncommon for parties to determine in advance the extent of each party's responsibility and subsequent liability.

Manufactured goods are also subject to the *Consumer Product Safety Act*, which requires reporting of any hazards to the public and to the Consumer Product Safety Commission. It also requires the recall of potentially unsafe products, so the buyer needs to be sure that there is adequate financial compensation when any recall is necessitated by a supplier's defective parts or material.

The supplier should also be required to hold the buyer harmless from any liability arising out of its violation of patent or copyright laws. Since this is an area of great complexity and potentially great financial liability, it is critical that the buying organization obtain maximum indemnification, including the requirement that the supplier defend it from any infringement suits.

INDEMNIFICATION, INSURANCE, AND BONDS Another way to limit liability is by requiring suppliers to carry and show proof of adequate insurance when the potential for loss is very high so that your organization receives proper *indemnification* should a loss occur. Most important, of course, is the coverage for worker's compensation, and it is common for buyers to require suppliers that work on-site to maintain certain levels of coverage.

Chances are good that your company carries insurance coverage for its property in the event of fire, theft, or loss due to certain natural disasters. You should determine if this coverage applies to property owned by your organization but stored at a supplier's facility (e.g., tooling), and if not, you should require that the property be insured in your organization's favor in the event of loss or damage.

Numerous forms of bonds (a form of insurance) are also available to ensure against contract performance failure, such as when the supplier fails to pay its subcontractors for labor or materials or when the supplier fails to meet the terms of the contract altogether.

TRANSPORTATION AND TITLE   Risk of loss often depends on when the title to goods passes from the supplier to the buyer. The general rules covering ownership are specified in *Incoterms*, the widely accepted criteria for defining the passage of title in international trade. Procurement departments are generally aware of these terms and designate them on the face of their purchase orders. The Incoterms website provides a graphic view of how these terms affect title and thus risk of loss. For more detailed information, you may want to visit the International Chamber of Commerce (ICC) website at www.iccwbo.org.

Resolving Errors and Omissions

There are a myriad of problems that arise during the life of a typical PO or contract, generating a significant amount of supplier management duties for the Procurement Department. Here are some of the more routine problems you will encounter and be required to resolve.

MISTAKES   Most errors in order fulfillment come as a result of inaccurate, incomplete, or erroneous descriptions on the PO. When you consider the sheer volume of manual transactions performed by the Procurement Department, this should come as no surprise. How to eliminate these errors has plagued procurement professionals around the world. Seemingly, the only cure will arrive when all routine transactions are automated through computer-based systems. While mistakes are part of human nature, the UCC does not recognize the concept of an honest mistake. Case law dealing with court decisions regarding mistakes does not appear to provide a unanimous and clear set of guidelines. However, there a few principles that might be useful to understand:

- For the most part, the courts do not seem inclined to review mistakes that are not considered *material* to the purchase.
- When a supplier acts in reliance of a purchase order that is erroneous, by manufacturing the wrong item, for example, the buyer will likely not be granted any relief. This is called a *unilateral mistake*.
- If a mistake made by the buyer is so obvious that it reasonably should have been discovered by the supplier, relief will usually be granted.

SHIPMENT   Losses due to shipment errors or damages are so common in most organizations that it is often considered a standard element of cost. Indeed, in some organizations thefts during shipment can create a major problem. Despite the efforts of the best minds in logistics, it appears that this issue will continue.

However, there are some specific ways that you can minimize the risk of loss or damage in shipment. They include the following:

- Use a third-party logistics provider to leverage greater volumes for improved service and faster delivery.
- Specify terms that pass title to your organization only upon delivery to your facility. Keep in mind that the passage of title and who pays the freight are two separate specifications.
- Specify your own packaging requirements.
- Require shipment of the entire order prior to payment.

PRICING AND PAYMENT ISSUES　It has been said that the best way to maintain good supplier relations is to pay them on time. It has also been said that the more an organization owes to another, the greater the importance of servicing it becomes. Clearly, we are dealing with a double-edged sword.

It is equally important to pay suppliers in accordance with the contract as it is to refuse unwarranted and unjustified advance payments. Payments should always be made in accordance with some clearly defined event, such as receipt of goods or achievement of a specific milestone. Keep in mind that it is typical practice to invoice buyers upon shipment. If the shipment takes 10 days to arrive and you are on payment terms of net 30 days, you can improve your organization's cash position by as much as 33 percent through payment terms predicated on the receipt of the goods and not just the invoice.

In many organizations, the rework generated by inaccurate or incomplete invoices can result in horrendous added costs. Eliminating these problems should be a key focus for continuous improvement. One company we know of rejects about 30 percent of the incoming invoices due to errors in pricing or in simply failing to include the PO number so that payment can be tied to a specific order. With volumes in excess of 5,000 invoices per month, you can imagine the additional cost this generates.

Tips and Techniques

It is standard practice in most organizations to pay suppliers for returned materials and then wait until a credit memo is issued to the buyer. Unfortunately, many organizations fail to recognize who needs to do the follow-up to ensure that the credit is actually issued. If you are in a position to write procurement procedures, be sure to include this step; otherwise, you may have no assurance that the credit has actually been issued.

Overages can also present billing problems. Does your organization have a clearly defined policy for the percentage or value of overruns that are acceptable? Is it prominently displayed on the face of your PO? If not, you are an easy target for cost overruns due to an overly aggressive sales agent.

Here are some of the other issues with payments you will likely encounter:

- **Late payments that generate credit holds**. Payments are often delayed by a manual sign-off process or invoices are incorrectly entered into the accounts payable system or, worse, lost.
- **PO and receiving documents cannot be matched.** Often, the supplier uses one nomenclature or part number while your organization uses another. Aligning the two systems can pay off for both.
- **Invoices and POs do not match due to price variations.** This can be avoided through the use of automated catalogs and through buyer diligence in obtaining quotes prior to placing the order.

Resolving Supplier Conflicts

Conflicts are normal in any relationship. How you resolve your conflicts, however, can determine the quality of your relationship with suppliers. Through the judicious use of continuous improvement processes, you may be able to significantly reduce them and so foster even better relationships with your suppliers.

Best practices in contract compliance require a highly evolved, proactive approach to conflict resolution. To accomplish this, you must have precise and legally compliant documentation of your processes. You should review a number of key areas regularly to determine how well actual processes conform to standard operating procedures and legal requirements. Some specific areas for your attention such as contract modifications, rejection of nonconforming goods, termination, and dispute resolution are outlined in the following section.

CONTRACT MODIFICATIONS   Modifications and changes to a contract will likely occur throughout its life to fit changing requirements and market conditions. A modification, under the UCC, is typically treated differently from the original contract formation and does not require the presence of some of the key factors, such as consideration, that must be evident during the initial formation phase.

In the event that both parties are at general odds regarding the terms and conditions of a particular contract, they may simply decide to rescind it and renegotiate a new one. If it is discovered that a mutual mistake or fraud has occurred, the court may decide that reforming the contract is in the best interest of both parties.

EVALUATION AND ACCEPTANCE OR REJECTION OF GOODS   The buyer typically reserves the right to inspect all goods and to accept or reject them in accordance with the terms of the contract. Once the buying organization accepts the goods, however, it is generally not allowed to later reject them for quality or for quantity. Payment for goods does not evidence acceptance, though, so the buyer that subsequently rejects material in accordance with the contract has the right to recover payment.

Goods that are received and subsequently rejected may be returned. However, once accepted by word or deed (e.g., actual usage), then the goods cannot be subsequently rejected. As noted earlier in the chapter, a supplier generally has the right to remedy (through rework or replacement) nonconforming goods within a reasonable period of time and at its own cost. The buyer also has a duty to help mitigate the loss if there is a reasonable way of using the goods in another application or at a downgraded price.

The UCC requires that the buying organization provide the seller with timely notice of its intention to reject nonconforming goods and, if the seller does not act within a reasonable period of time, gives the buyer the right to return the goods freight collect or to store the goods in a public warehouse and charge for storage fees.

CONTRACT TERMINATION   Typically, contracts are terminated when both parties have fulfilled their obligations. However, contracts can also be terminated for the convenience of the buying organization (if such rights exist in the contract) but usually require that all reasonable costs incurred by the seller up to the cancellation point are borne by the buyer.

Contracts can also be terminated for cause and canceled as a result of breach. An inexcusable delay can result in contract termination, unless the delay was caused by uncontrollable events (*force majeure*). There are also occasions when one party can be excused from a contract because performance becomes commercially impracticable, such as when raw material supplies are unavailable. To be so excused requires some relatively stringent conditions, and these are probably best reviewed by legal counsel. However, the simple fact that a supplier is losing money is not sufficient cause to terminate a contract.

Often, a buyer will discover that a particular supplier is having deep-rooted financial problems. If these problems continue, they are quite likely to result in service cuts and diminished quality. It is possible that the buying organization may be willing to assist by offering progress payments based on the level of completion of the products or services or even to pay for and take ownership of the material prior to their completion.

Federal bankruptcy laws do not allow for a buying organization to cancel its contract simply on the basis of the bankruptcy filing, so the rules covering anticipatory repudiation do not apply. The law, however, does allow the supplier to choose which contracts it intends to complete and which ones it will cancel.

It is also not unusual for a contract to be terminated by mutual agreement or suspended for specific periods of time. As long as both parties agree, it is perfectly acceptable to do so.

DISPUTE MEDIATION AND ARBITRATION   When parties are unable to reach agreement on how to administer a particular aspect of their contract, they often turn to third-party sources for resolution. Many of these avenues are outside the formal court system.

Mediation is the most commonly used method outside of the court system for reaching settlement in a dispute. Contracts often contain a clause requiring mediation when the two parties cannot agree on a solution. Generally, the mediation is conducted by a facilitator selected with the approval of both parties. Keep in mind, however, that mediation is not legally binding on the parties.

Arbitration is a similar process but one that does render a binding judgment that can be later enforced in court. Typically, arbitrators have either a legal background or a strong technical and business background in the matter being submitted.

Arbitration tends to be less expensive than court systems since the same rules of evidence will not apply.

CHOICE OF LAW   When a dispute requires resolution, the question of jurisdiction becomes important: What law or rules should apply? What specific court and location should hear the case? Obviously, this could have a significant impact on the outcome or decision, so *choice of law* or legal venue is typically cited as part of the terms and conditions. The clause states the jurisdiction (in the United States, it is typically a state) that governs and in which disputes must be resolved. *Warning:* Since only a small fraction of purchases actually end in court litigation, you may think including this clause is unimportant. But be careful—if you use the supplier's terms and you *do* encounter a dispute requiring third-party resolution, you may be traveling to the supplier's location.

Summary

Forming and administering contracts is one of the key competencies of the procurement professional. In this chapter we reviewed how you can best manage contract compliance and what potential value this brings to the organization. Post–purchase-order monitoring goes a step beyond the simple administration of the contract and includes ensuring compliance by working to achieve continuous improvement and an atmosphere of collaboration with your suppliers.

There is, of course, much routine work to be dealt with, as well. In administering contracts, the Procurement Department is also responsible for processing change orders and the daunting task of negotiating the additional pricing for those changes when the supplier already has been awarded the business. In addition, the Procurement Department is responsible for administering price adjustments on cost-plus contracts and reviewing claims for additional fees or increases in percentages.

Monitoring warranties, filing claims, and processing returns is another of the Procurement Department's routine tasks, which, under common circumstances, adds a great deal of value and support to the internal customer. Along with this, the Procurement Department handles the tracking and monitoring of the ongoing processes for expediting deliveries and maintaining on-time delivery performance.

There are a number of circumstances in which suppliers will be likely to create contract breaches, and the Procurement Department is charged with resolving them. Along with this goes the task of resolving conflicts through a variety of avenues such as arbitration and mediation.

CHAPTER 11

Project Management

P *roject management* is regarded as the discipline of defining and achieving objectives while optimizing the use of resources such as time, money, people, materials, energy, and space over the course of a project. A project can be defined as a set of activities of finite duration.

Project management is quite often the responsibility of an individual project manager. This individual seldom participates directly in the activities that produce the end result, but rather strives to maintain the progress and the productive mutual interaction of various parties in such a way that overall risk of failure is reduced or eliminated. Many projects characterized as complex span both functions, and processes within and between business enterprises are managed by cross-functional project teams.

The Five Project Management Processes

The *Project Management Body of Knowledge (PMBOK)* is a collection of processes and knowledge areas generally accepted as best practice within the project management discipline. The organization that maintains and advances project management education and the body of knowledge is the *Project Management Institute (PMI)*.[1]

The PMBOK recognizes five basic process groups and nine knowledge areas typical of almost all projects. The basic concepts are applicable to projects, programs, and operations. The five basic process groups are:

1. Project initiation
2. Project planning
3. Project execution
4. Project controlling
5. Project closeout

These processes are linear; that is, they follow one another. The project leader should understand that many of these processes overlap and interact throughout a project or phase. "Neat" boundaries between these processes do not, in reality, exist. Nonetheless, project management processes are typically described in these terms:

Inputs: Documents, plans, designs
Tools and techniques: Mechanisms applied to inputs
Outputs: Documents, products

PMI provides a knowledge framework for the cross-functional and process management skills required to deliver a successful project and has organized nine broad project management knowledge areas:[2]

1. Project integration management
2. Project scope management
3. Project time management
4. Project cost management
5. Project quality management
6. Project human resource management
7. Project communications management
8. Project risk management
9. Project procurement management

The Unique Character of Projects

Projects differ from typical organizational operations activities in that *projects* are characterized as oriented to a single goal; they are of finite duration, employ precision coordination of a set of interrelated activities, and are—in the end—unique. Operations activities and events, on the other hand, are characterized as ongoing or repetitive (see Figure 11.1).

Managing projects requires great skill and knowledge not only of the many technical aspects of project management, but a keen awareness of individual and organizational behavior. The competencies required of project managers as well as members of a project team make project management a challenging endeavor (see Figure 11.2). Running a successful project has often been likened to leading and playing in an orchestra.

Projects are a means of organizing activities that cannot be addressed within an organization's normal operational limits. Projects are often utilized as a means of achieving an organization's strategic plan, whether the project team is employed by the organization or is a contracted service provider.

The five project management processes identified by the Project Management Institute serve as the foundation for an understanding of the elements that help to define a successful project and project management. These processes follow the span of the *project life cycle* (see Figure 11.3).

The project management processes may be viewed as a closed loop system, with process spanning activities focused on ongoing project risk assessment and mitigation, as well as continuous quality process improvement.

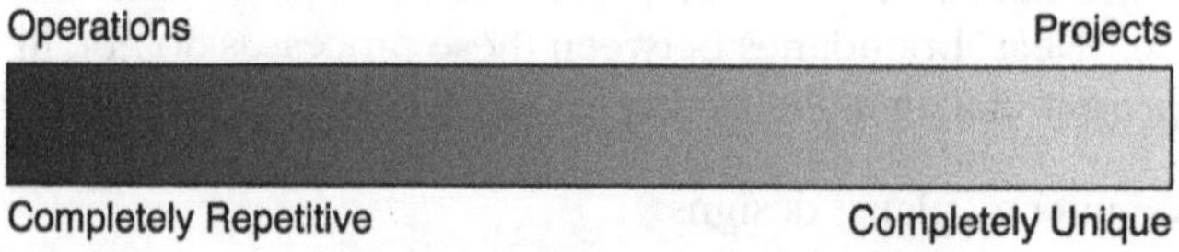

FIGURE 11.1   Operations versus Project Management Characteristics

FIGURE 11.2   The Challenging Project Management Environment

Stage One: Initiating a Project

The purpose of project initiation is to begin to define the overall parameters of a project and establish the appropriate project management and quality environment required to complete the project.

Development of the project charter is a pivotal starting point for the project, establishing the project definition statement that will serve as the foundation for all future efforts. The completion of this process is marked by the project kick-off meeting, in which the project manager presents the project charter. Successful projects begin with a detailed project definition that is understood and accepted by stakeholders. Putting everything down in writing helps ensure a commitment among project team members and between the team and the customers or stakeholders.

As part of project initiation, an initial project plan is developed, which consists of the *project charter*, cost, scope, schedule, and quality documents, and a preliminary risk identification list. These documents, once approved, ensure a consistent understanding of the project, help to set expectations, and identify resources

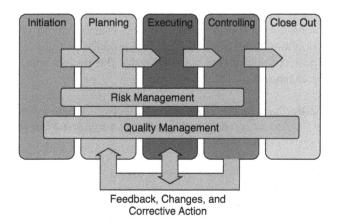

FIGURE 11.3   The Interrelationship among Elements of the Project Management Process

necessary to move the project to the next level of detailed planning. Potential problems are identified and ranked in importance so that they can be addressed early in the project.

Also during project initiation, a high-level project schedule is developed as the road map to more detailed project planning and project execution and control. This high-level schedule will be refined over time and will serve as the primary source of information regarding project status and progress. An accurate, realistic, and complete milestone schedule, rigorously maintained, is essential to the success of a project.

Sponsorship by management of the project must be confirmed or gained during project initiation. Having a project sponsor and securing approval early in the project management life cycle helps to ensure a commitment to the project.

This phase consists of the following processes:

- Prepare for the project: The project sponsor and initial project team are identified and work with the project manager to create the project charter.
- Define cost/scope/schedule/quality (CSSQ): The project manager, along with the project team, define the scope of the project and identify the preliminary budget, high-level schedule, and quality standards to complete the project.
- Perform risk identification: The project manager and project team begin to identify and document any risks or critical path constraints associated with the project.
- Develop the initial project plan: The project manager and project team identify all stakeholders, document their involvement in the project, develop means of communicating with them, and compile all documentation created during project initiation to produce the initial project plan.
- Confirm approval to proceed to the next phase: The project manager reviews and refines the business case, secures resources required for project planning, and prepares the formal acceptance criteria package for review and approval by the project sponsor.

The Project Charter

The project charter is a tool to obtain commitment from all affected groups and individuals associated with a specific project. It is a communication vehicle that can be referenced throughout all phases of the project. It provides a quick reference and overview of the project and lays the foundation for the project structure and how the project will be managed.

> *The Project Charter can be described as the agreement between the organization providing the product or service, and the customer organization requesting and receiving the project deliverable.*[3]

The project charter provides a consolidated and summary-level overview of the project. It allows all parties involved in the project (stakeholders) to document the agreed-upon scope and objectives, approach, and deliverables of the project. It also, at the outset of the project, documents the agreed-upon communications plans, control mechanisms, and responsibilities of team members. In other words, the project

TABLE 11.1   Relationship of Project Management Processes to the Project Charter

PMI PMBOK Process Areas	Location in Project Charter
Initiating	Project Purpose, Project Scope, Project Objectives
Planning	All sections
Executing	Project Deliverables and Quality Objectives, Stages, Project Schedule, Project Effort
Controlling	Project Control
Closing	Stages, Project Control

Source: James D. Reeds, Project Management Course, *Masters in Supply Chain Management Program,* University of San Diego: Supply Chain Management Institute, June 2003.

charter is a first-step communications tool within the project planning environment. It is an agreement that defines partners and external stakeholders; the project management framework to be used on the project; roles, responsibilities, accountabilities, and activities of the team members; management commitments (specifically in terms of communications and control); and the empowerment framework.

The project charter is the first step of project planning, following completion of the project initiation stage. The project charter does not change throughout the project life cycle, but rather is developed at the beginning of the project (immediately following project initiation approval and in the earliest stages of project planning). Further, the project charter can effectively serve to integrate all five stages of the project management process (see Table 11.1).

Stage Two: Project Planning

The basic steps in effective project planning require that a project team:[4]

Define the project scope. The project manager and the project team develop the statement of work, which identifies the purpose, scope (boundaries), and deliverables for the project and establishes the responsibilities of the project team.

Develop a risk management strategy. The project team evaluates the likely obstacles and creates a risk mitigation strategy for balancing costs, schedule, and quality.

Build a work breakdown structure. The team identifies all the tasks required to build the specified deliverables. The scope statement and project purpose help to define the boundaries of the project.

Identify task relationships. The detailed tasks, known as work packages, are placed in the proper time sequence.

Estimate work packages. Each of these detailed tasks is assigned an estimate for the amount of labor hours and equipment needed, and for the duration of the task.

Calculate initial schedule. After estimating the duration of each work package and figuring in the sequence of tasks, the team calculates the total duration of the project. (This initial schedule, while useful for planning, may need to be revised further down the line.)

Assign and level resources. The team adjusts the schedule to account for resource constraints. Tasks are rescheduled in order to optimize the use of people and equipment used on the project.

The Importance of the Work Breakdown Structure (WBS)

Once the project's scope has been determined, risk assessment has been performed, and the project has received approval from the firm's project sponsors, project planning may be initiated. A proven approach to effective project planning is the development of a project *work breakdown structure (WBS)*. The work breakdown structure identifies all the tasks in a project; in fact, a WBS is sometimes referred to simply as a task list. It turns one large, unique, perhaps mystifying piece of work—the project—into many small, manageable tasks. The WBS uses outputs from project definition and risk management and identifies the tasks that are the foundation for all subsequent planning. Work breakdown structures can be set up in either graphic or outline form, as shown in Figure 11.4. In either example, they list the various tasks involved.

The graphic WBS gives a picture that makes it easy to understand all the parts of a project, but the indented (list) WBS is more practical because you can list hundreds of tasks. The WBS clarifies and provides necessary details for a number of project management activities. Firms that standardize project management quickly identify similar types of projects and build WBS templates as a tool for their project managers. Building a WBS helps to:

- Provide a detailed illustration of project scope.
- Monitor progress.
- Create accurate cost and schedule estimates.
- Build project teams.

A project can best be understood by a thorough understanding of its parts. The work breakdown structure breaks the project down into many small, manageable tasks called work packages. The process of deciding who will perform these tasks and how they will be arranged provides the structure for the actual work of the project.[5] Without a well-defined and thought-through work breakdown structure, a project runs the risk of becoming disorganized, with the likely result that important tasks will be misscheduled, underallocated, or overlooked altogether.

After consulting the project's WBS, the next step in project planning is to identify *task relationships*.

The sequence in which detailed tasks—work packages—are performed is determined by the relationship between the tasks. This is best accomplished by establishing a link between an individual task's predecessor tasks and successor tasks. Scheduled through time, associating the sequence of a project's tasks with predecessor and successor relationships will provide a *project network diagram* (shown in Figure 11.5).

Network diagrams are commonly called PERT charts. PERT stands for *program evaluation and review technique*, one of the first formal methods developed for scheduling projects and programs. PERT relies heavily on network diagrams, so for many people the terms *PERT chart* and *network diagram* are synonymous.

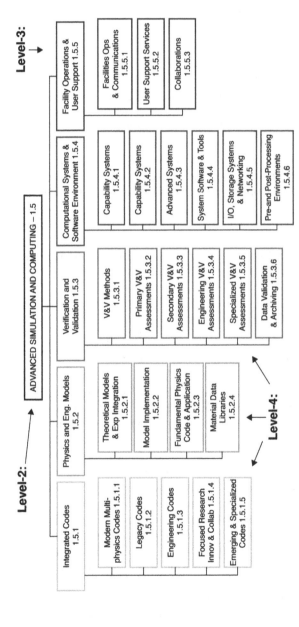

National Work Breakdown Structure

Level-1: DP

Level-2: ASC

Level-3: ASC Subprograms

Level-4: ASC Products

Level-5: ASC Projects

FIGURE 11.4 Example of a Graphic WBS and an Indented (List) WBS

Source: National Nuclear Security Administration (NNSA)

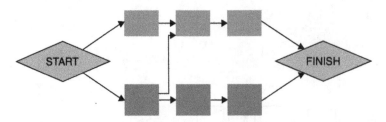

FIGURE 11.5   An Example of a Project Network Diagram

While a network diagram is essential in calculating the project schedule, it can be difficult to decipher on a large project. There is a good alternative that displays both the schedule information and the task relationships.

Gantt charts, named after Henry Gantt, who developed them in the early 1900s, have become the most common method for displaying a project schedule. The great advantage of the Gantt chart is its clarity: The horizontal axis shows the schedule, and the vertical axis lists the work breakdown structure. Figure 11.6 shows an example of a Gantt chart.

The initial schedule represents the combination of task sequence and task duration. But it's called an initial schedule because it hasn't taken into account people and equipment limitations. The next planning step uses the initial schedule as a starting point and balances it against the resources available to the project.

Assignment and Leveling of Project Resources

The goal of resource leveling is to optimize the use of people and equipment assigned to the project. It begins with the assumption that, when possible, it is most productive to have consistent, continuous use of the fewest resources possible. In other words, it seeks to avoid repeatedly adding and removing resources time and again, throughout the project. Resource leveling is the last step in creating a realistic schedule. It confronts the reality of limited people and/or equipment, and adjusts the schedule to compensate.

Every project faces the reality of limited people and equipment (resources). The idea is to avoid both over- and underallocation of project resources. Project overallocation can become serious if project managers believe that they have a large supply of a rare resource, such as the unlimited time of a subject expert. In this example, not only can a project schedule become unrealistic, but the manager may also overload a key resource. "Project managers must do their best to avoid resource peaks and valleys, and try to use a consistent set of people on the project at a consistent rate; this is not only more realistic, it is more efficient. This is because every upswing in resources has a cost."[6]

The process of balancing resource allocations for a project is known as *resource leveling* (see Figure 11.7). Resources are the people, equipment, and raw materials that go into the project. Resource leveling focuses only on the people and equipment; the materials needed for the project are dictated by the specifications and are planned by material planning and control systems, such as *enterprise resource planning (ERP)* information systems.

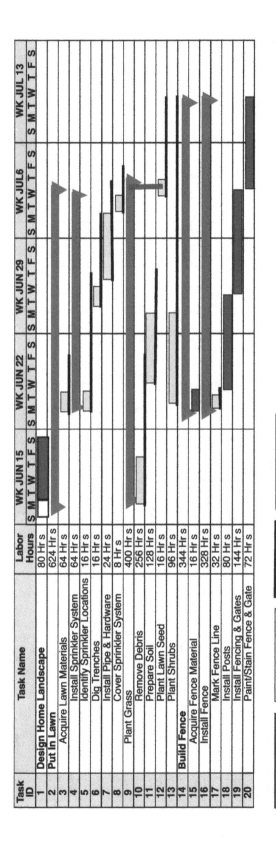

FIGURE 11.6   Example of a Typical Gantt Chart

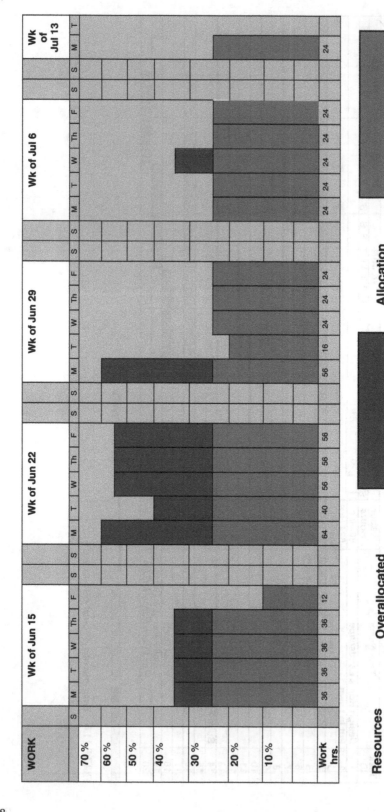

FIGURE 11.7   Resource Leveling

The wise project manager will seek to "level" the project's resources through actions such as consideration of scheduled overtime, additional funding for temporary labor, subcontracting, and so on.

Calculate a Baseline (Initial) Project Schedule

The next step in project planning is to *calculate a baseline (initial) project schedule.* Today, due to the complexity and information requirements of most projects, project management software is employed not only to plan a project schedule, but to continuously replan the project schedule throughout the life of the project. The initial schedule is calculated by using the network diagram and the duration of each work package to determine·the start and finish dates for each task, and so forth for the entire project. Schedule calculation provides a set of detailed schedule data for every work package:

- **Early start.** The earliest date a task can begin, given the tasks preceding it.
- **Early finish.** The earliest date a task can finish, given the tasks preceding it.
- **Late start.** The latest date a task can begin without delaying the finish date of the project.
- **Late finish.** The latest date a task can finish without delaying the finish date of the project.

A powerful project planning tool of the initial schedule is the determination of the project's *critical path.* When outlined on a network diagram, the critical path is the longest path through the network. A project's critical path information is most often portrayed as either a network diagram or as a Gantt chart.[7]

It is important to be able to calculate a project's critical path, and to keep a focus on maintaining control over critical path tasks and time allocations. Not every task on a typical complex project is "critical." Noncritical tasks in a project can in reality fall behind schedule without consequence to the overall on-time success of the project. The importance of the critical path is that it highlights those tasks of a project that cannot fall behind schedule or contribute to unplanned expenditures. In other words, to risk falling behind schedule on any critical path task is to risk falling behind schedule for the entire project.

An example of a critical path is shown in Figure 11.8. As you can see, there are several ways to get from the starting point to the end point. The critical path is calculated as the path that takes the longest amount of time to traverse, in this case A-E-F. The other paths take eight weeks and therefore have an additional week available to complete at the same time as the critical path.

Stage Three: Project Execution

Project execution is typically the part of the life cycle of a project when the majority of the actual work of the project is performed and the majority of the *project budget* is expended. The purpose of project execution is to manage every aspect of the project plan *as work is being performed* to make certain the project is successful. Project execution follows a *project execution plan (PEP)*, which is a key document

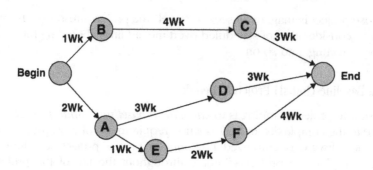

FIGURE 11.8   Calculating the Critical Path

for the management of a project. It is a statement of policies and procedures defined by the project manager and is usually developed by the project manager for the project sponsor/project director's approval. It sets out in a structured format the project scope, objectives, and relative priorities.

Before formally beginning project execution and control, the project team should review recent project status reports and the project plan. At this point in the project, the project plan comprises all deliverables produced during project initiation and project planning:

- Project charter.
- Project quality plan (scope, schedule, quality plan, budget).
- Risk management worksheet.
- Description of stakeholder involvement.
- Communications plan.
- Time and cost baseline.
- Change control process.
- Acceptance management process.
- Issue management and escalation process.
- Project organizational management plan.
- Project team training plan.
- Project implementation and transition plan.

Project execution may be viewed as an outcome of effective project scheduling—and rescheduling. However, the transition is often transparent, as project rescheduling and the actions that flow for rescheduling are prominent in the project execution stage. Thus, a realistic project schedule will emphasize the following ongoing characteristics throughout the project's life cycle:

- Communicate detailed presentation of the work to be done.
- Apply task sequences in the correct order.
- Account for external constraints beyond the control of the team.
- Accomplish on time, given the availability of resources.
- Consider all the objectives of the project (deliverables).

Projects require the engagement of a project team. This team is a composite of individuals with shared values, norms, and standards of behavior, who work together to achieve a common objective. Each team is unique, because it consists of individuals, each with their own personality, knowledge, and experience. The knowledge and experience of the team members are usually considered during the building of the project team, as to complete any task, especially a project, particular skills are required.[8]

Establish a Team Environment

Project team members must learn to work together to achieve project goals. They must recognize that there is more to teamwork than simply having team members feel good about each other. High-performing project teams are disciplined. Team members participate in all required meetings, are willing to suppress their egos for the good of the group, take their assigned tasks seriously, and continuously strive to improve their skills. High-performing project teams are either empowered to make decisions or are included in decision-making processes. This is the essence of project ownership.

There can be at least three levels of team participation (plus the customer level) and involvement that typically work on a project:[9]

1. **The primary group.** These are the team members who work face-to-face and know everyone else in the group. On a project, they are the immediate project team, or task force, whether full time or seconded part time.
2. **The secondary group.** These are the people who work part time on the project and contribute to the work of the primary team, but are not part of the task force. On a project, these are the functions that contribute through the network organization. However, they must be treated as part of the larger project team, if the team is to be effective.
3. **The tertiary group.** These are people who influence the work of the primary and secondary teams, or who are affected by their work, but have no direct contribution. The tertiary group has three parts: those influencing the work of the project, and those affected by the facility delivered or by the product of the facility. The first may consist of family and friends, peer groups, or professional bodies. The second group are people who live in the neighborhood in which the facility is to be built (NIMBYs—not in my back yard) or who will use or operate the facility after it is commissioned, or they may be people whose lives will be irreversibly changed (even by being made redundant) by the operation of the facility.
4. **Customers (consumers).** The final group are the customer(s); the people who will become the recipients of the output of the project deliverables. (Sometimes they are the users, but often not.) The expectations of all of these groups of people must be managed if the project is to be successful, as they have a powerful ability to disrupt.

A problem often encountered by project managers, especially at project startup, is getting a group of individuals to act collectively, to think as a team, and to commit to the idea of both individual and team responsibilities.

The Project Communications Plan

During project execution, the project manager, project team, and stakeholders will share information using a variety of communication mechanisms. These were defined during project planning and may include the following:

- Status meetings
- Status reports
- Memos
- Newsletters
- Executive correspondence
- Meeting notes
- Executive meetings
- Steering committee meetings

This information is collected, stored, and disseminated based upon procedures established and documented in the communications plan. While executing the plan, the project manager must be aware of how the organization will use the information and whether the plan is effective. He or she must be flexible and ready to modify the plan if portions of it are not working as expected or communication needs change within the performing organization.

Using the progress reports prepared by the project team, the project manager should complete a status report to be presented to the project sponsor. In this report, the project manager measures the "health and progress" of the project against the project plan. It is the primary communication vehicle between the project manager and the project sponsor, and it should contain the following information:

- Summary of progress to project schedule—a high-level glance at the major project deliverables, with their intended and actual start and end dates.
- Issues and action items—a running list of open and closed issues, including the name of the person responsible for taking action to resolve them.
- Significant accomplishments—a list of the most important completed tasks, or a description of work done toward their completion.
- Significant planned accomplishments for the following weeks—a description of the most important tasks scheduled for completion during the following weeks.
- Deliverable acceptance log—a running diary of actions taken toward acceptance of deliverables.
- Change control log—a running diary of actions taken toward acceptance of change control.
- Lost time—a description of any situation that occurred that resulted in the project team being unable to perform work.

Other project documents that should be attached to the status report include any change requests, deliverable acceptance forms, meeting notes, and the risk management worksheet. The status report becomes the point of discussion for the status meeting, the regularly scheduled forum in which the project manager presents the project status and discusses issues with the project sponsor.

Project Issues

Managing issues involves documenting, reporting, escalating, tracking, and resolving problems that occur as a project progresses. During project planning, the project manager and project sponsor agreed upon and documented the process for managing issues and included the process in the project plan.

The issue escalation and management process addresses the following:

- How issues will be captured and tracked.
- How issues will be prioritized.
- How and when issues will be escalated for resolution.

Issues are usually questions, suggestions, or problems raised by project team members, including the project manager and customer. They are different from changes in that they do not usually have an immediate impact on the project scope or schedule.

More intractable issues or problems/conflict must be addressed more expeditiously by the project manager and the project team. The same communications tools are used, but the urgency in addressing conflict and its resolution is necessary; otherwise, there will likely be serious risk to the project's success.

Stage Four: Project Controlling

The controlling functions include a broad cross-section of management skills and activities. These cover common areas such as quality control, budget management, risk analysis, acceptance of project deliverables, communications planning, and change management. We explore these aspects in the following section.

Implement Project Quality Control

Quality control involves monitoring the project and its progress to determine if the quality assurance activities defined during project planning are being implemented and whether the results meet the quality standards defined during project initiation. The entire organization has responsibilities relating to quality, but the primary responsibility for ensuring that the project follows its defined quality procedures ultimately belongs to the project manager. Quality control monitoring should be performed throughout the course of the project. Some of the activities and processes that can be used to monitor the quality of deliverables, determine if project results comply with quality standards, and identify ways to improve unsatisfactory performance are described below. The project manager and project sponsor should decide which are best to implement in their specific project environment.

- **Conduct peer reviews.** The goal of a peer review is to identify and remove quality issues from a deliverable as early and as efficiently as possible. A peer review is a thorough review of a specific deliverable, conducted by members of the project team who are the day-to-day peers of the individuals who produced the work.

- **Use quality checklists.** Both the project manager and project team members can create and make use of various checklists to be sure items are not overlooked while a product is being developed. Checklists may be simple hardcopy lists of "things to do," or they may be generated using more formal, electronic-based tools.
- **Maintain and analyze the project schedule.** This activity should never be taken lightly, regardless of the size of the project. Updating the project schedule on a regular basis while keeping a close watch on the timeline and budget is the basic means used to measure the quality of the schedule.
- **Conduct project audits.** The goal of a project audit is to ensure that the quality assurance activities defined in project planning are being implemented and to determine whether quality standards are being met. It is a process to note what is being done well, to identify real or potential issues, and to suggest ways for improvement.

Manage the Project Budget

Part of the project manager's job is to ensure that the project is completed within the allocated and approved budget. Budget management is concerned with all costs associated with the project, including the cost of human resources, equipment, travel, materials, and supplies. Increased costs of materials, supplies, and human resources, therefore, have a direct impact on the budget. The project manager must know the extent of his or her authority to make budget decisions. For example, is the project manager allowed to authorize work that requires additional hours of salaried personnel time, or must employee time extensions go through the same approval process as contract personnel or equipment purchases? Often, the project manager must work closely with fiscal and contract personnel in other divisions to track and control costs. A few budget-related characteristics the project manager should examine each time the schedule is updated include the following:

- **Original contract value.** The original estimated budget (cost) that was approved by the project sponsor.
- **Total approved changes.** The total cost of approved changes as a result of change control.
- **Total current budget.** The sum of the original contract value and the total approved changes. This is the most current approved project budget.
- **Cost to date.** The actual dollars (cost) expended to date on all tasks and materials in the project. The labor costs can be calculated by the scheduling tool based on the time the project manager tracks against the tasks in the project schedule.
- **Estimate to complete.** The dollars (cost) estimated to be expended to complete remaining project tasks. The project manager must verify and assess the impact of team members' revised effort estimates to complete tasks.
- **Forecast total.** The sum of the cost to date and the estimate to complete.
- **Project variance.** The difference between all estimated and all actual dollars. It is calculated by subtracting the forecast total from the total current budget. A positive variance means that the actual cost of the product is less than the budgeted cost. A negative variance means that the actual cost of the product is greater than the budgeted cost.

Project Risk Analysis

Risks are potential future events that can adversely affect a project's cost, schedule, scope, or quality (CSSQ). In prior phases, the project manager defined these events as accurately as possible, determined when they would impact the project, and developed a risk management plan. As the impact dates draw closer, it is important to continue reevaluating probability, impact, and timing of risks, as well as to identify additional risk factors and events. The project manager must continually look for new risks, reassess old ones, and reevaluate risk mitigation plans. The project manager should involve the whole project team in this endeavor, as various team members have their particular expertise and can bring a unique perspective to risk identification and mitigation. As the risk management is integrated into the status reporting process, this review and reevaluation should take place automatically with the preparation of each new status report. The risk management plan needs to be constantly reevaluated.

The Project Change Control Process

During project planning, the project manager, project sponsor, and customer agreed on a formal change control process that was documented and included in the project plan. The change control process describes:

- The definition of change and how to identify it.
- How requests for change will be initiated.
- How requests for change will be analyzed to determine if they are beneficial to the project.
- The process to approve or reject change requests.
- How funding will be secured to implement approved changes.

Although changes can be expected to occur throughout every project phase, any negative effect on the project outcome should be avoidable if the change control process is executed and managed effectively. The need for change is usually discovered during project execution, as actual task work is being performed. It is during execution that the project team may discover their original effort estimates were not accurate and will result in more or less effort being required to complete their work.

Manage Acceptance of Deliverables

The goal of this task is to manage the acceptance of deliverables according to the acceptance criteria management process developed during project planning. The acceptance management process is part of the project plan and documents:

- The definition of "acceptance."
- The criteria that must be met for each deliverable to be considered "acceptable."
- The number and identity of customers designated to be reviewers of each deliverable—typically reviewers are experts in the subject matter the deliverable covers.

- The number and identity of customers designated to be approvers—approvers have the authority to sign the approval form, indicating acceptance.
- The number of business days in which deliverables must be either approved or rejected by the reviewers and approvers.
- The number of times a deliverable can be resubmitted.
- The escalation process that will be followed if a timely decision on approval or rejection of a deliverable is not met.

The acceptance management process must be followed throughout the project.

Execute Communications Plans

During project execution the communications plan is carried out so that required information is made available to the appropriate individuals at the appropriate times, and new or unexpected requests receive a prompt response. Communications must continue to be bidirectional during project execution. The project manager must provide required information to the project team and appropriate stakeholders on a timely basis, and the project team and stakeholders must provide required information to the project manager. The project manager should periodically assemble the project team to review the status of the project, discuss their accomplishments, and communicate any issues or concerns in an open, honest, constructive forum.

Managing Organizational Change

The project manager, with the active participation and support of the customer and project sponsor, must be able to manage the specific activities that will adequately prepare the performing organization for any anticipated changes.

- **People.** Planned workforce changes must be executed in careful coordination with the Human Resource Department.
- **Process.** The redesign of existing business processes affected by the implementation of the product of the project and the development of corresponding procedures must be effectively managed.
- **Culture.** Specific plans were developed based on the extent of the "culture shock" the product of the project was expected to introduce into the performing organization and its business strategy, established norms for performance, leadership approach, management style, approach to customers, use of power, approach to decision making, and employee roles.

Stage Five: Project Closeout

Often, the most neglected project management activity is closing out the project. The reporting and accounting tasks associated with the closeout are not often viewed as being as exciting as developing the product of the project.[10] The real evidence that the project is complete will come from the customer of the project.

Formal acceptance of the finished product or acknowledgment of project phase completion signifies that the work is complete. The project manager must plan for customer acceptance from the very beginning of the project—and acceptance criteria should be found in the project charter itself.

The purpose of the *project closeout stage* is to formally acknowledge that all deliverables produced during project execution and control have been completed, tested, accepted, and approved by the project's customers and the project sponsor(s), and that the product or service the project developed was successfully transitioned from the project team to the performing organization. Formal acceptance and approval also signify that the project is essentially over and is ready for project closeout. Some project closeout activities may be classified as project objectives. These typically include the following:

- Obtain acceptance by the customer of the project deliverables.
- Document lessons learned.
- Facilitate project closure.
- Preserve project records and tools.
- Release resources.

To facilitate project closeout objectives, the project manager should conduct the following activities:

- Notify all project participants of the change in status of the project.
- Communicate product or service improvement ideas that may not have been implemented during the project.
- Detail any open tasks or unresolved issues.

Methods used for the accomplishment of these objectives would include the following:

- **Conduct final status meeting.** Once the product of the project has been successfully transitioned to the performing organization, the project manager should prepare the final status report and conduct the final status meeting. The project schedule must be up-to-date for all completed project and project management life-cycle phases. This is the final opportunity for all participants to confirm that the product of the project has been successfully developed and transitioned. Any outstanding issues or action items must be transitioned from the project team to the performing organization.
- **Preserve project materials, tools, and information.** Storage, archival procedures, and retrieval mechanisms for all aspects of the project should be ensured as a part of acceptance and closeout activities. The project manager must ensure that all documents or records that will be provided with the product are produced. Examples of documentation include:
  - User manuals
  - Online help
  - Assembly or usage instructions

A Key Knowledge Area: Project Procurement Management[11]

The Project Management Institute has adopted a planning view of the knowledge area related to procurement and its fundamental engagement in the project management process. The steps identified in project procurement management follow the project management five-stage process discussed earlier in this chapter. Taken from a contract management overview, the knowledge "steps" are:

1. Plan purchases and acquisitions.
2. Plan contracting.
3. Request sellers' responses.
4. Select sellers.
5. Contract administration.
6. Contract closure.

Plan Purchases and Acquisitions

The "plan purchases and acquisitions" process identifies which project needs can be met by purchasing or acquiring products, services, or results outside the project organization and which project needs can be met by the project team during project execution. This phase includes a review of the risks associated in each make or buy sourcing decision. This also includes a decision on which contract type is most appropriate for the needs of the project. A critical component of the procurement planning process is the formulation of the *contract statement of work* (CSOW). The CSOW is written to be clear, concise, and complete. It includes a description of any collateral services required. The CSOW may be modified as required as it moves through the procurement process until it is incorporated in a signed contract.

Plan Contracting

The approach taken to perform the plan contracting process is to collect information from the following project processes and their documents: the procurement management plan; the CSOW; project make-or-buy analyses; and the project management plan. The use of standard procurement forms will greatly enhance management of the procurement process during the project's life cycle.

EVALUATION CRITERIA   Evaluation criteria are developed and used to rate or score proposals. They can be objective (e.g., "The proposed project manager needs to be a certified project management professional [PMP]") or subjective (e.g., "The proposed project manager needs to have documented previous experience with similar projects"). Evaluation criteria are often included as part of the procurement documents.

The evaluation of bidder response to the contract solicitation can rest on many elements. A few of these are:

- **Understanding of need.** How well does the seller's proposal address the contract statement of work?
- **Overall or life-cycle cost.** Will the selected seller produce the lowest total cost of ownership (purchase cost plus operating cost)?
- **Technical capability.** Does the seller have, or can the seller be reasonably expected to acquire, the technical skills and knowledge needed?

- **Management approach.** Does the seller have, or can the seller be reasonably expected to develop, management processes and procedures to ensure a successful project?
- **Technical approach.** Do the seller's proposed technical methodologies, techniques, solutions, and services meet the procurement documentation requirements or are they likely to provide more than the expected results?
- **Financial capacity.** Does the seller have, or can the seller reasonably be expected to obtain, the necessary financial resources?
- **Production capacity and interest.** Does the seller have the capacity and interest to meet potential future requirements?
- **Business size and type.** Does the seller's enterprise meet a specific type or size of business, such as small business, women-owned, or disadvantaged small business, as defined by the buyer or established by governmental agency and set as a condition of being award a contract?
- **References.** Can the seller provide references from prior customers verifying the seller's work experience and compliance with contractual requirements?
- **Intellectual property (IP) rights.** Does the seller possess the IP rights in the work processes or services they will use or in the products they will produce for the project?

REQUEST SELLERS' RESPONSES   A few of the possible approaches used in the collection of seller's responses are bidders' conferences, advertising, and the development of a qualified bidder's list.

SELECT SELLERS   The select sellers process receives bids or proposals and applies evaluation criteria to select one or more sellers who are both qualified and acceptable. There are many possible selection elements: price, total cost of ownership, technical competencies, single or dual sourcing, sole sourcing, and others. Evaluation tools can employ any of the following techniques: a weighted decision matrix, independent estimates, a formal screening system, contract negotiation, a supplier rating system or matrix, expert judgment, and proposal evaluation scoring. At the end of this process, a contract is awarded to the selected supplier or suppliers.

CONTRACT ADMINISTRATION   Both the buyer and the seller administer the contract for similar purposes. Each party to the contract ensures that both it and the other party meet their contractual obligations and that their own legal rights are protected. The contract administration process ensures that the seller's performance meets contractual requirements and that the buyer performs according to the terms of the contract. Contract administration includes application of appropriate project management processes to the contractual relationship and integration of the outputs from these processes into overall management of the project. Contracts can be amended at any time prior to the close of the contract by mutual consent and negotiation. For more detail regarding contract administration, refer to Chapter 10.

CONTRACT CLOSURE   The contract closure process supports the close project process, since it involves verification that all project work and deliverables were acceptable. The contract closure process also involves administrative activities, such as records maintenance to reflect final results. Early termination of a contract is a special case of contract closure, and can result from a mutual agreement of the parties or from the default of one of the parties. The rights and responsibilities of the parties in the event of an early termination are contained in a termination clause of the contract.

Using a Matrix Model for Project Staffing

Organizational structure is at the very root of human activities, tracing back to our tribal hunting and gathering cultures in which the need for coordinating activities was virtually a matter of survival. The early approach to social organization was hierarchical and likely developed from the need for protection, with its obvious application to military operations.

There has been very little change over the centuries to alter our hierarchical approach to managing affairs until late in the nineteenth century and throughout the twentieth century. During this period new forms of organization were explored, mostly based on behavioral concepts, such as work standardization, bureaucratic organization, and motivational theories.

Matrix organizational structure grew out of this relatively recent focus on efficient management. It has been in use since the early 1950s and widely adopted, so there is a good deal of history and practice for us to draw from.

Matrix Structure

Before concluding this chapter, perhaps it might be useful to examine a common element of the project management organization—the matrix structure.

Traditional management structures are hierarchical. Employees are organized by function and report up to a single manager. Matrix structure is a management *system* in which workers report to more than one person, effectively having two or more supervisors at the same time. In a project environment, where team staffing is relatively fluid, the matrix organizational structure is fairly common.

In a matrix organization, professionals with different types of expertise are brought together to work on a project. They report to the managers of different projects, as well as to functional managers. The idea is to share knowledge and personnel to maximize effectiveness. Figure 11.9 provides an outline of a typical matrix organization.

The Benefits of a Matrix Organization

Matrix staffing offers a number of useful advantages:

- Maximizes resources.
- Facilitates rapid response to change in two or more environments at the same time, in the project and in the functional group.
- Permits more efficient exchanges of information, again through the project organization and the functional group.
- Addresses complexity in tech-driven companies.
- Highly specialized employees and equipment are shared by a number of groups.
- Improves motivation.

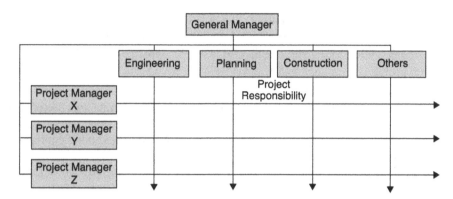

FIGURE 11.9   Example of a Matrix Organization

- Decision making becomes more participatory in groups.
- Each member is valued for the specialized knowledge he or she brings to the group. As a result, members are more likely to experience higher levels of motivation and commitment to the goals of the operations to which they are assigned.
- Leads to better management.
- As functional group leaders, decision makers become more knowledgeable about the day-to-day operations of the company through their project team members.

There are some requirements to employing an effective matrix structure. Clear communication is required so that everyone understands priorities, and there must be open lines between functional and project managers. Collaboration and consensus become the hallmark of the matrix, requiring managers to develop sound teamwork principles and organize their teams for participatory planning and decision making … especially critical in a lean organizations where staffing is at a minimum. It's not uncommon for only one procurement person to work on a team; that person must be prepared to implement all company policy and procedures to guide the project team.

Of course, the key benefit is centralizing and maximizing shared resources. When implemented effectively, this means that functional and line management plan jointly, developing processes for contingencies and unexpected supplier failures.

In the planning phase of the project, the procurement professional must ensure that priorities and expectations are realistically set by the team: establishing clear objectives, defining roles and responsibilities, and identifying required skill sets. The following are just some of the requirements to enable a successful matrix operation:

Individual Capability Requirements
- Ambiguity management: Work effectively in structures without clarity.
- Conflict handling: Resolve conflict with and between stakeholders.
- Leadership accountability: Take responsibility for making decisions.
- Entrepreneurial creativity: Provide entrepreneurial solution across the organization.

- Political intelligence: Navigate the political landscape.
- Relationship intelligence: Develop and maintain a range of stakeholders.
- Stakeholder alignment: Strategically and tactically align stakeholders.

Organizational Capability Areas
- Goal alignment: Ability to align goals with other business units and the organization.
- System and process: How do we reinforce, support, and encourage centralized systems and processes?
- Change management: Acknowledge the need for and the importance of putting steps in place.
- Cultural differences (understanding): Acknowledge that many cultures respond differently to the same incentives/challenges.

Summary

The Project Management Institute (PMI) has developed the project management body of knowledge (PMBOK). It identifies processes and knowledge areas generally accepted as best practice within the project management discipline.

The PMBOK recognizes five basic process groups and nine knowledge areas typical of almost all projects. The basic concepts are applicable to projects, programs, and operations. The five basic process groups are project initiation, project planning, project execution, project controlling, and project closeout.

Procurement in a project management environment has unique challenges in keeping pace with the process. While planning for purchases and contracts is required both in the context of sound business principles and the tightly integrated project, execution to planned timing is paramount. The key is to incorporate best procurement practices into project management activities.

Notes

1. See www.pmi.org/.
2. Project Management Institute, *A Guide to the Project Management Body of Knowledge (PMBOK)*, 4th ed. (Newtown Square, PA: Project Management Institute, 2008).
3. James D. Reeds, Project Management Course, *Masters in Supply Chain Management Program* (University of San Diego: Supply Chain Management Institute, June 2003).
4. Eric Verzuh, *The Fast Forward MBA in Project Management* (New York: John Wiley & Sons, 1999), 101–119.
5. Ibid., 120–152.
6. Ibid.
7. Ibid., 140–152.
8. J. Rodney Turner, Kristoffer V. Grude, and Lynn Thurloway, *The Project Manager as Change Agent: Leadership, Influence and Negotiation* (London: McGraw-Hill, 1996), 80.
9. Ibid., 81.
10. Verzuh, 243.
11. Project Management Institute, 284–310.

PMI publishes the standard PMBOK, Project Management Body of Knowledge, and offers two levels of certification:

- A *Certified Associate in Project Management* (CAPM) has demonstrated a common base of knowledge and terms in the field of project management. It requires either 1,500 hours of work on a project team or 23 contact hours of formal education in project management.
- A *Project Management Professional* (PMP®) has met specific education and experience requirements, has agreed to adhere to a code of professional conduct, and has passed an examination designed to objectively assess and measure project management knowledge. In addition, a PMP must satisfy continuing certification requirements or lose the certification.

CHAPTER 12

Quality

Virtually all organizations strive to improve the quality of their products and services. In fact, quality is often the most critical aspect of the product or service we buy, so it is not surprising to learn that a great deal of effort is spent identifying the degree to which our purchase conforms to the established quality requirements.

In its supplier management role, one of the key responsibilities of the Procurement Department is to ensure that the organization's quality requirements are being met consistently in order for it to maximize the value from its purchase. But "quality" itself seems to be so broad a subject that we are often at odds as to what exactly we mean when we speak of it.

We turn, therefore, to a review of the basic concepts of quality management in this chapter to ensure you understand what quality means, how it is measured, and how we go about achieving its full value. Here, let's look at how you will generally manage your quality activities, how you will measure your suppliers' performance, and how you will go about ensuring that your organization's overall quality objectives are being achieved.

Managing Quality Performance

Managing quality performance has a number of aspects: First, we need to define what we mean by quality and how it fits into our overall organizational strategy. Second, we need to understand where our organization is currently operating in the range of acceptable performance. And third, we need to determine how we intend to improve it.

Quality Assurance

Quality assurance plays a significant role in the procurement department's daily activities. To a large extent, it drives many of our fundamental processes. Taken in its broadest functional terms, quality assurance is a set of activities through which we define, measure, evaluate, and accept the products and services we purchase, often within the structure of the organization's policies and standard operating procedures. Quality assurance also includes the formal process of identifying and correcting specific problems and deficiencies, and the methodology used to do so.

Larger organizations usually have separate departments called *quality control* or quality assurance and often have special job titles that accompany the function, such as quality engineer or supplier quality engineer. Supplier quality and manufacturing quality sections are typically distinct within the enterprise, with the supplier quality function generally included within the procurement organization. In addition to maintaining incoming inspection processes, *supplier quality engineering (SQE)* groups have the responsibility of identifying, monitoring, and correcting quality problems originating within suppliers' operations.

Defining Quality

In procurement, when we speak of quality, we generally refer to the contractual obligation we've formed with the supplier to provide products or service that conform to a given specification or statement of work. Generally speaking, there are two aspects to this conformance: First, we consider how closely a product or service matches our requirements, referring to our specification as the baseline metric. In this aspect, we measure the precise deviation (or allowable *tolerance*) from a given number to determine if it meets the specification. Second, we consider the actual frequency with which a product or service meets the specification. Here, we want to know how often individual elements in a given lot of goods falls outside the acceptable limits.

As an example of how we might look at conformance to specifications, please consider this: If the wall of an aluminum tube is specified to be 1/32 of an inch thick (0.03125) with a tolerance of +/− 0.0001 of an inch, a tube measuring between 0.03124 and 0.03126 would be within an acceptable range. One measuring 0.031265, however, would not. So, in this particular case, any submission outside the specified range would not meet our requirements.

However, we recognize the fact that there are inherent variances produced in the manufacturing of aluminum pipe that prevents the absolute conformance to this specification all the time. Therefore, we measure how often within any given shipment we can expect to find individual tubes that do not meet this tolerance. We might specify this by requiring that 99.9997 percent (*Six Sigma*) of the material sampled falls into the + /− range. If it does, we accept the entire lot; if it does not, we reject the entire lot.

Employing Quality Systems

Measuring and sampling incoming material, then, is one way to control and manage our suppliers' quality, especially in a product-focused, manufacturing environment. A system most often used for this is *statistical process control (SPC)*, and it will be discussed in some detail later in this chapter. However, for your reference, the following paragraphs discuss some other commonly used quality system tools.

CERTIFICATION   *Supplier certification* is one way of reducing (or eliminating altogether) the need for incoming inspection. In certifying a supplier, the buying organization typically determines that the supplier's internal system for measurement and control of quality is sufficient to ensure it will meet the minimum quality level required without performing further incoming inspections. Often, certification will be provided on a part by part basis rather than as an overall blanket endorsement, so suppliers will need to "qualify" or recertify for each new part they produce.

When a supplier has been certified, it means that your organization will rely solely upon their internal controls to produce acceptable quality. This process usually works fine, but there is one significant caveat: Since certification is based on the supplier's current processes (and equipment), your organization will need to know in advance when a supplier changes any production processes so that you can either recertify the process or reintroduce incoming inspection. The need for a proactive, compliant communication system to monitor these activities is evident, and you should carefully include this as a requirement in your supplier certification agreement.

You should understand, also, that the Uniform Commercial Code (UCC) requirement to inspect incoming materials in a reasonable period of time after receipt will still apply, and your organization will assume responsibility for the goods even if no incoming inspection is actually performed. In your agreement, you should extend liability for nonconforming parts to the supplier until the materials are actually used.

ACCEPTANCE TESTING   Used most frequently when purchasing capital equipment, *acceptance testing* is a method used for determining if a particular piece of equipment is functioning at its expected output level. This usually requires an engineering or manufacturing signoff and a formal acknowledgment of acceptance (or rejection) communicated to the supplier.

The acceptance testing process is also commonly used for testing the first article submitted for approval prior to the supplier's actual manufacture runs and may represent a first step in the certification process.

INSPECTION PROCESS   When used, the inspection process will usually specify a range of inspection frequency, extending from 100 percent inspection of all products to no inspection at all, or any level in between. In most cases, the buying organization may specify routine lot sampling on a random basis or at specific lots or time intervals, or it may require actual, on-site audits of the process used by the supplier to measure quality metrics.

The location of the inspection is important, too. It is generally agreed that the earlier in the production process the inspection can take place, the less costly will be the corrective action. As a result, requirements may specify that the inspection will take place on the supplier's manufacturing line or at final assembly, or even as a separate process prior to shipment. Inspection may also be called for at your plant at various operational stages, as well: at the receiving dock, upon release to manufacturing, or even at your final assembly stage.

Similarly, in a service environment, the results or output of the service can require inspection at a variety of times and places. While it is not usual to perform acceptance testing as one might for equipment, there may be a requirement within the statement of work (SOW) that calls for some method of services inspection at specified time intervals as part of gathering the metrics for a service-level agreement.

Measuring Quality Performance

It's an old adage that you tend to get what you measure for, since we have a known tendency to work toward specific goals. For this reason, the ongoing measurement of quality performance becomes critical to the success of any serious effort to generate improvements, keeping in mind, of course, that there are numerous methods for measurement in common use today. Choosing the right measurement depends, to a large degree, on what we intend to accomplish.

Most of the time, the measurements we receive relating to quality performance will be based on some specific testing sequence. These measurements will tell us if the material we are receiving conforms to our specifications or if the process being used to produce the products has the capability of doing the job. In the section that follows, we will examine briefly those methods you are most likely to encounter.

STATISTICAL PROCESS CONTROL (SPC)   SPC has been previously defined in Chapter 2 as a system that measures the actual distribution of events from the beginning to the end of a given process. It is a method of monitoring, controlling, and, ideally, improving a process through statistical probability analysis. Its four basic steps include (1) measuring the process, (2) eliminating variances in the process to make it consistent, (3) monitoring the process, and (4) improving the process to its best target value.

When applied to quality measurement, it allows us to determine if the output of our process is within the desired range of control. As you will recall, two key measures are used in SPC: the upper control limit (UCL)—the highest point of measurement at which performance is acceptable—and the lower control limit (LCL)—the lowest point of measurement at which performance is acceptable. Between these two points, events are considered acceptable and the process is considered to be in control.

We generally use statistical process control (SPC) to measure the tolerances of products produced during rapidly repeating operational cycles, such as the output from automated machinery. In this environment, we determine the range of tolerance mathematically as three *standard deviations* above or below the average of the process.

Tips and Techniques

Standard deviation is a statistical measure of the variability or dispersion within a set of data points. It is calculated from the deviation or mathematical distance between each data value and the sample statistical mean, and it is usually represented by the Greek letter "S" for sigma. The more dispersed the data is, the larger the standard deviation. For data that follows a normal distribution, approximately 68 percent of all data will fall within one standard deviation of the sample mean, 95 percent of all values will fall within two standard deviations, and 99.7 percent of all data will fall within three standard deviations.

TOLERANCES   By definition, tolerance refers to the amount of deviation from our specification data points we are willing to accept. Tolerance is usually given in the same unit of measure or dimension as the specification, as we noted in the example given earlier in the chapter in the section "Defining Quality."

The concept of *tolerance stack-up* is used to measure the cumulative variations of each of the items in an assembly that goes into a final product. Tolerance stack-up analysis is used to determine if a form, fit, or function problem exists when manufacturing tolerances combine in a finished part or assembly. Tolerance stack-up analysis is typically performed either by assuming worst-case allowable dimensions, or by using statistical analysis of tolerances.

PARETO CHARTS The Pareto chart is a type of quality analysis used to determine if a few categories or units account for the majority of the total occurrences. The chart simply displays events in the order of their frequency.

Tips and Techniques

The commonly used Pareto principle (or 80/20 rule) was originally defined by J. M. Juran in 1950 and named after Vilfredo Pareto, a nineteenth-century Italian economist who studied the distribution of the world's wealth. Pareto concluded that the majority (80 percent) of the world's wealth was in the hands of a minority (20 percent) of its population.

Figure 12.1 represents an example of a Pareto chart showing the percentage by category and the cumulative percentage of defects in a hypothetical failure analysis.

C_{pk} C_{pk} is a process *capability index*. *Process capability* analysis entails comparing the performance of a process against its specifications. A process is capable if virtually all of the possible variable values fall within the specification limits. This is

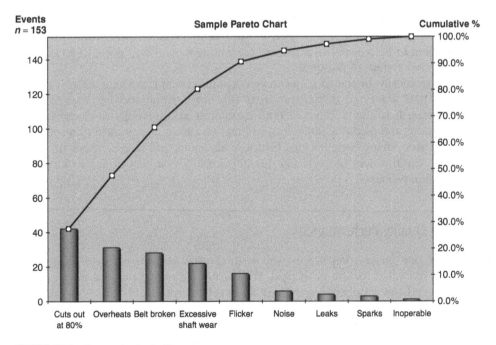

FIGURE 12.1 Pareto Analysis Chart

Source: www.qualityspctools.com/parresults.html.

measured numerically by using a capability index, C_p, with the formula:

$$C_p = \frac{USL - LSL}{6s}$$

where USL = upper specification limit and LSL = lower specification limit and $s =$ standard deviation

This equation indicates that the measure of process capability is how much of the observed process variation (USL minus LSL) is covered by the process specifications. In this case the process variation is measured by 6 standard deviations (+/− 3 on each side of the mean). If C_p is greater than 1.0, then the process specification covers almost all of the process observations.

However, the C_p index does not account for a process that is off-center. This equation can be modified to account for off-center processes to obtain the C_{pk} index as follows:

$$C_{pk} = \min\left[\frac{USL - \bar{x}}{3s}, \frac{\bar{x} - LSL}{3s} \right]$$

This equation takes the minimum distance between our specification limits and the process mean and divides it by 3 standard deviations to arrive at the measure of process capability.

BENCHMARKING As it relates to quality considerations, *benchmarking* is the process of measuring your organization's performance against others within the same business sector or industry to determine what constitutes *best-in-class performance* and how it has been achieved. This comparison can form the basis for a quality improvement program targeting those areas where quality gaps or deviations exist. Benchmarking is also frequently used in conjunction with strategic *value analysis* and planning to help establish goals and allocate resources according to an overall organizational system of priorities.

Philosophically, benchmarking can be considered simply as the search for better methods. It is a way of identifying areas that need reengineering, change, and improvement. It is also a blend of both qualitative and quantitative research that can be tedious and painfully difficult to gather, consuming a great deal of resources. For this reason, many organizations turn to consultants and research organizations that are in the business of gathering this information as a way of accelerating the improvement process.

Ensuring Quality Performance

Doubtless, one major compliance issue in most organizations involves the notion of getting full value for the price paid. So it is not surprising that ensuring quality performance from suppliers is generally an excellent way to improve the value of purchased goods and services. You should continually ask the question: How do I know that my organization is receiving the full value of its contractual spending? Ensuring quality performance is certainly one proven way.

Let's examine, then, some of the concepts and tools relating to ensuring quality performance from your suppliers.

Enforcing Quality Requirements

The process that *enforces* quality compliance is the key to successfully ensuring that your organization's quality policies and requirements are met by your suppliers. In most organizations with a formal quality program, the central tool for this is the *corrective action process*. Surrounding this process is the accurate documentation of quality standards and their conveyance to the supplier as well as developing an analysis of the root cause of the issue so that ongoing progress toward resolution of the problem can be properly monitored.

DOCUMENTING QUALITY REQUIREMENTS Without proper documentation, quality requirements are rendered virtually meaningless. In most cases, documentation will be related to supplier conformance issues and incoming inspections, but don't overlook the need to maintain accurate records of supplier site visits (when performed) and the history of their qualification or certification process. The qualification process establishes the supplier's level of capability, and it is important that you refer to this (as a baseline) when assessing its ongoing level of support. In many organizations, quality reporting is required on a periodic basis and is usually incorporated into the formal supplier business review process.

CONVEYING STANDARDS As part of the documentation process, your organization needs to have a system in place that defines the standards of conformance so that all parties will have a baseline point of reference when reviewing quality performance. Often, these will take the form of a set of written specifications and a system for organizing them, usually some body of *standard operating procedures (SOPs)*, where the measures of conformance we use are typically referred to as *key performance indicators (KPIs)*.

CORRECTIVE ACTION PROCESS Many organizations employ the *corrective action* process whenever standards of quality conformance are not met by suppliers. This tool is traditionally used to document and convey notification of supplier nonconformance and to similarly document the requirements and steps necessary to correct the noncompliant situation. The goal of the process is to eliminate the cause of the problem.

Note

Many organizations have robust and well-defined procedures for handling corrective actions. One example of a Supplier Corrective Action Request (SCAR), used by the Harris Corporation, can be found at www.govcoom.harris.com /suppliers/become/H-450-2.pdf.

ISO 9000:2000 defines corrective action as an action to eliminate the cause of a detected nonconformity or other undesirable situation. Accordingly, the component steps for the process include the following:

1. Recognize the problem and its effect.
2. Determine the root cause.
3. Determine and implement a short-term action plan (often called the "containment" phase).
4. Determine and implement a comprehensive action plan.
5. Determine and implement a preventive action plan.
6. Follow up to ensure compliance.
7. Audit to ensure the plans are effectively eliminating the problem.

DEVELOPING ROOT CAUSE ANALYSIS   Before you can fully resolve any quality discrepancy, you will need to identify and understand its root cause. A *root cause* is the element (or sequence of events) that, if corrected, will prevent a recurrence of the problem in the future. What is the underlying and fundamental element or chain of events that gave rise to the problem in the first place? For tracing the causal relationship of quality issues, we use a process called *root cause analysis*. Root cause analysis thus provides a structured methodology for determining the causal relationships of various elements in the process being used that may be ultimately responsible for the problem.

As with the corrective action process, root cause analysis also follows a sequential methodology that includes the following steps:

1. **Data collection.** This procedure should take place as close in time as possible to the initial discovery of the problem to minimize the loss of information.
2. **Assessment.** The assessment phase includes analyzing the data to identify causal factors, summarizing the findings, and organizing them according to logical categories.
3. **Corrective action.** Identify and implement viable solutions. This means finding answers to several questions, including these:
   a. How will the corrective action prevent recurrence?
   b. What new risks will this action introduce?
   c. Does the action fit in with overall objectives?
   d. Are resources available to properly implement the correction?
   e. What are the secondary consequences of implementation?
   f. Can the corrective action be implemented within an appropriate time frame?
   g. Will the results be measurable?
4. **Follow-up.** Determine if the corrective action has had the desirable effect in resolving the problem. If the problem recurs, the original instance should be reinvestigated to determine if it was properly analyzed.

OTHER CORRECTIVE ACTION OPTIONS   When suppliers are responsible for nonconforming goods or other quality issues, there are a number of options open to you:

- **Return.** Nonconforming goods can be returned to the supplier for further action. (Keep in mind, your organization may be responsible for any further damage while the goods are in its care.) Under the UCC, both the buyer and the supplier have a number of options regarding correction including repair or replacement. If services are involved, however, the likely remedy will be to redo the work, or some accept some form of discount.

- **Rework.** Under some circumstances, the buyer may be authorized to rework nonconforming goods or services at the supplier's expense. While this requires a negotiated settlement with the supplier, it might prove less expensive than having the products returned or redeploying personnel to correct the deficiency.
- **Renegotiate.** In the case of nonconforming goods or services that are partially usable, the buyer may choose to accept the existing performance and negotiate a reduced rate.
- **Re-source or retrain.** Ultimately, you will need to decide how the nonconformance or continuing nonconformance affects your organization's relationship with the supplier. Should you consider having the supplier retrain its employees as part of the corrective action, or should you simply find another source for your purchase?

Total Quality Management (TQM)

Total Quality Management (TQM) is an enduring process of continuous improvement focused on increasing customer satisfaction. As a philosophy, TQM requires the active participation of all members of the organization in working toward the improvement of processes, methods, and services, as well as the culture in which they are fostered.

Tips and Techniques

The Power of TQM

In 1993, the Boeing Corporation was placed on a limited production status, a form of probation, by the Air Force as a result of admitted quality problems, late deliveries, cost overruns, and an adversarial relationship. Boeing's leadership stepped in and implemented TQM with the stated goals of total customer satisfaction, incorporating quality in everything they did, and involving the entire team in the optimization of processes. The team focused on the systematic and integrated framework of TQM.

So successful was this approach that in 1998, this team was the winner of the National Quality Award, and today they are contenders for the *Malcolm Baldrige National Quality Award.*

DEPLOYING TQM IN PROCUREMENT   Likely the most commonly used implementation of TQM in procurement is the use of the *supplier scorecard* combined with the supplier business review. It is through this process that procurement has the opportunity to address ongoing product quality or quality of service issues in a meaningful way. By measuring and monitoring performance on a regular basis and by utilizing the dynamics of a cross-functional team, continuous improvement processes can become extremely effective tools for developing greater customer satisfaction.

KAIZEN   *Kaizen* is a discipline very closely related to TQM. We generally understand Kaizen to mean "improvement." Originally a Buddhist term, Kaizen comes from the words "renew the heart and make it good." Closely related to the Western concepts of TQM and continuous improvement, adaptation of the Kaizen concept also requires changes in "the heart of the business," corporate culture and structure, since Kaizen enables companies to translate the corporate vision in every aspect of a company's operational practice. Thus, in the workplace Kaizen means continuous improvement involving everyone as a group or team, from the CEO to the delivery van driver. Proponents of this way of thinking believe that continuous development and improvement is critical to the organization's long-term success.

QUALITY FUNCTIONAL DEPLOYMENT (QFD)   *Quality functional deployment (QFD)* is another adjunct of TQM. As a system, it links the needs of the customer or end user with the design, development, engineering, manufacturing, and service functions. The concept develops from a consideration that in today's industrial society there is a growing separation between producer and consumer. QFD is meant to help organizations discover both spoken and unspoken needs, translate these into actions and designs, and focus various organizational efforts on achieving a common goal of customer satisfaction. QFD thus seeks to create a culture where organizational goals are formulated to exceed normal expectations and provide a level of enthusiasm that generates both tangible and perceived value.

Employing Quality Systems

Two major quality standard systems are in use today that, in many ways, complement each other and enable organizations to provide greater customer-focused quality assurance. The key elements of these systems, Six Sigma and ISO, are briefly outlined in the section that follows.

SIX SIGMA   *Six Sigma* is a quality movement and improvement program that has grown from TQM. As a methodology, it focuses on controlling processes to +/− six sigma (standard deviations) from a centerline, which is the equivalent of 3.4 defects per million opportunities (where an opportunity is characterized as chance of not meeting the required specification). Six Sigma fundamental tenets include reducing the variation within a process, improving system capability, and identifying essential factors that the customer views as crucial to quality.

Six Sigma methodologies incorporate five steps corresponding to the acronym *DMAIC*:

Define customer requirement and improvement goals.
Measure variables of the process.
Analyze data to establish inputs and outputs.
Improve system elements to achieve performance goals.
Control the key variables to sustain the gains.

You can obtain further information about this process by visiting the American Society for Quality's website at www.asq.org.

ISO STANDARDS   *ISO*, the *International Organization for Standardization*, was established in 1947 as an effort to consolidate widely dispersed methods of approaching quality standards. Its stated goal was to facilitate a means of coordinating, developing, and unifying industrial and technical quality standards. Based in Geneva,

Switzerland, ISO is staffed by representatives from standards organizations in each of its member countries, working through committees that establish standards for industry, research, and government.

ISO 9000   In 1987, ISO issued a series of quality management and quality assurance standards as the ISO 9000 series that has, today, seen adoption by more than 500,000 organizations in 149 countries. This body of standards now provides a framework for customer-focused quality management throughout the global business community and has been widely acknowledged as providing the paradigm of assurance that customers will consistently find uniform quality in the products and services they purchase. Organizations are today certified as having achieved the standard through examination by an ISO registrar and may then use that certification as an assurance that standardized methods are being employed.

The 1994 editions of ISO 9001, ISO 9002, and ISO 9003 have been consolidated into a single revised document, which is now represented by ISO 9001:2000. ISO suggests that the greatest value is obtained when organizations use the entire family of standards in an integrated manner. It is suggested that, beginning with ISO 9000:2000, organizations adopt ISO 9001:2000 to achieve a first level of performance. The practices described in ISO 9004:2000 may then be implemented to make the quality management system increasingly effective in achieving organizational goals. ISO 9001:2000 and ISO 9004:2000 have been formatted as a consistent pair of standards to facilitate their use. ISO maintains that using the standards in this way will help relate them to other management systems and many sector-specific requirements (such as ISO/TS/16949 in the automotive industry) and will assist in gaining recognition through national award programs.

For the Procurement Department, ISO compliance generally means implementing a series of quality assurance procedures that cover the following:

- An evaluation process for the selection of qualified vendors.
- A periodic review of supplier performance, along with remedial action for unsatisfactory performance.
- Documentation of quality requirements in the purchase order.
- Quality control procedures for incoming material.
- Establishment of quality systems and monitoring at suppliers' plants.
- Procedures for tracking supplier defects and resolving quality issues with them.
- Implementation of supplier training programs.
- Collaboration in establishing joint quality assurance programs.

ISO 14000   *ISO 14000* is a series of international standards on environmental management. It provides a framework for the development of an environmental management and evaluation system, and the supporting audit program. The standard does not prescribe environmental performance targets, but instead provide organizations with the tools to assess and control the environmental impact of their activities, products, or services. The standards currently address environmental management systems, environmental auditing, environmental labels and declarations, environmental performance evaluation, and life-cycle assessment.

To learn more about this important set of standards, you might want to visit the ISO website at www.iso.org.

Summary

Managing quality at the supplier level is one of the key areas where procurement departments can add value. This generally means working closely with your internal quality assurance team to ensure that your suppliers are fully measuring up to their contractual obligations.

Understanding quality management requires that you first have a clear definition of your organization's quality objectives and improvement programs. You can then use this information to develop and manage supplier certification and qualification programs as well as monitoring the day-to-day quality performance of suppliers through statistical processes and inspections. Some of the common methods you will be expected to work with include SPC, C_{pk}, Pareto charts, and benchmarking the performance of other organizations to determine best-in-class measures.

Ensuring the quality performance of your suppliers will include documenting and conveying your organization's standards and requirements as well as your participation in remediation activities such as corrective action processes, root cause analysis, and exercising a variety of other options available to supply management under the UCC.

You will also be required to understand various TQM processes (along with Kaizen and QFD), how they are structured, and how they are deployed in procurement. This will mean developing a working knowledge of the principles and objectives of the predominant quality systems such as Six Sigma and ISO.

CHAPTER 13

The Procurement Function's Internal Relationships

The Procurement Department's organizational support role requires extensive co-ordination and collaboration with other internal departments. While some of these departments—for example, legal and finance—actually provide services to your procurement team, all of them constitute the collective customer base that depend on you to provide critical procurement and supply management functions. You will be working collaboratively with many of these groups on cross-functional teams engaged in the development of a new product or service. You may also work with them in resolving quality issues in a manufacturing operation, or, even more likely, selecting a new supplier. Consequently, you will probably spend a major portion of your time working with them. For this reason, it is important that you understand other internal departments' corresponding roles in your organization and the common activities they perform in fulfilling their missions.

In this chapter, you will first examine the roles of the major organizational groups you are likely to encounter and how these roles interface with those of your department. We then review the processes used to communicate with other departments and how you can best initiate and reinforce collaborative working relationships with each of them. And, finally, we examine how you can drive operational improvements within the Procurement Department to better serve your internal customers.

Understanding Key Departmental Roles

During your career, you will quite possibly never encounter two enterprises with exactly the same organizational structure. However, in the section that follows, we will try to describe the roles of the departments you will most commonly encounter so that you can gain a better understanding of how best to develop good working relationships with them. To provide some logical structure, you will find these grouped by their broader functional responsibilities: administrative and support, production or service, sales and marketing, and engineering and design.

Figure 13.1 shows an organizational chart for a typical manufacturing organization. You might find this useful as a reference map as you go through this section.

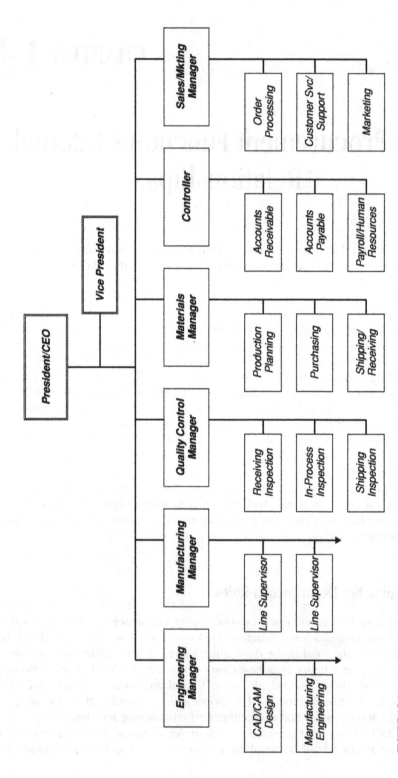

FIGURE 13.1 Organizational Chart

Administrative and Support Functions

Administrative and support departments generally include those groups that provide the foundation for the smooth, day-to-day tactical operation of the organization as well as those that perform general management activities that serve the entire organization. Typically, within this subsection you will find the following.

SENIOR MANAGEMENT Senior management includes the organization's major executive functions such as the chief executive officer (CEO) and president. In public corporations, it also applies to the board of directors, typically led by a chairperson.

Increasingly, procurement departments have been gaining visibility at the senior management level as a result of the need for improved cost structures and the expanding complexity of managing the supply community for competitive advantage. As a result of this visibility, procurement professionals are finding that they must develop more finely tuned communication skills and the ability to deliver highly effective summary presentations. Generally speaking, you will find that senior management, as a result of the very nature of its role, has less time to spend on individual subjects than other organizational managers. To maintain credibility at this level, you will need to address your presentations to the competitive forces driving overall organizational mission and strategy.

FINANCE, ACCOUNTING, AND TREASURY These three groups manage virtually all of the organization's monetary funds and provide the foundation for substantiating procurement performance. They are often the audit compliance watchdogs of organizational spending, and they plan the cash flow that ensures your suppliers are paid in a timely manner. Establishing close communications and good working relationships with these groups will enhance your department's fiduciary performance by helping to ensure the effectiveness of decisions that create financial obligations.

LEGAL Much of the Procurement Department's activities are based on legal principles, and these principles are in continual flux, being modified often by actual decisions of the judiciary branches of state and federal governments. Consequently, you will find your organization's Legal Department to be an excellent support function for guidance on how specific legal technicalities can affect your business relationships with suppliers and how courts are currently interpreting statutory law. Through this guidance you will be able to provide more effective support to your internal customers by mitigating risks to the organization and ensuring that decisions with potential legal implications are being made correctly.

FACILITIES Facilities departments are responsible for maintaining the physical infrastructure of the workplace and planning for effective space utilization. To the extent that your needs for inventory storage will vary with changing economic conditions, close coordination with this group can be important. You will also find that this department provides a large amount of your transactional processing workload due to the wide variety of materials and services required to support the organization's physical facilities.

HUMAN RESOURCES   Human resources (HR) departments are generally responsible for recruiting new employees, as well as developing and managing personnel policies and employee benefits. Often, HR departments also support training as part of the employee development process, so you may find that your department's training needs can be coordinated and assisted through its resources. As a professional, you will find that HR offers support by providing up-to-date information on employee management affairs and regulations governing the workplace.

INFORMATION TECHNOLOGY   Your information technology (IT) group is generally responsible for all the computer and telecommunications requirements in the organization. It supports the organization's internal data and communications networks and enterprise resource planning (ERP) systems and can provide the integration services necessary to interface with multiple software platforms should you be working toward automating your supply base. In addition, the IT organization is a large user of procurement services, so it is increasingly important that you are tuned in to planning for its future needs.

LOGISTICS   Frequently an integral part of the supply management function, logistics services support the organization by handling finished goods distribution (in a manufacturing environment) and inbound freight. An effective logistics group can add significant value to procurement activities by supporting the just-in-time (JIT) processes that reduce inventory and by providing support for reduced costs associated with inbound shipments. The Procurement Department can assist logistics operations by ensuring close adherence to shipping policy and using preferred carriers.

Production Functions

Production is a term widely used to refer to manufacturing, mining, or services that otherwise generates tangible goods or materials (such as baking and brewing). Production operations generally include the functions of manufacturing operations planning, quality assurance, and the maintenance of related equipment.

MANUFACTURING OPERATIONS   Procurement supports manufacturing operations by ensuring delivery of the proper supply of quality materials in the required quantity and at the right time. Failure to do so often result in unfortunate conditions where orders are unable to ship on time and the organization loses revenue. In extreme cases, the inability to ensure supply can lead to plant shutdowns, loss of customers, and layoffs. For this reason, the Procurement Department's responsibility to its manufacturing partners becomes very clear, and its management of the supply community is a mission-critical obligation.

Procurement is also charged with the responsibility of reducing the costs of materials used in the manufacturing operation. This, too, is a mission-critical function since often an organization prices its end product relative to the costs of materials and labor. Improved supplier pricing can lead to a more competitive pricing strategy.

PLANNING Planning is one of the keys to the successful operation of most manufacturing operations. Unless customer demand can be accurately forecasted, there is no guarantee that the available supply of materials will be sufficient to meet production objectives. In most operations, demand planning includes forecasting the mix of the various products customers might order, as well as the quantities that will be needed.

In some operations, the buying function is combined with the planning function in the form of a *buyer-planner,* so there are times when the planning function actually falls in the Procurement Department. In these situations, it is not unusual to find the Procurement Department itself reporting to manufacturing management and becoming an integral part of the production environment.

QUALITY ASSURANCE Quality assurance is a production function tasked with ensuring a given standard of quality. In manufacturing environments there are generally two groups engaged in quality assurance: an internal group monitoring manufacturing performance and a supplier-focused group monitoring the quality of incoming materials used in manufacturing. Considering the critical nature of these functions, procurement departments are typically closely allied to quality management teams and often work collaboratively on cross-functional teams. As the role of outsourcing expands and organizations find themselves more closely tied to outside manufacturing sources, this function takes on an even greater importance. Today, the management of quality from subcontracting service organizations—whose products are often shipped directly to the customer and never seen at the plant site—is becoming an increasingly important issue, leading to the increased use of supplier quality engineers deployed directly to procurement departments.

MANUFACTURING MAINTENANCE The Procurement Department also closely supports manufacturing operations by ensuring that spare parts and tools are available so that maintenance activities can take place when needed. In machinery-intensive manufacturing operations, down time due to the loss of even one piece of equipment can severely limit production capacity. Ensuring the supply of spare parts and maintenance-related supplier services becomes as critical as the material that goes directly into manufacturing the organization's products.

Sales and Marketing

Sales and marketing activities impact procurement in a variety of ways: Increased sales activities and merchandising campaigns generally create added demand that requires planning for additional flows of material, and slower market demand requires greater agility in manufacturing to support the increased customer service required to gain business in a highly competitive environment.

The potential benefit from strong relationships between supplier management groups and the sales and marketing efforts of the organization are frequently overlooked. The supplier community represents a special source of potential sales for your own organization for rather obvious reasons: Purchasing your goods or services increases their sales. What could be simpler? Yet it might be surprising to learn that few organizations have programs to market to their supply bases.

Tips and Techniques

There is nothing illegal or unethical about selling to your suppliers as long as the sales are not directly related to your specific purchases. A so-called "tying contract," where a purchase of goods or services from the supplier is contingent upon a corresponding purchase from your organization, is usually illegal. However, there is nothing wrong with saying, "My organization prefers to purchase goods and services from its own customers."

PRODUCT/BUSINESS DEVELOPMENT Product managers and business development managers are generally charged with overseeing specific product lines within the enterprise and have broad responsibilities for developing new business opportunities. Consequently, the groups they manage often have important roles in the development of new products and end-of-life discontinuation of existing ones. As a source of information regarding the potential needs of the organization, these groups can provide the Procurement Department with invaluable information that can be useful in formulating supply strategies and determining future directions for supplier partnerships.

PUBLIC RELATIONS The public image of your organization can significantly affect your relationships with suppliers. A strong, positive public image suggests that businesses associated with your organization will benefit beyond the direct profit they earn from their dealings with you, and they are more likely to offer concessions to gain your business. You can leverage this even further by ensuring that key executives of your suppliers are on the mailing list for press releases and other public relations materials . . . but be sure to send them only as long as the news continues to be favorable.

ADVERTISING/SALES COLLATERAL Most of the advertising done by your organization will be placed with professional advertising agencies by staff members with marketing backgrounds and expertise, since vendor selection for this service can be highly subjective. Nevertheless, there can be significant opportunity for cost savings through the purchase of printed materials and promotional merchandise that should not be overlooked. Sourcing and supplier management can work very well when you stick to providing collaborative input on the business aspects of procurement and consider that aesthetic considerations may be the key driver in a successful marketing campaign.

DISTRIBUTION Distribution is one of the key physical aspects to sales management whose importance should be evident. Physical distribution processes—conveying goods or services to the customer—typically involve a host of disciplines such as warehousing, packaging, inventory management, security, transportation and *traffic*, information technology, and customer service, just to mention a few. Distribution is a critical strategic function in any organization that generates a strong demand for purchased services and will often require the Procurement Department's assistance. You should work closely with this group to ensure that you have a clear understanding of its needs.

Similarly, distribution groups are in an excellent position to forecast incoming demand and sales trends, and so they represent a primary source of planning information that can assist you in developing relevant supply strategies.

Engineering and Design Functions

Engineering and design functions are typically separated into those groups working on new products and technical research and development, and groups working with manufacturing operations and factory systems. Early involvement by the Procurement Department in the new product introduction process can assist in aligning future strategies with sourcing needs and provide a smooth transition to new materials or suppliers. The Procurement Department can often help accelerate the process by introducing potential suppliers to the organization's business requirements and taking the initial steps toward qualification.

RESEARCH AND DEVELOPMENT (R&D)   The research process focuses on the discovery of new technology and methods, while the development process seeks ways to exploit them through practical application. The Procurement Department's ability to identify and develop new sources of supply can become a strategic resource to the organization when it is employed early in the design specification process.

NEW PRODUCT/SERVICE INTRODUCTION (NPI)   *New product or service introduction* is the complete business process of developing new products for the market. It typically covers the complete product life cycle from initial discovery of opportunity, product/service conception, design and development through to production, market launch, support, enhancement, and even retirement.

Other titles are often used to describe the NPI process, such as new product development (NPD). The exact meaning of the terms vary with different organizations; however, today the NPI process is characterized by a distinct functional division, notably between marketing, engineering (or R&D), and production, and NPI is likely to be seen as a cross-functional business process, involving both internal groups and external suppliers or partners.

In conjunction with the R&D functions, the introduction of new products or services requires a great deal of planning by the Procurement Department to ensure that new suppliers have been properly qualified and have the required capability to deliver. Early involvement by Procurement is no longer just desirable; it has become a necessity to the organization to ensure a smooth product introduction ramp-up from the development phase to actual marketing and distribution.

Developing Good Working Relationships

Throughout the procurement process, your effectiveness and your department's effectiveness will depend largely on the strength of your relationships with suppliers and your internal customers. For this reason, it is critical that you understand how to engage others proactively and how to establish the foundation for effective collaboration.

In this section, we review the ways good communication skills can assist your efforts and how you might better assist your organization as a participant in a collaborative working environment.

Communicating within the Organization

Good communication skills are the essential cornerstone to building meaningful relationships with other internal departments. Unless your customers clearly understand your goals and objectives and how you work to achieve them, you run the risk of being held at arm's length and excluded from critical internal communication activities. Similarly, those in your department need to have a clear understanding of the activities of other groups you will provide services for in order to more effectively meet their needs. If the communication is not clear and timely, both groups run the risk of misunderstandings that can result in ineffective team performance. Keep in mind that improving total operational performance is your primary objective in developing effective communications. To do so, you will require the active participation of those with whom you interface.

ESTABLISHING CREDIBILITY AND TRUST   Your ability to execute to plan can be the key to establishing credibility and trust with other groups. Thus the need to accurately communicate your performance objectives and progress toward them frequently and appropriately becomes apparent. To the extent that you can do this prior to engaging in activities that affect other departments and solicit their input regarding your approach and how best to meet their needs, you will find that you are effectively establishing credibility and trust. You can do this best by aligning your activities to support the departmental goals of your internal customers.

Gaining visibility also assists your efforts in developing credibility and trust. The more your customers know about your value-adding activities, the more likely they are to engage you in future sourcing efforts. Far too often, the Procurement Department is viewed as being stuck in administering meaningless details and transactional processes that seldom amount to any significant benefit to other departments. You can change this perception by creating frequent opportunities to "market" your strategic services and communicating success stories.

In this age of communication, there are virtually unlimited tools available to exchange information. In fact, there are so many avenues for information delivery, buyers often complain of information overload. To avoid inflicting numbing overcommunication on your customers, you will want to select the most effective channels for gathering and disseminating information and use only those most appropriate to individual situations. Here are some of the more common methods.

CUSTOMER SURVEYS   The customer survey is one method commonly used for gathering information. Properly employed, the survey can focus input on specific issues and root out problems before they interfere with operations. The survey can also gather opinions and assess the perceptions customers have regarding departmental performance and effectiveness.

Tips and Techniques

Leveraging an Effective Survey

A national biotech company used several dozen travel agents in the 20 states where they had either a sales office or manufacturing operation. Because the company utilized so many travel agents, the level of service it experienced was relatively low, while the cost of service was high. Some of the travel agencies even proposed a consolidation, offering lower prices. To ensure that the company used the best travel services and agents, its Procurement Department polled all end users of travel services via a survey that the Procurement Department developed and distributed. The results of the survey showed which of the many travel agency service providers met the expectations of the internal end users and which service providers did not. The survey input enabled the Procurement Department to eliminate the nonperforming suppliers much more objectively because it was based on the input of the end-user customers. At the same time, additional business was moved to the service providers that met the expectations of the end users. The result: greater user satisfaction, improved supplier performance, and less procurement management (and fewer travel agents).

ONE-ON-ONE MEETINGS Individual meetings with your key customers can provide an opportunity to exchange information and ideas in a private setting. Personal conversations are often very productive simply because, by the nature of their privacy, they encourage collaboration and an open exchange of opinion. Although these meetings tend to be somewhat informal, it is always a good idea to prepare an agenda in advance so you and your customer can stay organized, and both of you can come away with a sense of having accomplished a meaningful dialogue.

TEAM MEETINGS Held periodically, team meetings can be an excellent venue for communication. One of the greatest advantages is that you are able to pass along exactly the same information to all members of the team. You will also benefit from the interchange of ideas that typically occurs in a team environment, and you will find it an opportunity for gaining consensus in reaching decisions.

NEWSLETTERS AND WEBSITES Newsletters and information posted on a Procurement Department website, while certainly less personal than face-to-face meetings, can offer the advantage of reaching large numbers of readers with relatively minimal effort. When used regularly to convey relatively important information rather than minutiae, these tools can provide a focal point for dispensing up-to-date information. Keep in mind, however, that typically these tools provide only one-way communication and are not often effective substitutes for the interaction that goes along with face-to-face interaction.

Gaining Early Involvement

Early involvement by the Procurement Department in sourcing and new product introduction activities benefits the organization in several ways. Involving the Procurement Department in the initial stages of supplier contact enables the organization to leverage cost reduction and supplier management efforts at a time when they can be best influenced. Then, as the buying organization gains a clearer understanding of the product needs and cost restraints, sourcing strategies and negotiating tactical plans can be more highly focused on achieving the customers' goals rather than simply reacting to compliance issues. With the procurement team focusing on the business requirements, the technical team's time and energy is available to pursue optimal solutions.

From the supplier's perspective, early involvement by the Procurement Department enables a smoother transition from the development phase to the operational working environment. When the procurement professional explores terms and conditions early in the process, he or she can resolve potential contracting obstacles prior to their becoming "deal-breaking" roadblocks. By establishing solid relationships early, the procurement professional also clears the way for more collaborative negotiations with suppliers since both parties will have a better understanding of each other's needs and a greater opportunity to produce mutually beneficial results.

Strategic leverage increases with early involvement in the procurement process. As suppliers gain certainty that their company will receive the order, the incentive for creative solutions tends to diminish. You might want to use Table 13.1 as a guide

TABLE 13.1   Influence at Stages of Involvement

Stage	Areas of Influence
PRODUCT CONCEPTION	
	Commodity strategy
	Alternative materials
	Supplier investment
	Comarketing development
PRODUCT DESIGN	
	Sourcing strategy
	Total cost of ownership
	Quality requirements
	Partnerships and alliances
PRODUCT ENGINEERING	
	Supplier qualification
	Make-or-buy decisions
	Value analysis
	Negotiation of cost-based pricing
PRODUCTION PLANNING	
	Negotiation of availability
	Schedule creation
INTRODUCTION	
	Negotiation of volume-based pricing
	Negotiation of schedule allocations
	Schedule influence

because it outlines the specific development stage (in the left column) and the areas readily influenced through the Procurement Department's active role in the process at that stage (in the right column).

Participating in Cross-Functional Operations

A cross-functional team is composed of representatives from various segments of the organization with complementary skill sets and perspectives. In most organizations, the cross-functional team shares a common goal, and its members are equally accountable for the team's results. Typically, projects related to strategic sourcing activities and the ongoing management of critical suppliers is where you will most likely participate and where your input can be most valuable. In many cases, you will even find yourself leading these teams, so it is important that you understand the role you bring to the team and where you can be expected to add value.

In the section that follows, we will review the various roles and responsibilities of the Procurement Department in cross-functional team participation and how you can be most effective in helping to build successful teams.

Supply Management Roles and Responsibilities

The Procurement Department works with a number of typical operational and development teams where specific supply management expertise is useful. The most common of these teams are described here.

NEW PRODUCT DEVELOPMENT As we discussed earlier in the chapter (in the "Engineering and Design Functions" section), procurement departments have an important role in new product development teams to provide sourcing and supplier management assistance.

SOURCING AND NEW SUPPLIER DEVELOPMENT Closely related to developing and introducing new products is the development of new suppliers. Typically, procurement departments will take a leading role in this business process, sourcing and helping to qualify potential new suppliers.

COST REDUCTION Specific products or service lines may require reduced cost to effectively compete with others in the marketplace. Cross-functional teams review all aspects of internal and supplier-related costs with the objective of reducing the purchase price. Often, teams will adopt the value analysis methodology by looking at all the parts that are used in a particular product with the objective of reducing cost without impairing functionality.

CYCLE TIME REDUCTION The cycle time for ordering and receiving purchased parts and service can often become the gating factor in delivering to the end customer. Organizations have come to realize that there are trade-offs of value to simply achieving the lowest possible price, and you will frequently find yourself discussing the need for cycle time reduction with your suppliers.

BUDGET   Input from the Procurement Department on budget teams focuses on pricing trends and expected pricing in the future. Often, the Procurement Department will be asked to forecast prices for areas of major commodity or category spending.

CAPITAL EQUIPMENT   The procurement group is often asked to participate in the selection of capital asset equipment as the business lead in negotiating price and delivery terms.

INFORMATION TECHNOLOGY   Procurement departments take part in IT sourcing activities, both as a using group and as the buyer. As organizational computer and telecommunications systems become more fully integrated and more resources are dedicated to them, Procurement spends increasingly more time working with this group.

QUALITY ASSURANCE   Since the quality of your own product or service is often largely dependent upon the quality of purchased goods and services, the Procurement Department will be asked to assume an important role in ensuring that the specified quality requirements are met by suppliers.

EVALUATING TEAMS   Under what conditions will a cross-functional team likely produce value? This, of course, is a topic for organizational design debate. However, there are circumstances that are generally recognized as favoring the use of a team and others that tend to reduce its benefits. From a procurement perspective, you should be able to distinguish those desired outcomes that will benefit from team involvement and those that will be hindered. Here are just a few aspects you should consider:

- **Speed.** Overall, cross-functional teams tend to reduce the time it takes to reach objectives, especially in the product development process where ongoing coordination between functional elements can be critical. Speed is a critical factor in product and system development, and cross-functional teams allow many parts of the development process to take place concurrently.
- **Degree of change.** Massive degrees of change generally require a great deal of communication, and teams can become excellent tools for introducing and communicating change throughout the organization. By jointly developing a plan for communication and through joint crafting of the messages, teams can help ensure that the rest of the organization is in sync with the overall objectives of the change.
- **Organizational culture.** To a large degree, organizational culture determines the effectiveness of team outcomes. In cultures where teams actually manage processes and have the decision-making authority, team outputs are extremely effective. In cultures where tradition prevails, the teams may need to develop additional management buy-in for its recommendations, thus slowing the process considerably.
- **Decision making.** It has been shown that collectively teams make better decisions and produce more effective outcomes than any of their individual members, substantiating the adage that "two heads are better than one." However,

teams can often take a lot more time debating issues prior to reaching a decision than an individual would take to reach a decision alone.

■ **Leveraged expertise.** In a team environment, individual members gain the benefit of having subject matter experts to rely upon for technical information. This often reduces the time it takes to understand a specific problem. However, there is a down side: Frequently, individuals feel that the circumstances in their organizations are unique and substantially different from others in the industry. This thinking tends to restrict the options available to the team and often generates friction. Procurement professionals often refer to this as the NIH syndrome—not invented here—to describe the reluctance of some to use new ideas.

■ **Consensus building.** Consensus generally means that everyone on the team agrees to support an action or decision, even if some of them are not in full agreement. Consensus contrasts with voting where the majority rules. To the extent that teams are responsible for making strategic and operational decisions, consensus building has an important function because individual members of the team are required to provide public support for its decision. If the disagreement is strong, members will not be inclined to provide the needed effort and consensus will not be achieved.

■ **Complacency.** Teams, especially those of long standing, have a tendency toward entropy and can become complacent. Generally, one finds that goals are not updated and perhaps are no longer as valid as they were in the past. Under these circumstances, it is difficult for meaningful action to take place, and the individual members of the team lose motivation. This is one of the major pitfalls of the team process and seems to suggest that teams should be project oriented with a clearly established time for disbanding.

DEVELOPING EFFECTIVE TEAMS   There is a tendency for teams to develop within a specific growth pattern, similar to that often referred to in organizational development literature as the four phases: forming, storming, norming, and performing. Table 13.2 provides examples of these phases and what you might expect to encounter in each of them.

Team effectiveness depends upon establishing measurable goals early and developing a timeline with milestones for their achievement. These measurements

TABLE 13.2   Typical Stages of Team Development

Stage	Development Steps
Initial team organization	The team is chartered and formed. Team members learn about the project and one another.
Defining needs and goals	The team establishes goals and objectives consistent with its assignment. The team develops a preliminary timeline for completion.
Developing solutions and action plans	The team develops and refines potential solutions and builds consensus for one of the alternatives.
Achieving objectives	The team implements its plan, measures progress, adjusts actions to meet situation, and celebrates success.

work best if they parallel the team's expected deliverables. For example, if the team was established to develop cost savings, you would want to identify and measure:

- Anticipated cost savings.
- Method of measuring cost savings.
- Timeline for producing cost savings.
- Milestones.
- Duration of the project or completion criteria.

Reengineering Supply Management

As part of your duties, you will likely be called upon occasionally to lead or participate in formulating new procedures or revising existing ones. As organizational policy changes to meet changing economic or regulatory conditions, elements within the organization, such as supply management, also require realignment. Change also sometimes develops from newly available technology that offers greater efficiency or from new processes rolled out organizationally.

Dealing with change is a necessary skill that must be learned and continually employed as part of our professional lives. In procurement departments, change has an even more profound effect on others, and you must also learn to continually consider how to assist internal customers as well as suppliers through these changes. This section reviews the scope of operations in most procurement departments so that you can more clearly understand the functions that you will be responsible for improving. This section also discusses how change is best managed throughout the organization and supply base.

Understanding the Scope of Operations

When you consider the overall scope of procurement and procurement operations, you can easily understand how it touches virtually every function within the organization. For the purpose of providing some reference points and as an aid to understanding how typical procurement activities usually relate to one another, we've provided the following listing, which contains most of the common roles and responsibilities carried out in procurement departments. Notice that they are grouped into three main categories: procurement, materials management, and other supporting roles.

PROCUREMENT The procurement function manages the acquisition of goods and services, conducting a broad range of functional services that are used by all departments in the organization, as shown in Table 13.3.

MATERIALS MANAGEMENT The materials management function is responsible for the planning of supply requirements and the internal handling of purchased materials, as shown in Table 13.4.

OTHER SUPPORTING ROLES The Procurement Department indirectly supports a variety of activities within the organization. They are shown in Table 13.5.

TABLE 13.3   Procurement Functional Services

COMMODITY EXPERTISE

        Industry analysis
        Market analysis
        Commodity analysis
        Benchmarking
        Forecasting

SOURCING

        Locating potential suppliers
        Supplier prequalification
        RFx preparation and response analysis
        Evaluation of supplier capabilities
        Competitive bidding
        Supplier selection leadership

CONTRACTING

        Contract formation
        Negotiation of terms and conditions
        Management and administration of contract compliance
        Termination

SUPPLIER DEVELOPMENT AND MANAGEMENT

        Conducting performance reviews
        Implementing continuous improvement programs
        Developing cost reductions
        Auditing

RISK MANAGEMENT

        Risk assessment and evaluation
        Risk mitigation
        Ensuring supply
        Supplier ratings and approved supplier list
        Regulatory compliance

LICENSING

        Protection of intellectual property rights
        Licensing compliance

QUALITY MANAGEMENT

        Supplier qualification
        Quality assessments
        Quality improvement programs

TRANSACTIONAL PROCESSING

        Issuing purchase orders
        Expediting supplier shipments
        Returned goods documentation
        ERP and systems implementation
        Procurement card management
        E-procurement solutions

TABLE 13.4   Materials Management Function

LOGISTICS/SUPPLY CHAIN MANAGEMENT

Transportation and customs management
Receiving
Packaging
Physical distribution of finished goods
Internal movement of materials

PLANNING

Production planning and master scheduling
MRP management
Capacity planning
Forecasting
Just-in-time manufacturing

INVENTORY MANAGEMENT

Warehousing and stores operations
Part master maintenance
ABC inventory control
Economic ordering quantity analysis

SURPLUS DISPOSAL

Hazardous materials handling
Scrap sales
End-of-life product sales
Surplus equipment sales

Managing the Change Process

Charles Darwin, the nineteenth-century British evolutionist, is perhaps the preeminent student of change and one of the first to explore the way in which change affects our lives. "It is not the strongest species that survive," he wrote, "nor the most intelligent, but the ones who are most responsive to change."

TABLE 13.5   Other Supporting Roles

PROJECT MANAGEMENT

New product introduction projects
Information technology and systems projects
Manufacturing/services improvement programs
Plant engineering and relocation projects
Policy and procedure revisions
Audit preparation
Value analysis

FINANCE AND BUDGET

Cost center maintenance
Pricing forecasts for budgets
Spending analysis
Cost analysis
Accounts payable support
Return on Investment analysis

In order to improve organizational effectiveness, especially when responding to dynamic changes in the business environment, you must learn to master change. Despite its seeming randomness, change must be managed so that you can implement new methods. To a large extent, this means developing clear plans for structuring changes and communicating them to those within the organization who will be affected. People are generally resistant to change unless they fully understand it and even then only accept it with some trepidation. Unless you can manage change in measured increments, you run the risk of overwhelming them.

There are several factors that influence the effectiveness of change that you should take into consideration:

- The impetus for significant change needs to come from senior management, or it gains little support.
- Your agenda for change must be shared by everyone, and you need to have a mutual vision of how the change will provide benefits to the entire organization.
- You need to have access to the resources—time, money, staff, and expertise—to implement the changes smoothly.
- Plan ahead, define each step, check before acting, and communicate so that there are no surprises; absorb feedback and make allowances to correct mistakes as required.
- Whenever possible, introduce change at the prototype level first, testing to see if it will work as expected and making any needed changes before going forward. Choose opportunities for learning rather than just attempting to prove the concept through a successful first test. Mistakes are opportunities for learning.
- It is important to deal with emerging issues as soon as possible so that dissatisfaction and frustration do not take root.
- Provide continual feedback to your team on progress—both success and failures.
- To the extent possible, avoid micromanagement. Overstructuring finite details can be disenfranchising to team members and will only serve to slow the process by reducing initiative.
- Remember that if change moves too quickly, you may end up leaving a good many employees confused and in the dark as to what is expected of them. It is probably best to include in your plan a segment of time for feedback and questions as a way of ensuring you are moving ahead smoothly.

In your procurement role, you will most likely encounter the need for change that results from new or redefined Procurement Department roles and from changes in organization policy required by legislation such as that recently encountered through the Sarbanes-Oxley Act.

REDEFINING THE ROLE OF PROCUREMENT As transactional processing methods improve efficiency, fewer procurement employees are being assigned to routine buyer duties. More and more, organizations are coming to rely on their procurement departments to drive profitability improvement programs that translate to increased shareholder value and introducing innovation.

FORMING AND COMMUNICATING ORGANIZATIONAL POLICY Organizational policies need to receive periodic reviews to ensure that they reflect up-to-date thinking. This is especially true for procurement activities, which must adapt to continually changing legislation and regulatory requirements, as well as industry standards such as ISO. Ethical conduct has recently come under serious scrutiny in the business sector, and many organizations—especially those publicly held—are struggling to revise policy to conform to new criteria. Recently, the Institute for Supply Management published a set of guidelines called "Principles of Social Responsibility" to provide guidance on what constitutes socially responsible conduct. (You can find an outline of the program at the Institute of Supply Management's website: www.ism.ws.) Since its intention is to include this criteria in supplier selection and qualification audits, this will likely result in a flurry of new internal policies to ensure compliance.

Procurement Policy and Procedures Training

Internal organizational procurement policy and procedures are often complex and not readily accessible, so they need to be supplemented with training and extended communication activities. Fostering a better understanding of the requirements and benefits of compliance with these policies will greatly assist you in carrying out the organization's procurement strategy and objectives. Directing this task falls naturally in the hands of the procurement professional.

Meeting external regulations for public corporations has become a real issue with the passage of the Sarbanes-Oxley Act (SOX). Policies and procedures must be documented. SOX requires that key financial and accounting processes must be clearly stated and presented. In addition, all financial software applications must be documented.

FORMULATING TRAINING NEEDS   Internal procurement training requirements address two main areas, each with a somewhat distinct focus:

1. **Procurement Department standard operating procedures (SOPs).** SOPs address the "how-to" of procurement, defining the specific tasks required to perform any given operation. Examples of typical procurement procedures include how to qualify a supplier for inclusion on the approved supplier list or how to add a new supplier to the database. Training is typically required when new procedures are implemented and when existing procedures are revised. It is also important to have a structured training program to initiate new employees into the Procurement Department to reduce the risk of costly mistakes.

   Additionally, SOX requires organizations to standardize and update their procedures to ensure SOX documentation compliance. As a result, many organizations are discovering that their procedures are either incomplete, outdated, or do not adequately conform to regulatory requirements. It is clear that much training will be needed to ensure compliance with regulatory requirements as broad-based as this.

2. **Organizational policy regarding procurement.** Most organizations have policies regarding who can purchase materials and services and who can approve purchases and their limit of authority. Policies also typically specify who can obligate the organization to contractual relationships in the course of business activities. In addition, many organizations specify codes of ethical conduct for dealing with suppliers and for maintaining internal confidentiality.

While much of this policy may be strictly common sense, it is, nevertheless, prudent to ensure compliance through some method of organized training.

DEVELOPING TRAINING MATERIALS The format for training materials is generally determined by how the materials are intended to be used. Procedural and policy materials are often developed for classroom training or on-the-job training since this type of material often requires detailed explanation and coaching. Technical materials are often developed in manuals and used primarily for reference as needed. You will find that there are occasions when both systems will be useful.

DELIVERING THE TRAINING How the training is delivered is often as important as the content of the training itself. Some training is best handled in a classroom environment, while other training can be delivered through *computer-based training (CBT)* or other methods of self-directed study. Sometimes it is more effective to develop combinations of training types such as instructor-led, Web-based training (known as *blended learning*) or classroom training followed by on-the-job coaching.

It is widely accepted, however, that formal training should be provided only "as needed" to reinforce a specific skill requirement at the time of implementation. Skills are most effectively learned when they are introduced, where there is some previous context on which to base their value. Thus the focus of training should be developmental rather than purely remedial and should be presented in that context.

Summary

Successful interaction with other departments within the organization should be a key element in the Procurement Department's strategy. To accomplish this, you will need to develop a thorough understanding of the roles and duties of your internal customers and process partners. While no two organizations have exactly the same structure, most can be organized according to broad operational categories: administration, production (or service), sales and marketing, and engineering and design.

Your effectiveness within the organization will depend, to a large extent, on how well you can develop strong working relationships. Developing relationships with other departments (and employees) requires that you employ sound communication and trust-building techniques. Using appropriate channels and tools effectively is also an important element in this process. By building trust you will be able to gain early involvement in the sourcing and contracting processes, which will further enable you to contribute effectively in your organizational role.

Procurement departments typically participate in or lead cross-functional teams in most areas of the organizations, so you will be required to understand your role and responsibilities as a member of these teams. You will also need to know how these teams are formed, how the team process is carried out, and what the requirements are for effective team management. In order to improve operations and better meet organizational expectations, you should completely understand the scope of operations in the Procurement Department and the major functions that go along with it. This will assist you in managing the change process, helping to formulate policy and procedures, and providing communication and training to your staff and other departments within the organization.

CHAPTER 14

Supplier Relationship Management (SRM)

In the multifaceted business climate of today, information gained from supply chain partners is often the key to competitive success. Consequently, managing supplier relationships is one of the most important functions performed by the procurement department. It requires strategy, skill, and patience; it is a complex process that demands comprehensive attention in order to prove successful. And, most importantly, it has to be learned and practiced.

This chapter reviews several key aspects to managing supplier relationships. To begin with, we examine the steps you can take to develop the groundwork for more productive strategic supply relationships. Then, we review the more common day-to-day tactical activities of a procurement department in its interface with the supplier community and how you can make these activities more meaningful. Finally, we look at how you can effectively represent your organization through interaction with external supply groups.

Managing Productive Supplier Relationships

Productive supplier relationships do not just happen: As with any relationship of value, they demand effort and perseverance. In your role as procurement professional, there are a number of disciplines you will have to master in order to better encourage strong supply relations. In this section, we review the more commonly used processes that enable and improve relations with your suppliers.

Creating Good Working Relations

You create good working relations with your suppliers through fair and consistent treatment, enhanced by the judicious use of communication tools and by holding regular meetings. The benefits of building solid relationships can be enormous. When your working relationship is strong, suppliers are more likely to cooperate with you by moving up lead times when a product or service is needed immediately or by taking a return of product for your convenience. A close, collaborative relationship also makes it easier to negotiate terms and prices with your suppliers and helps avoid disputes since your organization's business will be highly regarded.

The following sections outline some of the more common ways to enhance working relationships.

MEETING WITH SUPPLIERS REGULARLY You will want to arrange meetings with your key suppliers on a regular basis. Often, these meetings will take the form of a formal supplier review or an executive conference. Such meetings provide the opportunity for the management of both organizations to get together to exchange technology or business development road maps so that strategic relationships can be better aligned and leveraged. At other times, you may want to meet less formally to review your immediate plans and ways that the supplier can provide support. Sometimes, you may be able to help the supplier resolve an internal problem that your organization has already solved.

While it is impossible to meet regularly with all of your suppliers, there are a number of other ways you can maintain regular contact:

1. **Supplier surveys.** Periodic surveys of suppliers can provide information on how effective your organization has been in developing them as a resource. They can also help identify problem areas that are generating additional cost to your organization. Sometimes, it is just good business practice to be open and listen to how suppliers view you as a customer.

2. **Improvement teams.** Regardless of the criticality of their role in supplying your organization, with good working relationships you provide an extra incentive for suppliers to participate in cost reduction projects and to work on multifunctional teams to help improve overall operations, keeping in mind that your best suppliers do not have a monopoly on good ideas. Inviting a talented supplier representative to participate in an improvement project, even if it does not directly relate to the product or service supplied, makes good business sense since it is another way to leverage the talent within your supply base.

3. **Reciprocal visits.** You should visit the supplier's facility as often as possible. By putting a face to a name, you will be inviting the supplier's personnel to connect with your organization and create a common bond. Visits will also enable you to become more familiar with how the supplier's operation works so that you can better leverage its capabilities and strengths, as well as understand its limitations.

   Holding a supplier open house—Supplier Day, as it is sometimes called—will introduce the supplier's team to your organization and enable them to see firsthand how their products or services are employed. This can be an extremely powerful tool for personalizing your organization's needs, thus strengthening the bonds between you.

IMPROVING COMMUNICATION Interorganizational communications are most effective when they are bidirectional and when they involve all levels of personnel. Effective communication can produce remarkable results. For example, forecasts of trends affecting your organization, even generalized ones, can reduce cycle time by preparing your suppliers to respond more rapidly to anticipated needs. To the extent that information such as this can be collaboratively shared, you will find that fill rates improve and that service levels rise. Information that provides a window into your operations can also be reassuring to supplier sales teams. Knowing which of your product lines are moving quickly, what products you intend to discontinue, and what new products you intend to introduce can be valuable intelligence to its sales organization, especially when it correlates with information from other sources.

You will also want to tap your suppliers as resources for trend information that will assist your internal customers by helping to determine the best time to place their orders. Often, sales departments have better access to market information that can be valuable assets when properly used.

There are a number of other ways your department can work with suppliers to better leverage information and improve communication. Here are just of few of the more commonly used methods:

- **Website.** Information about your company and your procurement team can be posted on a public website. Some organizations actually establish a supplier section where information of special interest to suppliers—invitations to bid, for example—can be distributed. Visit the HP website at http://h30173.www3.hp.com if you would like to see a good model of one.
- **Focus groups.** The *focus group* is a useful method for gaining supplier feedback. Typically set in a somewhat structured environment led by a professional facilitator and consisting of between 9 and 12 individuals, the group is brought together to examine a specific subject and share opinions. It can be a particularly effective way to test new ideas and gain feedback prior to implementation.
- **Newsletter.** A newsletter can be used to address the supply community specifically with information that will help them better understand what is happening inside your organization. Using word processing software makes it relatively easy to publish one at your desk, and it can be quite effectively distributed at no cost through e-mail.

REVERSE MARKETING Michiel R. Leenders and David L. Blenkhorn[1] identified the concept of *reverse marketing* by pointing out that the traditional relationship where the seller takes the lead by seeking out the buyer is being replaced in many instances by one where the buyer actively searches for suppliers to fill a specific need. This practice occurs when there are few or no suppliers available, and you will have to employ some aggressive recruiting and persuasion in order to develop a source to meet your organization's needs. Reverse marketing generally sees the buyer making the offer, even to the point of suggesting the selling price.

Monitoring Supplier Performance

Expected *supplier performance* levels are generally included in the general terms and conditions, product specifications (in the case of goods), or in the statement of work (in the case of services) for any given purchase. Often referred to as service levels, they can also be included in a separate addendum to the contract known as a *service-level agreement (SLA)*. Within the SLA, *metrics* (sometimes referred to as *key performance indicators*, or KPIs, as discussed in Chapter 1) are included to define the expected performance of the supplier.

Performance measures by themselves have little intrinsic value, so they are generally reviewed in terms of actual progress toward a specific goal or compared with a stated baseline standard. For example, if you are measuring cost reduction, you might indicate a KPI in terms of dollars per part or dollars per hour. Your goal would likely be stated in these same terms or perhaps as a percentage reduction. In this way, data and assessments can help reduce spending and risk and improve operations in quality, delivery, and service—the key goals of the supply management process.

In many organizations, supplier performance monitoring is automated through the use of some software system. Organizational procedures generally define what types of monitoring techniques are to be used and the frequency of reporting. The procurement and quality teams then implement a supplier review process through regular meetings, site visits, product testing, and customer surveys to determine where gaps exist in reaching the desired objective. Once gaps are identified, the next phase of enhancing supplier performance is the execution of corrective action plans.

MANAGING SUPPLIER ACTIVITIES   In general, a fairly wide variation exists within the scope of typical supplier activities, and you may find that in your organization only the key elements of their duties are actually being measured on a routine basis. Yet, as a procurement professional, the responsibility for ensuring that all supplier commitments are met will be yours. With hundreds of suppliers and thousands of events taking place daily, how can you possibly manage them all?

There are several ways you might consider for managing a broad scope of activities such as the following:

- **Management by exception.** One method of managing supplier activities relies on an automated reporting system and alerts you only when exceptions to the required standard occur. This is called *management by exception*. You receive notification only when events occur outside of the expected range of possibilities. For example, if you use a computer-based system for documenting receipts, you may be able to get notification of late deliveries whenever shipment is overdue by a specific amount of time.
- **Input from internal users.** You might solicit regular input from your internal users, either through surveys or through direct reporting methods. Or you might consider spending time with the users of the materials and services you purchase. This way, you observe the problems when they actually occur and from the perspective of your customer. It helps you understand the impact of actual failures (or successes) and enables you to better communicate them to your supplier.
- **Site visits.** It is not uncommon to find buyers monitoring activities directly in the supplier's facility so that they can become more actively involved in resolving issues. As Yogi Berra, the retired coach of the New York Yankees baseball team, once said, "You can observe a lot just by watching."

REVIEWING PERFORMANCE   Performance reviews are generally presented in a report format, outlining the supplier's actual performance to goal or standard for a specific period of time. Often, these are conducted in a formal meeting environment and within the framework of a standard predefined agenda. Since extensive reviews are typically very time consuming, it is common to hold them on a quarterly basis, especially when the supplier's team must travel a long distance to visit your facility. Use of your organization's business review process, in fact, is probably one the most widely accepted formats. Often, these are supplemented with an annual *executive* *review* where senior managers come together to exchange forthcoming *business plans* and *technology road maps*.

The use of a performance *scorecard* is a popular communication method for delivering supplier reviews. The scorecard is a compilation or summary of the supplier's performance to the preestablished metrics called for in the SLA. It is common to generalize performance into categories such as quality, cost, on-time delivery, and service on the scorecard, touching on the high points and low points of actual results.

It is important that you also allow time to obtain supplier feedback on problems from the supplier's perspective and to garner ideas on how your organization can better align their processes. While you want to avoid reducing the process to a sales presentation, you should also consider asking for feedback on how the supplier feels it can better serve you.

DEVELOPING PERFORMANCE IMPROVEMENTS While many variations of continuous improvement exist, the basic steps are fairly well defined:

1. Analyze existing conditions.
2. Determine the gaps that exist between the actual conditions and the desired state.
3. Develop plans to eliminate (or reduce) the gaps.
4. Implement the plan.
5. Measure improvements.
6. Repeat the cycle.

These steps are generally conducted within the framework of a *commodity management* team that is sponsored by the *business unit* leader. We've found it useful to manage improvement initiatives as projects, using Gantt charts and assigning specific actions and timelines to individual team members. This creates both accountability and a sense of understanding of all the elements that are required to make the project successful.

Note

The identification of business process gaps that have a financial ramification to an organization, along with the identification of a plan to remedy the gaps, is a key element of the Sarbanes-Oxley Act of 2002, Section 404, which was discussed in Chapter 1.

No progressive organization can operate in a vacuum. The procurement professional is uniquely positioned for adding strategic value to the organization by finding business opportunities to build strong relationships with other organizations in the supply chain, leveraging their innovation to seed fresh ideas and business processes. These supply relationships foster new learning that helps develop improved methods and generate new business opportunities.

Resolving Relations Issues

Reinforcing good business relationships with your supplier takes some measure of attention to detail and effort as there are numerous daily activities that, when not well performed, can lead to disputes and concerns. Normally, these issues are relatively minor and part of the normal course of business; however, when failure to perform routine supplier support activities becomes the rule rather than the exception, you will run the risk of having them result in diminished performance levels.

While it is difficult to generalize the kinds of problems you may encounter, here we discuss some of those that have been frequently mentioned in procurement literature.

PAYING INVOICES ON TIME   Cash flow is important to every business enterprise, and the finance team at your supplier will continually monitor and rate your account on how timely the payments are made by your organization. Accounts that are continually past due present a problem. If you consider that money has a time value, the longer it takes to collect the payment, the lower will be the actual profit. As a result, late payments actually cut into the supplier's operating margin. While an occasional late payment can be overlooked, a pattern of late payments may require the supplier to raise its prices in compensation.

An associated issue related to late payments is the handling of invoices. It's extremely frustrating for the supplier's accounts receivable staff to find an overdue payment and discover that the buying organization has no record of ever receiving it. No matter how you look at it, this will require significant duplication of effort to correct. To reduce lost invoices, be sure suppliers have the correct address for submitting them to your organization and, if needed, have the suppliers include an individual's name or a mail stop in the address.

Tips and Techniques

Organizations can maintain effective alignment with their suppliers by exchanging *aging* reports. The supplier's aging report shows when the invoice was submitted and how many days old it is, while the buyer's shows how long the invoice has been received and when payment will be made based on the existing terms. In this way, each party can proactively identify problem payments before they get out of hand.

MAINTAINING CONFIDENTIALITY   Any information given to you by the supplier should always be considered confidential and never disclosed to third parties outside your organization. Most of the time, buyers and sellers exchange confidentiality agreements or nondisclosure agreements early in their relationship that require both to maintain certain levels of confidentiality. Regardless of the existence of such legal documents, it is of the utmost ethical importance that information given you in confidence never be shared with your suppliers' competitors.

DEALING FAIRLY AND EQUALLY WITH SUPPLIERS   To maintain credibility requires that you treat all suppliers fairly and consistently, avoiding the perception that you favor one over the others. If your organization maintains a system of priorities based on the level of supplier qualification or certification, you will be obliged to follow it. However, you should continually encourage suppliers to work toward the preferred status, offering help and guidance as needed.

Many organizations develop close partnerships with some of their suppliers, including joint ventures and similar programs. Be sure to disclose this to suppliers who are new to doing business with you so that they do not waste effort in focusing on areas that will likely yield no results.

Tips and Techniques

Trust is a key element in relations with your suppliers. One way to establish and continue to maintain trust is by always keeping your word.

AVOIDING ILLEGAL SITUATIONS On the opposite end of the spectrum, there are many actions that may superficially appear to be solidifying relationships, but that may bring up issues with restraint of trade. Providing preferred treatment to suppliers who also buy your products can be one of them. While it is legal, and often preferable, to buy from one's suppliers, trading purchase for purchase can be seen as a tying contract, which is illegal. So long as price, quality, delivery, and the other fundamentals of supplier selection override decisions of personal preference, you will likely be viewed as exercising sound ethical judgment.

Certifying New Suppliers

Every organization has its own method for certifying suppliers. Some are general and based on conformance with specific qualifications, such as being ISO certified. Some require certification by a third-party examiner. Others are more specific to the needs of your particular organization, such as ISO/TS 16949, which is an international quality management system standard for manufacturers of automotive parts. Perhaps you require a specific environmental policy or conformance to specific rules of social responsibility in order for your suppliers to reach certified status. You may find that some of these requirements are readily achievable, while others may be established only by your own organization. In this case, you may need to develop a program for communicating your requirements and assisting the supplier in achieving them.

Tips and Techniques

Certification should not be confused with qualification. Supplier qualification is a process used to determine if a particular supplier is capable of handling a specific job. Certification means that the supplier has met certain criteria and levels of performance—often determined through field audits—that enable it to be considered by your organization as an ongoing applicant for business.

MENTORING *Mentoring* is a form of teaching and guidance that assists individuals and organizations reach a certain level of performance. Often, mentoring is an educational process in which the mentor serves as a role model or teacher, providing opportunities for growth to less experienced organizations. It is based on encouragement, constructive comments, openness, mutual trust, respect, and a willingness to learn and share.

Often, an established organization will assist a newly developing one through this kind of mentorship, but for the process to work well, there has to be some mutual benefit. In some cases, the benefits can be an additional source of supply that makes an otherwise closely held industry more competitive. At other times, it can be the means to support small, minority businesses to ensure that they get a fair share of your business.

Developing Continuous Improvement

Continuous improvement as a quality concept was discussed in Chapter 12 in relation to the buyer's responsibility in managing suppliers. In this section, we look at it a bit further from the aspect of obtaining alignment with supplier activities.

Gaining Early Supplier Involvement

Early supplier involvement in new product design can beneficially influence both cost and cycle time by leveraging the supplier's process strengths and relying on the expertise of its staff to enable optimal solutions. Often, it makes sense to involve multiple tiers of suppliers so that you can assure alignment of processes within the immediate supply chain. This is best accomplished through cross-functional, multi-organizational teams that search out the methods and processes that best leverage all of their strengths.

WORKING COLLABORATIVELY   Supplier involvement in your organization's operations will generally focus on areas of mutual goals. Activities can range from the typical unilateral problem solving to participation in activities that reach far into your organization. The benefit of this close collaboration is that both organizations are able to leverage their individual strengths toward the development of a single process that divides the workload and responsibilities accordingly. Real gains, however, occur when technology and expertise pass freely among partners so that knowledge is shared as it is jointly developed, providing a competitive advantage to the entire supply chain. From this effort, products that are brought to the marketplace are likely to add more value and, because they are not easily copied, offer greater sustainability.

FORMING PARTNERSHIPS AND ALLIANCES   Partnerships and business alliances are generally formed to fill specific needs, such as the joint development of a new product or service that would fall outside the capabilities of each of the participants if they were to attempt to go forward alone. This need is generally defined through some specific market research or opportunity analysis, following a formal path of internal examinations and recommendations by management. Typically, a business case is prepared prior to approval outlining the strategic benefits and potential threats.

For the supplier's contribution, the alliance generally requires an additional investment in equipment or staff. The buyer's contribution usually comes in the form of an exclusive contract to buy certain volumes of specific items. When the alliance involves joint development, cross-organizational, cross-functional teams are generally formed, having the effect of bring the two organizations' strategic objectives into alignment.

It is typical for organizations engaged in partnerships or alliances to form contracts governing roles and responsibilities, as well as the accrual of benefits. Successful partnerships are based on the full involvement of each of the partners, so it is important to develop clear measurements for how effectively each partner is meeting its commitments.

MAINTAINING PARTNERSHIPS AND ALLIANCES   To maintain the relationships, there must be continuing benefit to both parties. Successful long-term partnerships generally have high management visibility and support, so resources continue to be made available as long as there is a clear willingness by the working teams to continue to engage.

STRENGTHENING SUPPLIER RELATIONS   There is no general rule for strengthening supplier relationships: Many of the processes outlined earlier that are used to form the initial relationship can continue to be used to strengthen it. However, please keep in mind that it is the Procurement Department's responsibility—your responsibility—to develop and maintain valuable working relationships with suppliers.

Experience shows that one of the most important ingredients in strong relationships is trust. Trust is a characteristic and quality that typically develops when there is open and honest communication between parties, and when both respect each other's behaviors. Fundamental to this is keeping one's word and honoring all of your commitments.

Implementing Small/Disadvantaged Business Programs

In order to have an effective corporate supplier diversity development program, both commitment and involvement from senior management is usually required. The major goal of developing a supplier diversity program is to provide all potential suppliers equal access to procurement opportunities generated by your organization.

A written supplier diversity development policy is used to formalize the goals and objectives of the program. By formalizing the program with senior management support, you can generally ensure the dedication and support of the procurement staff. In order to meet the formalization of the process, a comprehensive buyer training and accountability road map must be developed. This accountability road map must include tracking and reporting systems that show the results of awarding procurement business to small and disadvantaged suppliers. To ensure success, effective communication of the program objectives needs to be developed to internal customers, existing suppliers, and potential suppliers.

Tips and Techniques

Minority Business Defined

The National Minority Supplier Development Council defines a minority-owned business as a for-profit enterprise, regardless of size, physically located in the United States or its trust territories, which is owned, operated, and controlled by minority group members. "Minority group members" are United States citizens who are Asian, Black, Hispanic, and Native American. Ownership by minority individuals means the business is at least 51 percent owned by such individuals or, in the case of a publicly owned business, at least 51 percent of the stock is owned by one or more such individuals. Further, the management and daily operations are controlled by those minority group members. See www.nmsdcus.org.

LOCATING QUALIFIED MINORITY SUPPLIERS   Effective identification and sourcing from minority suppliers is paramount to long-term success. There are many minority supplier directories that can assist in this effort. Attendance at small business and minority and female-owned trade shows is also effective in identifying such suppliers. Various industry contacts can also serve as informational networking in locating qualified minority suppliers within various commodities.

The following URLs can assist in sourcing minority suppliers:

- Diversity Information Resources, Inc., www.DiversityInfoResources.com
- DiversityBusiness.com, www.div2000.com
- DiversityInc.com, www.diversityinc.com
- Dynamic Small Business Search, http://dsbs.sba.gov/dsbs/dsp_dsbs.cfm
- Industry Council for Small Business Development, www.icsbd.org
- Minority Business Development Agency, www.mbda.gov
- Minority Business Entrepreneur Magazine, www.mbemag.com
- Minority Business News, www.minoritybusinessnews.com
- National Minority Business Council Inc., www.nmbc.org
- National Minority Supplier Development Council Inc., www.nmsdcus.org
- Women's Business Enterprise National Council, www.wbenc.org

DEVELOPING AND MANAGING PROGRAMS   Making small business and minority suppliers known within your organization is core in the development of any comprehensive procurement diversity program. The identification of the potential suppliers' capabilities is the domain of any procurement policy and supplier development strategy. To be truly effective, such information must be effectively communicated to the entire organization.

In order to determine if your supplier diversity development strategy is effective, a measurement and reporting system must be established to monitor results in a timely fashion. Many corporations use such reporting systems to establish various types of rewards and recognition programs for outstanding results for diversity suppliers and procurement commodity groups alike.

See Chapter 6 for more detailed information.

Pricing Factors and Supply

The basics of supplier selection based on pricing were initially discussed in Chapters 2, 3, and 4. In this section, however, we will round out those discussions by reviewing some of the factors that govern the actual pricing you will encounter.

Understanding Market Conditions

While strong relationships, as well as negotiation skill, have an important role in determining the prices your organization will be asked to pay for any particular product or service, *market conditions* at the time will also play a major role, too. Market conditions consist of a number of factors such as supply and demand, the overall economic climate, production capacity, competition, and numerous other elements that affect even the psychology of buyers and sellers. Since pricing is often a measure of your ability to manage the supply base, let's look more closely at some of the elements that affect your ability to control pricing from your suppliers.

SUPPLY AND DEMAND You will recall that in Chapter 2 we examined the role of market forces through supply and demand and stated that the imbalance of one in relation to the other directly affects pricing. "The ratio of supply to demand always affects prices. When supply is more plentiful than demand, suppliers must lower prices to make buying more attractive; when demand outstrips supply, buyers compete for the few available resources and prices rise." This is a fairly timeless concept.

However, there are times when an increase in pricing does not result in a corresponding decrease in demand. Automotive fuel is a paradigm example, with consumers purchasing the same amount regardless of the fluctuation pricing. When this occurs we say that the price is "inelastic," that is, it does not move in direct relationship to supply and demand.

ECONOMIC FACTORS Overall economic conditions are generally what drive supply and demand. When the economy is strong, consumers tend to have ample cash to spend. This generally strains production capacity, creating shortages and raising prices. Conversely, when consumers have little cash to spend, capacity is plentiful and prices tend to spiral downward.

What causes these cycles? Good question! The best answer is that any given time, no one really knows. Economic cycles have been noted since the beginning of recorded time but, while theories abound, no agreement is readily available. In hindsight, however, we can always point to situational factors such as "the market was oversold" as causes for creating a downturn. Overall, though, we consider upturns and downturns to be naturally occurring phenomena that will always be with us.

Industry Capacity Within any given industry, capacity can be measured by the percentage of utilization of resources. As we approach 90 percent of utilization, overtime tends to rise, and orders that were once profitable require increases in prices to sustain them. If you can adequately forecast these trends, you will likely be able to take very productive steps to take advantage of them.

Supplier Capacity   Individual supplier capacity can be constrained from time to time, as well, based on an influx of large orders or the unexpected loss of production capacity due to disaster. This may require you to move orders to a secondary source without the benefit of favorable pricing. Effective procurement professionals are always alert to the conditions affecting their most important suppliers and generally tend to avoid sole-sourcing situations for this very reason.

Available Labor   In unionized environments, conditions can change whenever a contract is under negotiations. Negotiation failure frequently results in strikes and work stoppages, followed by resultant shortages. Stockpiling in advance of a potential labor dispute can drive prices up even before the negotiation has concluded.

Cost-Based Pricing Models

In addition to general market conditions, prices can be governed by supplier costs and *markup* strategies. Despite the fact that we may never have full access to the supplier's costs, there are a number of profit models we can examine to get the full picture.

STANDARD MARKUP MODEL   Using a typical markup model, the supplier calculates the unit cost and then adds a percentage to cover overhead and profit. The overhead is generally comprised of all the operating expenses for the organization and converted to a percentage of direct costs. For example, if an organization allocates 20 percent of its costs to direct materials and labor and 40 percent of its costs to overhead, the cost ratio of overhead costs to direct costs is 2:1 (40 / 20 = 2). This means that the supplier determines the price by adding an overhead and profit factor to its estimated product or service cost. Let's look at an example where the supplier's desired profit is 10 percent and the direct cost of the product is determined to be $1.80.

$$\text{Selling Price} = \text{Total Cost} + \text{Profit}$$

$$\text{Total Cost} = (\text{Direct Cost} + (\text{Direct Cost} \times \text{Overhead}))$$

$$= (1.80 + (1.80 \times 2))$$

$$= 5.40$$

$$\text{Selling Price} = 5.40 + .54$$

$$= 5.94$$

SPECIFIC RATE OF RETURN MODEL   When the supplier expects to receive a specific rate of return for an investment, the calculation is based on the total cost of the investment plus the cost to produce the product or service. This figure is then multiplied by the rate of return desired in order to arrive at the selling price. As a simplified calculation it might look like this, given a 15 percent rate of return:

$$\text{Selling Price} = \text{Average Cost} + \text{Desired Rate of Return (15\%)}$$

$$\text{Average Cost} = \frac{(\text{Total Investment} + \text{Total Cost to Produce})}{\text{Anticipated Sales Volume}}$$

$$= \frac{\$150{,}000 + \$100{,}000}{100{,}000 \text{ Units}}$$

$$= \$2.50 \text{ per unit}$$

$$\text{Selling Price} = 2.50 + .375$$

$$= 2.875$$

Price Analysis Methods

While there are many elaborate ways to analyze prices, in your day-to-day activities you will likely have only little time to do overly academic studies. From a practical point of view, the easiest and most productive method of analysis is to compare the prices being offered with some form of benchmark. Here are some of the more commonly used tools to consider:

- *Trend analysis* employs statistics methodology to determine where prices are heading or how one price compares to another. Some of the more commonly used statistical methods used in procurement include the following:
  - *Linear regression analysis* calculates a mathematical formula for the best-fitting straight line through a series of data points. By extending the calculation of this line to an event in the future, we can develop a forecast. The upper chart in Figure 14.1 shows the actual prices paid for purchases over a 26-week period. This data can then be used to calculate a trend line, which is shown as the dotted line in the lower chart. We can then use this trend line to forecast anticipated volumes, shown as the extension of the trend line in the lower chart.
  - *Exponential smoothing* is an adjustment technique that takes the previous period's forecast and adjusts it up or down based on what actually occurred in that period. It accomplishes this by calculating a weighted average of the two values. As a historical projection, it allows the user to give more weight to most recent data.
- *Comparative analysis* can take a number of forms, ranging from benchmarking industry standards to a side-by-side comparison of quoted prices. Table 14.1 shows an example of a price list analysis that compares the prices from three suppliers at different volume levels. As you can see, no single supplier has the best price throughout the volume range. How you make your selection will depend upon the volume you purchase and how well you can negotiate aggregated volumes over a period of time to obtain the highest discount.
- *Product analysis* or *functionality analysis*, as it is sometimes called, examines products or services in terms of the functionality they provide, evaluating each element as a separate cost factor so that a comparative analysis of features can be made. This comparison helps determine the value and desirability of added

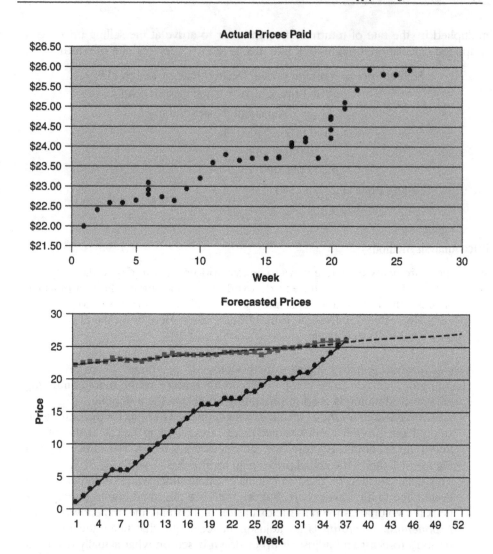

FIGURE 14.1   Example of Linear Regression Analysis

TABLE 14.1   Side by Side Comparison of Prices

Quantity	Supplier A	Supplier B	Supplier C
1,000	1.10	1.12	1.09
2,500	0.84	0.88	0.84
5,000	0.78	0.80	0.80
10,000	0.64	0.66	0.68
25,000	0.52	0.51	0.54
50,000	0.48	0.46	0.49

functionality and can also help compare products considered to be as disparate as apples and oranges.

Representing the Organization

One of the key functions of the procurement staff is managing the interface with suppliers and others outside the organization. This function requires an extremely tactful approach, since in many ways your contacts are the "public," and you must be certain the messages you give are in alignment with organizational policy. Close contact with your organization's public relations or communications teams will help ensure you are up-to-date on your current positioning of correct messages.

Meeting Sales Personnel

When effectively organized, meetings with sales personnel should always prove productive. While you have only the perspective of your own organization from which to gauge industry developments, your sales counterpart typically meets with several organizations during the normal course of business. Without compromising confidentiality, the sales representative can provide you with a host of ideas on how to improve operations.

As a result, it is important that you follow some specific protocol in dealing with sales personnel. To do so requires that you clearly understand the role of the sales professional.

THE ROLE OF THE SALES PROFESSIONAL Sales methods, of course, vary from organization to organization, industry to industry, and country to country. There are, however, a certain set of roles that are universal to virtually all those in sales. These roles generally include the following:

- Researching and prospecting for potential customers.
- Establishing rapport with a potential customer.
- Identifying the customer's needs.
- Matching the customer's needs with product offerings.
- Presenting the offer, asking for the sale, overcoming objections.
- Making the sale and closing.
- Providing ongoing customer support.

Tips and Techniques

Sales training can be an extensive and detailed process, often quite mysterious to the buyer. For an excellent resource for learning more about selling techniques and the selling profession, go to www.businessballs.com/salestraining.htm.

Keep in mind, however, that unlike the procurement agent or buyer, the salesperson is rarely an agent of the organization and is therefore not empowered to commit the organization to contractual obligations. To do so generally requires an individual at the management level.

THE ROLE OF PROCUREMENT   The Procurement Department provides the initial interface with sales personnel and is responsible within the organization for responding to initial sales inquiries. In this role, the Procurement Department must decide if there is any potential in the offering and if the salesperson has the ability to add value to the process. In addition, it is the procurement department's function to work with the sales representative to further identify organizational needs that might fit and to introduce the sales rep to others in the organization that may have an interest in the products or services being offered.

The procurement team also has the opportunity through its interface with sales personnel to learn how others in the same marketplace may be conducting operations (without asking for confidential information) and can pass along this information to others in the form of intelligence.

It is also worth noting that Procurement should be informed of any supplier visits paid directly to the user so that it can monitor information being disclosed. This helps ensure that other suppliers, should there be a competitive situation, gain access to the same information.

EXTENDING ORGANIZATIONAL HOSPITALITY   Sales staff should be treated at all times with courtesy and respect, as valued representatives of their organizations. Here are some guidelines you might want to refer to when meeting with sales personnel:

- Meet promptly and courteously with sales representatives making scheduled calls.
- Offer as much hospitality as possible during your meeting.
- Provide equal opportunity for all representatives to present their products when you have a specific need.
- Maintain confidentiality at all times.
- Show concern for the representative's time and expense.
- When unable to provide the business being sought, explain the reasons as clearly as possible.

HANDLING INQUIRIES, PROTESTS, AND COMPLAINTS   The Procurement Department handles numerous inquiries in the normal course of conducting business. Obviously, it is important that these be reviewed promptly and handled expeditiously as well as courteously. While many of these inquiries are simply prospecting efforts by sales personnel, many of them involve pending business and often require coordination with other departments in the organization.

When an inquiry refers to a current bid process or an open request for proposals (RFP), the buyer must be certain to respond accordingly to all participants as a measure of fairness and good business conduct. If the question materially affects the bidding, it may be necessary for the buyer to publish a formal addendum to the bid solicitation or the RFP addressing the issue.

From time to time, suppliers will want to protest an award decision or file a complaint regarding unfair treatment. Most organizations have well-defined processes to handle this, including requirements for filing the objection in writing along with appropriate documentation. As part of an appeals process, some organizations provide for an escalation path to management or a standing committee for further review and action. In many cases, a contract or policy calls for a formal dispute resolution process involving a neutral third party.

Regardless of the process used by your organization, it is important both that the suppliers understand the review process and that it be conducted expeditiously so as not to disrupt normal operations for either party.

PROFESSIONAL CONDUCT   Professional conduct is paramount to maintaining credibility with suppliers. Many organizations have a specific code of conduct, but if yours does not, consider using the one established by the Institute for Supply Management (see the accompanying box).

Tips and Techniques

Principles and Standards of Ethical Supply Management Conduct

Loyalty to Your Organization
Justice to Those with Whom You Deal
Faith in Your Profession

From these principles are derived the ISM standards of supply management conduct. . . .

- Avoid the intent and appearance of unethical or compromising practice in relationships, actions, and communications.
- Demonstrate loyalty to the employer by diligently following the lawful instructions of the employer, using reasonable care and granted authority.
- Avoid any personal business or professional activity that would create a conflict between personal interests and the interests of the employer.
- Avoid soliciting or accepting money, loans, credits, or preferential discounts, and the acceptance of gifts, entertainment, favors, or services from present or potential suppliers that might influence, or appear to influence, supply management decisions.
- Handle confidential or proprietary information with due care and proper consideration of ethical and legal ramifications and governmental regulations.
- Promote positive supplier relationships through courtesy and impartiality.
- Avoid improper reciprocal agreements.
- Know and obey the letter and spirit of laws applicable to supply management.
- Encourage support for small, disadvantaged, and minority-owned businesses.
- Acquire and maintain professional competence.
- Conduct supply management activities in accordance with national and international laws, customs, and practices, your organization's policies, and these ethical principles and standards of conduct.
- Enhance the stature of the supply management profession.

Source: Institute for Supply Management, approved January 2002

PARTICIPATING IN MEETINGS AND EXTERNAL EVENTS   From time to time, procurement department staff will be required to represent the department or the organization in meetings and at outside events. For this reason, it is important that you understand how to conduct an effective meeting and how to prepare successful presentations.

Meetings   There are a few simple rules for conducting meetings that will help you make them more effective:

- Select the right participants based on the topic and input from others who might be interested in attending.
- Extend invitations in sufficient time to assure everyone who wishes to attend will have ample time to make arrangements.
- Prepare an agenda and distribute it in advance of the meeting.
- Ensure that the meeting facilities are sufficient to the number invited and have the necessary supplies.
- During the meeting, ensure that those who wish to participate in the discussion are provided with ample opportunity.
- Follow the agenda, including starting and ending on time.
- Maintain focus during the meeting.
- Periodically evaluate progress during the course of the meeting.
- Take and post notes as appropriate.
- Reach consensus or decisions if and as planned.
- Following the meeting, publish notes and provide an opportunity for further input.

Presentation   Preparing and delivering an effective presentation is one of the most important skills you can develop and should not be difficult to achieve if you follow a few basic rules consistently. Many guides to effective presentations list the following as important considerations:

- Define the desired outcome of your presentation.
- Stay focused on your topic.
- Prepare your presentation with your specific audience in mind.
- Be in touch with your surroundings.
- Prepare carefully; use a script if needed.
- Organize material and present it in a logical sequence.
- Deal with one concept at a time.
- Leverage appropriate visual aids; be simple.
- Test regularly for clarity to be sure you are communicating with your audience.
- Deliver your material clearly.
- Define acronyms and unfamiliar terms.
- Maintain your audience's attention through eye contact.
- Encourage participation.
- Stay on schedule.

Ultimately, the most important consideration in meetings and presentations to bear in mind is to maintain your sincerity at all times. Most audiences feel uncomfortable around affectation.

Summary

In this chapter, we reviewed the requirements for managing productive supplier relations and how creating good working relationships required a measure of effort. Meeting regularly with your suppliers, conducting surveys to garner input, and initiating reciprocal site visits are just a few of the ways to enhance relations. We also reviewed many of the tools available for improving communications with suppliers and how best to resolve ongoing relationship issues.

We then turned our attention to ways in which new suppliers could be certified and how to develop continuous improvement programs for existing suppliers. We looked at how early supplier involvement assisted better performance in procurement and the advantages of working collaboratively through supplier partnerships and alliances.

This chapter also covered the fundamentals of establishing and managing a supplier diversity program, including sourcing minority suppliers, as well as developing and managing programs.

As a key part of supplier relationship management, we examined how supplier pricing operates in response to market conditions and profit strategies. This included a look at pricing methods and analysis of pricing trend data.

We concluded the chapter with an examination of how the Procurement Department represents the organization with suppliers and handles supplier inquiries and protests, and we reviewed a standardized code of ethical conduct. And, finally, we reviewed how to conduct effective meetings and prepare presentations.

Note

1. Leenders, Michiel R., and David L. Blenkhorn, *Reverse Marketing: The New Buyer-Supplier Relationship* (New York: Free Press, 1987).

CHAPTER 15

Leveraging Computer Systems

The supply management landscape has changed rapidly over the past several years, largely as a result of computerization and Internet utilization. Procurement departments are becoming increasingly inclined to move routine transactional processes, such as placing purchase orders (POs), to computer-based platforms to gain efficiency and better utilization of employee time management. This *reengineering* process has paralleled, for the most part, the widespread acceptance of automated systems across the entire spectrum of our organizations and the increasing use of the Internet for business.

Today, organizations are increasingly turning to computerized tools to integrate all of the elements in the *procure-to-pay* process. By doing so, they are realizing the financial benefits of increased productivity and reduced cycle times generated through the automation of routine processes such as requisition and purchase order generation, quotation, bidding, order tracking, expediting, supplier payment, and procedural compliance. Today, tools are widely available to assist procurement departments to time their buying decisions based on market trends in pricing and availability. Indeed, the current trend to *Web-based sourcing* using tools that automate and speed up many of the more tedious procurement processes such as requests for information (RFIs) and requests for proposals (RFPs) have enabled organizations to improve their supplier selection and reduce prices through standardization methods that would otherwise be cost prohibitive. Using these tools, organizations have even been able to manage their buying power in some of the smaller spending areas, such as maintenance, repair, and operations (MRO), which would have been impossible just several years ago.

Buyers and sellers have shared equally in these benefits through the transparency of supply capacity and product demand, producing greater collaboration and alignment between their organizations. Partners are now able to share supply and demand data in real time and the result has been savings for both. This has been especially apparent in the recent trend to supplier-managed inventory programs (or *consignment inventory*), where inventory is stored at the buyer's site and paid for only as used. Widespread adoption of methods such as this has freed enormous resources across the *supply chain.* Just as buyers have benefited from the ability to find more sources more easily, suppliers have benefited from the ability to reach larger markets without additional cost.

In this chapter, we review the most commonly used computer-based technology applications and their function in the organization. We also cover the computerized system tools being used in supply management and how they link to the organization's broader *information technology* structure.

Using Basic Information Technology Processes

Before delving into the specifics of procurement applications, and by way of an introduction to the subject matter, it would be worthwhile to go over some of the fundamentals of computerized systems by looking at the basic terminology, along with the types of *platforms* in use and the nature of the *software applications* developed for them.

Computer Basics

As computer systems evolve, the language describing their individual elements naturally changes, too. However, you will need to be familiar with some of the basic terminology to effectively manage your internal systems, regardless of their brand or configuration. Here are some of the terms most commonly used.

DATA PROCESSING TERMS   Basic data processing terms describe the fundamental principles used in information technology:

- *Bits/bytes* are the basic building blocks of computer technology. A bit is one binary digit—the smallest unit of computer programming—taking the form of a one or a zero. A byte is a grouping of eight bits that make up a single character.
- *Data* represents the basic information assembled from bits and bytes that is put into a computer.
- A *record* consists of an individual set of data, such as a name or an address.
- A *file* contains a set of related records that are usually stored in one place.
- A *digital system* is a system in which information is conveyed as data in a series of bits and bytes.

HARDWARE TERMS   Computer hardware refers to the elements of a computer system that you can actually touch. The major terms used to describe computer hardware include:

- The *central processing unit (CPU)* is really the brains of the computer and is responsible for performing most of the computational work.
- *Storage media* consists of a variety of products such as hard disk drives, memory chips, magnetic tape, CD-ROMs, and DVDs on which data is stored either optically or magnetically.
- *Input devices* are the hardware tools used to enter data into the system. They include keyboards, scanners, readers, memory devices, and disks.
- *Output devices* are the hardware components used to store or display information such as printers, monitors and the devices listed above as storage media.
- *Communication devices* are used to transmit data between computers and across networks. They include modems, broadband routers, switches, and wireless receivers.

COMPUTER TYPES   There are a traditional set of computer types that we commonly refer to when we describe the kind of devices we commonly use. Today, however, virtually all appliances and automobiles use embedded computers to one extent or another, so the list that follows is incomplete to the extent that it does not attempt to describe all computational devices.

- The *personal computer (PC)*, desktop or laptop, is the most visible computer in use today and makes up the majority of devices we employ.
- The *minicomputer* is one step above the PC and is designed for limited multiuser applications, such as those that might be found in smaller organizations.
- The *mainframe* is used to run major applications that require a great deal of computational power and storage capacity. They are also used to run large networks that communicate with thousands of terminals, sometimes located around the world.
- *Workstations* are devices that generally consist of dumb terminals used to access data on a mini or mainframe computer in a client/server environment. However, in today's networking systems, quite frequently PCs are used as both stand-alone systems and as workstations.
- The *personal digital assistant (PDA)* is a relatively small, portable device with only limited processing capability that connects to a computer to obtain information from calendars, address books, and lists of project items. PDAs are often combined with cell phones to provide maximum utility.

NETWORK TERMS   Computer networks consist of a series of computers linked together to exchange information. Some of the more common terms that reference computer networks include:

- *Local area network (LAN)* is a geographically restricted network, most commonly contained in one building.
- *Wide area network (WAN)* is a network that covers a large geographical area.
- The *Internet* is the largest computer network in the world, connecting millions of computers
- *Transmission control protocol/Internet protocol (TCP/IP)* is a networking standard. Transmission control protocol refers to that segment of the standard that is used to move data between applications; Internet protocol refers to the standard governing the movement of data between host computers.
- *Virtual private network (VPN)* is a data network that uses telecommunication lines and the Internet to exchange information but is secured by a *tunneling protocol* and secure firewalls.
- *Network operating system (NOS)* is the software used to operate the network.
- *File transfer protocol (FTP)* is a standard used in moving information across a network or the Internet.
- A *firewall* is a specialized software application that prevents unauthorized access to the network at the point where it connects to public systems.

Platforms

The term "platform" refers to the various underlying elements of a computer system: the software being used (such as the *operating system*), the hardware being used

Client/Server Configuration

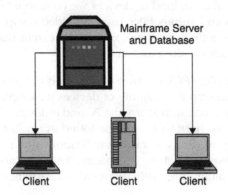

FIGURE 15.1   Client Server System

to run the software, and the method of storing and distributing data. This section addresses the latter usage and describes the fundamental configurations used in automated procurement systems.

CENTRALIZED SYSTEMS   A *centralized computer system* is a single computer—often called a *mainframe*—operating from one location but usually serving many users. These are most commonly used in a *client/server* configuration, where a *workstation* (or "dumb" terminal) without any processing capability is linked to a mainframe that does all the computational work. This model, in its simplest form, is shown in Figure 15.1. The major advantage of the centralized computer system is that it can be maintained and operated by fewer personnel since it is located in one place.

DISTRIBUTED SYSTEMS   *Distributed systems* are a collection of computer systems (both hardware and software) dispersed across several sites but operating as one cohesive unit. Their interaction is generally transparent to the users.

   Networks are a form of distributed system that consists of a group of computers linked together electronically so that their users can share information. The most common types of networks are the LANs, where computers are geographically close to one another (typically at the same location) and WANs, where they are further apart and generally linked by some form of telecommunications media.

   The major advantage of the distributed system is that it is modular and can be built or reconfigured fairly easily over large distances.

Software Applications

Software is a program or set of instructions that make the computer run or perform specific functions. As you know, software can be purchased as off-the-shelf items (sometimes referred to as "boxed") or as customized applications. Typically, the more common software applications such as word processing or spreadsheet software will be purchased in its packaged form through distributors or directly from the manufacturer. However, buyers always have the option of downloading the software directly from the producer's website or buying it already installed on their computers. In some states, boxed software is taxable, while the same software downloaded from a website is not, making it an attractive way to save money.

When buying mission-critical applications—such as financial or manufacturing software—organizations often find that the "packaged" version does not meet all of its needs. Consequently, applications are quite typically modified—customized—by the original or third party programmers so that they can meet these special needs.

It is sometimes helpful to categorize software types so that you can understand where a particular program fits in the computing process. There are two basic types of software:

1. **Systems software.** *Systems software* provides the instructions that make the computer run. Utilities and operating systems such as Microsoft Windows, MacOS, and Linux are typical examples. Systems software also manages the communications and interface aspects of the network.
2. **Applications software.** *Applications software* enables the user to carry out specific tasks such as writing letters using word processing programs or performing financial analysis using spreadsheets programs. The term also applies to the broader, more scalable systems such as *enterprise resource planning (ERP)* applications used to manage an entire organization.

Using Software for Procurement

You will likely find that while much of the software used in procurement applies to processes used by everyone in the organization, some of it is naturally dedicated to the procurement process only. Procurement professionals need to become familiar with virtually all the software used by the organization since the procurement team will be responsible for its purchase. In addition, you should also understand that your role requires particular expertise in applications used primarily for procurement and supply management. When your organization seeks to acquire new or upgraded programs that impact your area, you should expect to be called upon for your knowledge of software tools dedicated to the procurement function.

This section outlines the software applications most commonly used by organizations, grouping them by general applications and applications specific to procurement operations.

General software applications encompass a broad spectrum of software used in today's organization. Here are just a few of them.

Desktop Applications

So-called "desktop applications" include a variety of commonly used software programs, many of which are released and sold in bundled configurations called suites. Microsoft Office is an example of this, containing word processing, spreadsheets, e-mail, database, and presentation software—all typically designed to be used by the general public as well as the experts. In addition to the traditional office suites, there are numerous others available to manage files, scan documents, keep track of appointments and contacts, and manage finances. Some of the more commonly used include the following:

- **Word processing** programs such as MS Word or WordPerfect enable the creation and editing of text materials for letters, documents, reports and tables.
- **Spreadsheets** allow the user to organize, analyze, and manage numerical data, create graphs and charts, and generally provide surprisingly powerful number-crunching capability, enabling the sorting and conversion of data through formulas.
- **Contact management** programs enable users to store and keep track of extensive lists of people. Typically, these tools are used in sales to manage customer relationships by maintaining records of contacts, projects under way, and customer preferences.
- **Database management** software allows for the management of relatively large amounts of data through powerful sorting and classification processes, enabling the user to organize and aggregate information logically. Typical *database management systems (DBMS)* in use today are those using relational models that organize data into rows and columns showing the relationship between elements. Two of the most common relational databases in use are Microsoft SQL and Oracle. The relational database has largely facilitated rapid access to large amounts of information, replacing the slower method of hierarchical databases that stored information in tree formats where data had to be accessed through its corresponding root element.
- **Project management** tools allow users to track complex projects by individual task and timeline. Project management software is often used as a "game plan" to ensure that all participants are aware of their responsibilities and as a means to inform management of the timely progress of the project.

Web Access and E-Mail

Web browsers such as Internet Explorer or Netscape provide yet another dimension to software applications, enabling users to effectively access the vast amount of information available through the Internet. As an adjunct to networks, the browser also provides the key user interface to the *World Wide Web* where information and profiles for just about any organization can be found.

Networks leverage the Internet through the use of a single, common standard: TCP/IP, which stands for transmission control protocol/Internet protocol. It is the basic communication language or protocol that allows computers to exchange information over the Internet.

Combined with browsers, *search engines* such as Yahoo! and Google provide some of the most powerful resources for the buyer. Search engines allow the user to quickly find and consolidate information found on the Internet for just about any specific subject, product, or service. Today, these tools have become so efficient that they can (and frequently do) return thousands of "*hits*" for a search objective in a fraction of a second.

Perhaps more than any other tool, *e-mail* has revolutionized the way we communicate in computer-enabled societies. E-mail allows the immediate transmission of individual messages across the Internet and instantaneously enables individuals or groups to communicate vast amounts of information in real time.

Tips and Techniques

Along with the vast potential tools such as these have for enhancing and accelerating business processes occurs a particularly unpleasant downside: *information overload*. Simply stated, this phenomenon occurs when individuals receive more information than they can process or absorb. While no official studies have yet been made public, information overload appears to be largely counterproductive and stress inducing.

Graphics

Graphics tools include programs for creating and viewing illustrations, photography, diagrams, and blueprints. We commonly use Adobe Acrobat, an application offered free by the publisher, to enable users to open and view document files that have been converted to a specific format that does not require you to have the original application in order to view it. Our engineers use AutoCad to design and document manufactured parts, and we typically use programs such as Visio to document process flows in graphical format.

Security

Ensuring that computer systems and files are maintained securely has become a major issue for organizations today. There has been a serious proliferation of malicious software distributed surreptitiously—*viruses, worms,* and *spyware*—that can have devastating effects on an organization's operations. So-called *firewalls* have been developed that allow limited access to a particular internal system by blocking material and users coming from systems outside the organization that do not have preauthorization to enter. In addition, software to filter viruses and worms are commonly deployed across networks to help block these attacks.

Additional security devices commonly used include *encryption* and *digital signatures*:

- **Encryption.** Involves the coding (or scrambling) of messages or data so that only the designated recipient can access them. The most common method in use is the *encryption key*. To decipher an encoded message, both the sender and receiver use the same code. In *public key encryption*, there are two keys: a public key, which is available to anyone, and a corresponding private key, which only the sender can access. Using this method, any party can send a message encrypted with the subscriber's public key, but only the subscriber has the private key needed to decrypt it.
- **Digital signatures.** Consist of encryption technology and a *public key infrastructure (PKI)* used to determine the authenticity of a message and the identity of the sender to ensure that it has not been changed. Often, third parties are used as the certificate authority to manage and certify the authenticity of the signature.

Supply Management Applications

In addition to those general applications and processes described above, you will also need to develop a basic knowledge and understanding of the specific applications available for procurement and supply management. These applications, described below, primarily address transactional uses such as requisitioning and purchase order placement, but they also include planning and strategic management tools, as well.

MRP/ERP *Material requirements planning (MRP)* and *manufacturing resource planning (MRPII)*, as stand-alone applications or as elements of the larger ERP system, are some of the most powerful tools available to organizations that need to plan and manage manufacturing operations and control inventory. In supply management, MRP systems are primarily used to determine when to place orders for standard materials so that they arrive exactly when needed. This helps to reduce the levels of inventory held by most manufacturing organizations and thereby improves cash flow.

Part of the MRP process involves forecasting demand for individual parts so that they can be ordered in advance of receiving actual customer orders. This complex process is generally handled by computer software programs through decision support models using calculated algorithms to predict future requirements. These requirements are, in turn, matched with the capacity of manufacturing centers using *computer-aided manufacturing (CAM)* software that controls the capacity and scheduling of equipment.

EDI *Electronic data interchange (EDI)* is the most widely used process for exchanging data related to procurement between computers. Supported by the *American National Standards Institute's (ANSI) X12* process, basic EDI has been in use in manufacturing organizations for more than 25 years. The ANSI X12 standard is used to define the data exchange process currently in use, defining terms and specifying the sequence and character length of each *field*. Figure 15.2 describes the organization of this process, showing how individual elements (fields defined in a special dictionary) are rolled into functional segments. An example of a segment would be a "Ship To" address, where SHIP TO NAME, SHIP TO CITY, and so forth would represent individual data elements. Segments are then incorporated in transaction sets (such as purchase orders) and then rolled up in functional groups and transmitted in an electronic "envelope."

X12 also specifies the format of processes through a system of numerically designated forms (14 in use by procurement), each of which provides for a specific function. This list provides some idea of the processes included in its scope:

Procurement-Related ANSI X12 Documents

840 Request for Quotation
997 Functional Acknowledgment
843 Response to Request for Quotation
832 Price/Sales Catalog
850 Purchase Order
855 Purchase Order Acknowledgment

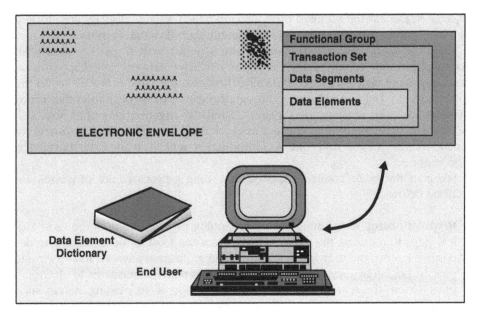

FIGURE 15.2   The ANSI X12 EDI Process

824 Application Advice
860 Purchase Order Change
836 Contract Award Summary
865 Purchase Order Change Acknowledgment
838 Trading Partner Profile
869 Order Status Inquiry
864 Text Message
870 Order Status Report
810 Invoice

EDI processing is conducted between trading partners who have already negotiated contracts with one another. It is managed through a *value-added network (VAN)* provider whose system translates the machine language from one trading partner's data processing system to another's, interconnecting the entire trading group. Setting up these systems can be quite costly, often in the range of $300,000 to $400,000, so it is understandable that only large organizations have found it cost effective to participate. Recently, however, ANSI has undertaken the conversion of its X12 standard to *XML (extensible markup language)* for use on the Internet. This should provide a far less costly alternative to VANs.

E-PROCUREMENT   *Electronic procurement* or *e-procurement* refers to the processes used to exchange various procurement-related information between organizations using the Internet as the data transfer tool. The Internet is, in part, a collection of networked parties known as the World Wide Web, who use the TCP/IP standard to access and transfer data between one another. The Web uses *hypertext markup* *language (HTML)* as the standard code through which website displays are enabled and a *uniform resource locator (URL)* for identifying individual websites.

Since the World Wide Web is essentially a public system, parties often wish to connect privately to one another using an exclusive network called an *extranet* or *virtual private network (VPN)*. Basically, these use the same protocols as do the public networks, but general access through the use of passwords and other forms of coding excludes unrecognized visitors. Similarly, organizations often establish procurement networks within the confines of their firewall, called *intranets*, to maintain internal security and control of information until it is ready to be transmitted to the supplier.

Some of the more common applications using e-procurement processes are described below:

- **Requisitioning.** Automating the requisitioning process is one of the most logical steps to reducing the transactional processing load in the procurement department. Since the user has to complete the requisition anyway, this electronic process begins by converting the organization's paper requisitions to electronic ones. Often, these are created within the bounds of an existing system such as an Oracle or SAP ERP application. However, once the requisition has been submitted it can be approved electronically by authorizing parties (leaving a clear, auditable trail) prior to submission to the buyer.

  Upon receipt, the buyer can automatically convert the requisition to a purchase order and transmit it electronically to the supplier. Typically, *electronic purchase orders (EPOs)* are transmitted via e-mail or electronically created fax, although companies using EDI can transmit them through their VAN.

- **Electronic catalogs.** Often, the basis of an electronic requisitioning system is an electronic catalog, typically maintained by the supplier and stored on either its website or the client's intranet. An electronic catalog is similar in organization to a paper catalog but is stored and accessed through the computer. Typically, users access the catalog for selection, and once the item they wish to purchase has been identified, it can be submitted directly for approval. Following approval, it is routed directly to the supplier, bypassing procurement altogether since procurement has already approved the catalog's content and negotiated the pricing with the supplier. Except for its automatic transmittal to the supplier, an electronic catalog order is treated in exactly the same manner as any other order.

  By simplifying the ordering process for end users, the Procurement Department can often save significant costs by driving purchases through a single supplier under a contracted discount rather than using a variety of suppliers selling at list.

- **Automated RFP, RFI, and RFQ.** In addition to automating the purchase order process, many organizations have also tied their RFPs, RFIs, and RFQs to automated systems as well. This enables buyers to construct them from preexisting templates and transmit them electronically to a much wider supply base than would ordinarily be possible under traditional methods. The electronic method also allows for automated scoring of the suppliers' responses, removing the tediousness of detailed analysis by the buyer and speeding the process of selection enormously. This also helps avoid maverick purchasing of high-value items by using the excuse that the process just takes too long. It has been shown that an electronic RFP process can reduce the time it takes to go to contract from several months to only a couple of weeks.

- **Competitive bidding events and reverse auctions.** Automated methods for submitting bids have proven quite effective in obtaining cost reductions since the widest possible supply base can be easily accessed using the computer. With increasing popularity, competitive bidding has turned to the *reverse auction* (RA) to drive substantial price reductions.

    The RA is conducted in much the same manner as a traditional auction except for the fact that suppliers are bidding the price *down*. Buyers have the ability to set the highest acceptable bid (or reserve price) prior to the auction, and typically disclaimers give them the right to award to any party regardless of their position in the bidding.

Tips and Techniques

"What about relationships and special service?" is the typical question coming from the user. Well, experience has shown that while auctions provide significant savings, they typically result in the incumbent winning the bid!

Reverse auction companies have also developed ways to automatically transform bids from suppliers weaker in service or quality to the same level as their better counterparts, adding the extra cost to their bids by a predetermined factor. This results, for example, in adding a price factor to a supplier whose lower quality may result in 10 percent fewer usable parts of 10 cents per dollar bid to make it equal to the supplier who has perfect quality.

INVENTORY MANAGEMENT/SUPPLIER-MANAGED INVENTORY   In addition to the inventory management processes created by MRP that have enabled significant reductions in the volume of inventory, today we are experiencing a trend toward *supplier-managed inventory (SMI)* whereby the supplier manages the shipment of material to your facility based on usage forecasts you provide. This process is sometimes combined with consignment inventory and *evaluated receipts settlement (ERS)* whereby payment is initiated by the pull order, rather than a supplier's invoice. The advantage to the supplier is automatic payment, typically without delay, and the elimination of the need to initiate an invoice. Combined with *electronic funds transfer (EFT)*, which automatically transmits payment to the supplier's bank account, this system has led to tremendous reductions in transactional processing.

CONTRACT MANAGEMENT   Software that tracks and maintains updates to contracts can be extremely useful to larger organizations, where individual divisions may not be aware of existing contracts at other divisions and thus not able to take advantage of lower pricing. What is equally typical, often one division will go through the tedious process of contracting for something already under contract by another division, resulting in enormous time and energy drains with no payback.

COST MANAGEMENT, SPENDING ANALYSIS, AND SUPPLY BASE OPTIMIZATION   One of the keys to cost savings is through consolidating spending volumes going to several suppliers under one contract to obtain the greatest discount. This process is known as supply base optimization. Cost management software helps *rationalize* an organization's spending by analyzing the exact categories and suppliers of actual spending during a particular period. From this data, you should be able to formulate a strategy for combining purchases to leverage volume. Many organizations, unfortunately, have no idea of their spending by category or commodity since an analysis through manual processes would be nearly impossible. That, however, is changing and one of the most rapidly growing categories of software is in this area.

Before an effective program of supply base optimization can be implemented, an organization needs to develop a sourcing strategy. A sourcing strategy defines how many suppliers the organization deems as appropriate and the circumstances in which it is willing to depend on a single source. Without a clearly articulated sourcing strategy, an organization will not be able to establish its procurement objectives in a prioritized manner. The supply base optimization program can then be charged with identifying spending categories and key suppliers, reviewing and measuring contract compliance, monitoring changes within critical industries through supply intelligence and market research, and tracking cost savings.

Identifying spending data is the tedious task of tracking down the internal and external systems that have spend data in them. Fortunately, specialized software is available today to assist with the process of locating and consolidating information from multiple sources and "translating" that information to a common, reliable database. In system terms, the software standardizes and enriches spending data so that organizations can utilize it to determine commodity spending patterns.

SUPPLIER SCORECARDS   Another of the key benefits from automation is the maintenance of *supplier scorecards*. These are typically the basis for the periodic business review and the ongoing evaluation of supplier performance, and they normally require a great deal of clerical time in tracking and recording specific data. Use of automated tools, combined with a centralized processing system such as ERP, enables buyers to pull period reports for on-time delivery, pricing trends, and returns at the touch of a key.

ASSET TRACKING   Asset tracking is most often maintained by the finance department, so procurement had only limited ability to determine when assets were approaching the end of their useful life so that replacements could be efficiently planned. In addition, organizations often find themselves purchasing new equipment for one location when surplus exists in another. Currently, greater effort is being given to enabling the involvement of procurement in the management of assets so that these costs can be further reduced.

PREVENTIVE MAINTENANCE   In environments where equipment is frequently used, the ordering of spare parts has placed heavy burdens on the Procurement Department. Increasingly, however, software is becoming available that ties the scheduled replacement of parts directly to an electronic ordering system, eliminating the need for buyer involvement on a day-to-day basis.

SOCIAL MEDIA   The twenty-first century, so far, can be characterized by the trends toward individual interconnectivity through sites such as Facebook, Twitter, LinkedIn,

Angie's List, and a host of others. How this will eventually affect the world of supply management is, at this writing, anyone's guess. However, it's clear that social media have tremendous potential to improve professional networking communication and provide up-to-date reviews and benchmarks for buyers. And the fact is, social media have already become a significant tool in consumer-oriented marketing, with many companies using media such as YouTube to provide overviews and demonstrations of their products.

Impact of Automation on Procurement Organizations

The overall impact of current trends toward automation of the transactional processes has led to a transformation in recent times of the procurement function itself. With the burden of processing purchase orders largely removed from the buying team, organizations are beginning to find more use for their staff in the strategic functions of cost reduction, risk mitigation, and supplier development. This has resulted in a general trend toward upgrading the quality of the procurement staff and placing more of a burden on the procurement professional to recruit talented staff and to reengineer existing process to enable a more strategic, proactive approach. In today's organization, the enlightened procurement professional has been given more and more responsibility as an overall business manager charged with ensuring that best practices are implemented throughout the supply community.

Sourcing Supply Management Tools

The Procurement Department plays a dual role in the selection and acquisition of supply management software: providing domain expertise for the development of the statement of work and the typical support role in supplier selection. Generally, the Information Technology (IT) group will handle the actual specification development, since their team will be providing ongoing support and maintenance for any software installed.

The following section reviews some of the basic aspects the procurement professional should consider when engaged in this process.

Software

As outlined in the sections above, the software requirements for supply management generally include systems related to MRP processes and systems related to e-procurement. From a sourcing standpoint, organizations generally opt for inclusion of new or additional modules in their existing ERP framework. However, many of the applications for e-procurement have been developed only recently—spending analysis, for example—so organizations find that they are faced with a number of issues: Should they create applications themselves or should they acquire third-party systems that may not be compatible with their existing systems? Or should they postpone acquisition for the present time and wait until the provider of their existing software platform gets around to developing the process as an additional module?

MAKE OR BUY   The make-or-buy decision for software largely depends on the immediacy of the return on investment and the availability of market-based applications that suitably meet the organization's requirements. In addition, you must also assess the risk factors that may be involved.

Tips and Techniques

Questions to Ask before the Make-or-Buy Decision

Expertise Available
- Can you successfully engage commercial resources that will be able to develop applications to meet your organization's needs?
- How well you can define your requirements?

Potential Risks
- What issues are related to the successful implementation of the project?
- What potential risk exists down the road?

Costs
- Are the costs fully understood?
- What potential exists for unknown costs surfacing during the project?
- Will customization add significantly to the overall cost?
- What are the ongoing costs for maintenance?
- How do licensing fees compare?

Fit
- To what extent will customized software better fit the organization's specific needs?
- How easy will it be to migrate to your platform?

CUSTOMIZED VS. OFF-THE-SHELF   Similar to the make or buy decision is the consideration of whether to customize purchased software to meet the perceived special needs of your organization. The temptation, of course, is to bring in the new system to operate exactly like the old system to increase the comfort level of the users. However, you should consider not only the initial cost to customize but the ongoing cost of maintenance, since the publisher's upgrades to existing software may eliminate the customization already installed or require additional prior to deployment. You should also keep in mind that there will be ongoing support required and consider the impact of potential turnover of the supplier's staff.

Training

During the selection process for software, training issues should not be overlooked. At the very least, you will want to determine the overall cost of training and if it will be held in-house or at a remote location requiring travel. You should also determine the impact to existing operations during the training as a result of lost time.

Outsourcing

Outsourcing IT applications has become relatively common today, especially favoring suppliers who manage networks, help desks, and websites. Most organizations feel that it is no longer part of their core competencies to manage the complex infrastructure required to support fully developed systems. In addition, the coming of age of *application service providers (ASPs)*—software providers who, in effect, rent software that they then maintain on their site—has lent additional credibility to the improved return on investment of leasing as these suppliers move into supporting essential functions for the organization. As the IT function moves offshore to find less expensive labor, the outsourcing formula becomes even more attractive.

While outsourcing continues to remain a risk-focused decision, organizations are increasingly finding that where core competencies are not involved, the benefits of dedicated expertise and reduced cost far outweigh the loss of control.

Summary

Automation is becoming a way of life for today's procurement professional as the variety of tools available for transactional processing expands. As a result, the procurement professional has had to learn new skills to manage technology, including a basic understanding of how computer technology works. The procurement professional's vocabulary should include standard data processing terminology and a familiarity with the hardware and network requirements common in contemporary organizations. In addition, it is increasingly accepted that the procurement staff will have adequate facility with the more commonly used business software applications such as word processing and spreadsheet management.

Supply management applications are changing rapidly as well, and virtually every function has seen some form of automation. Organizations are increasingly turning to ERP to ensure process uniformity across operations to supplement their original implementations of financial and human resource programs. MRP and EDI are now becoming simply modules in a broader spectrum of applications. The recent trend to Web-based processes has also affected procurement, and buyers are learning that the automation of traditional methods such as competitive bidding provides significant advantages. However, along with the benefits these processes offer is the downside of potential information overload.

One of the side effects of this process is that the procurement professional is increasingly becoming the organization's domain expert when it comes to selecting software and systems that automate supplier management. As a result, you will find that you are now applying the same decision-making processes (such as make or buy) to your own department that you previously applied to your customer.

CHAPTER 16

Financial Decisions for Sourcing

During the normal course of business, you will be required to assist in making many financial decisions related to the acquisition of goods and services for the organization. Many of these decisions will involve determining whether to acquire the goods and services from suppliers through direct purchase or if the organization can more efficiently provide them itself by using internal resources. In addition, determining whether to buy or lease is another typical business decision that must be made on an ongoing basis. These decisions are generally referred to as *make or buy* and *lease or buy* because they require a comparative analysis of those alternatives.

In addition, there are numerous other financial leveraging strategies that you will need to understand, such as how commodity markets operate and how the cost of money through interest rates is determined—factors that are most often driven by conditions in the marketplace. In this chapter, we will explore the processes for preparing for some of these key financial decisions and their importance to the modern organization.

Performing Make-or-Buy Analysis

Make-or-buy analysis, as its name implies, is the process that determines if the organization should produce a particular product or service in-house or if it should turn to a third-party supplier and simply purchase it from them. Many companies in the semiconductor industry, for example, have increasingly turned to "fabless" operations, choosing to outsource the production of silicon die products, which requires large investments in sophisticated tools and equipment, to third parties who have already invested huge amounts of money in developing their state-of-the-art facilities. Today, approximately two-thirds of all semiconductor companies delegate manufacturing operations to outside foundries, focusing instead on what they consider to be their own core competencies and design and marketing strategies.

In the following section, we will examine the dynamics of make-or-buy analysis, looking at the process dynamics as well as the strategies behind them.

Make-or-Buy Dynamics

There are numerous opportunities for *outsourcing* the products your organization manufactures or the functions your organization performs internally by contracting them to third parties. Commonly targeted services include business functions such as information technology, facilities management, payroll management, logistics, and with more increasing frequency, procurement itself. It is also becoming increasingly more common for manufacturing operations to outsource entire product-line assembly functions to firms specializing in material procurement, assembly, and testing. The benefits of outsourcing generally include reduced labor costs resulting from the transfer of operations to lower-paid workers, along with lower material prices due to the larger economies of scale with consolidated volumes purchased by third manufacturers. The offsetting disadvantages include loss of control and, sometimes, loss of scheduling flexibility.

Generally, make-or-buy decisions are conducted by a cross-functional team so that the benefit of all perspectives can be obtained and evaluated. Before deciding the viability of buying products or services currently handled internally, the team will need to look carefully at a number of factors and gather information from a number of sources.

VIABILITY STUDY   The first step in a make-or-buy decision is determining if buying the product or outsourcing the service is viable. This depends largely on the existing supply base. You will likely find that this is actually a sourcing process involving finding suppliers capable of handling your organization's business. You will need to locate suppliers that have personnel with the proper skill set, as well as available equipment and facilities, to handle your needs. If you and your team are unable to locate viable suppliers, you are faced with either developing existing suppliers to handle your needs or continuing to do it in-house.

If the marketplace for your requirement has a limited number of suppliers, you will also want to analyze the risk involved. Are there viable backup alternatives should the supplier you choose encounter difficulties? Do the physical logistics involved add significantly more costs and process complexity to your operations? How financially solvent are the potential providers—are they capable of making the financial investments required by developing technology?

You will also want to look into the resources required for managing the supplier. Will the supplier become a critical factor in producing your end product, requiring close audit tracking and frequent business reviews? Will the outsourcing engagement require engineering or quality staff to work closely with the supplier on a continuing basis? Will these support resources be available?

REQUIREMENTS   The next step in the process is determining your organization's exact needs. This part of the process is very similar to the one we outlined in the section on establishing requirements in Chapter 2. You will need to develop a clear specification or statement of work (SOW), as well as an estimate of future requirements volume or frequency of service. This is necessary for two reasons: first, to establish a baseline for the current costs to your organization, and second, to enable a relatively accurate quote from potential suppliers. Without either of these, you may not be able to determine accurately if there are financial advantages to buying.

CONDUCTING ANALYSIS   Having located viable sources and defined the exact requirements, the final step is actually conducting the analysis. To do this, you will first need to prepare a request for proposal (RFP) or request for quotation (RFQ) to go out to the potential suppliers. Once the RFP and RFQ are returned and analyzed, you will have enough data to do a comparative analysis between your current operating values—primarily cost—and those of the proposed outsourcing. As with any RFP or RFQ comparison, you will want to analyze and compare the elements of quality, cost, technology, and service. Most importantly, you must be certain you are receiving equal or greater value from the supplier before making a final outsourcing decision.

The team's initial analysis will likely focus on those elements you consider tangible, such as cost, lead times, and scheduling flexibility. If, following this analysis, the team continues to find potential value in an outsourcing engagement, it should continue with the analysis and turn to a number of subjective criteria before making the actual decision.

In performing a basic analysis—with a new product, for example—cost and capacity may be the critical factors. In the analysis of cost, you will want to be sure to consider direct costs such as material, labor, and freight and indirect costs such as receiving, inspecting, and stocking, as well as scrap and the cost of resolving quality issues.

Subjective Make-or-Buy Analysis Factors

There are several intangible factors that should be considered by the team before coming to a final conclusion as to whether or not to actually go forward with the outsourcing engagement.

STRATEGY In the long term, your team will want to determine how well the proposed outsourcing fits with the overall organizational strategy. Prior to making a recommendation, you will want to explore a number of questions such as these:

- Is the process or product a critical part of the organization's core competency? If so, your team must weigh the pros and cons of placing this in the hands of a third-party supplier.
- Does learning from the development of this product or service drive learning in other business function areas? You will want to determine if this will weaken any existing technology development.
- Will your outsourced business provide adequate incentive to suppliers to continue participating? If there is not sufficient revenue from the outsourcing to continue to engage suppliers, you should consider the effect that future capacity constraints might place on the supplier.
- Can you actually reduce internal costs sufficiently to offset the acquisition costs? You need to analyze the true cost reduction to the organization as a result of outsourcing. Unless buying can produce reduced staffing by eliminating existing head count, the calculated savings may be "soft." You will also want to be certain that reduction in staffing in one area does not result in the need for increased staffing in another. For example, will outsourcing a manufacturing operation require additional quality and procurement personnel due to quality or delivery issues?
- To what extent will the organization be able to reverse its sourcing decision in the future, bringing back in-house the product or service if the supplier should fail? This is often a key strategic decision because the equipment and expertise needed to produce the outsourced item may require heavy investment to replace at some future date.

RISK   Although risk assessment is difficult or impossible to quantify, its evaluation is a critical part of any outsourcing determination. In the words of the famous Murphy: "Anything that can go wrong will go wrong." Therefore, when conducting any risk analysis, one should not hesitate to evaluate each and every one of the factors and assumptions made in the initial sourcing comparative analysis.

In performing risk analysis, you need to carefully balance the specific, expected benefits of the engagement with factors that you may not be able to control. For example, you will need to determine the effect of capacity constraints in the supply community hampering future production operations. Conversely, you will want to gauge the impact that a business downturn will have on your selected supplier. Will your supply needs continue to be met?

You will also want to analyze, where possible, the potential impact that changing technology may have on future requirements. With relatively low volumes, you may be unable to convince a supplier to invest in future research and technological development. This condition might favor keeping the product or service in-house. Similarly, with a new product or service about to be introduced to the market, your organization will want to determine if the resources that must be acquired to produce the product or service will result in an internal return on that investment. In these circumstances, turning to a supplier with existing capability may prove more effective.

Tips and Techniques

Some elements of risk cannot be tolerated at any level. Lack of statistical process control (SPC) tools, for example, should immediately disqualify a potential supplier for technology-driven parts.

QUALITY CONSIDERATIONS   There is virtually no factual data to support the assumption that buying a product or service rather than making it will result in diminished quality. According to a recent survey, in fact, the majority of companies outsourcing found that work skill quality actually improved following the engagement, and 70 percent reported an increase in the quality of outsourced business processes.

As always, successful buying programs require a clear definition of quality and the definitive documentation of the business processes required for its support. Many organizations choose to outsource simply because they have little or no documented control of subordinate processes in the first place. Suppliers often have better process documentation in place and greater control of quality simply because the product or service is a core competency for them.

SUPPORT CAPABILITY   Support capability refers to the ability to develop advanced product technology. Supporting new product development in some areas is often a financial burden for the buying organization but a core competency for the supplier engaged in providing the service to a wide spectrum of customers. Suppliers are usually in a better position to absorb the costs of development simply because they can distribute it over a wider customer base.

Similarly, supporting business processes has become, for some organizations, a core competency due to their large customer base. Many have dedicated engineering staffs to work with customers during the product development cycle to ensure alignment between the design and the manufacturing process. Many are global and have multinational support. Most have sophisticated customer service systems capable of tracking customer orders and repair status on a 24/7 basis.

Outsourcing Business Processes

Today, outsourcing entire business processes, such as manufacturing assembly, information technology, or logistics, is a common occurrence. While the process sometimes appears more complex and the resulting risk may be higher because of the broadened scope, it invariably follows a process similar to the make-or-buy analysis.

Outsourcing is defined as the transfer of a previously performed function from the organizational staff to a third-party supplier. As we noted earlier in this chapter, there are a host of such functions within the organization that have become subject to potential outsourcing. The prime drive appears to be lowered cost from the engagement, likely as a result of efficiencies the supplier is able to achieve by spreading the overhead across a larger group of users. However, many organizations are experiencing improved service as a result of the greater human resources available to the supplier in times of customer need.

The following sections discuss the make-or-buy process and some important elements you should consider when sourcing these services.

NEEDS ANALYSIS   Needs analysis should be performed by a cross-functional team composed of subject matter experts and those familiar with the processes being used internally at the current time. Be sure to include stakeholders as well, so that all user groups are represented.

Your team must define the requirements in terms of a statement of work (SOW), just as it would with any other service. At a minimum you will want to have:

- A detailed description of the work to be performed.
- Costs of the present operation, by function.
- Required service levels—how you intend to measure performance.
- Critical risks in the engagement.

DECISION-MAKING PROCESS   From these elements, your team should be able to incorporate its needs into an RFP and submit it to qualified or qualifiable suppliers. Be certain to include your typical contract terms for this type of engagement so you can determine quickly if suppliers are not willing to accept your existing business and legal terms. You should also be able to construct an assessment criteria matrix to objectively rate the suppliers' responses to your RFP once received.

Based on the initial responses (or noticeable lack of response), your team will need to decide if the potential exists to actually conduct the proposed outsourcing. You'll base this on the nature of the responses and the costs being proposed. If it appears to be feasible, proceed to the supplier selection process; if not, consider revising the SOW or dropping the outsourcing project.

TABLE 16.1   Benefits of Buying vs. Leasing

Benefits of Buying	Benefits of Leasing
No fees for early termination	Little or no cash to obtain the equipment
Can be sold at any time	Payments are considered expenses and may provide tax advantages
Total costs are usually lower over time	Several disposal options at end of lease
Use of the equipment can extend far after it is paid for	Does not affect bank line of credit
	Little fear of obsolescence

SUPPLIER SELECTION   Many organizations use preestablished selection criteria based on comparative rating methodologies that rates suppliers on the basis of proposed cost, service levels, technology capability, quality, and the level of ongoing investment in the process you are outsourcing. We reviewed this in Chapter 4, and you may want to refer back to it for further details.

Performing Lease-or-Buy Analysis

Leasing is an alternative to buying that's used primarily when acquiring capital equipment. In many respects, leasing can be considered similar to renting.

Lease-or-buy analysis is the process of comparing the overall costs associated with leasing compared to owning a particular asset. Depending on the cost of capital for a given organization, the lease may provide significant advantages. Lease payments are typically expensed rather than capitalized so they can be directly related to the accounting period in which they occur. While it is common for an equipment lease to require a long-term contract, there is usually little or no down payment needed.

Consider Table 16.1 and the comparison between the two options.

Leasing Features

A lease agreement grants the *lessee* possession of equipment or property for a stated period of time and at an agreed-upon rate of payment. The lessee is not the owner of the asset but commonly bears all responsibility for maintaining it in good working order. At the end of the lease, the lessee may have the option of purchasing the equipment at a *fair market value* or at a previously agreed upon amount if such a clause is included in the contract.

LEASE TYPES   There are several common types of leases that you should become familiar with:

- *Finance lease*. A financing device whereby a lessee can acquire an asset for most of its useful life. Generally, a finance lease is noncancelable during the term of the lease. Leases of this type are generally net to the lessor, so the lessee is responsible for maintenance, taxes, and insurance.

- *Full payout lease.* A lease in which the actual cash payments will return the lessor the full equipment cost plus a satisfactory return over the lease term.
- *Leveraged lease.* A lease in which the lessor borrows a portion of the purchase price of the leased equipment from institutional investors. In a typical transaction, 20 to 40 percent of the purchase price is provided by one or more investors, who become owners and lessors of the equipment. The balance of the purchase price is borrowed from banks or other sources of capital.
- *Net lease.* A lease in which the fees are payable net to the lessor; that is, the lessee pays all out-of-pocket expenses such as taxes, insurance, and maintenance. The lease, therefore, only addresses the equipment itself. All costs in connection with the use of the equipment (usually hard to predict) are to be paid by the lessee over and above the agreed rental payments. Most finance leases are net leases.
- *Operating lease.* A short-term lease whereby a user can acquire an asset for a fraction of the useful life of the asset. The lessor may provide services in connection with the lease such as maintenance, insurance, and payment of personal property taxes. From a strict accounting standpoint, the specific requirements of Financial Accounting Standards Board (FASB) Standard 13 (discussed later in the chapter) must be met for a lease to be qualified as an operating lease.

LESSORS *Lessors* are persons or entities who own the property being leased (e.g., real estate or equipment), which a lessee receives use and possession of in exchange for a payment of fees. Lessors typically include banks, manufacturers of equipment, third-party owners, and capital funding organizations.

Decision-Making Factors

As with any decision, leasing provides a number of considerations, both favorable and unfavorable. The next sections discuss some of those you should usually consider.

ADVANTAGES OF LEASING Some of the advantages to leasing include:

- **Better cash flow.** Leasing gives you access to the asset with minimal up-front payments and spreads the cost over time. You can pay for the asset with the income it generates while minimizing the drain on your working capital.
- **No debt.** An operating lease preserves your credit options and does not influence your credit limit because it is generally classified as expense, not debt.
- **Maximize financial leverage.** Your lease can often finance everything related to the purchase and installation of the asset and may free up cash flow to pay for items such as training.
- **Cash flow management.** Lease payments are usually constant, making cash management more predictable.
- **Tax advantage.** Operating lease payments are generally tax deductible just like depreciation charges but are made with pretax money. Cash purchases, in contrast, are made with after-tax money.

- **Flexible time frames.** Leasing contracts can be structured to fit your requirements. You can use an asset as long as you need it without owning it forever.
- **Protection against obsolescence.** Depending on your end-of-lease option, you can return the asset to the lessor.

DISADVANTAGES OF LEASING   Some of the disadvantages to leasing are:

- **More expensive.** A finance lease is usually more expensive than an outright cash purchase because the payments include finance charges. However, leasing may cost less than other forms of financing.
- **Additional guarantees required.** Depending on the credit rating of your company, the lessor might require additional guarantees. These may be provided by officers of your organization or your bank and could affect your organization's credit rating or financial standing with bankers reviewing debt-to-asset ratios.
- **Fixed term.** It may be impossible or very costly to terminate a leasing contract early.
- **Locked interest rates.** Interest rates are usually fixed throughout the lease, which may prove a disadvantage in times of falling interest rates.

COST FACTORS   Any lease analysis must consider typical total cost of ownership factors such as acquisition cost, operating costs, and maintenance and disposal. Acquisition costs typically include the down payment (if required), taxes, shipping costs, installation, and financing or loan fees. Operating costs typically include any enhancements to the original equipment, consumables, and energy/fuel consumption. Maintenance factors include preventive maintenance, spare parts, and down time. Disposal costs include reconditioning costs, facility removal costs, shipping, early lease termination fees, and "fair market value" salvage value.

Here are some of the more subtle cost factors that you will need to take into account in any complete analysis:

- **Return of asset reconditioning.** If you choose to return the asset at the end of your lease, the condition to which it must be reconditioned and the place where it must be returned are important cost factors to consider.
- **Notice period.** If your lease includes an automatic option to renew, take note of any time periods in which you must give notice in case you do not want to renew the contract. Some leasing companies will automatically renew the contract if you fail to give notice.
- **Purchase rights.** When returning the asset at the end of your lease, a predetermined fixed price offers more option than the fair market value, which theoretically is always available to you.
- **Maintenance responsibility.** Clarify which service and maintenance programs are included in the lease. If you are responsible for service and maintenance, make sure it is in line with the manufacturer's recommendations.

BUDGET CONSIDERATIONS   Organizations needing to balance the need for new technology with budget constraints find that leasing helps stretch budget dollars with monthly payments that are often lower than purchase installments. With a lease, organizational cash remains untouched and available for other profitable uses. In addition, leasing often expands financial resources without affecting established credit lines.

Many companies realize significant tax benefits from leasing their technology. Monthly lease payments are generally tax deductible and can be treated as a business expense. Conventional bank financing typically requires a minimum balance. With leasing, there is no minimum balance or down payment required.

FASB 13 The FASB established standards of financial accounting and reporting for leases by lessees and lessors for transactions and revisions entered into on or after January 1, 1977. For lessees, a lease is a financing transaction called a capital lease if it meets any one of four specified criteria; if not, it is an operating lease. Capital leases are treated as the acquisition of assets and the incurrence of obligations by the lessee. Operating leases are treated as current operating expenses.

For lessors, a financing transaction lease is classified as a sales type, direct financing, or leveraged lease. To be a sales type, direct financing, or leveraged lease, the lease must meet one of the same criteria used for lessees to classify a lease as a capital lease, in addition to two criteria dealing with future uncertainties.

Leveraged leases also have to meet further criteria. These types of leases are recorded as investments under different specifications for each type of lease. Leases not meeting the criteria are considered operating leases and are accounted for like rental property.

Formulating Financial Strategies

The Procurement Department is in one of the best positions in the organization to influence and improve the bottom line by leveraging relationships and information from the supply community. But to do so, the professional must understand existing processes and strategies within the organization so that, for example, creating a cost saving in one operating area does not resurface as a financial burden in another.

In this section, let's examine some of the finance-based avenues and tools available to you to better perform your job.

Organizational Considerations

The type of organization you are employed by will have a large influence on the nature of its financial strategies and will require different approaches from the Procurement Department. Consider some of the various ways organizations might respond to similar situations depending upon their sectors and organizational structures.

COMMERCIAL Commercial enterprises can be divided into two sectors:

1. **Public corporation.** Public corporations, businesses whose stock is publicly owned and traded on one of the many stock exchanges, owe a measure of fiduciary due diligence to their many stockholders. In addition to its efforts to reduce cost, the Procurement Department must follow standard operating procedures so that the public can rely on the management's ability to produce

profit. The department is always under audit scrutiny and must ensure that procedures are followed at all times.

2. **Privately owned enterprises.** Businesses that are privately held are free to develop financial strategies within the constraints of their mission and the direction provided by the owners. The Procurement Department's responsibility, however, remains the same: to provide value for the organization.

NONPROFIT Nonprofit organizations include schools, churches, charities, and other organizations working for the benefit of the community. Obviously, with nonprofit organizations, the "profit" motive is largely absent. Nevertheless, these organizations want to stretch their operating budgets as far as possible in order to better fulfill their mission, and the Procurement Department can serve the mission by enabling a fixed budget to be leveraged that much further.

GOVERNMENT Government procurement requirements are possibly the most stringent and certainly the most complex in regard to process and procedure compliance. Procurement departments in these environments must conform to a host of complex and sometimes obscure regulations originally designed to ensure that the public is protected while receiving the most value for its tax dollar and that suppliers are treated fairly and equally. This has unfortunately made the procurement process more cumbersome than most would like it to be, and it's certainly more difficult for the purchaser to achieve outstanding results. To many, conformance to the prescribed process and completion of proper documentation have become more important considerations than desirable results. While improvements in the system to make them more strategically responsive to financial objectives are taking place all of the time, it is by nature a slow process and we (the authors) have unbridled admiration for those who manage to consistently produce outstanding results despite the often formidable obstacles and roadblocks.

PROCUREMENT STRUCTURE How the procurement organization is structured and where it resides in the organization can definitely affect its performance and fit with the organization's overall financial and operational strategies. An astute procurement professional will make every possible effort to ensure that those in the organization developing the strategic goals will understand how the current structure of the procurement group both supports and hinders those goals.

While there are likely infinite variations of Procurement Department structure, the next sections list some of the standard types you are likely to encounter.

Centralized A centralized Procurement Department exists when it is the sole authorized agency to purchase goods and service for the organization. This group supports the entire organization, regardless of location or the nature of operations. The advantage of this structure is that it supports compliance with organizational policy, and it can better leverage the supplier community through combined volumes. The downside is that it is extremely difficult to find expertise capable of servicing a product or diverse organization.

Lead/Divisional In a lead/divisional Procurement Department, the procurement groups are distributed across the organization to support local user groups, and each procurement group places its own purchase orders. However, the group with the greatest expertise in a specific area is responsible for negotiating prices and contracts for the entire organization.

Cooperative Centralized buying services, known unofficially as cooperatives or *buying consortiums*, have become relatively popular recently. They are able to save money by combining the volumes of several customers and making one purchase. Several of these have become successful and quite well known.

Tips and Techniques

Consortiums need to have a common basis for organization in order to comply with antitrust regulations when receiving preferential pricing. One significant requirement is that the organizations participating in the buying have a significant similarity, such as being part of the same industry or being engaged in a similar nonprofit mission. Be sure to check with your legal counsel before proceeding with forming a consortium.

Monetary Considerations

Related to the development of financial strategies are a number of elements that will affect how and when purchases are made. Here, we'll look at some of the more common areas where procurement and financial influences overlap.

DEPRECIATION It is generally recognized that equipment and certain other assets purchased by an organization have a finite useful life, at the end of which they will theoretically no longer be of any salvage value. *Depreciation* is the process of allowing for and recording this decline in value over a specified period of time. If, for example, a copier machine cost $100,000 and has a recognized useful life of five years, then each year it would depreciate by another $20,000.

This has two important considerations: First, since depreciation is an expense for tax reporting purposes, it represents a *liability* on the organization's books. Second, the "book" value or asset value also declines at this rate, reducing the organization's book value on the *balance sheet* and, potentially, the possible resale or salvage value.

This needs to be taken into consideration when preparing return on investment (ROI) analysis and when calculating costs for a make-or-buy/lease-or-buy decision.

BOND AND CURRENCY MARKETS Purchasers involved in foreign trade understand that currencies fluctuate frequently, rising or declining in value against the U.S. dollar or other base currency. If you are purchasing in foreign currencies, you need to know how this can affect the future price of your purchase at the time of contracting. If your base currency—let's use U.S. dollars for this example—declines relative to the purchase currency, you will need more dollars to pay the invoice. If the opposite is the case, the supplier may receive less than expected in terms of global market value.

To maintain the stability of your transaction (and to some extent, the profitability of your purchase), you can often use a process called hedging. Hedging is a strategy designed to reduce the risk of fluctuations in forward-looking contracts requiring payment in a foreign currency. Your organization's actions will depend on how it forecasts currency changes: If it expects the foreign currency to decline in value relative to the dollar, it will place aside the dollars needed for payment, purchasing the foreign currency when it appears to be at its lowest point. However, if the currency is expected to increase in relation to the U.S. dollar, it might prove wise to purchase the foreign currency as soon as the contract is signed.

Tips and Techniques

Currency hedging is best left to experts because of its inherent financial risk. To date, no one has figured out how to predict the future value of any currency very far in the future. Most organizations rely on their treasury group to handle this or use an outside broker who is an expert in the currency under consideration.

COMMODITY MARKETS   To constitute a *commodity*, products must be relatively standardized, undifferentiated, and capable of trading in a formalized market environment, such as an exchange. In the past, typical commodities have been related to metals, lumber, agricultural products, chemicals, and fuels. They are typically traded on open exchanges where the price fluctuates according to supply and demand. In these open exchanges, it is possible to purchase a number of so-called "instruments" that can reduce risk of future fluctuations, including the purchase of contracts for future delivery at a designated date and at the price specified in the contract, regardless of the actual market price at the time of purchase. Contracts can be created and sold even for products not yet physically owned by the seller. Once created, these contracts can then be bought and sold as desired.

These financial instruments all have one aspect in common: risk. As you know, it is impossible to forecast where prices are heading from one period to the next. Expert advice, sound forecasts of demand, and lots of diligent scrutiny are the minimum requirements for success in mastering commodity markets.

INTEREST RATES   *Interest rates* can have a significant impact on purchasing decisions, especially those related to timing. As interest rates rise, companies pay more to the lenders for additional capital, thus raising their costs and their selling prices. For the same reason, buyers are under increased pressure to reduce inventory and the price of equipment purchased.

PAYMENT TERMS   *Payment terms* refer to the agreement between buyer and seller regarding the timing and method of payment for goods and services supplied. Payment terms are closely related to interest rates because in many senses they represent a loan to the buyer by the seller for the period between receiving the product or service and the time that it takes for the payment to actually reach the sellers' coffers.

Payment terms for purchases generally follow a standard format, indicating the number of days in which the payment is due and any discounts that can be taken for payment at some specific, earlier date. For example:

- Net 45 means that payment in full is due in 45 days.
- Net 10th prox means that payment in full is due on the tenth day of the following month.
- 2 percent 10/net 30 means that payments received within 10 days of the invoice date will receive a 2 percent discount, and the balance is payable in full in 30 days.

Some organizations maintain the policy that payment is due from receipt of the invoice rather than its date since this is easier to verify. Most sellers invoice upon shipment, so this does not seem unfair, especially in a situation where the product being shipped takes weeks to arrive.

BUYER FINANCING There are always situations where suppliers require advance payment, either to ensure that the contract can be started or to provide financing for equipment and materials in quantities not affordable at the supplier's current level of operation. Sometimes organizations advance loans to suppliers or provide equipment already owned in order to help them along. This practice has its pros and cons. Nonetheless, organizations must ensure fairness to other suppliers and conformance to applicable laws and regulations.

CASH FLOW The term "cash flow" is often used rather vaguely. Operating cash flow is the cash generated by the business after changes in working capital; net cash flow is the amount of money left after expenses at any particular time period. It may not be a good time to make large purchases when cash flow is at a low point because funds may need to be borrowed to cover the bill. Timing purchases to coincide with cash inputs can prove an effective tool in adding to the bottom line.

Legal Aspects

While most of the legal aspects affecting procurement have been outlined in Chapter 5, as a professional you should be reminded of the importance of tracking legal developments so that you are in full compliance with the law. Sarbanes-Oxley (SOX), for example, requires reporting commencing in November 2005.

TAX LAWS While you will not have direct responsibility for taxes, you will need to know some basic principles under which tax laws operate so that you can take them into account when making certain procurement decisions. For example, in many states, purchases for products being resold (or that go into products being resold) do not require the payment of sales tax. In many areas, taxes on inventory are assessed just as they would be for real property. Software downloaded via the Internet is usually exempt from sales tax (considered a service rather than a product), while the same software purchased in a box will be subject to tax.

Tips and Techniques

Use tax is a tax levied on goods that are bought outside the taxing authority's jurisdiction and then brought into the jurisdiction. This tax is designed to discourage the purchase of products that are not subject to a sales tax.

REGULATIONS As noted, most of the regulations governing procurement operations relate to commonly used processes. These include regulations governing antitrust, intellectual property, environmental health and safety (including hazardous materials), international trade, and the Uniform Commercial Code. You will likely be required to track changes to these regulations as the compliance source for your organization.

Summary

One of the Procurement Department's most frequently used analytical tools is the make-or-buy analysis. This comparative analysis enables you to determine whether or not outsourcing a product or service or manufacturing or performing it in-house is the most advantageous path for your organization. There are a number of dynamics that must be considered, including specific analysis of needs and requirements, technical viability, risk, quality, and service capability. There is also the ever-important aspect of price to consider.

Similar to considerations you must take to determine whether to outsource a product or service is the process of determining whether to lease or buy. Leasing has a number of additional considerations that should be taken into account, including the impact on cash flow, tax liability, cost factors, budget considerations, and regulatory requirements. There are various lease types to consider and they differ from one another significantly, each providing its own advantages and disadvantages.

There are also a number of financial tools you will be required to understand and use as part of developing strategies. Divided into two aspects—organizational and monetary considerations—these cover organizational and procurement structures and common financial factors such as depreciation, payment terms, interest rates, bond and commodity markets, financing, and cash flow.

CHAPTER 17

Source to Settle

Procurement sourcing concepts have changed significantly over recent decades. Where we used to see the procurement (or purchasing) function as a stand-alone process—isolated, as it were—to essentially transactional activities such as issuing purchase orders and expediting deliveries, we now see the overall function as consisting of multiple interconnected services. Today, many organizations view this expanded concept of procurement as a start-to-finish process that begins with supplier sourcing activities and concludes when the supplier is paid.

Forward-thinking organizations are adopting a *source-to-settle (S2S)* strategy that streamlines processes and integrates sourcing, procurement, and accounts payable. Typically, this integration occurs through an enterprise application software (EAS) application (such as SAP) or business process outsourcing (BPO), but as a discipline, the concept can be implemented in almost any automated business process environment. Figure 17.1 shows the evolution of S2S.

Why Source to Settle?

There are a number of compelling benefits to employing an S2S operational strategy. As an integrated process, S2S enables an agile approach to fulfilling customer demand and moves the organization toward the full scope of managing the entire supply chain effectively, while at the same time improving compliance through auditable processes.

Issues

If you carefully examine the acquisition processes of most organizations, you will likely find that they are highly fragmented and decentralized. Often the supply sourcing function is controlled by the end user; geographically dispersed organizations conduct sourcing and procurement operations independent of one another. Spend data are often nonexistent; when such data exist, often they are inaccurate due to the lack of quality in the data-gathering process. This fragmentation leads to costly inconsistencies, such as implementing multiple sourcing strategies across the organization and encouraging redundant activities.

LACK OF UNIFORM PROCESSES In this fragmented environment, there is little or no automation in the data collection process. Reliance on manual processes and

FIGURE 17.1   The Evolution of Source to Settle

paperwork thus adds unnecessary cost and mistakes to operations. Manual processes decrease visibility in supplier selection and spending patterns; the information that is available is often spotty and untimely. Without a centralized approach to contracting, compliance is generally not encouraged or, when it is, not effectively carried out, so we can expect to find multiple suppliers for the same products or services. We can also expect to find that approvals often occur after the actual purchase (maverick spending).

LACK OF COMPLIANCE   It is easy to understand how a fragmented environment makes auditing and compliance monitoring difficult. So-called maverick spending, which refers to purchasing actions outside existing contracts or from nonpreferred suppliers, plagues many organizations since it does not leverage the preferential cost benefits of buying through approved sources.

Lack of compliance extends beyond just off-contract spending. In fact, many organizations have a host of procurement policies that are not being followed:

- **Approval work flow.** Most organizations have a policy that requires some form of approval for virtually all products and services purchased by the organization. Although this is sometimes a blanket approval (as in the case of direct materials used in manufacturing), approval is typically required for any other purchase. Circumventing the required approval work flow by using expense accounts, for example, is a frequently cited occurrence that hinders the process of consolidating purchases to improve pricing. In a publicly held company, this form of circumvention can lead to unreported obligations as outlined under the Sarbanes-Oxley Act (SOX) if the problem is significant enough. Many organizations also refer to the enterprise risk management (ERM) process known by its acronym as COSO (Committee of Sponsoring Organizations of the Treadway Commission, a framework for risk management), which emphasizes the importance of identifying and managing risks across the enterprise.

- **Conflict of interest.** Following conflict-of-interest guidelines as a code of conduct is another procurement policy that is extremely important to the organization's health. A conflict of interest occurs in any situation where the individual puts his or her personal interests ahead of the organization's needs. Favoring one supplier over another as a result of perks or favors provided, such as meals or tickets to a football game, becomes a conflict of interest, if not in actuality, certainly in the perception of others.

The Consequences of Foul Play

A former corporate buyer and a former vice president (VP) for a subcontractor pleaded guilty to conspiracy, violating the antikickback statute, mail fraud, money laundering, and federal income tax fraud. The VP also pleaded guilty to engaging in a racketeering enterprise.

The subcontractor's VP paid the corporate buyer kickbacks; in exchange, the buyer agreed to steer business from the corporation to a wholly owned subsidiary of the subcontractor. The buyer then directed approximately $6 million in repair contracts from the corporation to the subcontractor's subsidiary and was paid approximately $100,000 in kickbacks.

- **Open competition.** When was the last time a high-value product or service was opened for competitive bids: three years ago, five years ago? Many organizations, especially those in the public procurement sector, require competitive bidding to ensure they are receiving prices and terms that are current in their industries.

Compliance is considered a major issue in government as well. The Department of Defense, for example, has an entire organization dedicated to ensuring full contract compliance called the Defense Contract Management Agency (DCMA). According to a statement on its website, the agency "monitors contractors' performance and management systems to ensure that cost, product performance, and delivery schedules are in compliance with the terms and conditions of the contracts." This is a rather unique role for any governmental agency; it not only manages performance but the systems used to ensure it. Thus DCMA also monitors the competitive bidding *process* to ensure that taxpayers' money is spent as frugally as possible.

Objectives and Benefits of an S2S Process

In addition to resolving the issues just noted, the S2S system enables organizations to achieve a number of other objectives. Many of these are broad objectives that flow from the organization's overall strategic plan while others can be considered purely operational. We examine the most important of these objectives next.

COST REDUCTION/COST AVOIDANCE   At the heart of any business strategy is the need to operate profitably. Doing this involves more aspects than the scope of this book, but it also clearly refers to reducing the cost of purchased goods and services as well as avoiding any additional cost through wise decision making.

SPEND VISIBILITY   The S2S process focuses on employing automated methods to help analyze the organization's spending patterns and rationalize supplier consolidation or aggregation. Aggregating purchases made from many suppliers to one or two typically results in financial leverage in terms of cost savings. To do this effectively, however, requires clean and reliable data covering historical spending patterns, both in commodity categories and by supplier. This is a difficult requirement; even with the best data collection and reporting system, it has been estimated that only 85 percent of the line items purchased can be properly identified by automated analysis of a given spend category. The rest, if it accounts for any significant spending, must be identified and processed manually.

STANDARDIZED PROCESSES   The source-to-settle structure demands repeatable and consistent processes throughout the organization in order to ensure that it can be managed properly. Gaining the maximum advantage of its benefits requires standardization in all key areas of the acquisition process *before* implementation. If we simply convert our faulty manual processes to one that is automated, we will likely create even more chaos than we already have. Areas of particular importance include sourcing methodologies such as market research, eRFx (an electronic request for proposal, quotation, and so on, signified here as "x"), e-Auctions (online auctions), supplier selection, procurement and contract administration, supplier relationship management (SRM), supplier performance reporting and improvement, and accounts payable or electronic payment.

Specifically, standardization in sourcing requires uniform methods of analysis for assessing suppliers during the qualification, bidding, and selection phase. Doing this calls for establishing a set of metrics to evaluate and qualify suppliers (often referred to as scorecards). These are measures that, if properly chosen, can be used after the supplier is selected for ongoing supplier performance evaluations and reviews.

Other important elements of standardization include formats for eRFxs, e-Auctions, requests for proposals, and requests for quotes, along with general terms and conditions for each of the major categories of goods and services. Uniform contracts for *master supply agreements* and *master service agreements (MSAs)* would also fit into this standardization category. In short, all elements in the S2S process must be governed by organization-wide policy and procedures, with automated systems and analytical software helping to ensure ongoing compliance.

REDUCED TRANSACTIONAL COST   Automation is the first rule of reducing transactional costs both in procurement and payables. Numerous automated procurement systems are available, and they extend all the way to small businesses. We focus first on the requisitioning process, automating purchase requests through online catalogs created by suppliers with whom we have existing contracts. With an automated system, the user selects the items needed from a consolidated catalog that enables a search for products he or she is eligible to purchase. The request is then routed via automated work flow for approval. Once approved, it can be electronically directed to the supplier via electronic data interchange (EDI) or extensible markup language (XML) data feeds. The sourcing group's involvement is with the selection of the suppliers and the negotiation of pricing and terms.

We can also automate invoicing using e-commerce technology or EDI, often at very little or no cost, depending on our existing level of automation. For example, an automated accounts payable is easily implemented with installed *ERP (enterprise resource planning)* or S2S software, such as Oracle, SAP, and a host of others. Recently, XML has become a payment standard that enables the global use of electronic business information in an interoperable, secure, and consistent manner by all trading partners. And of course, using purchasing cards (P-cards) to reduce low-price or one-time purchases have been a standard practice for some time. Both of these methods not only reduce tactical hands-on transactions, but they enhance supplier relations through consistent, on-time payments.

SUPPLIER INTEGRATION   Many S2S systems include a module or section for SRM. This module is designed to provide stronger collaboration with suppliers by increasing the level of integration with your organization. To a large extent, doing this means reducing payment cycles to agreed-on terms through monitoring and cash flow planning, which goes a long way to improve good relations. It also better enables buying organizations to leverage discounts offered for early payment, which often adds up to a substantial annual amount of cost savings.

Effective supplier integration often helps both organizations reduce the cost of transaction processing through readily available electronic methods. At the same time, it can also improve transaction accuracy. Fewer errors improve the quality of operations since less time is required to resolve or rework them.

RISK MANAGEMENT   Lately, supply chain business risk has become a major focal point in organizations. We are recognizing that the success of any program typically depends on events occurring as we planned. But often we find that is just not the case. Delays occur in supplier delivery, products and services are not available when we need them, or the quality of our purchase is not up to agreed-on standards. As a result, costly production delays eat away at our profit and, worse still, we have disappointed customers.

How does the S2S process help organizations meet their overall risk management objectives? A number of S2S monitoring tools are available as of this writing, but keep in mind that financial markets are currently in turmoil and new processes will likely emerge to deal with contemporary situations.

- **Contract exposure.** Contractual obligations, especially financial ones requiring the buyer to pay for a certain amount of goods or services whether used or not, are a significant financial concern and require close monitoring. Consumer spending habits often change rapidly, so work or materials in the pipeline can become obsolete in a very short time. Because of this, dealing with suppliers who have the ability to meet demand quickly, with relatively short lead times, is an absolute necessity to reduce the financial exposure inherent in a long supply chain or in long lead times. This case applies equally to buyer and seller.

Example of Contract Risk

Toward the end of the dot-com boom, in the summer of 2001, Cisco Systems, a leading computer network company, startled analysts with the announcement that it had its first loss of earnings in more than 10 years. Sales of its products were down by about 30 percent.

As a result, Cisco had to write off inventory, both on hand and committed to purchase, with an estimated worth of $2.2 billion. This write-off occurred despite the sophisticated technology Cisco had in place to monitor economic conditions.

The fault in this example lies not only with poor demand forecasting but with the integration of its entire procurement system. Obviously, the supply-side planners were not provided with the information pointing to a decline in the macroeconomy and a fall-off in customer demand orders. A demand planning system integrated with production planning might have solved the problem to some extent. However, it was just a matter of time before a disaster such as this one occurred without a fully enabled, completely integrated sourcing system that places high value on an agile supply chain. An S2S system that monitors suppliers' lead times and inventory availability against sourcing criteria will likely go a long way toward solving this type of situation.

- **Financial stability.** Large-scale supplier financial failure is a very real possibility, as we have learned recently. In the future, "too big to fail" may no longer become an option. In accounts payable, for example, credit risk can be related to the stability of the buyer's bank or line of credit. A bank closing often means a total disaster for a company's cash flow if its business or its suppliers' businesses are linked directly or indirectly to that financial institution. Credit risk changes very rapidly now, and as we have seen, supplier credit lines can disappear virtually overnight. In the past, systemic risk—where a domino effect of bank closings occurs and affects the entire system—has been managed largely by central banking regulators, but, as we have seen in the recession of 2007 to 2009, temporary interruptions are likely possible. In this case, risk monitoring systems tied to the organization's financial monitoring system will likely become the tool of choice.
- **Doing business with governments.** Governments also create uncertainty in some markets when they run out of money toward the end of their budget year. A good case in point is California, which began to issue IOUs to its suppliers when its budget ran out and its legislature was unable to act. Consider how you would react when you receive an IOU from a customer instead of payment.
- **Financial globalization.** Markets that have become globalized have additional risks in terms of changing exchange rates, timing, and settlement that are generated by differences in their legal system. Bankruptcy for the supplier as well as the buyer must be understood and monitored in terms of the laws of a

particular country. A sourcing team must constantly monitor conditions within the geographical area of its suppliers (captured in an S2S system).

Implementing an S2S Process

"The devil is in the details," as the saying goes. When an organization decides to implement a system such as S2S, it has the option of purchasing and installing an existing software package from an outside source or creating its own. Sometimes it becomes apparent that we need to modify the existing software so that it more completely meets our operational needs. In doing so, we must pay particular attention to our business objectives so that we avoid overspecification (paying for features that are not required) and bog ourselves down in developing tactical minutiae. The benefit of an S2S system is its ability to drive process standardization and capture actionable information that is usually strategic in nature. This system typically includes supplier performance, order status, spend analysis, cost control, outstanding contract obligations, and accounts payable status. We want this information so that we can meet strategic objectives, fulfill existing commitments to our end user customers, reduce business and supplier risk, and work toward continuous process improvement.

Installing an S2S system is a means to an end objective(s) rather than the other way around. It is important to understand your organization's needs fully and analyze the market to determine exactly what sourcing is available to meet them. There is no substitute for thorough preparation: fully understanding our objectives and what we need to meet them. Such a process will reduce the cost of implementation, improve its chances of success, and provide the shortest path to a successful operational system. The point is simply this: Do your research homework.

This section provides a skeletal methodology for implementing an S2S process. Our goal is to help familiarize you with the overall requirements so that you know what to expect and can develop your own model for successful implementation.

Elements of a Source-to-Settle Process

Virtually all S2S software is modular. This means that the system can be implemented in multiple stages, depending on its architecture, of course. While all systems differ to one extent or another, a general pattern appears to emerge that establishes these key modules that need to be implemented.

SOURCING Somewhat of a misnomer, most sourcing modules do not contain all the elements typically found in the process. Instead, they are most often designed to handle the simpler activities, such as supplier competitive bidding, requests for proposal, quotations, and perhaps electronic reverse auctions. However, suppliers must already be included in the system in order to participate. The systems we surveyed did not include important functions such as comparative supplier analysis, financial profiles (for risk management), capabilities, and current operational capacity levels. Some do include submodules for supplier rationalization (although most include this function in the analysis section).

PROCUREMENT S2S software varies widely in this area, although most is characterized by electronic methodologies and applies only to indirect (maintenance, repair, and operations) spending. The procurement module typically contains processes for these activities:

- Electronic catalogs containing prenegotiated items (stock-keeping units) for use in selecting products (and, sometimes, services).
- Requisitioning by internal users and accompanying electronic work flow routing for approval that is based on preassigned levels of sign-off authority.
- Assignment of purchases to department and general ledger codes.
- Purchase order generation and electronic transmission to the supplier using various methods, such as e-mail or "punch-out" (access to the supplier's portal along with the ability to select and order products) or through EDI.
- Supplier order acknowledgment and advance shipping notices.
- Shipping notice, delivery tracking, and receiving.

INVENTORY CONTROL Typically used for manufacturing (direct spending), this module includes:

- Order releases to suppliers (on blanket purchase orders or master agreements).
- Receipt to stock and stock on hand (available and promised).
- Scheduled releases to manufacturing floor or stockrooms.
- Valuation of inventory, on hand or in transit.
- Inventory reconciliation with physical counts.
- Returned authorizations to the supplier.

ACCOUNTING AND SETTLEMENT This module includes all of the accounts payable functions:

- Invoice receipt and entry (or eInvoice).
- Debit memos and credit processing.
- Electronic matching or invoice approval routing (for services).
- Discrepancy reconciliation.
- Payment (by check or electronically).
- Tax accounting and payment.
- Purchasing card management.
- Financial cost accrual against purchase order commitments.
- Budget interface.

ANALYSIS Using a variety of data mining management techniques, the analysis module provides standardized reports and information on demand. It typically includes:

- Spend analysis by product and supplier.
- Usage data by cost center or department.
- Supplier performance metrics.
- Spending with noncontractual suppliers (maverick spending).
- Spending against budgets.
- Spend variance of actual costs versus cost standards.

Implementation Process

In order to smoothly implement an S2S system (or any complex process, for that matter), we need to utilize a cross-functional team consisting of stakeholders (users), subject matter experts, internal customers, and representatives from the information technology (IT) department. (In some cases, it might prove useful to have one or two supplier representatives as well.) The project team must be in place prior to the system selection to ensure buy-in and business continuity. Here are the other recommended process steps.

REQUIREMENTS ANALYSIS The using group typically establishes the requirements analysis via a business requirements document (BRD) for the S2S system. Understanding the particular need based on factual data is critical to obtaining approval and funding. If you are part of the group leading the project, you will have already prepared a needs analysis to gain approval for the application from your management. If you are not part of this group, you will want to ensure that the project has been funded or appears likely to be funded so that you and your team can provide full support. If you are also a member of the sourcing team, you will want to see the BRD converted to a statement of work so that you can clearly determine the deliverables.

If a requirements analysis has not yet been performed, utilize the team to develop a detailed profile of existing conditions and the desired objectives. Gather the facts carefully so that there are no concerns regarding its accuracy:

- Create a process flow map; assess the cost and time it takes to perform the S2S process in its current state across the organization, using acceptably accurate data.
- Outline the key bottlenecks as pinch points.
- Determine how the project supports strategic business objectives.
- Estimate the resources needed (internal and external) to acquire and implement the S2S and support it going forward.
- Prepare an analysis of the return on investment and other benefits, such as improved customer support and supply management.

Two common traps should be avoided:

1. **Simply automating your current process because "it has worked in the past."** Implementing an S2S platform provides a unique opportunity to examine everything you do and to benchmark with best practices before going forward. Start from the ground and justify the value of every element that will go into the new process, whether it is an existing one or not. And listen to the provider of the proposed software: There may be new areas of metric tracking that you are not aware of and technology that can enable processes not considered previously.
2. **Failing to consult with your suppliers (existing or new) and to engage them in your analysis efforts.** Suppliers may have domain knowledge that you can leverage; some may have already implemented a similar system. You may even consider adding one or two to the S2S analysis team.

MANAGEMENT SUPPORT   Before going further, ensure that there is sufficient management support and that the project is funded. This should be done before investing time in performing the requirements analysis via a BRD from a logical viewpoint. It would be virtually impossible to gain management support without a justification analysis. Paradoxically, we may need some management buy-in before using any resources to go forward with the initial requirements analysis. However, if this is necessary, you may be able to present some compelling benchmarks (best practices) from other organizations that have already installed an S2S system or from published articles in various research organizations, trade magazines, and blogs.

MARKET RESEARCH   It would be impossible to review all of the available solutions on the market. You can accelerate the selection process by using some basic approaches to finding the best solutions for your organization. Use the Internet to identify all S2S systems available. Since ongoing support is critical, carefully review and filter providers with programs less than a year or two old. Ask for a list of customers; find providers with customers in your industry or of your business size. Your short list should contain no more than five names; think of the aggregated amount of time you and the team will have to invest in reviewing each of them.

Avoid asking for a demonstration before you have finished your review and know which systems will best fit your organization's needs. It's easy to get side-tracked by some sales-oriented bells and whistles. Stick to your short list and provide each of the potential suppliers with your requirements documentation. Do this formally, using a request for proposal. Be sure to require respondents to use the format you have provided so that you can compare all of the proposals easily. Document everything, including conversations (formal and informal). Remember that verbal commitments must be included in the finalized written contract.

It will become apparent in reviewing proposals which providers can and cannot meet your requirements. Conduct a final shoot-out with no more than three that appear to have the systems closest to your needs. (Customization will be costly, so keep it to a minimum.) Ask for demonstrations within a specified time period. Check references with questions such as (but not limited to):

- How long did it take to implement your system?
- Did the supplier meet your timeline?
- Were costs in line with your expectations?
- Did you require more customization than expected?
- How well did your employees adapt to the new system?
- Have you achieved all of your sourcing objectives?
- Which sourcing objectives did you have to abandon?
- Does the supplier technology work as expected?
- Was the training effective and sufficient?
- Are you receiving the benefits you expected?
- Is the system operating to everyone's satisfaction?
- What do you believe could have been done better by the supplier?
- What do you believe could have been done better by your implementation team?

SELECTION In making the final S2S supplier selection, thoroughly evaluate the proposals, reference feedback, and the impressions of how close the systems come to matching stated requirements. Conduct a measured evaluation by each team member, summarize the findings, and select two suppliers (one primary and one fallback). There will not be full consensus; there rarely is. But you should be close enough to get buy-in from all user groups. If there are gaps between your needs and the system's capability, negotiate a solution that satisfies key internal customers. Make the award based on the viability of the system, the supplier's commitments to meeting the milestones in your timeline, and the supplier's proposed cost.

IMPLEMENTATION If the selection process has been conducted properly, project implementation will be an extension of the processes outlined, and you can expect it to go smoothly—if you have a plan that everyone on the team agrees with. Here consensus is critical; you must mitigate any concerns by key users (including IT) regarding implementation methods, training, timelines, and communication. Some project management tips you might want to consider include the following:

- Develop the implementation plan, with an associated project timeline (with critical path items), in enough detail so that it can be used as the guiding milestone document.
- Ensure that personnel resources will be available when needed.
- Establish a training plan and select superusers (subject matter experts) and end user testers.
- Develop a communication plan. Determine who needs to know what and when.
- Implement the training and communications roll-out plans.
- Run a complete pilot on a test system.
- Populate the new system with required data.
- Run a pilot on the installed system.
- Have superusers try out the system with mock data.
- Run the new system in parallel with the existing system.
- Cut over to the new system and retire the old one.
- Monitor operations with metrics to ensure service-level contract compliance.
- Review or survey the level of satisfaction by end users.
- Plan for additional tweaking and installation of planned module add-ons.

Please keep in mind that this list is not a guideline for implementation in itself. It is just meant to stimulate initial thought processes. And remember that rarely does an implementation go exactly as planned. Flexibility will stand everyone in good stead.

Managing the S2S Process

Aside from implementation, ongoing monitoring is one of the most important keys to achieving success with a process such as S2S. You must continually assess its effectiveness and iron out any wrinkles that appear.

A centralized management structure makes the process much easier to control; decentralization common to multiple operating units generally leads to a lack of adherence to the principles that drive anticipated benefits. We have come to recognize that decentralization results in redundant suppliers (and higher prices) and a decrease in contract compliance due to maverick spending.

Fully leveraging an S2S system requires some very tough management decisions. The organization can centralize operations under a single S2S officer and with a unified sourcing team. The sourcing team must become familiar with each unit's specific requirements so that it can develop relationships with suppliers that can effectively respond to the needs of each unit.

We often find that organizations are not willing to collectively buy in to a fully centralized sourcing, procurement, and contract administration group. This is quite understandable from an internal user's perspective. So what is the solution? Many organizations find that a central sourcing group, with team members located in each of the major business units, can effectively unify the supplier selection and management and the initial selection and contracting process. Individual business units usually maintain a dedicated procurement team to handle local requirements. The enabling factor is linking all groups together through the same system and process. In this way, all sourcing and procurement personnel have access to the same data at the same time.

Supplier selection and supplier management is often conducted by dispersed sourcing and commodity management teams. For geographically dispersed units, suppliers must have the capability of serving all of them, or at least those that account for 90 percent utilization and above. This requirement for suppliers to serve all of an organization's location tends to provide some management challenges for them but the challenges so far have proven manageable through increased communication via today's online collaboration tools and additional travel for face-to-face meetings by the staff.

Outsourcing the S2S Process

Organizations today are increasingly turning to business process outsourcing for many of the services they use that do not fall within the scope of their core competencies. Sourcing and procurement of indirect goods and services, along with the management of the S2S system, are becoming more and more prevalent, and with increasingly effective results.

There must be a clear benefit to outsourcing these functions in order to gain management's interest. BPO providers must be selected on their demonstrated ability to ensure operational effectiveness. But as experience increases, organizations are better equipped to make the right decisions, select outsourced groups with excellent track records, and acquire the ability to become effective managers of the outsourced business processes.

Despite the somewhat increased risk, organizations still find many benefits in outsourcing the acquisition of indirect goods and services. Reduced operational cost is quite possibly the most important benefit organizations seek. Most outsourcing services are simply better at what they do than most of their customers. Outsourcing companies are also better equipped to effectively absorb spikes in transactional volume since they generally employ a larger staff than their customers. From a finance perspective, this outsourcing means that a variable cost can be transferred to a fixed cost, and we always know the cost of outsourced operations.

In the sourcing and procurement functions, outsourcing can also provide a smoother overall operation. Outsourcing providers are able to hire more focused and highly specialized employees since they work with larger overall volumes. Working with many customers and many suppliers gives them access to benchmarking information previously available only to major consulting firms (many of which are today engaged in providing outsourced services themselves). As a result of their increased volumes, outsourcing firms are also better able to acquire the best technology, generally unaffordable by most small and midsize organizations.

As a start, if you have a need for outsourcing the S2S process, here is a list of resources along with their URLs:

- **BravoSolution,** www.bravosolution.com/cms/us
- **Enporion,** www.enporion.com/solutions/source-to-settlement.html
- **SAP Supplier Relationship Management,** www.sap.com/solutions/business -suite/srm/index.epx
- **SciQuest Inc,** www.sciquest.com
- **Source to Settle: Compliance Clues for the CFO (Aberdeen Group, Inc.),** aberdeen.com/link/sponsor.asp?cid=3590
- **Source-to-Settle Group | LinkedIn,** www.linkedin.com/groups?home=&gid=2946468
- **The Future of Procure-to-Pay—eProcurement (Part 1),** cporising.com/2010/10/01/the-future-of-procure-to-pay-eprocurement-part-1/
- **The Future of Procure-to-Pay—eProcurement (Part 2),** cporising.com/2010/10/01/the-future-of-procure-to-pay-eprocurement-part-2/
- **The Future of Procure-to-Pay—eProcurement (Part 3),** cporising.com/2010/10/01/the-future-of-procure-to-pay-eprocurement-part-3/
- **The Hackett Group,** www.thehackettgroup.com

Summary

We began this chapter with a detailed analysis of the reasons why organizations need an S2S system. The issues presented included the lack of uniform processes and the lack of compliance with business process policy.

The objectives and benefits of an S2S process include cost reduction/cost avoidance, increased spend visibility, better regulatory compliance, standardized processes, reduced transaction cost, improved supplier integration, and risk management.

Then we covered the basics of implementing an S2S process, describing the elements of an S2S process, including sourcing, procurement, inventory control, accounting and settlement, and analysis. The implementation process includes a requirements analysis, management support, market research, system selection, and bringing the system online.

We concluded with some notes on managing the S2S process and important considerations in outsourcing.

CHAPTER **18**

Material Management and Supply Operations

Controlling the flow, storage, and stocking levels of materials is another of the key functions of supply management. Organizations, particularly those engaged in manufacturing operations, consider material management a core competency because production processes and materials go hand in hand. The effective flow of materials can, and often does, significantly affect the overall productivity—and thus the costs—of the manufacturer.

Because, in many instances, there is a great deal of capital invested in stored inventory, how the inventory is controlled and managed can also affect the organization's profitability. When profit is viewed as a return on the investment, it becomes clear that maximizing that return will depend largely on how rapidly existing inventory can be consumed and converted back into cash. Obviously, if all other conditions are equal, the organization with the smallest ratio of inventory to sales is the organization that will likely be the most profitable.

In this chapter, we will examine the various methods of controlling inventory so that it can be used as a valuable resource to support operations rather than as a black hole for cash. These controls include strategies and methods for ordering and stocking materials, as well as effective processes for disposing of inventory that is no longer needed.

Inventory Control and Management Systems

Organizations that own and manage *inventory* are constantly seeking ways to reduce the size of that inventory in order to reduce the amount of nonproductive funds that are thus tied up. As most of you know, inventory generally doesn't do anything except consume valuable space and require a lot of cycle counting. For organizations that require inventory for perhaps justifiable reasons, such as using it as a buffer for unreliable supply or large swings in demand, the challenge comes with managing it so that as little as possible is needed. From this effort, a number of systems have been developed for determining when to order inventory and automating the management process. We'll describe some of these systems in this section.

Types of Inventory

Inventory is generally classified according to its functional type and, if used in manufacturing, its current state of production. Thus it is typical for material to be classified as *raw material (RM)*, *work-in-process (WIP)*, or *finished goods (FG)*. Raw material, in turn, can be classified as *direct material* (i.e., material that goes directly into the product being manufactured) or *indirect material* (material that supports manufacturing operations but does not ship out with the final product). In addition, there are inventories of materials you maintain that are not directly related to any production functions, such as MRO (*maintenance, repair, and operations*) as well as supplies and marketing support materials.

Before we look at how these inventories are managed, it might be useful to define their various natures. Let's start with raw materials.

RAW MATERIAL CLASSIFICATIONS   Raw materials, as the title implies, are materials in their basic state as they have been received and to which no manufacturing operations have been performed. They are in the first stage of the transformation process to the final manufactured product.

There are two major categories of raw materials:

1. **Direct material.** Direct material is the primary classification for raw materials in manufacturing operations. It is only the material that, after manufacturing processes are applied, ships out to a distributor or the final customer. If, for example, you manufacture hammers, then steel would be your primary direct material.

    The level of inventory for direct material is considered one of the manufacturing organization's key financial indicators. To demonstrate effective management of inventory, organizations use the term *turns,* referring to the number of times the inventory of direct materials will turn over during a period (usually a year). In simplest form, inventory turnover is calculated as the number of times the inventory is sold during the period or as the ratio of inventory to sales. Inventory turnover is also calculated as the cost of goods sold divided by the average level of inventory on hand.

2. **Indirect material.** Indirect material is the class of materials in the manufacturing process that does not actually ship to the customer as part of the final product. For example, the gas used to heat the furnaces that melt the steel in the manufacture of hammers is an indirect material. Similarly, the water that cools the metal is also an indirect material.

WORK-IN-PROCESS (WIP)   Work-in-process describes manufactured goods that have not yet been completed. However, in order to be considered WIP, some labor other than handling and storage must have been directly applied. Components and assemblies are the typical types of WIP in most manufacturing operations.

FINISHED GOODS   Finished goods are those products that have completed the manufacturing production process and for which all necessary labor operations have been completed. Depending on the industry, finished goods are usually packaged and ready for shipment.

NONPRODUCTION–RELATED MATERIALS Nonproduction–related materials are those not used in manufacturing at all, but rather that support the administrative operations of the organizations. MRO items such as light bulbs, copy paper, maintenance, construction, and janitorial supplies are a few examples. Nonproduction materials may also include inventories of promotional materials such as advertising flyers and catalogs. Many of them are managed by the same *inventory management* methods used in manufacturing so that their levels can remain as low as possible.

Capital goods are also a form of large expenditure assets tracked by the organization as though it were inventory. Capital goods are assets purchased for long-term use, such as machinery and other equipment that *depreciate* or lose value over a predetermined period of time.

The Role of Inventory

Inventory has a specific role in manufacturing entities, and inventories are maintained by these organizations for a number of specific reasons:

- Inventory protects the organization from the uncertainties of supply and ensures that material is readily available when it is needed. Inventory buffers are most common in operations where demand and lead times vary considerably and are hard to predict.
- Inventory is often held in anticipation of a seasonal demand or other specific increase in demand or for a particular customer order. It can also be the result of canceled sales orders.
- Some situations result in inventory being created by the minimum quantity of orders required by a supplier or as a result of ordering larger amounts to receive special price breaks.
- Extra-large WIP inventories are often created through long production cycle times.

Regardless of the specific reason for maintaining the inventory in the first place, inventory must be closely controlled and monitored since it absorbs a great deal of the organization's available working capital. For a review of inventory management, let's turn to a look at the systems typically used to keep inventory to a minimum.

Systems for Managing Inventory

Inventory management systems are tools used to control inventory so that materials are on hand when needed while at the same time minimizing the financial liability to the organization. Fundamental to these tools are the various ordering strategies you ultimately employ and the automated systems that support these tools.

ORDERING STRATEGIES An inventory ordering strategy is basically a method for determining the quantity of materials to be ordered and the timing for delivery of that order. There are several common methodologies in use that you should be familiar with that we will discuss in this section.

TABLE 18.1   Fixed Quantity Order Method

WEEK #	1	2	3	4	5	6	7	8
Demand	150	0	70	0	175	0	90	60
Net Balance	110	110	40	40	(135)	65	(35)	(135)
Planned Receipts	0	0	0	0	200	0	200	0
On Hand End of Week	110	110	40	40	65	65	165	30
Quantity to Order	0	0	200	0	200		0	?

Order Point Reordering   The *order point* method of inventory replenishment establishes a predetermined minimum level of inventory that, when reached, will trigger a reorder. The calculation subtracts incoming orders from the stock on hand to determine when the reorder point has been reached. This method may require the calculation of a *safety stock*, typically based on the anticipated amount that will be used during the lead time it takes to replenish the stock. The actual formula is:

> On-Hand Inventory − Incoming Orders − Safety Stock (if used)
> = Reorder Point

Fixed Order Quantity   The *fixed order quantity* rule (sometimes called FOQ) states that the quantity ordered is the same fixed amount each time an order is required to cover a potential shortage, regardless of how much is actually needed to cover that shortage. Table 18.1 shows the incoming demand for a number of given weeks and the effect of this demand on the available balance of inventory at the end of each week. From the information in the bottom row, you can see that, based on a lead time of two weeks and a fixed order quantity of 200 parts (a number determined, perhaps, by the minimum order the supplier requires)—you will need to place an order in Week 3 to cover a planned deficit of 135 parts in Week 5 and in Week 7 to cover a planned deficit of 35 parts. Notice that while the shortages are different quantities, the amount ordered is always the same. Week 8 shows a question mark in the quantity to order because you do not have demand figures to cover the two-week lead time.

Periodic Order Quantity   The *periodic order quantity* rule (sometimes called POQ) requires that the quantity ordered be enough to cover requirements for a fixed number of periods. Table 18.2 shows the same demand as Table 18.1, and you can see that orders are placed in the same intervals (every two weeks), but the orders are placed in the amount needed to cover the shortage during the two-week period following receipt. Notice that, in Week 5, 150 parts need to be ordered to cover the cumulative demand for Weeks 7 and 8 (90 + 60). Since you are ordering every two weeks exactly, your next scheduled order in Week 7 shows a question mark because you don't know what the demand will be in Week 9, at the end of the two-week lead time.

Lot for Lot   As the title implies, with a *lot for lot (L4L or LFL)* system, you order exactly what is needed for a given period. With respect to the quantity, you always order exactly enough to avoid a stock outage while ordering as little as possible. With

TABLE 18.2 Periodic Order Quantity Method

Week #	1	2	3	4	5	6	7	8
Demand	150	0	70	0	175	0	90	60
Net Balance	110	110	40	40	(135)	0	(90)	60
Planned Receipts	0	0	0	0	135	0	150	0
On Hand End of Week	110	110	40	40	0	0	60	0
Quantity to Order	0	0	135	0	150	0	?	0

respect to timing, you always order in time to ensure that no outages occur. Using the same figures in Table 18.3 used for Table 18.2, you can see that the only change is that the order originally placed in Week 5 for 150 parts is split into two orders one week apart, for 90 and 60 parts, respectively.

Economic Order Quantity   *Economic order quantity (EOQ)* is another inventory ordering model that attempts to minimize total inventory cost by answering the following two questions.

■ How much should I order?
■ How often should I place each order?

This model assumes that the demand faced by the firm is linear, that is, the rate of demand is constant or at least nearly constant. It also assumes that the purchase price of the product is not dependent on the quantity ordered at any given time but determined between purchaser and supplier in advance based upon the anticipated number of units to meet the demand over the coming period, typically annually.

The goal of the EOQ formula is to minimize total inventory cost. Inventory costs are assumed to be made up of total holding costs and ordering costs. Holding costs include the cost of financing the inventory along with the cost of physically storing and managing the inventory. These costs are usually expressed as a percentage of the value of the inventory. Ordering costs include the costs associated with actually placing the order. These include a labor cost as well as a material and overhead cost.

The basic economic order quantity formula is calculated as the square root of twice the annual usage times the ordering cost, divided by the carrying cost per unit.

TABLE 18.3 Lot for Lot Ordering Method

Week #	1	2	3	4	5	6	7	8
Demand	150	0	70	0	175	0	90	60
Net Balance	110	110	40	40	(135)	0	(90)	60
Planned Receipts	0	0	0	0	135	0	150	0
On Hand End of Week	110	110	40	40	0	0	60	0
Quantity to Order	0	0	135	0	90	60	?	0

It's shown in the following formula:

$$E00 = \sqrt{\frac{2(\text{Annual usage in units})(\text{Order cost})}{(\text{Carrying cost per unit})}}$$

As an example, say that the usage for a particular part is 15,000 per year. Let's also assume that the organization orders the parts three times per year and that the average cost of placing an order is $129. Thus, the numerator in this calculation would appear as:

$$2 \times (15,000 \times 129) = 3,870,000$$

Carrying cost, the denominator in the formula, consists of the cost of storage and handling plus the theoretical cost of interest for the value of the inventory should it be financed. Calculating the carrying cost is a bit more difficult. Let's take some shortcuts in establishing the interest cost by assuming the average daily inventory volume is 7,500 parts, and each part costs $1.10. This means that there is an average daily value of $8,250 on hand ($7,500 \times 1.10 = 8,250$). If interest rates were 5 percent per year, the interest for one day would be approximately $1.13 per day (($.05 / 365) \times 8,250 = 1.13$). Calculating the annual interest cost per unit is as follows:

$$\text{Average Interest Cost/Unit} = (1.13 \times 365)/7,500 = \$0.055$$

Continuing the calculation requires a determination of the storage and handling costs. Let's assume that 7,500 parts (the average daily inventory) uses 50 square feet of storage at a monthly cost of $0.45 per square foot or $22.50 per month. If you multiply this by 12 months and then divide by the average number of parts stored, you can calculate the average storage costs per unit:

$$\text{Average Storage Cost/Unit} = (22.50 \times 12)/7,500 = \$0.036$$

The remaining calculation requires an estimate of the handling costs per unit. Let's assume that the handling costs are simply the cost of cycle counting. If you cycle count four times each year (once per quarter), and it takes 10 minutes (0.1667 hour) at an average labor cost of $18 per hour, the cost would be calculated as follows:

$$\text{Handling Cost/Unit} = ((18 \times 0.1667) \times 4)/7,500 = \$0.002$$

You now have the denominator for the formula:

$$\text{Carrying Cost} = \text{Interest Cost} + \text{Storage Cost} + \text{Handling Cost}$$
$$= (0.055 + 0.036 + 0.002) = \$0.093/\text{Unit}$$

Using these numbers to complete the formula:

$$\text{Square Root of } (3,870,000/0.093) = 6,451 \text{ parts per order}$$

Using this formula, you would then order parts approximately twice per year at an interval of 157 days. To calculate this, you divide the parts per order by the annual requirements and then multiply 365 by that fraction:

$$\text{Days to Reorder} = 365 \times (6,451/15,000) = 156.95$$

Using EOQ effectively requires strict adherence to a number of requirements:

- Demand is known with certainty.
- Demand is relatively constant over time.
- No shortages are allowed.
- Lead time for the receipt of orders remains constant.
- The order quantity is received all at once.

If you are lacking any one of these criteria, use caution because your calculation will probably have a wide margin of error.

AUTOMATED PROCESSES   Managing inventory through automated processes has become fairly common as a result of the widespread use of ERP systems. Most organizations maintain computerized *perpetual inventories* that automatically add incoming receipts to the quantity on hand and then subtract issues from that amount to provide an up-to-the minute tally of the inventory on hand. In addition to using automated systems, many organizations today also rely on their suppliers to manage and keep track of inventories that are held on consignment. Ultimately, this may prove to be the most effective way of managing inventory because, among other factors, it enables the supplier to integrate usage in its customer's facility with its own planning strategy. (Supplier-managed inventory is discussed later in this section.)

MRP and MRPII   As discussed in Chapter 8, material requirements planning (MRP) and manufacturing resource planning (MRPII) are computerized, time-based priority planning techniques that calculate material requirements and schedule supply to meet changing demand across all product lines. MRP, the initially developed system, was created in the United States and Canada during the 1960s. MRP takes into consideration customer orders and planning forecasts to determine inventory requirements. MRPII is essentially MRP but with some additional features. Typically, an MRPII package includes elements such as cost information, management reports, and the ability to model situations through "what-if" analysis. It may also include *capacity requirements planning (CRP),* a tool that determines the loading at a workstation or throughout the entire factory so that capacity constraints can be reflected in the planning process).

Tips and Techniques

MRPII stands for manufacturing resources planning, signifying a concentration on the planning of all manufacturing resources, rather than limiting planning to just the material requirements. The "II" designation is used to distinguish this form from its MRP predecessor.

When relevant data has been gathered regarding the status of parts, assemblies, and resources, the lead time of every component can be determined based upon a variety of manufacturing conditions. As soon as an incoming customer order is received, the backlog for the manufacturing organization and the delivery time for product can be calculated. An MRP system can call attention to constraints such as overloaded production centers, the effect of incoming orders, changes in capacity, shortages, delays in manufacturing, and delays by suppliers so that effective action can be taken to reduce them in a timely fashion.

From a systemic perspective, MRP relies on two basic types of information to calculate requirements:

1. **Structural information.** Structural information is information about the organization's items (parts or components) and how each of the different items is related. It includes important ordering information for each item such as lead time, lot (or batch) size, and where the item is obtained (for example, whether it's purchased or manufactured in-house). The key point about structural information is that it changes relatively infrequently.
2. **Tactical information.** Tactical information is information about the current state of manufacturing; for example, sales orders (real and forecast) pending, the master production schedule, on-hand inventory levels, and unfilled purchase orders. Obviously, the key point about this information is that it changes frequently.

Demand Concepts   In procurement, *demand* generally means the actual or projected usage of the items you are monitoring. The concept of demand is very closely related to the MRP process and is an integral aspect of inventory management. For this reason, demand is typically classified in terms of the conditions that generate it. Thus, there are two basic types of demand:

1. **Independent demand** is any demand for a product or service that is generated externally, usually by customer orders. It is usually difficult to predict and quantify.
2. **Dependent demand** is dependent in quantity, quality, and timing on its related independent demand, usually in the form of an incoming customer order or aggregation of orders. The materials needed to fulfill such incoming orders are by nature dependent upon that order in the first place. An independent order for a computer from an assembly facility, for example, creates a dependent demand for a motherboard and a certain set of other specific subassembly components. MRP and MRPII systems are primarily dedicated to tracking these dependencies and calculating dependent demand patterns as a primary function in inventory control.

In most MRP systems, the dependent demand generated by "exploding" the bills of material (BOMs) for incoming orders does not assume an infinite capacity for capacity-constrained resources (such as machines and people). Therefore, specific methods are required to schedule capacity-constrained resources. This scheduling process usually generates a manufacturing plan, and it is the responsibility of the Procurement Department or materials control group to ensure that the materials are available as required by the plan.

Demand Planning Demand planning is a process of collaboration among all of the participants—sales, operations, finance, as well as affected groups in the supply community—in the demand forecasting process. Each needs to receive and provide data.

Demand planning is also a critical element in enabling a more comprehensive processes like a *collaborative planning, forecasting, and replenishment (CPFR)* process. It employs the demand forecast as the foundation for its planning and offers guidance on how the forecasted elements will be actually used. Demand planning allows the organization to make accurate customer demand predictions to better manage inventory replenishment with forecasting.

CPFR is a set of standardized business processes shared between trading partners. As in demand planning, collaborating partners develop forecasts and operational plans based on mutual objectives and measures.

JUST-IN-TIME INVENTORY MANAGEMENT Meeting the requirements of a manufacturing plan and at the same time allowing for maximum flexibility and last-minute changes due to customer order changes requires a truly flexible *demand management* system. *Just-in-time (JIT)* inventory management processes (also known as *lean* or stockless manufacturing) were developed for just this reason.

JIT and MRP are two distinctly different systems for controlling production. While MRP is based on meeting predicted demand during a period of time, JIT is based on actual usage. JIT is a means of market pull inventory management conducted in an environment of continuing improvement. Use of JIT methods results in considerably reduced inventory and enhanced customer response time. However, to be successful it requires a systemic and highly cooperative approach to inventory receipt, throughput, and delivery.

Although JIT was developed for production environments, the process can be extended to all business environments. The basic concept is to receive what is needed just in time for it to be used. This, in effect, places the responsibility on the supplier to get what is needed to where it is needed, just before it is needed.

JIT is also a management philosophy that works to eliminate sources of manufacturing waste by producing the proverbial "right part in the right place at the right time." In theory, waste results from any activity that adds cost without adding value, such as moving and storing. JIT is thus designed to improve profits and return on investment (ROI) by reducing inventory levels (increasing the inventory turnover rate), improving product quality, reducing production and delivery lead times, and reducing other costs (such as those associated with machine setup and equipment breakdown).

SUPPLIER-MANAGED INVENTORY (SMI) The concept of SMI or *vendor-managed inventory (VMI)*, whichever you prefer to call it, is a logical progression from ideas that generated JIT inventory management in the first place. The goal of both is to build enough flexibility into the manufacturing system (or the supply chain itself) so that customer demand can be met in as short a time frame as possible. In today's business environment, the customer wants immediate gratification and will likely turn to another product if the one chosen is not available relatively instantly.

SMI places the responsibility on the supplier to meet incoming customer demand (or rapidly changing forecasts). Often working from the manufacturer's MRP outputs, the supplier assesses incoming demand and plans operations accordingly to ensure that material is available for production exactly when it is needed. Although in most SMI applications the supplier is responsible for managing the inventory, the buying organization pays for it when received as it would if it had ordered the material directly. Consequently, there must exist a very close partnership built upon mutual trust in order for the management of materials to be confidently turned back to the supplier. In these situations, however, the materials management group (or Procurement Department) must closely monitor activities, working with the supplier on a continuous improvement process.

The ultimate extension of SMI is *consignment inventory*. Managed in essentially the same way as SMI, the major difference is that the supplier owns the inventory until it is actually withdrawn from stock for production. To be considered true consignment, the stock must be located at the buyer's facility and owned by the supplier with no contingencies for automatic purchase of obsolescent stock.

Inventory Economics

Since manufacturing organizations often have a great deal of capital resources tied up in inventory, minimizing inventory can result in better overall financial performance. However, there should always be a balance maintained between inefficient use of inventory and the needs of meeting market demand. In general, you will want to consider how to maximize the return on the organization's investment in inventory. In this evaluation, you may want to consider that ROI is a ratio that measures how much over how long. So you can conceivably improve the performance of inventory investment both by reducing the overall size of the inventory, and therefore its value, and by shortening the length of time your organization owns it, and thereby its rate of return.

INVENTORY TURNOVER   One typical measure of the efficient use of inventory is its *turnover* ratio. Inventory turnover measures the speed that inventory is used relative to sales. It's typically calculated by dividing annual sales by average inventory, using the average inventory over an accounting period rather than just an ending-inventory value. Inventory turnover can also be calculated by dividing the total annual value of all inventory used (or issued) by the amount of inventory currently on hand:

$$\text{Annual Inventory Used/On-Hand Inventory} = \text{Turnover}$$

For example, if the annual inventory used was \$100 million and the current inventory is valued at \$10 million, the turnover rate would be 10 times annually. Low turnover is an indication that inventory is too high for the accompanying level of sales.

Lead-Time Considerations

As noted earlier in this chapter, inventory can be used to buffer stock outages caused by suppliers and to support variable customer demand. Strategically, the consideration of when to carry inventory and how much should be held can be rationalized according to the service levels the organization is attempting to achieve. Service levels can be measured in terms of the frequency of stock outages and the seriousness of the effects of the outages, such as production stoppages or order cancellations. For the most part, these effects can be financially evaluated and related to the cost of carrying various levels of inventory, with strategic decisions made according to the degree of support desired.

Physical Management and Inventory Accounting

In order to effectively manage inventory, it must be properly maintained, reported, and carried on the business records. Automated systems rely on a virtual accuracy of 100 percent in order to properly maintain minimal amounts of inventory. In a JIT environment, even the smallest discrepancy can result in a planning or financial disaster. In this section, we review some of the methods and tools available to maintain accurate records and account for discrepancies.

Controlling Inventory

Inventory control refers to the activities and methods used by organizations to receive, track, maintain, and issue materials. It also includes the management of inventory from a financial standpoint to ensure that it is accurately accounted for and valued. This process involves the actual physical storage, handling, and issuance of materials, as well as the record keeping that goes along with it.

STORES   Organizations that maintain substantial amounts of inventory usually manage it by keeping it in specific locations. These stocking locations are usually referred to as *stores*. The general function of the stores operation is to physically manage and issue parts and supplies to internal groups as they are needed. There are two broad systems for managing stores:

1. **Open stores.** When the value of inventory or the need for security is relatively low, or when access to it is required quite frequently, materials may be stored in open locations that are accessible directly by production staff, known as *open stores*. Record keeping is typically loose, relying primarily on physical cycle counting to reconcile on-hand inventory levels.
2. **Closed stores.** Conversely, when inventory must be tightly controlled because of its value, scarcity, or potential safety issues, it is generally maintained in a limited access stockroom, called *closed stores*. Here, receipts and issues are closely recorded and often require authorized signatures or approvals before inventory release.

STORAGE AND RETRIEVAL SYSTEMS   Within the storage facility, and regardless of its type, material is physically stored using various systems for stocking and retrieval:

- **Specified locations.** In some storage schemes, designated bins or storage shelves are allocated for the same specific items of inventory. This enables rapid retrieval when goods are uncontrolled because the staff becomes familiar with where materials are actually located and can find them quite easily.

- **Random access locations.** In automated storage and retrieval systems, inventory locations are stored on a computer system. When inventory is received, it is automatically allocated the first open space designated on the computer system and physically placed in that location. When it is needed, the material is found by using the computer system to report its exact location.
- **Automated storage and retrieval systems.** Automated storage and retrieval systems rely on computerized mechanical systems—often robotic—to store and retrieve material with little human intervention. Parts are delivered to specified locations either on demand or in accordance with a manufacturing schedule.

RECORD SYSTEMS   Today, most inventory record keeping systems are automated. However, depending on the system used for controlling inventory—open or closed stores, for example—inventory records are updated on *periodic* or *perpetual* basis.

Periodic updating requires that physical counts are taken at designated intervals and used to update the records of quantities on hand. This system is most commonly used for small parts such as nails or screws or liquids that are difficult to account for precisely.

Perpetual inventory is used when precise and up-to-date accounting is required. This system records exact receipts and issues as they occur so that the on-hand inventory is precise.

CYCLE COUNTING   *Cycle counting*, physically counting inventory to ensure its accuracy, is used to update inventory records when usage varies imprecisely or is nonstandard (as may be the case with commodities, liquids, and fasteners), and when inventory accuracy is critical. It is also commonly employed when auditing or verifying the actual value of the inventory at a specific time.

The timing for cycle counting often follows a specific schedule based on the value of the inventory as segmented according to the typical Pareto principle of *ABC analysis*, where the most valuable materials are counted most frequently: A items may be counted monthly, B items quarterly, and C items annually. Cycle counts are also taken more frequently for parts that are used more frequently since there may be a higher risk of inaccuracy.

Reconciling Discrepancies

The difference between the recorded inventory and the actual inventory found on hand when it is physically counted requires some form of reconciliation. Most commonly, the recorded inventory is adjusted to reflect the actual inventory counted during the cycle count. However, you should always keep in mind that such variation has financial implications and how it is accounted for financially depends upon the organization's policy. Low-value errors associated with high volumes of transactions are common and typically tolerated. Generally, such losses are absorbed by an overhead variance account. However, loss of valuable inventory through damage or theft can become a serious financial issue if it becomes commonplace, so you will want to ensure that proper safeguards are in place so that it does not become a serious issue. Judicious use of closed stores for inventory security may circumvent such problems.

Disposition of Surplus Assets

Most organizations, at one time or another, generate surplus materials, scrap, or obsolete equipment that may have value to others outside the organization. Surplus materials and equipment can be generated in a number of ways:

- Scrap or waste generated by manufacturing operations.
- Excess purchases.
- Obsolete material and supplies.
- Discontinued finished products.
- Decommissioned equipment.

Converting these nonproductive assets to cash or, at the very least, minimizing the cost of their disposal can certainly add financial value to the organization. Nevertheless, it is surprising to learn that many organizations have no process or system at all for effectively handling these assets.

Tips and Techniques

One of Our Authors (Fred Sollish's) First Visit to Corporate Storage

As a newly appointed procurement manager, Fred was assigned the task of supervising the revamping of his organization's 5,000-square-foot storage facility. He was told it was used mostly for retired records. Although it sounded simple, he was immediately challenged: On his first visit, Fred was unable to open the door because it was apparently blocked by something inside. With some help, he was able to raise the rollup receiving door and was presented with a startling scene: Equipment and surplus materials were randomly piled everywhere, from floor to ceiling in some places, covering every available square foot of the facility. It was impossible to enter without climbing upon or over something.

Fred hired a disposal firm who inventoried the usable equipment and placed it in an already scheduled auction for a similar firm. The company recovered close to $90,000. What's more, with all the equipment and surplus removed, they found that the records occupied a very small portion of the warehouse. The company sent them to a records storage facility and turned in the lease on the warehouse, saving another $2,200 per month.

Disposal Strategies

The Procurement Department is a natural resource for surplus disposal since it has continuing contact with both internal users and suppliers. With knowledge of the needs of internal users, Procurement has an opportunity to find secondary uses for surplus within the organization. Procurement may also have specialized knowledge about where the material or equipment was purchased from initially and may have access to reselling channels through them. There are two main concerns you'll have as a procurement professional when it comes to disposal of materials: The first are your legal obligations, and the second is the disposal of hazardous materials. Let's discuss these in more detail.

LEGAL ASPECTS   Before beginning any disposal operations, you should first acquaint yourself with any key legal aspects that might be associated with the specific items you are proposing to dispose of, such as transfer of legal title, liabilities, and implied warranties. You will also want to be certain that you prepare the appropriate sales "as is" documents. Since legal requirements can be as varied as the materials and equipment you are giving up for disposal, it is imperative to get the proper legal counsel prior to going forward.

HAZARDOUS MATERIALS DISPOSAL   Hazardous materials must be disposed of in accordance with applicable laws and regulations. In the United States, the U.S. Environmental Protection Agency (EPA) defines the nature of specific hazardous materials and prescribes the methods for their disposal. The U.S. Department of Transportation (DOT) prescribes the method for transporting hazardous materials and their required documentation. There are also numerous state and local regulations governing the disposal of hazardous waste. New York State, for example, has enacted a series of regulations that is intended to supplement those of the federal government. (For more information, visit www.dec.state.ny.us/website/dshm/regs/370parts.htm.)

OTHER ENVIRONMENTAL CONSIDERATIONS   *ISO 14000* is a group of environmental management standards developed by the International Organization for Standardization in 1996. It is designed to provide an internationally accepted framework for environmental management, measurement, evaluation, and auditing, to provide organizations with the tools needed to assess and control the environmental impact of their activities. In addition to environmental management systems, the standards address environmental auditing, environmental labels and declarations, environmental performance evaluation, and life-cycle assessments.

In Europe, the *WEEE (waste electrical and electronic equipment)* regulation, which was designed to tackle the issue of surplus TV and computer equipment recycling, requires the original equipment manufacturer to take back all surpluses for disposal. With an effective date of August 2005, this regulation requires manufacturers and importers to recycle a large variety of equipment from customers ranging from mobile phones to tea kettles. Further, businesses are expected to provide for the recycling of existing electrical and electronic equipment that will become waste in the future.

The *Basel Convention*, an international agreement on the control of cross-boundary movements of hazardous wastes and their disposal, was adopted in 1989 by a United Nations–sponsored conference of 116 nations held in Basel, Switzerland. It restricts trade in hazardous waste, some nonhazardous wastes, solid wastes, and incinerator ash.

The *Kyoto Protocol* (unfccc.int/resource/docs/convkp/kpeng.html), also known as the *Kyoto Agreement*, is a United Nations–sponsored agreement to prevent global warming signed by 38 developed countries. At a summit held in 1997, those signing the treaty agreed to reduce their emission of *greenhouse gases* by the year 2012. Greenhouse gases are gases such as carbon dioxide (CO_2), water vapor, methane (CH_4), nitrous oxide (NO_2), and other trace gases that trap heat in the atmosphere and produce a greenhouse effect that causes an increase in global temperatures. However, by 2002, several countries, including the United States and Japan, had all but reneged on their promises. The use of public areas for landfill has also come under tighter regulation all around the globe by local governments, and many countries have enacted regulations supplementing those issued by their respective governments. By focusing on landfills, environmental movements have addressed two major issues: First, there is an urgent need to develop more sustainable resources through recycling, and one way to drive recycling is through limitations on the amount of solid waste allowed in landfills. Second, the gases emitted by landfills are considered a source of global warming.

Disposal Methods

Depending on their nature and the legal and environmental considerations governing them, surplus materials and equipment can be disposed of in a variety of ways. To be truly effective, however, the process requires proper planning, organization, and assessment. Not surprisingly, the market demand for surplus materials and equipment follows a similar pattern as its newly manufactured counterparts. It would be wise for you to understand the nature of the marketplace so that you can make informed decisions on the value and salability of your organization's surplus.

The methods for asset disposal are fairly common and are listed below. The challenge lies in matching the material with its optimum method of disposal, which will, of course, depend on the nature of the materials and the needs of your organization. Following are some of the disposal methods you may utilize as a procurement professional:

- **Return.** One of the easiest alternatives is to return excess material or equipment to its original manufacturer. Often this also provides the best value since the supplier can offer a credit on future sales that can be timed to the actual revenue generated by your organization. Keep in mind, however, that if you are a small buyer of these items, you will not likely have a great deal of leverage to compel the supplier to accept the return.
- **Reuse.** Another excellent method of disposal is to transfer the materials or equipment internally to another department that can use it. This not only avoids the expense of disposal, it may also save money by avoiding the direct purchase of similar materials.
- **Sale.** Sale of excess assets provides an excellent way to generate cash. However, keep in mind that your sale of this material will likely compete with the sale of new products and may be discouraged by your supplier. Also keep in mind that it might be costly to find potential buyers and to make the sale.

  One alternative is to consign the material to a third-party reseller who already has channels for moving this. You will likely have to pay a large percentage of the revenue, but using a third party might provide the path of least resistance for you.

  You may also want to explore surplus auctions. These are conducted both live and online. Be cautious, however, of the effort involved not only in selling but in collecting the funds.

- **Trade-in.** Trading in old equipment for credit toward the purchase of similar new equipment may also prove effective, if the need to purchase new equipment actually exists. Even when the value of the surplus is low, this may be an easy way for the supplier to offer you a discount and may save you the trouble of actually having to go through the physical disposal process yourself.
- **Donation.** Depending on the material or equipment, donating it to a charitable operation may provide excellent community relations and may also offer a tax deduction (if your organization is otherwise profitable). Donating surplus materials and usable equipment fulfills a social responsibility, as well.

Tips and Techniques

Don't count on your ability to give the surplus away to charity. Many charities are inundated with such donations and have little ability to use or accept them.

- **Cannibalization.** If you have no use for the entire surplus product (or equipment), you might want to consider tearing it down for usable spare parts. While this is not a preferred use for excess assets, it may prove more profitable than having to put it in a landfill or sell it for scrap.
- **Scrap.** Again, depending upon the exact nature of the surplus, scrap dealers may have a use for it and may be willing to purchase it and pick it up if the price is right. You can expect, at best, to realize a few pennies on the initial dollar your organization has spent for its initial purchase. However, as previously noted, regulations such as WEEE may soon spawn new recycling industries that of necessity find increasing value in scrap materials.

Summary

Managing and controlling inventory, often one of the major assets of the organization, is another key area where the Procurement Department can add value. To accomplish this effectively requires an understanding of the various reasons for keeping inventory, such as safety stock and economic ordering methods, as well as being familiar with the specific classifications of inventory such as direct and indirect materials, work-in-process, and finished goods. The procurement professional must also be able to implement and utilize various common systems for managing inventory levels and reordering stock. These systems are often automated and include MRP and MRPII, along with various demand-based strategies such as JIT and SMI.

In this chapter, you also looked at various methods for managing and controlling inventory, including stores, storage and retrieval systems, and records systems. In this role, the procurement professional will also need to know how to maintain accurate inventory counts and reconcile discrepancies that may occur.

As a central focus for managing the disposal of surplus and obsolete assets, the procurement team is frequently responsible for determining the most valuable method of disposal for the organization.

CHAPTER 19

Logistics

The term *logistics* derives from an ancient French military term for soldiers' barracks or quarters, *loger*. Interestingly, the early supply arm of the military was known as Quartermasters, a group markedly inefficient during Napoleon Bonaparte's historic march to Moscow, during which the lack of an effective supply management process resulted in the loss of an entire army. Barely 5,000 of the original force of over 500,000 returned home; starvation and cold resulting from the inability to properly supply the army accounted for the majority of the losses.

In the business world, logistics can be equally important and can have the same fatal effects if managed poorly, although the victim is typically the corporate entity rather than its individuals. Today's concept of supply chain management recognizes this importance and seeks to develop effective, efficient processes that focus on controlling the flow of materials from origin to end user. This process is critical to the effectiveness of globalization.

The Logistics Process

In this section, we turn our attention to the multiple aspects of *logistics* to examine how the discipline affects the commercial organization.

Definitions of Logistics

In today's complex commercial environment, with its ever-expanding global reach and a focus on process integration between business enterprises, it is hardly surprising that definitions associated with the term *logistics* have likewise evolved. The views of what constitutes the boundaries of the study and practice of logistics are varied. One definition describes logistics as:

> ... *The process of strategically managing the procurement, movement and storage of materials, parts and finished inventory (and the related information flows) through the organization and its marketing channels in such a way that current and future profitability are maximized through the cost-effective fulfillment of orders.*[1]

The Council of Supply Chain Management Professionals (CSCMP, previously known as the Council of Logistics Management [CLM]), offers a more expanded view that logistics is intimately intertwined with supply chain management processes:

Logistics Management is that part of Supply Chain Management that plans, implements, and controls the efficient, effective forward and reverse flow and storage of goods, services and related information between the point of origin and the point of consumption in order to meet customers' requirements.[2]

From a supply management perspective, it is most important to consider the *management* of logistics as a body of knowledge and practice:

Logistics Management activities typically include inbound and outbound transportation management, fleet management, warehousing, materials handling, order fulfillment, logistics network design, inventory management, supply/demand planning, and management of third party logistics services providers. To varying degrees, the logistics function also includes sourcing and procurement, production planning and scheduling, packaging and assembly, and customer service. It is involved in all levels of planning and execution—strategic, operational and tactical. Logistics Management is an integrating function, which coordinates and optimizes all logistics activities, as well as integrates logistics activities with other functions including marketing, sales, manufacturing, finance and information technology.[3]

The scope of *logistics management* requires that we should view logistics as an integrative, process-oriented set of activities. This requires the orchestration of materials, human resources, and information not only within a business enterprise, but also between the numerous enterprises that constitute a supply chain/supply network.

The Military Dimension of Logistics

In military logistics, experts manage how and when to move resources to the places they are needed. In military science, maintaining one's supply lines while disrupting those of the enemy is a crucial element of military strategy, since an armed force without food, fuel, and ammunition is defenseless.

Logistics has been around for as long as there have been armies and navies with which cities, territories, and nation states have attempted to exert their will via military force on others. The earliest known standing army was that of the Assyrians at around 700 B.C. The need to feed and equip a substantial force along with the means of transportation (i.e., horses, camels, mules, and oxen) would mean that it could not linger in one place for very long.

The United States Department of Defense places a strategic emphasis on the study and application of logistics. The U.S. Air Force Institute of Technology identifies the acquisition of materials and the management of information associated with the deployment and sustainability of its weapons systems as *Acquisition Logistics*. This view encompasses everything involved in acquiring logistics support equipment and personnel for a new weapons system. The formal definition is "the process of systematically identifying, defining, designing, developing, producing, acquiring, delivering, installing, and upgrading *logistics* support capability requirements through the acquisition process for Air Force systems, subsystems, and equipment."[4]

The U.S. Department of Defense also emphasizes the ongoing support of its weapons systems in the field, long after manufacture and delivery. Critically, this view of military logistics stresses the critical nature of spare parts provisioning. *Integrated logistics support (ILS)* encompasses the unified management of the technical logistics elements that plan and develop the support requirements for a weapons system. This can include hardware, software, and the provisioning of training and maintenance resources.[5]

The Commercial Dimension of Logistics

From organizations such as Toyota came the then-revolutionary philosophies of just-in-time (JIT) and Total Quality Management (TQM). From these philosophies have arisen and developed the competitive strategies that world-class organizations now practice. Aspects of these that are now considered normal approaches to management include Kaizen (or continuous improvement), improved customer-supplier relationships, supplier management, vendor-managed inventory, customer focus on both the specifier and user, and, above all, recognition that there is a supply chain along which all efforts can be optimized to enable effective delivery of the required goods and services. This means a move away from emphasizing functional performance and a consideration of the whole chain of supply as a total process. It means a move away from the "silo" mentality to thinking and managing "outside the (functional) box." In both commercial and academic senses the recognition of supply chain management as an enabler of competitive advantage is increasingly to the fore. This has resulted in key elements being seen as best practices in their own right and includes value for money, partnering, strategic procurement policies, integrated supply chain/network management, total cost of ownership, business process reengineering, and outsourcing.

However, the history of logistics in the United States commercial sector is best characterized as a view of logistics as a loose collection of functional specialties, with little integrative ability. While this may be said of many business enterprise functions, the problem of "functional silos" has been particularly acute in the field of logistics. In many ways, the evolution of modern logistics has paralleled the development of emergence of process integration both within business enterprises, and more recently, throughout the supply chain. This trend is demonstrated in Figure 19.1.

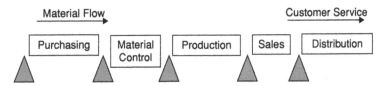

FIGURE 19.1   Stage One: Functional Silos

Source: Adapted from Martin Christopher, *Logistics and Supply Chain Management: Creating Value-Adding Networks*, p. 19.

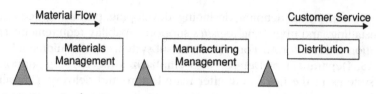

FIGURE 19.2   Stage Two: Internal Functional Integration

In traditional organizations, work within a firm was performed by specialists who often worked in isolation from one another and, most frequently, competed with one another for scarce resources and funds. Additionally, functional isolation was complicated by fragmented information flows and transactions. Consequently, little attention was paid to the needs of the customer. Under the umbrella of logistics, organizational silos were further fragmented as evidenced by further organizational specialization, such as warehousing, material handling, transportation (often organized as inbound freight and receiving, and outbound freight and shipping), fleet operations, where applicable, and distribution operations.

After World War II, the concept of materials management introduced some degree of functional integration internal to the firm (Figure 19.2).

In this stage of development, many firms reduced the organizational conflict in consolidating many of the functions associated with the manufacturing process and the acquisition and planning of material requirements. Further, links with distribution requirements driven by customer demand were organizationally linked within the firm. This internal integration was mostly driven by acquired information capabilities with the development of *material requirements planning (MRP)* and *distribution requirements planning (DRP)* information systems in the late 1950s through early 1980s. The next stage in the integration of business logistics may be characterized by effectively linking internal functional information systems, as shown in Figure 19.3.

Once again, the potential of the integration of previously isolated functional silos and their activities was made possible by the introduction of more powerful information systems, such as manufacturing resource planning (MRP II) and distribution resource planning (DRPII). The introduction and development of these powerful planning systems continued throughout the 1980s and early 1990s.

The next evolutionary stage in the integration of logistics processes may be illustrated as shown in Figure 19.4.

During the period of the mid-1990s and today, powerful enterprise resource planning (ERP) information systems have enabled the integration between suppliers, the business enterprise, and its customers. The potential for vastly improved planning

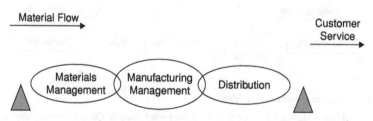

FIGURE 19.3   Stage Three: Internal Process Integration

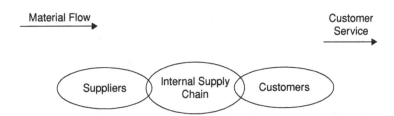

FIGURE 19.4   Stage Four: Process Integration between a Firm, Its Suppliers, and Customers

and scheduling of materials and finished goods to better serve the enterprise's customers is still emerging. This potential has demonstrated the effectiveness of a process view of not only a particular business, but has given rise to a realization that customer satisfaction may be best served through the application of the concept of supply chain management (SCM).

Logistics Management and Supply Chain Management

Modern logistics management has evolved into a potent strategic competitive weapon in global business. The contemporary view of SCM lends itself to a continued evolution of logistics as a core competency for any business enterprise. To understand this point, one must examine supply chain management as a concept that demands the utmost in the seamless integration of information regarding manufacturing and production capabilities, supplier performance, inventory, customer service, and demand management. Instead of viewing logistics management and its processes as a series of functional relationships, it is more appropriate to view the set of complex and seamless relationships between a firm's suppliers, the internal competencies of the firm, and the needs of its customers as a "network" that spans all functions of all constituents of a "chain."

The supply network model in fact suggests integration well beyond a supply chain management model. The collaborative efforts of multiple channel members assemble to meet the real needs of the end customer, so that the requirement for seamless value-added processes is very real. When we seek to further integrate the entirety of the processes in such an environment, we are combining the objectives of both *customer relationship management (CRM)* and *supplier relationship management (SRM)*. The result is a concept known as *value chain management*. Thus, VCM may be defined as:

> *... The integration and optimization of all resources, starting with the vendor's vendor. It integrates information, materials, labor, facilities, logistics, etc. into a time responsive, capacity managed solution that maximizes financial resources and minimizes waste, i.e., optimizes value for both the Supply Chain Network and the customer's customer.*[6]

Further, the characteristics of global value chains requires coordination between all network processes. Such networks are typically fast, virtual, highly flexible, oriented toward future customer demand, and uniquely positioned and configured along product lines. The implication is that such network relationships must address

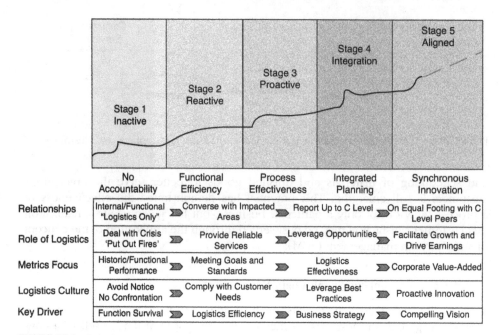

	No Accountability	Functional Efficiency	Process Effectiveness	Integrated Planning	Synchronous Innovation
Relationships	Internal/Functional "Logistics Only"	Converse with Impacted Areas	Report Up to C Level		On Equal Footing with C Level Peers
Role of Logistics	Deal with Crisis 'Put Out Fires'	Provide Reliable Services	Leverage Opportunities		Facilitate Growth and Drive Earnings
Metrics Focus	Historic/Functional Performance	Meeting Goals and Standards	Logistics Effectiveness		Corporate Value-Added
Logistics Culture	Avoid Notice No Confrontation	Comply with Customer Needs	Leverage Best Practices		Proactive Innovation
Key Driver	Function Survival	Logistics Efficiency	Business Strategy		Compelling Vision

FIGURE 19.5   Five-Stage Model of Supply Chain Awareness

Source: Karl B. Manrodt, Brian Gibson, and Stephen Rutner. "Communicating the Value of Supply Chain Management to Your CEO." Oak Brook, IL: The Council of Supply Chain Management Professionals, 2005, p. 12.

highly complex and changing customer demand and supply patterns. The idea of a "one-size-fits-all" supply chain management business strategy is not realistic.

Modern logistics management will most likely evolve toward a greater use of highly focused and flexible cross-functional and cross-enterprise teams to accomplish its objectives. As a result of this trend, logistics management will receive top management attention and occupy a strategic focus in the business enterprise. This is an important challenge for logistics management, as not all business enterprises have developed an integrated view of the study and application of logistics. This is illustrated in a recent study aimed at increasing the awareness of top business executives of the strategic potential of logistics management (Figure 19.5).

While there has been considerable development in the integration of logistics processes *within* many firms, the CSCMP study indicates that the biggest challenge that lies ahead for the majority of business enterprises is the attainment of effective process alignment *between* firms.

Modes of Transportation

When we think of methods to manage the flow of goods, we immediately think of transportation and how we can best move the equipment and materials we need for operations into our facilities, and how we can move the products we make to the consumer. In most cases, the decisions we make are likely based on trade-offs between cost and time; air freight, for example, is faster than ocean vessels but proportionally more expensive.

The role of transportation under logistics management has changed significantly over the past three decades. The deregulation of the United States' transportation industry in 1980 proved an important departure from a previous time wherein transportation was viewed as mostly a commodity to be purchased from the lowest bidder. In the scenarios of supply and value chain management discussed earlier, it is imperative that the selection of the very best transportation service providers have an important impact on successful business strategy.

A Logistics Perspective on Transportation

A consideration of transportation capabilities will focus on the movement of products, the storage of products, the costs of transportation, and the various players in a typical transportation cycle.

PRODUCT MOVEMENT   Goods may be moved by a number of means and methods, commonly referred to as transportation *modes*:

- **Air.** Aviation or air transport refers to the activities surrounding mechanical flight and the aircraft industry. Aircraft include fixed wing (airplane) and rotary wing (helicopter) types. Air transport capability is limited by load size, weight lift capacity of an aircraft, and aircraft availability. Dedicated airfreight services such as Federal Express, UPS, and DHL have managed to become profitable, despite the inherent limitations of airfreight capabilities. No particular commodity dominates the traffic of goods carried by airfreight.
- **Water transport.** Goods carried by ship fall into three distinct waterborne categories of transport: internal river, coastal and intercoastal freight, and international freight. Additionally, categories such as barge and powered versus nonpowered shipping vessels should be considered.
- **Pipeline, oil and gas.** Pipeline transportation is a significant element of the United States's transportation system. In addition to petroleum products, the other major product that is transported by pipeline is natural gas. Similar to petroleum, natural gas pipelines are owned and operated by private business enterprises. In comparison with other modes of transportation, pipelines are unique in that they operate on a 24-hours-per-day, 7-days-per-week basis. Unlike other modes, there is no empty container that must be returned. Pipelines have the highest fixed costs and lowest variable costs among transportation modes. High fixed costs result from the right of way for pipelines, construction, and other requirements for safety and control.
- **Rail.** Rail transport refers to the land transport of passengers and goods along railways or railroads. Rail transport makes highly efficient use of space: A double-track rail line can carry more passengers or freight in a given amount of time than a four-lane road. As a result, rail transport is the major form of public transport in many countries. Many millions use trains as regular transport in India, South Korea, Japan, China, and in European countries. However, outside of New York City, rail transport as a form of public transit in the United States is rare. Very few major U.S. cities other than New York, Chicago, Boston, and

Philadelphia can lay claim to any significant use of local rail-based passenger transport; meanwhile, Amtrak is the only nationwide passenger rail system in the country. Commercially, world rail transport has had a mixed record. Most rail systems, including urban rapid transit (metro/subway) systems, are highly subsidized and have never or rarely been profitable; however, their indirect benefits are often great. With the advent of containerized freight in the 1960s, rail and ship transportation have become an integrated network that moves bulk goods very efficiently with a very low labor cost. An example is that goods from east Asia that are bound for Europe will often be shipped across the Pacific and transferred to trains to cross North America and be transferred back to a ship for the Atlantic crossing.

- **Road** (motor or "highway"). Highway transportation in the United States has greatly expanded since the end of World War II. A road is an identifiable route or path between two or more places. Roads are typically smoothed, paved, or otherwise prepared to allow easy travel, though they need not be, and historically many roads were simply recognizable routes without any formal construction or maintenance. In urban areas, roads may pass along and be named as streets, serving a dual function as urban space and route.

- **Intermodal transportation.** Intermodal transportation combines two or more transportation modes to take advantages of economies of scale, with an objective of providing service at the lowest total cost. For example, *piggyback service* combines the flexibility of motor freight for short distances with the low line-haul cost associated with rail transport for longer distances. The most common example of *piggyback* transport is the trailer-on-a flatcar (TOFC) or container-on-a-flatcar (COFC). Another example of intermodal transportation is that of the *containership*. The *fishyback*, *trainship*, or *containership* concept loads a truck trailer, railcar, or container onto a barge or ship for the line-haul move.

TRANSPORTATION PARTICIPANTS   One way in which to better understand the scope of logistics is to examine the participants in a typical transportation transaction.

Most transportation decisions involve at least six parties: a shipper, a destination party (usually called a consignee), carriers and agents, governments, the Internet, and the public.

- **Shipper and consignee.** The shipper and consignee have a common interest in moving goods from origin to destination within a period of time at the least possible cost. Related services would include scheduled pick up and delivery times, estimated or actual delivery transit time, and a guarantee of accuracy in information between the parties.

- **Carrier agents.** The carrier represents a business that performs a transportation service. They desire to maximize their revenue while moving goods, while at the same time reducing labor, fuel, and vehicle costs. To further reduce costs, most shippers seek to consolidate shipments and coordinate pickup and delivery times in order to achieve economies of scale.

- **Governments.** Governments have a vested interest in transportation because of its effects on the economy and general social well-being of its citizens. Because of the direct impact of transportation on the economy, governments have been traditionally involved in the practices of carriers. In the United States, a more recent emphasis on carrier safety and security in addition to traditional financial review is evident in the formation of the Department of Homeland Security in 2001.

- **Internet.** A wide assortment of Internet-based transportation information services have developed in the last decade. These transportation information capabilities are most typically referred to as aspects of *e-commerce*. Two distinct e-commerce marketplaces have emerged that greatly simplify transportation information flow. One area of transportation e-commerce involves matching carrier carrying capacity to available shipments. Yet another form of transportation e-commerce provides information on the purchase of fuels, equipment, spare parts, and related operating supplies. Also, real-time traceability of goods is now possible as the result the adoption of bar code and radio frequency identification technologies.
- **The public.** The public is concerned with transportation accessibility, expense, and effectiveness as well as environmental and safety standards.

Traffic Management

In its simplest form, traffic management governs the scheduling of shipments and receipts, managing the overall transport of goods and material. Many changes have taken place in this area since 9/11, and the impact of increased worldwide security has been profound.

The Trend toward the Outsourcing of Logistics Services

The question of outsourcing all or a part of the logistics management function for any firm should be the result of an extensive, strategically driven decision by a business enterprise's top management. In all likelihood, such an important decision should also take into consideration valued inputs from a firm's key customers and suppliers as well.

A third-party logistics provider (abbreviated 3PL) is a firm that provides outsourced or "third-party" logistics services to companies for part or sometimes all of their supply chain management function. Third-party logistics providers typically specialize in integrated warehousing and transportation services that can be scaled and customized to the customer's needs based on market conditions and the demands and delivery service requirements for their products and materials. A 3PL provides integrated logistics services (i.e., the complete set of logistics activities from the buyer to the seller).

"A 4PL is an integrator that assembles the resources, capabilities, and technology of its own organization and other organizations to design, build and run comprehensive supply chain solutions." Every organization has their own interpretation of the term *4PL* and ideas on what exactly a 4PL should offer. To add more complexity to the interpretation, the following groups of service providers actually provide "4PL type" services:

- Consultants
- IT service providers
- "E" marketplaces

- Financial institutions
- Private organizations
- Logistics service providers (3PL activities)

A true 4PL organization would then build a set of activities focused around a specific set of supply chain initiatives and goals. While 4PL architecture is still in the conceptual stage as a logistics planning and intermediary surrogate for the client organization, it is designated to provide logistics visibility, transportation control, performance metrics and status reporting. Additionally, as a planning and control group, it manages specific logistics issues, often linked to functional support and business development.

Customs

For various reasons—generally revenue generation and market regulation—nations have established tariffs for products and materials entering (and departing) their countries. These tariffs are typically regulated by the respective national customs agency. There is no universal system that applies to all countries and all situations, despite the fact that many countries today adhere to some community of regulation, such as the European Common Market (EC) or the North American Free Trade Agreement (NAFTA), explained in their respective sections, below.

Scope of U.S. Customs Reorganization

Established in 1927, the U.S. Customs Service and its organizations were formed to regulate immigration into the United States, as well as regulate the traffic of goods both into and out of the country. In the United States since the terrorist attacks of September 11, 2001, there has been a considerable reorganization and integration of customs functions at the federal government level. The various functions are now under the organizational control of the U.S. *Department of Homeland Security*.

The United States Customs Service (now part of the U.S. *Customs and Border Protection, CBP*) was the portion of the U.S. federal government dedicated to keeping illegal products outside of U.S. borders. It also regulated what could leave the United States and was partially responsible for who could enter the United States.

Operations were divided into two separate sections, the first of which was the Office of Field Operations (OFO), which handled duties and tax penalties along with helping to prevent contraband from entering the United States. It was primarily made up of inspectors that served as the "front-line" of customs by monitoring and policing all international ports of entry into the United States (land, sea, or air); by screening incoming and outgoing international shipments of cargo; and by inspecting informal entries of dutiable goods by individuals through personal transport or shipment through international postal carriers (government and private). Inspectors also handled operations regarding smuggling of contraband into the United States and the exportation of controlled or strategic resources from the United States. Other OFO personnel included import specialists, intelligence officers, and other contracted personnel responsible for record keeping and handling protest and tax penalty arbitration, along with other record support functions.

Import specialists provided the backbone of OFO by providing expertise concerning proper classification of goods for the purpose of charging duties. The primary resource for determining duty classifications is the two-volume Harmonized Tariff Schedule for the United States (HTSUS), which is updated annually. Import specialists were divided into commodity teams (CTs), which are assigned specific types of goods to specialize in. For example, one team may be assigned vehicles, vehicle components, and ball bearings, and another may be assigned clothing, textiles, and toys. Each CT is assigned a more senior import specialist, whose job it is to train import specialists who are new to a particular commodity team. These individuals are usually *de facto* experts in the analysis of goods to which they are assigned and are often called upon to physically inspect goods entering (or petitioning to enter) the United States. They are primarily engaged in activities concerning formal entries, which are handled by customs brokerage houses, but they also provide assistance in informal entries.

The other half of the U.S. Customs and Border Protection Service was the Office of Investigation (OI). The OI consisted of specialized sections of special agents that are divided by common crimes regarding international affairs. Primary sections included financial crimes, narcotics, strategic, and computer forensics. The OI also included an internal affairs section that monitored and investigated allegations of misconduct and criminal activity within both the OI and the OFO. As part of the reorganization associated with the creation of the Department of Homeland Security, the OI was transferred to U.S. Immigration and Customs Enforcement on March 1, 2003.

Global Customs Issues and Logistics

It is sufficient to repeat that each nation engaged in today's global commerce maintains its own set of customs laws, regulations, and organizational infrastructures. This fact makes it a challenge to effectively engage in the seamless, efficient, and effective transfer of goods among the world's many trading nations. For example, moving goods across a border often requires the payment of excise tax, often collected by customs officials. Animals (and occasionally humans) moving across borders may need to go into quarantine to prevent the spread of exotic or infectious diseases. Most countries prohibit carrying illegal drugs or endangered animals across their borders. Moving goods, animals, or people illegally across a border, without declaring them, counts as smuggling. The rationalization of trading agreements between international and regional trading partners, as well as an unprecedented trend toward the disaggregation and outsourcing of the various aspects of the means of production and distribution has resulted in an overall simplification or "harmonization" of customs regulations and procedures.

Within the environment of global trade, however, it should be noted that each nation is unique in how it executes its own customs requirements—and it is recommended that for any international trade and customs transaction, the specific customs authorities in each nation must be consulted. Frequently, such specialized and comprehensive knowledge is provided by third-party service providers (customs agents, freight forwarders, or brokerage firms). The trend toward harmonization—alignment—of international customs procedures and regulations is generally encouraged by:

- The similarity of consumer demand for like goods throughout the world (examples: cell phones, television sets, and consumer electronics in general).

- The increasing scarcity of raw materials and the continuing search for new sources of supply.
- The need to serve growing consumer demand in new markets with great sales potential to a rising middle class (examples: the People's Republic of China and India).
- The availability and access to standardized high-speed data transmission and associated technologies (examples: bar-coding and radio frequency identity tags).
- Cost advantages in both labor and materials offered by global strategic sourcing.

The World Customs Organization

For more than 50 years, the World Customs Organization (WCO) has provided leadership in expanding the avenues of international trade. The WCO's accomplishments are both numerous and varied. The organization's success has been driven by a clear-minded adherence to a simple principle: The more simple and harmonized the world's customs procedures, the more prosperity for international trade and the world at large. By following this principle, the WCO has scored many triumphs across the entire spectrum of customs-based issues. For example, the WCO created and administers several international agreements that facilitate world trade. The major international conventions created or administered by the WCO include:

- The *Harmonized System Convention* (the basis for the U.S. import and export schedules).
- The General Agreement on Tariffs and Trade (GATT) Customs Valuation Agreement.
- The Nairobi and Johannesburg Conventions, both dealing with the sharing of information.
- The 1973 Kyoto Convention on customs procedures.
- The 1999 revised Kyoto Convention, formally known as the International Convention on the Harmonization and Simplification of Customs Procedures.

In June 2002, the WCO Council unanimously adopted a resolution on the security and facilitation of the international trade supply chain proposed by the United States that has resulted in the development of numerous guidelines, benchmarks, and best practices. Together with the WCO, U.S. Customs and Border Protection (CBP) has been actively drafting and writing best practices, guidelines, and standards relating to the security of international supply chains. While much has been accomplished, the work continues both at CBP and the WCO.

As in a domestic logistics environment, important decision elements will be encountered in an international setting. Some of these are:

- Port selection.
- Desirability of free trade zones.
- Customs regulations and procedures unique to individual nation states and trading blocs.
- Total cost decisions.
- Financial and currency exchange considerations.

Logistics in the Context of International Trade

An emerging view of logistics and supply chain management as an appropriate strategic business perspective in the development and maintenance of global commerce and trade is noteworthy. SCM, with a high dependence upon the flawless execution of logistics strategies, is a vehicle that promises to lift the traditional views of logistics from a set of descriptive analyses focused on activities *within* a firm, to one that underscores the importance of high levels of organizational integration and interdependence. Further,

> *Global sourcing may be important to a firm's competitive position as a means to access raw materials, improve quality, lower cost, or access technology. . . . Pursuing a global procurement strategy successfully requires that a firm possess a supply chain orientation and the skills to deal with the complexities and uncertainties of the global environment.*[7]

The Influence of Globalization on Logistics

An ideal "globalized" business environment could be described as one in which neither distance nor national borders impede economic transactions. This would be a world where the costs of transportation and communications approached zero, and the barriers created by differing national jurisdictions (nation states or regional economic organizations) had vanished.

According to Sir Anthony Giddens of the London School of Economics and Political Science, the debate over both the meaning and consequences of globalization may be viewed from two perspectives:

1. The radical perspective:

   > *. . . not only is globalization very real, but . . . its consequences can be felt everywhere. The global marketplace, they say, is much more developed than even two or three decades ago, and is indifferent to national borders. Nations have lost most of the sovereignty they once had, and politicians have lost most of their capability to influence events. It isn't surprising that no one respects political leaders any more, or has much interest in what they have to say. The era of the nation state is over.*

2. The skeptical perspective:

   > *The notion of globalization, according to the skeptics, is an ideology put about by free-marketeers who wish to dismantle welfare systems and cut back on state expenditures. What has happened is at most a reversion to how the world was a century ago. In the late 19th Century there was already an open global economy, with a great deal of trade, including trade in currencies.*[8]

Degrees of Global and Regional Economic Integration

In surveying the global business environment, there are considerations beyond the context of the values and beliefs of the individual and the characteristics of the single business enterprise. Such considerations should focus on the array of economic interactions, and ultimately, the forms of economic interaction that take place at the regional and interregional level. Such an analysis must take into account the effects of globalization and the trend toward global economic integration. There are several degrees of economic integration, which range from loose trading affiliations to virtual full economic and political union. It is within this landscape that modern logistics management must operate. The following narrative is intended to provide a general familiarity with global trading issues the logistics professional will most likely encounter.

Regional Trading Alliances and Governing Bodies

There are numerous international trade agreements between global trading partners and numerous contracts between business enterprises. However, it is important to note the existence of the world's major trading blocs.

THE EUROPEAN UNION (EU)   The EU is an intergovernmental and supranational union of 27 democratic member states from the European continent. The EU was established under that name in 1992 by the Treaty on European Union (the Maastricht Treaty). However, many aspects of the EU existed before that date through a series of predecessor relationships, dating back to 1951. The EU nowadays has a common single market consisting of a customs union, a single currency managed by the European Central Bank (so far adopted by 17 of the 27 member states), a common agricultural policy, a common trade policy, and a common fisheries policy. A common foreign and security policy was also established as the second of the three pillars of the European Union. The Schengen Agreement abolished passport control, and customs checks were also abolished at many of the EU's internal borders, creating a single space of mobility in which EU citizens could live, travel, work, and invest. The most important EU institutions include the Council of the European Union, the European Commission, the European Court of Justice, the European Central Bank, and the European Parliament. The European Parliament's origins go back to the 1950s and the founding treaties, and since 1979 its members have been directly elected by the people they represent. Elections are held every five years, and every EU citizen who is registered as a voter is entitled to vote. The EU's activities cover all areas of public policy, from health and economic policy to foreign affairs and defense. However, the extent of its powers differs greatly between areas. Depending on the area in question, the EU may therefore resemble a federation (e.g., on monetary affairs, agriculture, trade and environmental policy, economic and social policy), a confederation (e.g., on home affairs), or an international organization (e.g., in foreign affairs). Many of the policies of the EU relate in one way or another to the development and maintenance of an effective single market. Significant efforts have been made to create harmonized standards, which are designed to bring economic benefits through creating larger, more efficient markets. The power of the single market reaches beyond the EU borders, because to sell within the EU, it is beneficial to conform to its standards. Once a nonmember country's factories, farmers, and merchants conform to EU standards, much of the cost of joining the Union has already been sunk. At that point, harmonizing domestic laws in order to become a full member is relatively painless and may create more wealth through eliminating the customs costs.

THE NORTH AMERICAN FREE TRADE AGREEMENT (NAFTA) The North American Free Trade Agreement, known usually as NAFTA, is a free trade agreement among Canada, the United States, and Mexico. NAFTA went into effect on January 1, 1994. NAFTA is also used to refer to the tripartite trading bloc of North American countries. NAFTA called for immediately eliminating duties on half of all U.S. goods shipped to Mexico and gradually phasing out other tariffs over a period of about 14 years. Restrictions were to be removed from many categories, including motor vehicles and automotive parts, computers, textiles, and agriculture. The treaty also protected intellectual property rights (patents, copyrights, and trademarks) and outlined the removal of restrictions on investment among the three countries. Provisions regarding worker and environmental protection were added later as a result of supplemental agreements signed in 1993. This agreement was an expansion of the earlier Canada-U.S. Free Trade Agreement of 1989. Unlike the European Union, NAFTA does not create a set of supranational governmental bodies, nor does it create a body of law that is superior to national law. NAFTA is a treaty under international law. (Under United States law it is classed as a congressional-executive agreement rather than a treaty, reflecting a peculiar sense of the term "treaty" in United States constitutional law that is not followed by international law or the laws of other states.)

ASSOCIATION OF SOUTHEAST ASIAN NATIONS (ASEAN) The Association of Southeast Asian Nations (ASEAN) is a political, economic, and cultural organization of countries located in Southeast Asia. ASEAN was formed on August 8, 1967, by Thailand, Indonesia, Malaysia, Singapore, and the Philippines, as a nonprovocative display of solidarity against communist expansion in Vietnam and insurgency within their own borders. Following the Bali Summit of 1976, the organization embarked on a program of economic cooperation, which floundered in the mid-1980s only to be revived around a 1991 Thai proposal for a regional "free trade area." The countries meet annually. The British protectorate of Brunei joined the ASEAN six days after the country became independent from the United Kingdom on January 7, 1984. The mainland states of Vietnam, Laos, and Myanmar were later admitted. Vietnam joined the ASEAN on July 28, 1995. Laos and Myanmar were admitted into the ASEAN on July 23, 1997. Cambodia became the newest member when it was admitted on April 30, 1999. The Melanesian state of Papua New Guinea has observer status in the ASEAN. Meanwhile, the former Indonesian province of Timor-Leste has applied for observer status in ASEAN. Timor-Leste is widely seen as a member state candidate. The association includes about 8 percent of the world's population, and in 2003 it had a combined gross domestic product (GDP) of about US$700 billion, growing at an average rate of around 4 percent per year. The economies of member countries of ASEAN are diverse, although its major products include electronics, oil, and wood. The ASEAN countries are culturally rich. It includes more Muslims than any other geopolitical entity. About 240 million Muslims live mostly in Indonesia, Malaysia, and Brunei. Buddhism constitutes the main religion of mainland Southeast Asia, and there are about 170 million Buddhists in Thailand, Myanmar, Laos, Cambodia, Vietnam, and Singapore. Catholicism is predominant in the Philippines. ASEAN has governments with widely differing views on governance and political process, including practices in areas such as suffrage and representation. It encompasses styles of government ranging from democracy to autocracy.

MERCOSUR   MERCOSUR was founded in 1988 as a free trade pact between Brazil and Argentina. The modest tariff reductions in its first years led to an 80 percent increase in trade between the two partners. Today, MERCOSUR consists of five member nations (Argentina, Paraguay, Bolivia and Venezuela) (pending, with five nations included as associate members: Columbia, Ecuador, Peru, Bolivia, and Chile). The members have committed to the formation of SAFTA (South American Free Trade Area). The ambitious goal is to encourage internal free trade for not less than 80 percent of the goods produced in the region. Some South Americans see MERCOSUR as giving the capability to combine resources to balance the activities of other global economic powers, perhaps especially the United States and the European Union. There are more than 250 million people in this region, and the combined GDP of the member nations is more than $1.1 trillion a year.

THE ANDEAN COMMUNITY   The Andean Community of Nations (in Spanish: *Comunidad Andina de Naciones*, abbreviated CAN) is a trade bloc comprising the South American countries of Bolivia, Colombia, Ecuador, and Peru). The trade bloc was called the Andean Pact until 1996 and came into existence with the signing of the Cartagena Agreement in 1969. Its headquarters are located in Lima, Peru. The Andean Community has 120 million inhabitants living in an area of 4,700,000 square kilometers, whose GDP amounted to US$260 billion in 2002.

ASIA-PACIFIC ECONOMIC COOPERATION (APEC)   The Asia-Pacific Economic Cooperation (APEC) is a group of Pacific Rim countries that meet with the purpose of improving economic and political ties. It has standing committees on a wide range of issues, from communications to fisheries. The heads of government of all APEC members meet annually in a summit called "APEC Economic Leaders' Meeting," rotating in location among APEC's member economies.

THE WORLD TRADE ORGANIZATION (WTO)   The World Trade Organization (WTO) is an international, multilateral organization founded in 1995, which sets the rules for the global trading system and resolves disputes between its member states, all of whom are signatories to its approximately 30 agreements. WTO headquarters are located in Geneva, Switzerland. As of February 2011 there were 153 members in the organization with the latest member (Cape Verde) joining in 2008. All WTO members are required to grant one another most favored nation status, such that (with some exceptions) trade concessions granted by a WTO member to another country must be granted to all WTO members.

GATT AND THE GOODS COUNCIL   *GATT* (General Agreement on Tariffs and Trade) covers international trade in goods (www.wto.org/english/tratop_e/gatt_e/gatt_e.htm). The workings of the GATT agreement are the responsibility of the Council for Trade in Goods (Goods Council), which is made up of representatives from all WTO member countries.

The Goods Council has 10 committees dealing with specific subjects (such as agriculture, market access, subsidies, antidumping measures, etc.). Again, these committees consist of all member countries.

Also reporting to the Goods Council are a working party on state trading enterprises and the Information Technology Agreement (ITA) Committee.

Foreign Currency and Exchange

The management of currency during the exchange of products and materials between countries is no insignificant task in global trade and is often best left to the finance function. However, it is frequently the role of procurement and logistics sections to negotiate the details of how and when rates are calculated.

THE FOREIGN EXCHANGE MARKET (FOREX)   The foreign exchange (currency or forex) market exists wherever one currency is traded for another. It is by far the largest market in the world in terms of cash value traded, and it includes trading between large banks, central banks, currency speculators, multinational corporations, governments, and other financial markets and institutions. Retail traders (small speculators) are a small part of this market. There is no single unified foreign exchange market. Due to the over-the-counter (OTC) nature of currency markets, there are a number of interconnected marketplaces where different currency instruments are traded. This implies that there is no such thing as a single dollar rate, but rather a number of different rates (prices), depending on what bank or market maker is trading. In practice, the rates are often very close; otherwise, they could be exploited by arbitrageurs. The main trading centers are in London, New York, and Tokyo, but banks throughout the world participate. As the Asian trading session ends, the European session begins, then the U.S. session, and then the Asian begins again. Traders can react to news when it breaks, rather than waiting for the market to open.

BANKS   The interbank market caters for both the majority of commercial turnover and large amounts of speculative trading every day. A large bank may trade billions of dollars daily. Some of this trading is undertaken on behalf of customers, but much is conducted by proprietary desks trading for the bank's own account. Until recently, foreign exchange brokers did large amounts of business, facilitating interbank trading and matching anonymous counterparts for small fees. Today, however, much of this business is moving on to more efficient electronic systems such as Bloomberg EBS, TradeBook, Reuters 3000 Matching, and EBS. The broker squawk box that lets traders listen in on ongoing interbank trading is heard in most trading rooms, but turnover is noticeably smaller than just a few years ago.

CENTRAL BANKS   National central banks play an important role in the foreign exchange markets. They try to control the money supply, inflation, and/or interest rates and often have official or unofficial target rates for their currencies. They can use their often substantial foreign exchange reserves to stabilize the market. Milton Friedman argued that the best stabilization strategy would be for central banks to buy when the exchange rate is too low and sell when the rate is too high—that is, to trade for a profit. Nevertheless, central banks do not go bankrupt if they make large losses, as other traders would, and there is no convincing evidence that they do make a profit trading. The mere expectation or rumor of central bank intervention might be enough to stabilize a currency, but aggressive intervention might be used several times each year in countries with a dirty float currency regime. Central banks do not always achieve their objectives, however. The combined resources of the market can easily overwhelm any central bank. Several scenarios of this nature were seen in the 1992–1993 ERM collapse and in more recent times in Southeast Asia.

COMMERCIAL COMPANIES An important part of this market comes from the financial activities of companies seeking foreign exchange to pay for goods or services. Commercial companies often trade fairly small amounts compared to those of banks or speculators, and their trades often have little short-term impact on market rates. Nevertheless, trade flows are an important factor in the long-term direction of a currency's exchange rate. Some multinational companies can have an unpredictable impact when very large positions are covered due to exposures that are not widely known by other market participants.

INVESTMENT MANAGEMENT FIRMS Investment management firms (which typically manage large accounts on behalf of customers such as pension funds, endowments, etc.) utilize the foreign exchange market to facilitate transactions in foreign securities. For example, an investment manager with an international equity portfolio will need to buy and sell foreign currencies in the "spot" market in order to pay for and redeem purchases and sales of foreign equities. Since these transactions are secondary to the actual investment decision, they are not seen as speculative or aimed at profit maximization. Some investment management firms also possess specialist currency overlay units, which have the specific objective of managing clients' currency exposures with the aim of generating profits while limiting risk. While the number of dedicated currency managers is quite small, the size of their assets under management (AUM) can be quite significant, which can lead to large trades.

RETAIL FOREX BROKERS Retail forex brokers handle a minute fraction of the total volume of the foreign exchange market. Standard retail services include 24-hour online currency trading and 100-to-1 leverage. Most retail brokers do not provide direct access to the interbank market, acting as dealers (buying or selling against the customer's order for their own account) rather than as true brokers (arranging a trade for the customer with a third party). The brokers earn money by offering a bid/offer spread that is wider than the interbank spread. Retail traders should be aware of the possibility of retail forex brokers manipulating quoted spot rates, improperly triggering their clients' stop-loss orders, or charging hidden fees.

In the United States, "it is unlawful to offer foreign currency futures and option contracts to retail customers unless the offeror is a regulated financial entity," according to the Commodity Futures Trading Commission. Legitimate retail brokers serving traders in the United States are most often registered with the CFTC as "futures commission merchants" (FCMs) and are members of the National Futures Association (NFA). Potential clients can check the broker's FCM status at the NFA. Retail forex brokers are much less regulated than stockbrokers, and there is no protection similar to that from the Securities Investor Protection Corporation.

Supplemental Information

Because logistics is such a broad-ranging and key function in procurement and supply management, it is impossible to cover all of the related topics *in their appropriate contexts* in a single chapter. In the following section, we provide some additional information out of context for the sake of brevity, which we hope will be useful.

The Reach of Intelligent Freight Technologies

Intelligent freight technologies monitor and manage physical assets and information flows. Five clusters of technologies can be applied individually or in tailored combinations:

- **Asset tracking** uses mobile communications, *radio frequency identification (RFID)*, and other tools to monitor the location and status of tractors, trailers, chassis, containers, and, in some cases, cargo.
- **On-board status monitoring** uses sensors to monitor vehicle operating parameters, cargo condition, and attempts to tamper with the load.
- **Gateway facilitation** uses RFID, smart cards, weigh-in-motion, and nonintrusive inspection technologies to simplify and speed operations at terminal gates, highway inspection stations, and border crossings.
- **Freight status information** uses Web-based technologies and standards to facilitate the exchange of information related to freight flows.
- **Network status information** uses services to integrate data from cameras and road sensors and uses display technologies to monitor congestion, weather conditions, and incidents.

See www.ops.fhwa.dot.gov/freight/intermodal/freight_tech_story/exec_summ _intro.htm.

Logistics Automation

Logistics automation is the application of computer software and/or automated machinery to improve the efficiency of logistics operations. Typically, this refers to operations within a warehouse or distribution center, with broader tasks undertaken by supply chain management systems and enterprise resource planning systems.

Logistics automation systems can powerfully complement the facilities provided by these higher level computer systems. The focus on an individual node within a wider logistics network allows systems to be highly tailored to the requirements of that node.

COMPONENTS   Logistics automation systems comprise a variety of hardware and software components.

Fixed Machinery

- Automated cranes (also called automated storage and retrieval systems) provide the ability to input and store a container of goods for later retrieval. Typically cranes serve a rack of locations, allowing many levels of stock to be stacked vertically, and allowing far high storage densities and better space utilization than alternatives.

- Automated conveyors allow the input of containers in one area of the warehouse, and either through hard coded rules or data input allows destination selection. The container will later appear at the selected destination.
- Sortation systems are similar to conveyors but typically have higher capacity and can divert containers more quickly. They are typically used to distribute high volumes of small cartons to a large set of locations.

    Typically, all of these will automatically identify and track containers based on bar codes, or increasingly, RFID tags.

Mobile Technology

- Radio data terminals are handheld or truck-mounted terminals that connect wirelessly to logistics automation software and provide instructions to operators moving throughout the warehouse.
- Many also have in-built bar code scanners to allow identification of containers.

Software

- Integration software provides overall control of the automation machinery and, for instance, allows cranes to be connected up to conveyors for seamless stock movements.
- Operational control software provides low-level decision making, such as where to store incoming containers and where to retrieve them when requested.
- Business control software provides higher level functionality, such as identification of incoming deliveries, stock and scheduling order fulfillment, and assignment of stock to outgoing trailers.

Tariffs

Customs duties on merchandise imports are called *tariffs*. Tariffs give a price advantage to locally produced goods over similar goods that are imported, and they raise revenues for governments. For more information, visit www.wto.org/english /tratop_e/tariffs_e/tariffs_e.htm.

RULES OF ORIGIN Determining where a product comes from is no longer easy when raw materials and parts criss-cross the globe to be used as inputs in scattered manufacturing plants. Rules of origin are important in implementing such trade policy instruments as antidumping and countervailing duties, origin marking, and safeguard measures. For more information, visit www.wto.org/english/tratop_e/roi_e /roi_e.htm.

ANTIDUMPING DUTY *Antidumping duty* is applied to imports of a particular good from a specified country in order to eliminate the harm being caused by the dumping to the domestic industry of the importing country. Article VI of the GATT 1994 permits the imposition of antidumping duties against *dumped* goods, equal to the difference between their export price and their normal value, if dumping causes injury to producers of competing products in the importing country.

If a company exports a product at a price lower than the price it normally charges on its own home market, it is said to be "dumping" the product. Is this unfair competition? The WTO agreement does not pass judgment. Its focus is on how governments can or cannot react to dumping. It disciplines antidumping actions and is often called the "Antidumping Agreement."

For more information, visit www.wto.org/english/tratop_e/adp_e/adp_e.htm.

AD VALOREM TARIFF An *ad valorem* tariff is a tariff that is imposed in percentage terms over the value of the good, for example, a 5 percent tariff, which means that the import tariff is 5 percent of the appraised value of the good in question.

RATES OF DUTY All goods imported into the United States are subject to duty or duty-free entry in accordance with their classification in the HTSUS.

There are three types of rates of duty that may be assessed on goods imported into the United States: ad valorem, specific, or compound (or mixed).

1. An ad valorem rate of duty is a percentage of the dutiable or customs value of the merchandise. (This is the rate of duty most often applied in the HTSUS.)
2. A specific rate of duty is a specified amount per unit of weight or other measure of quantity (e.g., 10 cents per pound or 5 cents per dozen).
3. Finally, a compound (or mixed) rate of duty is a combination of both an ad valorem rate of duty and a specific rate of duty (e.g., 5 percent ad valorem plus 10 cents per pound).

Freight Standards

- Economic Impact of Inadequate Infrastructure for Supply Chain Integration, www.nist.gov/director/planning/upload/report04-2.pdf
- Standards Setting Needs for Freight Management, www.ops.fhwa.dot.gov /freight/index.cfm
- Concept of Operations for an ESCM Standard, www.ops.fhwa.dot.gov/freight /index.cfm

Links

- California Center for Innovative Transportation (CCIT), www.calccit.org
- National Transportation Research Center, www.ntrc.gov
- Transportation Research Board (TRB), www.trb.org
- Defense Logistics Agency, www.dla.mil
- Foreign relations of the United States, www.state.gov/r/pa/ho/frus
- Foreign trade statistics, www.census.gov/foreign-trade/www
- Free Trade Area of the Americas (FTAA), www.ftaa-alca.org/alca_e.asp
- Hemispheric Trade and Tariff Database, www.ftaa-alca.org/NGROUPS /NGMADB_e.asp
- North American Free Trade Agreement (NAFTA), www.fas.usda.gov/itp /policy/nafta/nafta.asp

- United Nations Commission on International Trade Law (UNCITRAL), www .uncitral.org
- United Nations Conference on Trade and Development (UNCTAD), www .unctad.org
- World Customs Organization (WCO), www.wcoomd.org
- World Intellectual Property Organization (WIPO), www.wipo.org
- World Trade Organization (WTO), www.wto.org
- U.S. Customs Service, www.cbp.gov
- NAFTA Resources, www.cbp.gov/nafta/resource.htm
- WTO trade topics, www.wto.org/english/tratop_e/tratop_e.htm
- WTO Glossary, www.wto.org/english/thewto_e/glossary_e/glossary_e.htm
- Exporting Basics, www.export.gov/exportbasics/index.asp
- Trade Agreements, www.ustr.gov/Trade_Agreements/Section_Index.html
- Intermodal Association of North America, www.intermodal.org
- Council of Supply Chain Management Professionals, www.cscmp.org

Summary

In this chapter, we defined logistics in its broader sense as the segment of supply chain management concerned with the movement of goods and materials and provided a brief background on its historical importance. We also outlined the key role of logistics as a process in the business environment and how it is likely evolving toward the concept of value chain management.

The overview of transportation modes described the various methods of moving materials through stages from raw material to the consumer, pointing out the optimum use for each of them. In conjunction with transportation, traffic management is the administrative segment of logistics. In reviewing traffic management, we examined the role of the 3PL and 4PL providers.

Since all governments regulate the movement of materials into and out of their countries, knowledge of customs requirements is critical in the management of logistics. While duties are currently established by individual nations, there is an increasing movement to a harmonized system of tariffs. The "Supplemental Information" section included a summary of the various types of tariffs in effect today.

Global trade has become increasingly characterized by regional trade agreements such as NAFTA and the EU, with many treaties and pacts focused on improving trade relations and reducing restrictions within the immediate geographical area in response to competitive pressures from other regions. As global trade rapidly accelerates, global organizations such as WTO have stepped up efforts to unify widely regulated and disparate practices worldwide. In the United States, for example, literally dozens of federal and state agencies are involved in the regulation of trade to one extent or another, from the use of roads and waterways to regulating the traffic in endangered species.

Since money is the common denominator in trade activities, currency transactions also play a major role in logistic activities. Multiple markets exist for the exchange of currency, and we reviewed several of the more important of them.

In concluding this chapter, we examined several elements of logistics out of context, including technology and automation efforts, along with some common concepts in tariff administration.

Notes

1. Martin Christopher, *Logistics and Supply Chain Management: Creating Value-Adding Networks,* 3rd ed. (Harlow, Herts., UK: Pearson Education, 2005), 4.
2. Council of Supply Chain Management Professionals (CSCMP), "Supply Chain Management/Logistics Management Definitions" (Oak Brook, IL: 2006), www.cscmp.org /Website/AboutCSCMP/Definitions/Definitions.asp.
3. Ibid.
4. Air Force Institute of Technology, Graduate School of Acquisition and Logistics. Wright-Patterson AFB, Dayton, OH, 1997. In Matthew D. Cox, *Logistics World,* Logistics Dictionary. www.logisticsworld.com/logistics/glossary.asp.
5. Walter Cooke, University of Scranton/Defense Logistics Agency, from "Integrated Logistics," *HUM—The Government Computer Magazine* (December 1993). In Matthew D. Cox, *Logistics World.* Logistics Dictionary (1997), www.logisticsworld.com/logistics/glossary.asp.
6. Gergard Plenert, *The eManager: Value Chain Management in an eCommerce World* (Dublin: Blackhall Publishing, 2001), 30.
7. Nancy W. Nix, "Supply Chain Management in the Global Environment." In John T. Mentzer (ed.), *Supply Chain Management* (Thousand Oaks, CA: Sage Publications, 2001), 44.
8. Sir Anthony Giddens, *Runaway World: How Globalisation Is Reshaping Our Lives* (London: Routledge, 2000), 29–30.

CHAPTER **20**

Regulatory Compliance

As you may imagine, numerous laws and governmental regulations—federal, state, and local—affect procurement activities to one degree or another in the United States. Many of these play key roles in the way business organizations can function, while others establish the legal framework for buying and selling.

In your role as procurement professional, you will not only need to understand how laws and regulations affect business conducted domestically, but you will also need a thorough understanding of how the laws governing businesses in other countries vary widely from those in the United States. What is taken for common business practice in one country may be unheard of in another.

Regulatory Factors Governing Procurement

The laws regulating commerce in the United States (and likely elsewhere) are so extensive that it would be impossible to even begin to list them here. However, in this section we've outlined some of the most frequently cited laws and regulations that you should recognize as a procurement professional.

Uniform Commercial Code

The *Uniform Commercial Code (UCC)*, especially Article 2, the section governing sales, is perhaps the regulation most commonly used by procurement departments in conducting day-to-day business. The UCC was developed by the legal community early in the last century as trade between the states began to accelerate and the need for uniform laws became evident. It has subsequently been adopted and ratified by 49 U.S. states and the District of Columbia.

Tips and Techniques

The UCC applies in every state except Louisiana. Louisiana operates under a legal system more closely tied to French law than the English legal system that formed the foundation of law in the other states.

The UCC governs a variety of commercial areas, most importantly the sale and purchase of goods. It does not generally apply to services except in the case of combined purchases of goods and services and only if the product represents more than 50 percent of the total transaction value.

Section 2, governing sales, is the most applicable section of the UCC to procurement. Its scope is extremely broad and covers virtually every area related to the sale and purchase of goods between merchants. The section is divided into parts dealing with specific elements of the commercial relationship within the scope of business-to-business activities. For example, Part 2 covers the broader aspects of contract formation while Part 3 details specific aspects of contracts such as delivery, warranty, and shipping; Part 5 deals with the important aspects of performance; Part 6 covers contract breach and repudiation; and Part 7, the final segment, covers remedies.

Note

Appendix H on the companion website contains an index listing each of the parts of Section 2 and the subsections they cover.

You can find out more about the UCC and obtain the full text by visiting: www.law.cornell.edu/ucc/ucc.table.html.

Antitrust Legislation

While the system of conducting business in the United States requires open and fair competition to ensure economic justice, many individual assaults have been made on this system in an attempt to gain personal advantage. These have typically been met with appropriate legislation by the U.S. Congress. For instance, you might recall from U.S. history what happened when railroad monopolies began selective pricing of freight to favor businesses in which they held an interest. They were able to effectively reduce competition by charging exorbitant freight rates to competing companies, resulting in higher prices for their products compared to those in which the railroad owners had an interest. The result of these unethical business practices is government regulation, which we discuss in depth in this section.

SHERMAN ANTITRUST ACT (1890)   In response to increasing public concern over the formation of monopolies in the United States and their negative impact on commercial trade, Congress passed the Sherman Antitrust Act in 1890. The act banned business contracts made in the form of a trust, or those created under unethical circumstances such as through bribes, graft, or coercion. The act restricts "every contract and combination in the form of trust or otherwise, or conspiracy, in restraint of trade or commerce." The law was accompanied by sharp teeth in the form of criminal penalties and treble damages for violations. Included in the outlawed practices were conspiracies to fix pricing and to require reciprocal buying.

The Sherman Act has seen several amendments over the years designed to further refine its prohibitions, most significantly the Clayton Antitrust Act of 1914.

CLAYTON ANTITRUST ACT (1914)   The Clayton Antitrust Act of 1914 was designed to bolster the provisions of the Sherman Act and further reduce monopolistic practices.

It made certain corporate practices illegal, including price cutting to freeze out competitors, exclusive pricing arrangements, and tying contracts (where the purchase of specific goods and services by the buyer is contingent upon the purchase of other goods or services as a package). It also outlawed the holding of stock by one company so that it could gain control over another, thus reducing or eliminating competition, and the practice of interlocking directorates where a few influential individuals controlled an industry by sitting on the boards of related companies.

ROBINSON-PATMAN ACT (1958)   The key element of the Robinson-Patman Act of 1958 is that it barred direct or indirect price discrimination that would substantially reduce competition. This federal legislation prohibits suppliers from exclusively charging lower prices to certain customers simply because they purchase in larger quantities than other customers. While some specific exceptions apply, quantity discounts for exactly the same quality of like material (or services related to the purchase of the material) are basically illegal under this law unless all competing buyers are eligible for the same discount.

In addition, the provisions of Robinson-Patman prohibit the *purchaser* from knowingly receiving a discriminatory price or forcing the supplier to provide one. It also forbids the seller from providing and the buyer from accepting any commission related to the sale.

The law, however, does allow the seller to match the prices of its competitors and to lower prices when there is a valid justification—for example, when there are differences in distribution costs or when perishable goods have reached the end of their shelf life.

For the act to be enforced (which, by the way, it rarely is), it must be proven that the alleged price discrimination produced an adverse effect by limiting competition and at least one of the alleged discriminatory sales crossed state lines. In addition, the act applies only to goods and materials of a predominantly physical nature rather than intangibles such as services (unless related and subordinate to the goods being purchased), and the goods in question must be of "like grade and quality." Altogether, there are some 10 provisions that must be violated concurrently for enforcement to take place.

FEDERAL TRADE COMMISSION (FTC) ACT (1914)   The FTC Act, also created in 1914 along with the Clayton Act, established the FTC as the watchdog agency for restraint of trade activities and to investigate any alleged improprieties between buyers and sellers. The agency is empowered to root out and prosecute instances of illegal, unfair, or deceptive business practices. However, buyers rarely have dealings with the FTC, so it's unlikely that as a procurement professional you'll have much to worry about this regard.

OFPP (OFFICE OF FEDERAL PROCUREMENT POLICY) ACT (1974)   Though it's been through several amendments, the OFPP Act of 1974 established the official *Federal Acquisitions Regulations (FAR)*, the U.S. government's procurement policies, which are overseen by the OFPP.

OFPP oversees several statutes related to acquisitions for such government organizations as the Department of Defense, the General Services Administration, and the National Aeronautics and Space Administration.

Other Federal Government Legislation

Most governmental regulation affecting commercial business dealings is focused on eliminating collusion and conspiracy to fix pricing. However, a procurement professional should be aware of a number of other laws enacted by Congress that impact the conduct of routine procurement activities, such as the Small Business Act, the Davis-Bacon Act, the Walsh-Healey Public Contracts Act, the Service Contract Act, the Prompt Payment Act, the False Claims Act, and the Buy American Act.

Within government procurement processes, many regulatory requirements require equally close monitoring. The Federal Acquisition Regulations (FAR) is an extensive compendium of regulations that require compliance and, as anyone familiar with it will tell you, it is an exceptionally complex body of legislation that requires government contracting organizations and contractors doing business with the federal government to follow very strict procedures and to produce rather extensive documentation.

SMALL BUSINESS ACT (1953)   The Small Business Act represents an effort by Congress to foster the participation of small, disadvantaged, and female-owned businesses in federal contracting. It requires federal purchasers to assign a designated volume of procurement to small businesses (called "set asides") and to allow some contracts to be split between large and small businesses, where the small business has the opportunity to share part of the contract providing they can match the bid terms.

DAVIS-BACON ACT (1931)   The Davis-Bacon Act and its amendments require that federal construction projects over $2,000 contain a clause establishing the minimum wages to be paid to various classes of workers employed under the contract. Under the provisions, contractors and subcontractors are required to pay workers employed under the contract wages at least equal to the locally prevailing rates and fringe benefits for similar projects.

WALSH-HEALEY PUBLIC CONTRACTS ACT (1936)   Closely related to the Davis-Bacon Act, the Walsh-Healey Act applies to government purchases and contracts exceeding $10,000. Going beyond requiring minimum wage, the act limits the work week to 40 hours and attempts to ensure safe and sanitary working conditions. There is also a provision that, in effect, blackballs violators by making them ineligible for further government contracts for three years and distributing a list of their names to federal contracting agencies.

SERVICE CONTRACT ACT (1965)   The Service Contract Act empowers the Employment Standards Administration to predetermine the prevailing wage and benefit rates to be paid for federal service contracts that are over $2,500. It also provides the enforcement mechanisms for the Davis-Bacon and Walsh-Healey acts that include safety standards and record-keeping requirements.

PROMPT PAYMENT ACT (1982)   The Prompt Payment Act ensures that federal agencies pay suppliers and contractors in a timely manner and even allows for the assessment of late payment penalties and interest.

FALSE CLAIMS ACT (1863) Under the False Claims Act, those who knowingly submit, or cause another person or entity to submit, false or fraudulent claims for payment of government funds can be held liable for treble damages plus civil penalties.

BUY AMERICAN ACT (1933) The Buy American Act of 1933 was passed to ensure that the federal government supports domestic companies and domestic workers by buying goods manufactured in the United States that are made from materials mined or produced in the United States. The law provides exceptions for items not commercially available in the United States or if the price is more than 6 percent higher than comparable foreign products. It also allows exceptions for purchases under $100,000 or by department head waiver.

Tips and Techniques

Should the United States Waive the Buy American Act?

How important is it to ensure that the U.S. government support U.S. businesses during poor economic times and in a time of military climate? You'd assume it was very important, especially during the Iraq conflict. But the State Department decided to waive requirements that the military purchase U.S.-made cars and trucks for the war effort. This led to a strong complaint to the Secretary of State from a leading minority congressman stating that if U.S.-produced cars were good enough to win the war, they should be good enough to win the peace.

Do you agree? Is a law passed in the Depression of the 1930s to protect U.S. jobs still appropriate for the U.S. to follow today?

OCCUPATIONAL SAFETY AND HEALTH ACT The Occupational Safety and Health Act gives rise to a variety of rules and regulations governing safety in the workplace. Under certain circumstances, your organization will want to include a clause in its contracts that essentially shifts the burden of compliance to the supplier. A clause in the contract requiring compliance with applicable laws is generally sufficient protection, but it must be crafted by legal counsel since regulations are quite formal in this area.

SARBANES-OXLEY Corporate financial malfeasance has resulted in several scandals in recent years and, as a reaction, Congress enacted the Sarbanes-Oxley Act (or SOX, as it is called). This law, passed in 2002, affects only publicly traded corporations for now but will likely expand to include all corporate entities that have dealings with them, whether public or private. Section 404 of the act requires, among other things, that corporate policies and procedures be documented and that key accounting and finance processes be clearly stated. More importantly, the act requires that CEOs and CFOs attest to the veracity of the financial statement in a written statement. The firm's financial reports must include disclosure of all financial obligations, including procurement contracts that could create a liability for the shareholders. Penalties for violation include very stiff prison sentences.

The Sarbanes-Oxley Act also requires certain financial controls and reporting as part of a publicly traded corporation's responsibility to its shareholders and the

U.S. Securities and Exchange Commission. To meet these obligations, corporations must have in place a systematic procedure to gather the necessary procurement-related information during the S2S process. In addition, SOX mandated a number of reforms to enhance corporate responsibility, enhance financial disclosures, and combat corporate and accounting fraud, and created the Public Company Accounting Oversight Board to oversee the activities of the business process auditing profession.

The impact that this will have on procurement activities is still being sorted out, but it is clear that all risks associated with any significant supply agreement will need to be disclosed and steps taken to mitigate the risk included in reporting documents. For example, any high-dollar "take or pay" contract requiring payment regardless of whether or not the products or services are needed (often used as an inducement to the supplier to invest in capital equipment or engineering) will need to be disclosed, along with the rationale for entering into such an agreement and the steps that can be taken to minimize the loss to shareholders should the need for cancellation arise.

Foreign Trade Regulations

In addition to numerous domestic laws governing trade, Congress has enacted several key pieces of legislation affecting foreign trade, and the U.S. government has been signatory to a number of others that were negotiated internationally. Some of the more significant of those include the following.

GENERAL AGREEMENT ON TARIFFS AND TRADE (GATT)   This international agreement, first signed in 1947, has now become a significant element of the World Trade Organization (WTO). Affecting trade in goods only, the agreement was designed to help reduce restrictive tariffs and encourage international trade. Approximately 110 countries now participate.

NORTH AMERICAN FREE TRADE AGREEMENT (NAFTA)   This treaty was designed to enhance trade among the U.S., Mexico, and Canada, offering favorable tariffs and removing import and export barriers for goods that primarily originate in one of the three countries.

UNITED NATIONS CONVENTION ON CONTRACTS FOR THE INTERNATIONAL SALE OF GOODS (CISG)   Ratified by Congress in 1986, this treaty was initiated to provide uniformity to global sales and automatically applies to commercial sales between the signatory countries. It does not apply to trade for services only. The full text of the agreement can be found on the Internet at www.uncitral.org/english/texts/sales/CISG.htm.

TRADE AGREEMENTS ACT OF 1979   One of the stated purposes of this act is "to foster the growth and maintenance of an open world trading system." It was also enacted to expand opportunities for U.S. international commerce and to support and enforce the rules of international trade.

FOREIGN CORRUPT PRACTICES ACT   This law is primarily known for its antibribery provisions that make it illegal for any U.S. citizen to bribe a foreign official in order to obtain or sustain business. It is somewhat confusing because it applies only to officials and does not include payments made to facilitate routine duties (sometimes called "grease").

ANTI-KICKBACK ACT OF 1986 This law was passed to deter subcontractors from making payments and contractors from accepting payments for the purpose of improperly obtaining or rewarding favorable treatment in connection with a prime contract or subcontract relating to a prime contract.

The Act –

(a) Prohibits any person from—
1. *Providing, attempting to provide, or offering to provide a kickback;*
2. *Soliciting, accepting, or attempting to accept any kickback;*
3. *Including, directly or indirectly, the amount of a kickback in the contract price charged by a subcontractor to a prime contractor [and ultimately the government].*

Source: FAR 3.502-2

Import/Export Regulations

While international trade creates a wide array of financial benefits, those benefits are not without major obstacles. Regulatory initiatives such as Customs-Trade Partnership Against Terrorism (C-TPAT), CSI, Antidumping and Countervailing Duties (ADCVD) and Sarbanes-Oxley (SOX) have had significant impact on global trade by requiring more information from importers and new processes to meet the regulatory demand of such policies.

Regulations today have become more stringent and evolving, covering not only the shipment of goods but also the flow of funds. Exporting organizations are under greater scrutiny than ever before regarding their global trade practices and face multiple challenges that affect the entire company from sales to finance. The challenges facing export management businesses include the following:

- Restrictions on those with whom business is conducted, including financial and services providers, as well as buyers and consumers.
- Stiff fines and loss of ability to export goods for noncompliance with regulations.
- Increased regulatory requirements, such as mandatory
- New free trade agreements.
- Maintaining and increasing shipment tracking with little added cost.
- Compliance with multiple regulatory bodies, such as the Department of Commerce's Bureau of Industry and Security (BIS) and the State Department's Office of Defense Trade Controls (ODTC).
- Updating of supply chain information.
- Continually changing duty classifications.
- Maintaining accurate audit trails and ensuring the security and integrity of data.

Note

Appendix I on the companion website contains details on recent import and export legislation.

Government Organizations and Roles, Regulations, and Controls

Government has a vested interest in logistics, and in particular, its transportation component, as it is of critical importance to reliable service and the economic well-being of its citizens. Government desires a stable, secure, and efficient transportation environment to support economic growth.

Since the terrorist attacks on the United States on September 11, 2001, there has been an unprecedented reorganization and realignment of the U.S. government agencies and their various roles and duties as they apply to the movement of goods and services, both domestically and internationally. Some of the major federal agencies that deal with transportation and logistics issues are discussed in the next sections.

The United States Department of Transportation

The United States Department of Transportation (DOT) is a cabinet department of the U.S. government concerned with transport. It was established by an act of Congress on October 15, 1966, and began operation on April 1, 1967. It is administered by the United States Secretary of Transportation. Its mission is to "Serve the United States by ensuring a fast, safe, efficient, accessible and convenient transportation system that meets our vital national interests and enhances the quality of life of the American people, today and into the future."[1] The DOT consists of the Office of the Secretary and 11 individual operating administrations:

- Federal Aviation Administration (FAA)
- Federal Highway Administration (FHWA)
- Federal Railroad Administration (FRA)
- Federal Transit Administration (FTA)
- Maritime Administration (MARAD)
- Federal Motor Carrier Safety Administration (FMCSA)
- National Highway Traffic Safety Administration (NHTSA)
- Research and Innovative Technology Administration (RITA)
- Pipeline and Hazardous Materials Safety Administration (PHMSA)
- Saint Lawrence Seaway Development Corporation (SLSDC)
- Surface Transportation Board (STB)

The Homeland Security Act of 2002 authorized the establishment of the Department of Homeland Security, which, on March 1, 2003, assumed management of the United States Coast Guard and the Transportation Security Administration, formerly DOT Operating Administrations.

The duties of the chief U.S. DOT agencies are outlined in the following sections.

The Federal Aviation Administration (FAA)

The Federal Aviation Administration (FAA) has the authority to regulate and oversee all aspects of civil aviation in the U.S. Along with the European Joint Aviation Authorities, the FAA is one of the two main agencies worldwide responsible for the certification of new aircraft. The FAA issues a number of awards to holders of its licenses. Among these are demonstrated proficiencies as a mechanic, an instructor, a 50-year aviator, or as a safe pilot. The Air Commerce Act of May 20, 1926, is the cornerstone of the federal government's regulation of civil aviation. This landmark legislation was passed at the urging of the aviation industry, whose leaders believed the airplane could not reach its full commercial potential without federal action to improve and maintain safety standards. The FAA became more involved with the environmental aspects of aviation in 1968 when it received the power to set aircraft noise standards. Legislation in 1970 gave the agency management of a new airport aid program and certain added responsibilities for airport safety. During the 1960s and 1970s the FAA also started to regulate high-altitude (over 500 feet) kite and balloon flying. In 1979 Congress authorized the FAA to work with major commercial airports to define noise pollution contours and investigate the feasibility of noise mitigation by residential retrofit programs. Throughout the 1980s these charters were implemented. In the 1990s, satellite technology received increased emphasis in the FAA's development programs as a means to improvements in communications, navigation, and airspace management. In 1995, the agency assumed responsibility for safety oversight of commercial space transportation, a function begun 11 years before by an office within DOT headquarters.

For more information, visit www.faa.gov/.

The Federal Highway Administration (FHWA)

The FHWA specializes in highway transportation. The agency's major activities are grouped into two programs: the Federal-Aid Highway Program and the Federal Lands Highway Program. The FHWA's role in the Federal-Aid Highway Program is to oversee federal funds used for constructing and maintaining the National Highway System (primarily interstate highways, U.S. routes, and most State Routes). This funding mostly comes from the federal gasoline tax and mostly goes to state departments of transportation. The FHWA oversees projects using these funds to ensure that federal requirements for project eligibility, contract administration, and construction standards are adhered to. Under the Federal Lands Highway Program (sometimes called "direct fed"), the FHWA provides highway design and construction services for various federal land-management agencies, such as the Forest Service and the National Park Service. In addition to these programs, the FHWA performs research in the areas of automobile safety, congestion, highway materials, and construction methods. The FHWA also publishes the *Manual on Uniform Traffic Control Devices* (MUTCD), which is used by most highway agencies in the United States. The MUTCD specifies such things as the size, color, and height of stop signs.

For more information, visit www.fhwa.dot.gov/.

The Federal Railroad Administration (FRA)

The FRA was created in 1966 to promote safe, environmentally sound, successful rail transportation. The Office of Railroad Development (RDV) is responsible for federal investment and assistance to the rail industry as well as the development and implementation of administration policy concerning intercity rail passenger service and high-speed rail. It sponsors research and development activities to advance science and engineering to improve the technology for railroad safety and work. It provides investment opportunities for small freight railroad projects, primarily through the RRIF program. The Office of Safety promotes and regulates safety throughout the nation's railroad industry. It employs more than 415 federal safety inspectors, who operate out of eight regional offices nationally. FRA inspectors specialize in five safety disciplines and numerous grade crossing and trespass-prevention initiatives: Track, Signal and Train Control, Motive Power and Equipment, Operating Practices, Hazardous Materials, and Highway-Rail Grade Crossing Safety. The office trains and certifies state safety inspectors to enforce federal rail safety regulations. Central to the success of the rail safety effort is the ability to understand the nature of rail-related accidents and to analyze trends in railroad safety. To do this, the Office of Safety collects rail accident/incident data from the railroads and converts this information into meaningful statistical tables, charts, and reports.

For more information, visit www.fra.dot.gov/us/content/2.

The Federal Transit Administration (FTA)

The FTA provides financial and technical assistance to the local public transit systems. The FTA is one of eleven modal administrations within the DOT. The FTA functions through a Washington, D.C., headquarters office and 10 regional offices that assist transit agencies in all 50 states, the District of Columbia, Puerto Rico, the U.S. Virgin Islands, Guam, Northern Mariana Islands, and American Samoa. Public transportation includes buses, subways, light rail, commuter rail, monorail, passenger ferry boats, trolleys, inclined railways, and people movers. The federal government, through the FTA, provides financial assistance to develop new transit systems and improve, maintain, and operate existing systems. The FTA oversees grants to state and local transit providers, primarily through its 10 regional offices. These grantees are responsible for managing their programs in accordance with federal requirements, and the FTA is responsible for ensuring that grantees follow federal mandates along with statutory and administrative requirements.

For more information, visit www.fta.dot.gov/.

The Maritime Administration (MARAD)

MARAD administers financial programs to develop, promote, and operate the U.S. Merchant Marine; determines services and routes necessary to develop and maintain American foreign commerce and requirements of ships necessary to provide adequate service on such routes; conducts research and development activities in the maritime field; regulates the transfer of U.S. documented vessels to foreign registries; maintains equipment, shipyard facilities, and reserve fleets of government-owned ships essential for national defense; operates the U.S. Merchant Marine Academy at Kings Point, New York; and administers a grant-in-aid program for state-operated maritime academies in California (California Maritime Academy), Maine (Maine Maritime Academy), Massachusetts (Massachusetts Maritime Academy), Michigan (Great Lakes Maritime Academy), New York (SUNY Maritime College), and Texas

(Texas Maritime Academy). The Maritime Subsidy Board negotiates contracts for ship construction and grants operating-differential subsidies to shipping companies. The maritime administrator is vested with the residual powers of the director of the National Shipping Authority, which was established in 1951 to organize and direct emergency merchant marine operations.

For more information, visit www.marad.dot.gov/index.html and www.nvr .navy.mil/marad.htm.

The Federal Motor Carrier Safety Administration (FMCSA)

The FMCSA's primary mission is to reduce crashes, injuries, and fatalities involving large trucks and buses. In carrying out its safety mandate, the FMCSA:

- Develops and enforces data-driven regulations that balance motor carrier (truck and bus companies) safety with industry efficiency.
- Harnesses safety information systems to focus on higher risk carriers in enforcing the safety regulations.
- Targets educational messages to carriers, commercial drivers, and the public.
- Partners with stakeholders including federal, state, and local enforcement agencies; the motor carrier industry; safety groups; and organized labor on efforts to reduce bus- and truck-related crashes.

For more information, visit www.fmcsa.dot.gov/.

The National Highway Traffic Safety Administration (NHTSA)

The NHTSA is responsible for setting safety standards and verifying compliance by automobile manufacturers. It also issues recall notices that ensure full awareness of mechanical problems with cars sold in the United States, and publishes the results of safety tests of various automobiles, to allow buyers to evaluate the anticipated behavior of an automobile in a crash.

For more information, visit www.nhtsa.dot.gov/.

The Research and Innovative Technology Administration (RITA)

The RITA is comprised of the Bureau of Transportation Statistics (Washington, D.C.), the Volpe National Transportation Systems Center (Cambridge, Massachusetts), the Transportation Safety Institute (Oklahoma City, Oklahoma), and the Office of Intermodalism (Washington, D.C.). The main vision of the RITA is to identify and facilitate solutions to the challenges and opportunities facing America's transportation system. The RITA is part university research lab and part Silicon Valley entrepreneurial company. The agency fosters the exchange of ideas and information in a high-priority incubator committed to research and gets these innovative ideas from the laboratory into the field. The RITA allows the DOT the opportunity to realize greater collaboration, information sharing, coordination, support, and advocacy for its widespread research efforts.

For more information, visit www.rita.dot.gov/.

The Pipeline and Hazardous Materials Safety Administration (PHMSA)

The PHMSA has public responsibilities for safe and secure movement of hazardous materials to industry and consumers by all transportation modes, including the nation's pipelines. The agency also oversees the nation's pipeline infrastructure, which accounts for 64 percent of the energy commodities consumed in the United States.

For more information, visit www.phmsa.dot.gov/.

The Saint Lawrence Seaway Development Corporation (SLSDC)

The SLSDC is a wholly owned government corporation created by statute May 13, 1954, to construct, operate, and maintain that part of the St. Lawrence Seaway between the Port of Montreal and Lake Erie, within the territorial limits of the United States. Trade development functions aim to enhance Great Lakes/St. Lawrence Seaway System utilization without respect to territorial or geographic limits.

For more information, visit www.seaway.dot.gov/.

The Surface Transportation Board (STB)

The STB was created by the Interstate Commerce Commission Termination Act of 1995 at the same time the Interstate Commerce Commission was abolished. The STB was created to replace the ICC, which had been charged with playing to the interests of the trucking industry and being generally useless due to deregulation. The STB is an economic regulatory agency that Congress created to resolve railroad rate and service disputes and review proposed railroad mergers. The STB is decisionally independent, although it is administratively affiliated with the U.S. DOT. The STB serves as both an adjudicatory and a regulatory body. The agency has jurisdiction over the following:

- Railroad rate and service issues.
- Rail restructuring transactions (mergers, line sales, new line construction, and old line abandonment).
- Certain trucking company, moving van, and noncontiguous ocean shipping company rate matters.
- Certain intercity passenger bus company structure, financial, and operational matters.
- Rates and services of certain pipelines not regulated by the Federal Energy Regulatory Commission.

For more information, visit www.stb.dot.gov/.

The U.S. Department of Homeland Security

Homeland security refers to domestic governmental actions designed to prevent, detect, respond to, and recover from acts of terrorism, and also to respond to natural disasters. The term became prominent in the United States following the September 11, 2001, attacks; it had been used only in limited policy circles prior to 9/11. Before this time, such action had been classified as civil defense. Homeland security is officially defined as "a concerted national effort to prevent terrorist attacks within the United States, reduce America's vulnerability to terrorism, and minimize the damage and recover from attacks that do occur," according to the National Strategy for Homeland Security. Because the U.S. Department of Homeland Security (DHS) includes the Federal Emergency Management Agency (FEMA), it has responsibility for preparedness for, response to, and recovery from natural disasters as well. Homeland security is generally used to refer to the broad national effort by all levels of government—federal, state, local, and tribal—to protect the territory of the United States from hazards, both internal and external, as well as the Department of Homeland Security itself. Homeland security is also usually used to connote the civilian aspect of this effort; "homeland defense" refers to its military component, led chiefly by the U.S. Northern Command headquartered in Colorado Springs, Colorado. The scope of homeland security includes the following:

- Emergency preparedness and response (for both terrorism and natural disasters), including volunteer medical, police, emergency management, and fire personnel.
- Domestic intelligence activities, largely today within the FBI.
- Critical infrastructure protection.
- Border security, including both land and maritime borders.
- Transportation security, including aviation and maritime transportation.
- Biodefense.
- Detection of nuclear and radiological materials.
- Research on next-generation security technologies.

In the United States, the concept of "homeland security" extends and recombines responsibilities of much of the executive branch, including the Federal Bureau of Investigation (FBI), the National Guard, the Federal Emergency Management Agency (FEMA), the United States Coast Guard, the former Immigration and Naturalization Service (INS), the former U.S. Customs Service, the Secret Service, the Transportation Security Administration (TSA), and the Central Intelligence Agency (CIA).

For more information, visit www.dhs.gov/dhspublic/.

Tax Laws

While procurement will not have direct responsibility for taxes, you will need to know some basic principles under which tax laws operate so that you can take them into account when making certain procurement decisions. For example, in many states, purchases for products being resold (or that go into products being resold) do not require the payment of sales tax. In many areas, taxes on inventory are assessed just as they would be for real property. Software downloaded via the Internet is usually exempt from sales tax (considered a service rather than a product), while the same software purchased in a box will be subject to tax.

Tips and Techniques

Use tax is a tax levied on goods that are bought outside the taxing authority's jurisdiction and then brought into the jurisdiction. This tax is designed to discourage the purchase of products that are not subject to a sales tax.

FASB

The *Financial Accounting Standards Board (FASB)* established standards of financial accounting and reporting for leases by lessees and lessors for transactions and revisions entered into on or after January 1, 1977. For lessees, a lease is a financing transaction called a capital lease if it meets any one of four specified criteria; if not, it is an operating lease. Capital leases are treated as the acquisition of assets and the incurrence of obligations by the lessee. Operating leases are treated as current operating expenses.

For lessors, a financing transaction lease is classified as a sales type, direct financing, or leveraged lease. To be a sales type, direct financing, or leveraged lease, the lease must meet one of the same criteria used for lessees to classify a lease as a capital lease, in addition to two criteria dealing with future uncertainties.

Leveraged leases also have to meet further criteria. These types of leases are recorded as investments under different specifications for each type of lease. Leases not meeting the criteria are considered operating leases and are accounted for like rental property.

Conformance to Law

At the minimum, organizations are required to conform to antitrust, environmental, and health and safety laws. As you will recall, antitrust regulations were covered in Chapter 3, and some of the laws covering environmental and health and safety processes were outlined above. In addition, there are numerous laws governing intellectual property, and there are rules governing confidentiality such as the *Uniform Trade Secrets Act (UTSA)* that define rights for particular trade secrets. As a procurement professional, you will be required to have a working knowledge of all of these laws and regulations.

In addition, you should become familiar with the activities and regulations of certain governmental agencies that are empowered to protect the rights and welfare of the general population. One of these organizations, the Environmental Protection Agency (EPA), is charged with enforcing federal laws relating to hazardous materials, clean air, and water and waste disposal. Many of the regulations and laws enforced by this agency carry criminal charges if violated, so you should become very familiar with their overall requirements.

Preventing Workplace Discrimination and Harassment

What constitutes discrimination in the workplace? The precise definition of discrimination in the workplace and what is illegal discrimination varies somewhat from state to state. However, discrimination can be defined as treating one person unfairly over another according to factors unrelated to their ability or potential, such as age, race, disability, sex, sexual orientation, religion, or national origin. There are numerous laws and regulations that attempt to eliminate unfair discrimination, and many organizations have established policies and procedures to align with them. In this section, we'll outline some of the regulations you are most likely to encounter.

Administering Equal Opportunity Processes

While it would be hard for you as a manager to be completely up-to-date on all the specifics of existing laws, it is nevertheless your responsibility to ensure that discrimination and harassment are never present in your workplace. To accomplish this, you will need to be familiar with some of the key laws and regulations and how they operate to provide equal opportunity for all employees.

LAWS AND REGULATIONS The U.S. *Equal Employment Opportunity Commission (EEOC)* (www.eeoc.gov) is charged with the enforcement of the body of federal laws governing equal employment opportunity.

The key federal laws prohibiting job discrimination are discussed next:

- **Title VII of the Civil Rights Act of 1964, 1972, 1991.** Prohibits employment discrimination based on race, color, religion, sex, or national origin. It also allows employers to use a bona fide occupational qualification (BFOQ) to establish employment requirements where a need legitimately exists. (For example, an advertising director can require a female model for a bathing suit ad.)
- **Equal Pay Act of 1963 (EPA).** Protects men and women who perform substantially equal work in the same establishment from sex-based wage discrimination.
- **Age Discrimination in Employment Act of 1967, 1978, 1986 (ADEA).** Protects individuals who are 40 years of age or older.
- **Title I and Title V of the Americans with Disabilities Act of 1990 (ADA).** Prohibits employment discrimination against qualified individuals with disabilities in the private sector and in state and local governments.
- **Sections 501 and 505 of the Rehabilitation Act of 1973.** Prohibits discrimination against qualified individuals with disabilities who work in the federal government.
- **Civil Rights Act of 1991.** Provides, among other things, monetary damages in cases of intentional employment discrimination.

In general, the presence of a specific set of conditions can confirm the existence of illegal discrimination. Unfair treatment does not necessarily equal unlawful discrimination. Treating a person differently from others violates *Equal Employment Opportunity (EEO)* laws only when the treatment is based on the presence of a protected characteristic rather than on job performance or even on something as arbitrary as an employee's personality. Keep in mind, however, that discrimination claims can be highly subjective when reviewed by an arbitrator or a jury.

To avoid discrimination, you do not have to extend preferential treatment to any employee. The law requires only that you extend the same employment opportunities and enforce the same policies for all employees.

AFFIRMATIVE ACTION   *Affirmative action* became law with the passage of the Equal Employment Opportunity Act of 1972, whereby employers, labor unions, employment agencies, and labor management apprenticeship programs must actively seek to increase the employment opportunities for protected groups such as racial minorities and the disabled. Although Title VII of the Civil Rights Act of 1964 outlawed future discriminations in employment practices, it did nothing to redress already existing imbalances. The 1972 law, later strengthened by Executive Order 11246, required employers to draw up a detailed written plan for equalizing economic salaries, training programs, fringe benefits, and other conditions of employment. These plans included numerical goals and timetables for achieving such changes.

In recent decisions, however, the U.S. Supreme Court has significantly reduced the scope of federal affirmative action programs requiring that such actions serve a compelling interest and be narrowly defined. In 1994, the Fourth U.S. Circuit Court of Appeals rejected a University of Maryland scholarship program restricted to African-American students. In 2004, the Fifth Circuit rejected an admissions procedure at the University of Texas Law School that divided applicants into two groups—first, blacks and Mexican-Americans, and second, all others—and then applied different admissions quotas to each group. The court held that the law school's interest in diversity did not constitute a compelling state interest and that the school could not take race into account in any form in its admissions process. The Supreme Court let both decisions stand without further review. While as a matter of law other states are not absolutely debarred from continuing race-restricted scholarships or preferential admissions policies, the consensus is that these programs are unlikely to survive the all but certain legal challenges they will face.

Some areas of affirmative action are still being enforced, though. Title 5, Section 503 of the Rehabilitation Act does require that affirmative action be taken in employment of persons with disabilities by federal contractors.

AMERICANS WITH DISABILITIES ACT (ADA)   The EEOC provides an outline of the basic principles of the *Americans with Disabilities Act (ADA)*. We will discuss those principles next.

The ADA prohibits discrimination on the basis of disability in all employment practices. It is necessary to understand several important ADA definitions to know who is protected by the law and what constitutes illegal discrimination:

- **Individual with a disability.** An individual with a disability under the ADA is a person who has a physical or mental impairment that substantially limits one or more major life activities, has a record of such impairment, or is regarded as having such impairment. Major life activities are activities that an average person can perform with little or no difficulty such as walking, breathing, seeing, hearing, speaking, learning, and working.
- **Qualified individual with a disability.** A qualified employee or applicant with a disability is someone who satisfies skill, experience, education, and other job-related requirements of the position held or desired, and who, with or without reasonable accommodation, can perform the essential functions of that position.
- **Reasonable accommodation.** Reasonable accommodation may include, but is not limited to, making existing employee facilities readily accessible to and usable by persons with disabilities; job restructuring; modification of work

schedules; providing additional unpaid leave; reassignment to a vacant position; acquiring or modifying equipment or devices; adjusting or modifying
examinations, training materials, or policies; and providing qualified readers or
interpreters. Reasonable accommodation may be necessary to apply for a job,
to perform job functions, or to enjoy the benefits and privileges of employment
that are enjoyed by people without disabilities. An employer is not required
to lower production standards to make an accommodation. An employer generally is not obligated to provide personal use items such as eyeglasses or
hearing aids.

- **Undue hardship.** An employer is required to make a reasonable accommodation to a qualified individual with a disability unless doing so would impose an
undue hardship on the operation of the employer's business. Undue hardship
means an action that involves significant difficulty or expense when considered
in relation to factors such as a business's size, financial resources, and the nature
and structure of its operation.

- **Prohibited inquiries and examination.** Before making an offer of employment, an employer may not ask job applicants about the existence, nature, or
severity of a disability. Applicants may be asked about their ability to perform
job functions. A job offer may be conditioned on the results of a medical examination, but only if the examination is required for all entering employees in
the same job category. Medical examinations of employees must be job-related
and consistent with business necessity.

- **Drug and alcohol use.** Employees and applicants currently engaging in the
illegal use of drugs are not protected by the ADA when an employer acts on
the basis of such use. Tests for illegal use of drugs are not considered medical
examinations and, therefore, are not subject to the ADA's restrictions on medical
examinations. Employers may hold individuals who are illegally using drugs
and individuals with alcoholism to the same standards of performance as other
employees.

Eliminating Sexual Harassment

Sexual harassment in employment is any kind of sexual behavior that is unwelcome
and/or inappropriate for the workplace. The EEOC has defined sexual harassment
as "unwelcome sexual advances, requests for sexual favors, and other verbal or
physical conduct of a sexual nature . . . when . . . submission to or rejection of such
conduct is used as the basis for employment decisions . . . or such conduct has
the purpose or effect of . . . creating an intimidating, hostile, or offensive working
environment."

Sexual harassment is also defined as unwelcome sexual advances or conduct.
Sexual harassment can include verbal harassment (derogatory comments or dirty
jokes), visual harassment (sexually explicit posters, cartoons, or drawings), physical
harassment, and outright sexual advances or confrontation with sexual demands.
Sexual harassment also includes animosity that is gender-based and a sexually
charged work environment. In the workplace, sexual harassment can come from the
owner, supervisor, manager, lead person, foreperson, coworker, and/or customer.

In a series of major decisions in 1998, the United States Supreme Court clarified
and broadened the law. In a unanimous decision in March 1998, the Court ruled

that when the workplace is permeated with discriminatory intimidation, ridicule, and insults that are sufficiently severe or pervasive to alter the conditions of the victim's employment and create an abusive working environment, Title VII is violated.

Summary

This chapter focused on regulatory requirements that primarily apply to procurement operations. Obviously, commercial regulation is a topic that cannot be covered in a single chapter or even in a single work; however, here we attempted to post an overview of the most important regulations and agencies that govern them.

We first examined the Uniform Commercial Code and U.S. legislation directed to restraint of trade and monopolies. This was followed by a brief compendium of miscellaneous government regulations, including important recent ones such as Sarbanes-Oxley. We also covered significant U.S. foreign trade regulations along with import and export regulations

Next we covered U.S. and international efforts to regulate hazardous materials and global pollution through the establishment of environmental standards and protocols, including the handling and disposal of hazardous material and waste. This section also reviewed the agencies responsible for implementing these regulations.

We followed with a look at government agencies involved in regulating traffic in commercial trade and their responsibilities, and a very brief examination of important U.S. tax laws.

The chapter concluded with a section on preventing workplace discrimination and harassment, including an overview of applicable laws. We also covered civil rights actions, the Americans with Disability Act, and eliminating sexual harassment.

Note

1. See U.S. Department of Transportation website: www.dot.gov/.

About the Authors

Fred Sollish, MS, CPM (San Francisco, CA) is the Managing Director of eParagon, LLC, a consulting firm specializing in providing training and working tools for the supply chain management profession. He is a working professional in supply management and procurement with over 30 years' experience as a manager. Fred is former president and CEO of the Institute for Supply Management (ISM) Silicon Valley affiliate. He is also an instructor for sourcing and procurement–related courses.

John Semanik, MBA, CPM (San Jose, CA) is cofounder and Director of eParagon, LLC. He has served in senior corporate supply chain positions at leading-edge companies such as Hewlett-Packard and Sun Microsystems. He is the former Managing Director and instructor for San Jose State University's Professional Development curriculum in Supply Chain Management and Purchasing, and former CEO of the Institute for Supply Management (ISM) Silicon Valley affiliate.

About the Website

This book includes a companion website that can be accessed at www.wiley.com/go/procurementdeskreference2e.

It contains the following appendices:

- Appendix A: Sample Purchase Requisition Form
- Appendix B: Sample Purchase Order Form
- Appendix C: Electronic Catalog Example
- Appendix D: Common Auction Types
- Appendix E: Commonly Used Financial Ratios
- Appendix F: Request for Proposal (RFP) Example
- Appendix G: Request for Quotation Example
- Appendix H: Outline of Uniform Commercial Code and Article 2
- Appendix I: Important U.S. Import/Export Regulations
- Appendix J: Sample Terms and Conditions
- Appendix K: Links to Related Professional Organizations

The website contains a full glossary of commonly used procurement terms and terms used in the book, a suggested reading list, and flashcards with key terms and definitions organized alphabetically.

The password to enter this site is: Sollish.

Index